Winner of the Jules and Frances Landry Award for 1996

Revolution,
Romanticism,
and the
Afro-Creole
Protest Tradition
in Louisiana
1718–1868

Revolution, Romanticism, and the Afro-Creole Protest Tradition in Louisiana 1718–1868

CARYN COSSÉ BELL

LOUISIANA STATE UNIVERSITY PRESS
Baton Rouge and London

Manufactured in the United States of America
First printing
06 05 04 03 02 01 00 99 98 97 5 4 3 2 1

Designer: Michele Myatt
Typefaces: Granjon, Cornet
Typesetter: Impressions Book and Journal Services, Inc.
Printer and binder: Thomson-Shore, Inc.

Library of Congress Cataloging-in-Publication Data
Bell, Caryn Cossé
Revolution, romanticism, and the Afro-Creole protest tradition in Louisiana, 1718–1868 / Caryn Cossé Bell
p. cm.
Includes bibliographical references and index.
ISBN 0-8071-2096-0 (cl : alk. paper)
1. Afro-Americans—Louisiana—New Orleans—Politics and government. 2. Creoles—Louisiana—New Orleans—Politics and government. 3. Radicalism—Louisiana—New Orleans—History—19th century. 4. Radicalism—Louisiana—New Orleans—History—18th century. 5. Republicanism—Louisiana—New Orleans—History—19th century. 6. Republicanism—Louisiana—New Orleans—History—18th century. 7. Romanticism—Louisiana—New Orleans—History—19th century. 8. Romanticism—Louisiana—New Orleans—History—18th century. 9. New Orleans (La.)—History. I. Title.
F379.N59N43 1997
976.3'35—dc20 96-35429
CIP

Grateful acknowledgment is made to the Archives of the Sisters of the Holy Family, New Orleans, for permission to cite unpublished and published materials.

Portions of Chapters 2, 4, and 7 first appeared in "The Impact of Revolutionary Upheaval in France and the French Caribbean on Nineteenth-Century Black Leadership in New Orleans," by Caryn Cossé Bell and Joseph Logsdon, in the *Proceedings of the French Colonial Historical Society, Martinique and Guadeloupe, May 1989* (Lanham, Md., 1992), 142–53, and are reproduced by permission.

The paper in this book meets the guidelines for permanence and durability of the Committee on Production Guidelines for Book Longevity of the Council on Library Resources. ♾

For Ulysses S. Ricard, Jr.
(1951–1993)

Contents

Illustrations

Acknowledgments

Hurrying to class during my undergraduate days at the University of New Orleans, I thanked the courteous young man who opened the door for me. To my pleasant surprise, the polite stranger was Joseph Logsdon, my new history instructor. Since our first encounter on that fall day, Joe has opened countless "doors" for me. His pioneering insights and unflagging enthusiasm were essential to the evolution of this book.

Through Joe, I met Lawrence N. Powell of Tulane University, who advised me on this project from the beginning. His insistence on sound scholarship and a broad conceptualization together with his superb editorial skills made this book a far better work. My debts to both Larry and Joe are great. I will always be thankful for their wisdom and patience. Whatever shortcomings and flaws remain are a consequence of my own limitations.

Most of the fundamental sources for this book are stored in the Amistad Research Center at Tulane University and the Earl K. Long Library at the University of New Orleans. At Amistad, Alvery Rodney, Emanuella J. Spencer, and Director Clifton H. Johnson made my research a meaningful, productive experience. I am grateful for their support as well as the encouragement of the center's new director, Donald E. DeVore. I would also like to express appreciation to D. Clive Hardy, director of archives at the University of New Orleans, and archivists Marie E. Windell and Beatrice Rodriguez Owsley. Their efficiency and accommodation of my research needs eased my task considerably.

An intellectually stimulating and very happy spring, 1996, semester as a John E. Sawyer Fellow at the Longfellow Institute of Harvard University enabled me to complete this book. I am extremely grateful to Longfellow Institute directors Marc Shell and Werner Sollors for providing a superb working environment. Their support was essential. I am also indebted to Henry Louis Gates, Jr., and the W.E.B. Du Bois Institute for their generosity and for their interest in my work.

A grant from the Louisiana Endowment for the Humanities helped bring this book to publication. For the grant and for their support through the years, my sincere thanks go to LEH executive director Michael Sartisky, Kathryn Mettelka, Rhonda Miller, James Segreto, and all of the other members of the LEH staff and board of directors.

I would also like to express my appreciation to L. E. Phillabaum, John Easterly, Claudette Price, and the other staff members of Louisiana State University Press. I am especially grateful for Catherine Landry's sound editorial advice and Sarah Whalen's expert scrutiny of the manuscript. Their suggestions improved the text immeasurably.

I am also deeply indebted to Frances Landry and her late husband Jules Landry for their support. Their vision and generosity have provided a wonderful stimulus to research and publication, and I am grateful for their dedication to the study of southern history and culture.

Florence Edwards Borders at the Center for African and African American Studies of Southern University in New Orleans, educator Kathi Martensen, and Joe Louis Caldwell, chairman of the University of New Orleans history department, gave me their unswerving support through the years. Completing this book would have been a great deal more difficult without their encouragement and advice. I am profoundly thankful for their friendship.

Mary Boniface Adams of the Sisters of the Holy Family generously shared her research and her wonderful perspective with me. I would like to thank her as well as Eva Regina Martin, Sylvia Thibodeaux, and the other members of the congregation. I am also indebted to artist Sharon Lewis Hall, whose creative turn of mind and beautiful artwork sustained me as I neared completion of this study. My thanks go to her, as well as to Philip P. Boucher, William I. Shorrock, and the other officers of the French Colonial Historical Society for their gracious permission to reprint portions of an article that appeared in 1989 in their publication *Proceedings of the Fifteenth Meeting of the French Colonial Historical Society*.

In addition, I would like to thank the staff of several research institutions who took the time and trouble to help me: Collin B. Hamer, Jr., and Jean M. Jones of the New Orleans Public Library; Sylvia Verdun Metzinger, Joan G. Caldwell, and Wilbur E. Meneray at Tulane University's Howard-Tilton Memorial Library; Kevin L. Ray of the W. S. Hoole Library at the University of Alabama in Tuscaloosa; Florence Jumonville, head librarian of the Historic New Orleans Collection; Charles E. Nolan of the Archdiocese of New Orleans; and especially Xavier University archivist Lester Sullivan, who gave me invaluable assistance with freemasonry sources.

I also want to record my gratitude to my indispensable colleague and dear friend, Ulysses S. Ricard, Jr. (1951–1993). Ulysses' death cut short a brilliantly productive life and dealt a devastating blow to the study of Louisiana's unique cultural heritage. As senior archivist at Amistad Research Center, Ulysses attained international recognition for his expertise on Creole, Cajun, and African American history and language. With his death, Louisiana lost one of its most articulate, enthusiastic, and knowledgeable emissaries to the world.

Finally, I would like to acknowledge the support of my husband, Dennis Glen Bell, whose unsparing love and devotion made this book possible. I thank him with all of my heart.

Revolution, Romanticism, *and the* Afro-Creole Protest Tradition *in* Louisiana 1718–1868

Introduction

The most pressing and controversial question of the post–Civil War era was the place of southern blacks in the political and social order. The answer drawn up by delegates to Louisiana's constitutional convention of 1867 was arguably the Reconstruction South's most radical blueprint for change. Louisiana's 1868 constitution enabled black Louisianians to join society as equal participants. Given the traditions of the old regime, the newly drafted charter pointed the way to social revolution.

Resembling other state constitutions of the Reconstruction South, it guaranteed black citizens equal civil and political rights; it assured them of equal justice before the law; and it mandated the establishment of a state-funded system of public education. Unlike other state constitutions, however, it went to unprecedented lengths to achieve complete equality for black Louisianians. It required legislators and other state officials to recognize, by oath, the civil and political equality of all men. It alone among Reconstruction constitutions explicitly required equal treatment on public transportation and in licensed businesses and other places of public accommodation. And it forbade segregation in public schools. South Carolina with its overwhelming black voting majority was the only other state to adopt a constitution that prohibited segregated schools. But even there, black proponents of school integration acknowledged that the two races preferred separate schools and never extended the ideal to elementary or secondary schools. The school integration and public accommodations provisions of the Louisiana constitution were a century ahead of their time.[1]

1. Joe Gray Taylor, *Louisiana Reconstructed, 1863–1877* (Baton Rouge, 1974), 151–55; Eric Foner, *Reconstruction: America's Unfinished Revolution, 1863–1877* (New York, 1988), 319–22; Ted Tunnell, *Crucible of Reconstruction: War, Radicalism, and Race in Louisiana, 1862–1877* (Baton Rouge, 1984), Chap. 6; Charles M. Vincent, "Black Constitution Makers:

The driving force behind the Louisiana constitution's racial egalitarianism was the most politicized and articulate free black community in the South, the French-speaking black Creoles of New Orleans. Their republican idealism ensured that Louisiana's 1868 constitution would envision far-reaching change.[2]

The city's Afro-Creole leaders inaugurated their movement in the fall of 1862 with the founding of a French-language newspaper, *L'Union*. The paper's founders, Dr. Louis Charles Roudanez, his brother Jean-Baptiste Roudanez, and Paul Trévigne, published editorials, essays, and literary works that set the Civil War within the context of an ongoing age of democratic revolution.

In the first issue, the paper's editors urged everyone who "can lend intellectual or pecuniary support to the propagation of the cause of the rights of man and humanity to do so without delay." All those, the paper continued, "who aspire to establish everywhere an unblemished republican system, an unfettered democracy, hasten to us, contribute like us, your grain of sand to the construction of the Temple of Liberty!"[3]

A series entitled "Dictionnaire Féodal" ("Feudal Dictionary") offered a highly politicized account of eighteenth-century French history intended to draw a parallel between serf society in France and slavery in the South. Other essays pointed to the ideals of the American Revolution and the French Revolution of 1789 and urged the nation to follow the example of France in 1848, when the Second Republic abolished slavery and immediately extended suffrage to free men of color and former slaves.[4]

Black Creole intellectual Henry Louis Rey looked still elsewhere in the French world. A newly enlisted Union officer, Rey exhorted free men of color to join the army and take up "the cause of the rights of man" in the tradition of Saint Dominguan free men of color Jean-Baptiste Chavannes and Vincent Ogé. In Saint Domingue [present-day Haiti] in October, 1790,

---

The Constitution of 1868," in *In Search of Fundamental Law: Louisiana's Constitutions, 1812–1974*, ed. Warren M. Billings and Edward F. Haas (Lafayette, La., 1993), 69–80.

2. For the purposes of this study, the terms *free people of color, black Creole, Afro-Creole,* and *Creole of color* refer to native-born Louisianians of African and Latin European descent.

3. *L'Union,* September 27, 1862.

4. *Ibid.*, October 8, 25, November 1, 15, 1862.

Chavannes, a veteran of the American Revolution, and Ogé launched a revolt against the French colony's white planter regime. Though the ill-fated uprising resulted in the execution of Chavannes and Ogé, it nonetheless paved the way for the Haitian Revolution of 1791–1804. Rey praised the courage of the two rebels in his call to arms: "CHAVANNE [*sic*] AND OGE did not wait to be aroused and to be made ashamed; they hurried unto death; they became martyrs here on earth and received on high the reward due to generous hearts. . . . Hasten all; our blood only is demanded; who will hesitate?"[5]

Clearly, Afro-Creole activists viewed the Civil War as far more than a struggle to preserve the Union. It was a necessary step in mankind's progression toward a republican millennium. In destroying the South's despotic oligarchy, the North would set the nation's republican system on a solid foundation. Social reform, *L'Union* assured its readers, would commence with the war's end. Then the country would be able to propagate republican ideals around the world so that "our brothers in every country can profit from this divine gift." The new "millennium" would arrive before the end of the century. With such expectations, Afro-Creoles rallied to the Union cause.[6]

Under Federal occupation of the city, French-speaking white radicals also mobilized. In June, 1862, they launched a Unionist movement with the aim of reestablishing a loyal state government. By mid-1863, they had aligned themselves with free men of color and were pressing for free black voting rights. Early in 1864, after local Federal authorities threatened to undermine their interracial movement, the group took their campaign to Washington, thereby compelling the president and Congress to take up the issue of black voting rights even before the end of the war.[7]

As their radical agenda and bold actions revealed, the city's Afro-Creole leaders and their white allies possessed a well-developed philosophy of political radicalism at the time of the Civil War. Rooted in the egalitarianism of the age of democratic revolution, a Catholic universalist ethic, and

5. Rey's letter to *L'Union* is cited in the New York *Times,* November 5, 1862; Carolyn E. Fick, *The Making of Haiti: The Saint Domingue Revolution from Below* (Knoxville, Tenn., 1990), 82–83.

6. *L'Union,* December 6, 1862.

7. Foner, *Reconstruction,* 62–66.

Romantic philosophy, their republican idealism produced the postwar South's most progressive vision of the future. This study documents the eighteenth-century origins of their political and intellectual heritage, its evolution in antebellum New Orleans, and its impact on the war and Reconstruction.

Apart from two major studies of French-language writers in nineteenth-century Louisiana, Edward Larocque Tinker's *Les Ecrits de langue française en Louisiane au XIX siecle* and Auguste Viatte's *Histoire littéraire de l'Amérique Française des origines à 1950*, few works have noted the activities in the city of white proponents of republican revolutionary thought. In the nineteenth century, these white ideologues preserved revolutionary idealism in their Romantic literary works and their masonic lodges. Though their ranks produced some of the most radical leaders of the Civil War era, the nature of their political culture has remained largely unexplored. The present work seeks to fill this gap.[8]

By contrast, scholars have written extensively on the Afro-Creole intelligentsia. Instead of seeing them as the bearers of republican ideals, some observers have portrayed them as race-conscious extremists or aristocrats of color who identified with the state's slaveholding elite. One of their earliest critics, Henry Clay Warmoth, wrote in 1930 in his memoir, *War, Politics and Reconstruction: Stormy Days in Louisiana*, that during Reconstruction there "was a class of colored people in Louisiana who really hoped and believed that the change in affairs would result in the Africanization of the State." With their "Dominican and Haytian predilections," the former Republican governor continued, these Creole radicals, encouraged "by the protection that they expected from the United States Army, and realizing the helplessness of the formerly ruling white people . . . thought to establish an *African State Government*."[9]

In 1955, historian Donald E. Everett echoed Warmoth's harsh view of free black aspirations. During the antebellum era, Everett wrote, an insu-

8. Edward Larocque Tinker, *Les Ecrits de langue française en Louisiane au XIX siecle* (1923; rpr. Geneva, 1975); Auguste Viatte, *Histoire littéraire de L'Amérique Française des origines à 1950* (Paris, 1954); see also Auguste Viatte, "Complement à la bibliographie louisianaise d'Edward Larocque Tinker," *Louisiana Review,* III (Winter, 1974), 12–57.

9. Henry Clay Warmoth, *War, Politics and Reconstruction: Stormy Days in Louisiana* (New York, 1930), 52, 57.

lar group of French-speaking, free black property owners and slaveholders shunned contact with the majority of free blacks and identified their interests with those of governing whites. During the Civil War, this small clique of opportunistic leaders proposed to exchange their military support for political recognition. They joined the Confederate army and then switched their allegiance to the Union cause. Ultimately, anticipating their control of the freedmen's vote in the postwar era, Creole leaders entertained "visions of dominating the white population in the Reconstruction period."[10]

Another body of historical literature produced an entirely different appraisal of nineteenth-century free black leadership. Writer Rodolphe Lucien Desdunes, a contemporary of Warmoth's, included a highly flattering account of Afro-Creole Louisianians in his book *Our People and Our History*. Desdunes, one of the city's most distinguished black Creole spokesmen by the time of his book's publication in 1911, portrayed his community's Civil War leaders as unswerving patriots who "burned with the desire to take up arms for the cause of freedom." After the war these "generous servants of the common cause" devoted their talents and their personal finances to the campaign for universal suffrage. During Reconstruction, these same men, the "true friends of the people," sought the peaceful reorganization of the state.[11]

Most subsequent historians of black Louisianians have expanded upon Desdunes' interpretation, but David Rankin challenged their view. Rankin's studies have discarded the notion of French-speaking blacks conspiring to dominate white Louisianians, but his work has reinforced the image of a caste-conscious Creole elite. Basing his findings on a sample of approximately two hundred men, Rankin concluded that the dominant black politician in Reconstruction New Orleans was free before the war, probably French speaking, light complexioned, probably Catholic, literate and possibly well educated, and likely a veteran of the Civil War. In their struggle for political rights, this exclusive class of wellborn leaders aligned themselves with the former slaves only after the freedmen's support became crucial to their own advancement. This short-lived alliance

10. Donald E. Everett, "Demands of the New Orleans Free Colored Population for Political Equality, 1862–1865," *Louisiana Historical Quarterly,* XXXVIII (April, 1955), 64.

11. Rodolphe Lucien Desdunes, *Our People and Our History,* trans. and ed. Sister Dorothea Olga McCants (Baton Rouge, 1973), 124, 132, 134.

collapsed during the election of 1868, when French-speaking leaders betrayed their elitist inclinations by supporting ex-slaveholders for the state's highest political offices. Among the leaders of the suffrage campaign, Rankin noted an "aristocratic spirit" that, over time, "had never really disappeared at all."[12]

Both the positive and the critical accounts of French-speaking leaders as reactionary elitists have often ignored records in French and overlooked crucial aspects of free black protest. During the war, Afro-Creole spokesmen seized upon the ideals of the American and French Revolutions and images of revolutionary events in the French Caribbean. In literary works, newspaper editorials, and spiritualist séances, they recalled the unfulfilled promise of the age of democratic revolution. They demanded *liberté, égalité, fraternité*. The nature of their radical philosophy is a long-neglected aspect of the city's political history.

Chapter 1 of the present study establishes that the free black protest tradition originated in colonial New Orleans, where a Latin European religious culture, a tripartite racial order, and the outbreak of revolutionary upheaval in Europe and the Americas gave rise to one of the most assertive, prosperous, well-educated, and cohesive free black societies in nineteenth-century North America. The chapter traces events through the territorial period (1803–1812), when free black militiamen, emboldened by the terms of the Louisiana Purchase, demanded political rights.

Chapter 2 recounts the impact of free black veterans of the French republican army who entered Louisiana in the Saint Domingue refugee movement. Together with white veterans of revolutionary upheaval in

12. For references to Afro-Creole radicalism, see John W. Blassingame, *Black New Orleans, 1860–1880* (Chicago, 1973); Charles B. Roussève, *The Negro in Louisiana: Aspects of His History and His Literature* (New Orleans, 1937); Charles Vincent, *Black Legislators in Louisiana During Reconstruction* (Baton Rouge, 1976); C. Peter Ripley, *Slaves and Freedmen in Civil War Louisiana* (Baton Rouge, 1976); and David C. Rankin, "The Origins of Negro Leadership in New Orleans During Reconstruction," in *Southern Black Leaders of the Reconstruction Era,* ed. Howard Rabinowitz (Urbana, 1982), 173. Also see David C. Rankin, "The Politics of Caste: Free Colored Leadership in New Orleans During the Civil War," in *Louisiana's Black Heritage,* ed. Robert R. MacDonald, John R. Kemp, and Edward F. Haas (New Orleans, 1979); David C. Rankin, "The Impact of the Civil War on the Free Colored Community of New Orleans," *Perspectives in American History,* XI (1977–78), 379–416.

Europe and the Americas, they carried the ongoing current of revolutionary idealism forward. When military necessity forced Louisiana officials to enlist the services of the free black militia, black Saint Dominguans joined their ranks. The service of these soldiers in the American Revolution and the War of 1812 would be a key factor in future demands for equal citizenship.

Black New Orleanians had developed close ties to Catholic Church leaders by the time of the Louisiana Purchase. Chapter 3 discusses these ties and describes how events surrounding St. Louis Cathedral reinforced a spirit of dissent among French-speaking Catholics. During the early decades of the nineteenth century, the moderating influence of the city's religious culture together with economic and military necessities forestalled, to some extent, the erosion of the free black community's intermediate status within the city's tripartite racial order. After 1830, however, the decline of Latin European institutions, the in-migration of white laborers, and the imposition of a dual racial order eroded the social and economic position of the free black class. The harsh realities of Americanization fueled ethnic tensions. Afro-Creoles and other disaffected elements remained receptive to radical influences from Europe.

For French-speaking dissidents in Europe and the Americas, the Romantic literary movement, freemasonry, and spiritualism purveyed the ideals of the democratic revolutions of the late eighteenth and nineteenth centuries. Chapters 4, 5, and 6 discuss these movements.

Chapter 4 covers the period from 1830 to 1850, when revolutionary upheaval in post–Napoleonic France sent large contingents of political exiles fleeing to Louisiana. The influx of these emigrés strengthened an existing colony of French-speaking intellectuals. Together they established a remarkably productive French-language literary community. The city's free black writers, like Romantic writers in France and the Caribbean, employed their skills to challenge existing social evils. For black artists, literary Romanticism also served as a springboard to other forms of social and political activism. Antebellum Afro-Creole reform efforts involving free black writers and women of color included founding a school for indigent children and establishing a Catholic convent. Indeed, Catholic women of color exerted considerable influence upon the shaping of the Afro-Creole protest tradition. Although their activities are only touched upon in this work, women were key agents of change within the city's religious culture. A more focused and thoroughgoing examination of Catholic dissidence will yield a much fuller picture of the role of women in the city's social and intellectual history.

Chapter 5 recounts the activities in New Orleans of a circle of republican freemasons whose views paralleled those of their radical counterparts in France. The small cadre of white, French-speaking activists constituted an influential faction within the city's extensive network of masonic lodges. Acting upon their unorthodox religious convictions, they played a leading role in 1805 in establishing a schismatic congregation at St. Louis Cathedral. Until the mid-1840s, they appeared prominently in church affairs. Though ousted from control of the cathedral in 1844 by the American church hierarchy, freemasons continued to contribute to the city's strong undercurrent of political radicalism.

Alienated by the mounting conservatism of the Catholic Church, French-speaking white radicals and prominent black Creoles joined the spiritualist movement, a radical new religious sect. Spiritualism's unitive philosophy, its emphasis on personal empowerment, and its repudiation of orthodox religion appealed to liberal-minded activists. Chapter 6 discusses the spiritualist phenomenon and records the movement's spread, beginning in the late 1840s, among French-speaking intellectuals. The concluding chapter covers the period from 1862 to 1868, when black Creole leaders and their white allies attempted to translate their radical ideals into a concrete agenda for change.

This work began with a study of a number of French-language literary works written between 1830 and 1845, and a systematic reading of *L'Union*, a French-language Afro-Creole newspaper that began publication in 1862. Together with two previously untapped manuscript sources—freemasonry records in New Orleans covering the period from 1858 to 1873, and a collection of Afro-Creole spiritualist registers for a similar period—these materials indicated the presence in nineteenth-century New Orleans of a longstanding subculture of political radicalism that had links to corresponding movements in Europe and the Americas. What follows is an attempt to recover a biracial protest tradition that drew upon both French and American revolutionary traditions to produce a unique vision of republican equality in postwar Louisiana.

1

Revolution and the Origins of Dissent

In the summer of 1804, New Orleans officials demanded that Louisiana's territorial commissioner, William C. C. Claiborne, punish and banish black leaders who had attempted to assert the rights of free people of color. Instead, Claiborne met quietly with representatives of the free black community and insisted they abandon their plan to draft a petition to Congress. It seemed to the commissioner that "in a Country where the negro population was so great the Less noise that was made about this occurance [*sic*] the better." The anger of the "white inhabitants was so roused" that he feared violence and recalled "that the events which have Spread blood and desolation in St. Domingo originated in a dispute between the white and Mulatto inhabitants, and that the too rigid treatment of the former, induced the Latter to seek the support and assistance of the Negroes." The peculiar nature of conditions within the territory prompted Claiborne to gloomily predict that at some point in the future "this quarter of the Union must (I fear) experience in some degree, the Misfortunes of St. Domingo."[1]

The political and social complexity of the newly acquired territory forced Commissioner Claiborne to proceed cautiously. For over a decade, revolutionary upheaval in France and the Caribbean had contributed to volatile conditions. While white radicals from Bordeaux and Saint

1. Claiborne to James Madison, July 12, 1804, in *Official Letter Books of W.C.C. Claiborne, 1801–1816,* ed. Dunbar Rowland (Jackson, Miss., 1917), II, 234–45. William Charles Cole Claiborne (1775–1817), a native of Virginia, was appointed governor of the Mississippi territory in 1801 by Thomas Jefferson. In 1803, the president appointed Claiborne and General James Wilkinson co-commissioners to receive Louisiana from the French on December 20, 1803; in August, 1804, Jefferson appointed Claiborne to a three-year term as governor of the Orleans territory.

Domingue agitated against the American regime after the Louisiana Purchase of 1803, an influx of free people of color, refugees of the Haitian Revolution, fueled tensions. Even as the territorial commissioner forwarded his dispatches to Secretary of State James Madison in 1804, the discovery of a Haitian soldier, Marseille, among the new immigrants intensified fears of a slave uprising. The concern that Haiti's free black emigrés would infect the slave population with notions of freedom prompted city officials to discourage free black immigration. Ultimately, such fears and the discovery two years later of a plot by armed free people of color to overthrow the American regime prompted state legislators in 1806 to forbid entry to free black males from the French West Indies.[2]

In 1789, Saint Domingue, with a population of 30,000 whites, approximately 28,000 free people of color, and some 465,000 slaves, was France's largest and most prosperous Caribbean colony. With the onset of the French Revolution, the colony's free people of color, who possessed one-third of the plantation property, one-quarter of the real estate, and one-quarter of the slaves, demanded political equality and threatened to rebel. Rebuffed by the colonial plantocracy and assaulted by white reactionaries, prominent free black leaders organized an attack on Cap Français (present-day Cap-Haitien), a key colonial stronghold in the north, in October, 1790. When the uprising failed, leading free men of color in the south fortified their estates and armed their slaves. The ensuing turmoil sparked a massive slave uprising in the north in August, 1791, involving as many as 20,000 rebels in the plantation zone surrounding Cap Français. Black rebellion spelled the ruin of the slaveholding regime. By 1795, the French government had conceded racial equality and slave emancipation. In 1799, as the black revolutionaries moved toward independence, a civil war erupted. In the conflict, Toussaint Louverture overwhelmed the mulatto-led proponents of republicanism and forced large numbers of people of color into exile. Finally, on January 1, 1804, after expelling French forces, black revolutionaries proclaimed the independent nation of Haiti.[3]

2. H. E. Sterkx, *The Free Negro in Ante-Bellum Louisiana* (Rutherford, N.J., 1972), 91–93.

3. Robin Blackburn, *The Overthrow of Colonial Slavery, 1776–1848* (London, 1988), 163, 182; Fick, *The Making of Haiti,* 19, 106; C.L.R. James, *The Black Jacobins: Toussaint L'Ouverture and the San Domingo Revolution* (Rev. ed.; New York, 1963), 64–65, 370, and Chaps. 7 and 10.

In view of events in the French Antilles, New Orleans' free black militia was of great immediate concern to American authorities when they assumed control of the territory at the end of 1803. Like free men of color in the former French colony of Saint Domingue, many free men of color in New Orleans were armed. As members of the colonial militia, slave and free black soldiers had played a significant role in the defenses of Louisiana. During the revolutionary era, they had absorbed republican principles. With Louisiana's transfer to the United States, they pointed to American revolutionary ideals and demanded equal citizenship. The assertiveness and status of these men stemmed from their historical experience in colonial Louisiana.

The free black community had emerged from a frontier society characterized by a high degree of social and economic fluidity. In New Orleans, as will be shown, a Latin European religious ethic, an unbalanced sex ratio, and a shortage of skilled laborers and soldiers contributed to the city's fluid milieu and opened the way to freedom. Colonial policies designed to build a more rigid social order fueled the racial flux. By the end of colonial rule in 1803, there were 1,335 free blacks in New Orleans in a total population of 8,050 residents, of whom 2,775 were slaves. During the eighteenth century, the city's Latin European religious culture helped shape the outlook and character of native-born Creoles of color.[4]

Throughout the colonial era, Capuchin friars (members of the Franciscan order) dominated church affairs in Louisiana. Committed to missionary work and the rule of poverty, French and Spanish Capuchins devoted considerable attention to Louisiana's slave and free black populations. Latin European slave laws assured them of an important role in eighteenth-century New Orleans.

4. The population figures for 1803 are drawn from Jerah Johnson, "Colonial New Orleans: A Fragment of the Eighteenth-Century French Ethos," in *Creole New Orleans: Race and Americanization,* ed. Arnold R. Hirsch and Joseph Logsdon (Baton Rouge, 1992), 52*n*79. In 1769, there were only 99 free blacks in New Orleans in a population of 1,803 whites and 1,227 slaves. These figures would seem to indicate that the number of free blacks increased very little under the French regime. It has been convincingly argued, however, that Spanish census takers undercounted free people of color because of the high level of social fluidity (Gwendolyn Midlo Hall, *Africans in Colonial Louisiana: The Development of Afro-Creole Culture in the Eighteenth Century* [Baton Rouge, 1992], Chap. 8). Also see Paul F. Lachance, "The Formation of a Three-Caste Society," *Social Science History,* XVIII (Summer, 1994), 226. For the 1769 population figures, see table in Chap. 3.

Under the French regime, the period from 1718 to 1763, the Code Noir of 1724 had subordinated all settlers to Catholic precepts. Rooted in a legal and religious tradition that recognized the moral personality of the slave, the code required that bondsmen be instructed in the Catholic religion and administered the sacraments of baptism, marriage, penance, and extreme unction. Other provisions forbade the separation of a married couple and their children under fourteen years of age and prohibited slaves from laboring on Sundays and other Catholic holy days. The code sought to ensure social and political stability by assimilating slaves and free blacks into the Christian community.[5]

Sustained by the Code Noir, Capuchin missionaries incorporated black New Orleanians into the life of the church. Catholicism's doctrinal commitment to the spiritual equality of all Catholics informed their efforts. All of the city's inhabitants, regardless of race or condition, received the Catholic sacraments in the same place of worship, St. Louis Church. Capuchin friars baptized *negritte* and *negrillon* slave infants while their white slaveholding godparents bore witness to the sacred rites. In a baptismal ceremony in 1729, some of the city's most prominent leaders, including Bienville and De la Chaise, appeared as sponsors for their adult slaves.[6]

The church's inclusive religious practices applied to free blacks as well as slaves. In August, 1725, Father Raphael de Luxembourg, the new vicar general of the Capuchin mission in Louisiana, officiated at the wedding of Marie Gaspar, a free woman of color and the daughter of a drummer in Bienville's army, and Jean Baptiste Raphael, a free man of color from Martinique.[7]

5. Roger Baudier, *The Catholic Church in Louisiana* (New Orleans, 1939), 64–310; James T. McGowan, "Creation of a Slave Society: Louisiana Plantations in the Eighteenth Century" (Ph.D. dissertation, University of Rochester, 1976), 48–49, 120; Mary V. Miceli, "The Influence of the Roman Catholic Church on Slavery in Colonial Louisiana, 1718–1763" (Ph.D. dissertation, Tulane University, 1979), 53–58.

6. Baudier, *The Catholic Church,* 84; Miceli, "The Influence of the Roman Catholic Church," 72. After the church created the diocese of Louisiana on April 25, 1793, and designated New Orleans the cathedral city, St. Louis Church became St. Louis Cathedral.

7. Roussève, *The Negro in Louisiana,* 40; Roulhac Toledano and Mary Louise Christovich, "The Role of Free People of Color in Tremé" in *Faubourg Tremé and the Bayou Road,* ed. Christovich and Toledano (Gretna, La., 1980), 90, Vol. VI of Christovich, ed., *New Orleans Architecture*.

Church policies designed to assimilate the black population into the dominant social order were not intended to promote interracial intimacy. Nonetheless, frontier conditions forced the church to adapt to the social realities of an emergent slave society. In 1722, in New Orleans and the surrounding area, the population of 514 black slaves was nearly as large as the white population of 293 men, 140 women, and 155 *engagés* (French laborers). The scarcity of white women led the predominantly male population of French soldiers and adventurers to establish extramarital liaisons with slave women. Though the Code Noir and church doctrine forbade interracial marriage and concubinage, colonists ignored attempts by the clergy to halt the spread of such practices. By the middle of the eighteenth century, interracial liaisons were commonplace, and parish registers indicated the church's acceptance of social patterns within the city.[8]

In April, 1729, Jacques, an infant slave owned by Etienne Boucher de Périer, the governor of the colony, and the son of the slave woman Françoise, was baptized. The ceremony was the first recorded instance in which church transcribers publicly noted the absence of a known father. During the 1740s, the term *d'un père inconnu* (father unknown) appeared frequently in the baptismal records; in 1763, every page of the baptismal register contained at least one entry accompanied by the phrase. By the 1790s, many inhabitants of the city openly acknowledged their illegitimate, mixed-blood children in the church registry. In 1799, the Spanish minister, Joseph Antonio Caballero, reported that military officers lived "openly with their mulatto concubines as do many of the people, and they are not ashamed to name the children in the parish registers as their natural children."[9]

While the church's accommodation to interracial unions contributed to the city's fluid social milieu, conditions in the Capuchin friary suggested the ways in which close personal relationships developed. After France's cession of Louisiana, the Spanish, who governed the colony from 1763 to

8. Laura Foner, "The Free People of Color in Louisiana and St. Domingue," *Journal of Social History,* III (Summer, 1970), 409 *n*13; Ira Berlin, *Slaves Without Masters: The Free Negro in the Antebellum South* (New York, 1974), 108–109.

9. Miceli, "The Influence of the Roman Catholic Church," 72–92; Baudier, *The Catholic Church,* 244–45; James Alexander Robertson, ed., *Louisiana Under the Rule of Spain, France, and the United States, 1785–1807* (Cleveland, 1911), I, 356.

1800, sent a small group of Capuchins to join the existing community of French missionaries. On their arrival in New Orleans in 1772, the Spanish friars viewed the conduct of their French counterparts with extreme alarm. Contrary to the teaching of St. Francis and the spirit of Franciscan poverty, the Spaniards complained, the French clergymen owned a plantation and slaves and used silverware, porcelain, and snuff. Father Cirilo de Barcelona, the superior of the small group of Spanish friars, reported on "the indecency with which, in sight of the exposed Host, these priests demean themselves in the choir, where they are seen stuffing their noses with tobacco . . . scandalizing the people, and moving the very angels to wrath."[10]

Cirilo found living arrangements in the friary deplorable. Eighteen slaves—ten women, four men, and four children—lived in the friars' home. The Spanish governor, Luis de Unzaga, attributed the presence of the "young blackwomen and mulattresses, who are their [the Capuchins'] slaves, and who were born on their plantation" to the "excessive kindness of Father Dagobert [Dagobert de Longuory, head of Louisiana's Capuchin mission]." Father Cirilo, however, offered a far less charitable explanation for living arrangements in the friary:

> What is most deplorable is to see in the convent the concubine of the friars, for such is the reputation she bears. She has three sons, although who her husband is God only knows. They eat at our table and off the plates of Father Dagobert, who, without shame, or fear of the world at least, if not of God, permits them to call him papa. She is one of the mulattresses who are kept in the house. She is the absolute mistress of the whole establishment, and the friars have for her so much attachment, that they strive who shall send to the cherished paramour the best dish of the table, before any one of us is allowed to taste it.[11]

The woman's unmarried and pregnant sister also lived in the friary, and Cirilo had observed "a white man sallying out of the chamber of this mulattress" at four o'clock in the morning. Furthermore, "persons of high standing" had informed the Spanish friar that "the young negresses and mulattresses, immediately after having attended us at supper, go out of the

10. Charles Gayarré, *History of Louisiana* (New Orleans, 1903), III, 76.
11. *Ibid.*, III, 69, 74.

convent to meet their lovers, and spend with them the greater part of the night."[12]

Determined to impose a stricter religious discipline in the colony, Cirilo demanded that Dagobert correct conditions in the friary. Though the Spanish priest was of the opinion that "to expel these women from the convent, would be to inflict too painful a blow on Father Dagobert," Cirilo insisted that they be banished to the Capuchin plantation, where, if necessary, they could be sold. In the ensuing dispute, the Spanish governor sided with Dagobert. Determined to maintain peace in the colony, Governor Unzaga defended the popular spiritual leader in dispatches to colonial officials. In 1773, Unzaga explained Dagobert's continued refusal to expel the slave women. The friar refused to "throw out of doors a set of people whom he has raised and kept about him from the cradle."[13]

Practices within the friary surely typified the complex nature of race relations in the city. Clearly, the church's assimilationist policies reinforced the city's lax social regimen and guaranteed black New Orleanians a measure of acceptability that eased the transition to freedom. The city's Latin European religious culture and the racial makeup of the city's slave and free black populations provided the basis for the emergence and empowerment of an aspiring class of free people of color. Other colonial policies enhanced the relative status and social mobility of slaves and free blacks.

Under both the French and Spanish regimes, the city suffered a shortage of white skilled laborers. During the 1720s, the French colonial government addressed this shortfall by apprenticing slaves to experienced tradesmen. By 1732, slave artisans participated in a wide range of occupations. The presence of skilled black artisans in the urban workforce promoted a greater degree of occupational and personal contact between whites and blacks. Such interaction produced opportunities for many slaves to purchase their freedom.

After 1763, the Spaniards continued channeling black workers into the ranks of the skilled labor force. In their roles as *commandeurs* (slave foremen), masons, metalworkers, carpenters, and other craftsmen, many black laborers advanced to positions of authority and prestige. By the end

12. *Ibid.*, III, 64.

13. *Ibid.*, III, 85.

of the Spanish domination, slaves and free men of color monopolized many of the skilled trades. Other colonial policies also facilitated the emancipation and upward mobility of black New Orleanians.[14]

Throughout the eighteenth century, Louisiana's colonial militia suffered high rates of desertion and death. French authorities strengthened their forces with enslaved black soldiers and laborers. A number of these men earned their freedom on the battlefield, and military service became an important means of manumission. Bondsmen who acquired their freedom in this way became esteemed members of the black community.

During the Natchez War of 1730–1731 and the campaigns against the Chickasaw Indians between 1739 and 1740, French authorities created a permanent free black military force. By 1740, the Louisiana militia possessed a separate company of fifty free black soldiers, and after 1763, the Spanish government incorporated these soldiers into their military forces. The Spaniards divided free black soldiers into separate military units on the basis of color as part of a general policy of creating more rigidly defined racial categories. They separated dark-complexioned free black soldiers (*morenos*) from lighter-complexioned soldiers (*pardos*) in segregated companies.

Spanish officials awarded free black soldiers silver medals, cash bonuses, and military pensions for exemplary service. The Spaniards also advanced black soldiers to positions as commissioned and noncommissioned officers. Membership in the Spanish corps was considered a mark of high status by the city's Creoles of color. The free black officer Francisco Dorville proudly appended the title *commandante de mulatos* to his signature. At baptisms, weddings, and other social gatherings, a great deal of importance was attached to the presence of black officers. In Louisiana, as in other Spanish colonies, military service functioned as a principal means of free black advancement. By the time Spain ceded Louisiana to

14. Daniel H. Usner, Jr., *Indians, Settlers, & Slaves in a Frontier Exchange Economy: The Lower Mississippi Valley Before 1783* (Chapel Hill, N.C., 1992), 54–56; Berlin, *Slaves Without Masters,* 113–14; Thomas Marc Fiehrer, "The African Presence in Colonial Louisiana: An Essay on the Continuity of Caribbean Culture," in *Louisiana's Black Heritage,* ed. MacDonald, Kemp, and Haas, 18–23; Sterkx, *The Free Negro,* 51; Marcus B. Christian, "A Black History of Louisiana" (typescript in Marcus B. Christian Collection, Earl K. Long Library, University of New Orleans), Chap. III, 1–24.

France in 1800, the three companies of free black officers and soldiers comprised more than two hundred men.[15]

Although a shortage of white manpower had prompted the initial deployment of black soldiers, another important consideration persuaded colonial officials to arm black Louisianians. The plan to build a successful plantation society in lower Louisiana hinged on the white regime's ability to manipulate the region's large and diverse populations of African slaves and Native Americans. In 1731, after suffering a devastating Indian attack on Natchez (present-day Natchez, Mississippi), Governor Périer summed up French concerns: "The greatest misfortune which could befall the colony and which would inevitably lead to its total loss would be a union between the Indian nations and the black slaves, but happily there has always been a great aversion between them which has been much increased by the war, and we take great care to maintain it."[16]

As Périer's comments indicated, French administrators placed a high priority on encouraging antagonism between Indians and slaves. In 1729, with this policy objective in mind, Périer had dispatched a contingent of armed black slaves to destroy an Indian village downriver from New Orleans. Still, the divide-and-rule strategy involved concessions. At the time of the Natchez massacre, French authorities promised slave soldiers their freedom in return for their support. Ultimately, concessions that promoted black interests undermined the efforts of French officials and planters to build a more rigidly ordered colonial society.[17]

After 1763, Spanish authorities cultivated and exploited rivalries among contending factions as a matter of official policy. The relatively

15. Usner, *Indians, Settlers, & Slaves,* 86, 220–22; Hall, *Africans in Colonial Louisiana,* 240; Christian, "A Black History," Chap. XVI, 2–4, Chap. XII, 17; Marcus B. Christian, "Demand by Men of Color for Rights in Orleans Territory," *Negro History Bulletin,* XXXVI (March, 1973), 54–55; Fiehrer, "The African Presence," in *Louisiana's Black Heritage,* ed. MacDonald, Kemp, and Haas, 21; Berlin, *Slaves Without Masters,* 112; Roland McConnell, *Negro Troops of Antebellum Louisiana: A History of the Battalion of Free Men of Color* (Baton Rouge, 1968), 3–42. The suspension of the militia under the American regime prompted Dorville to add *que en Tiempo de la Dominacion Espanola* (during the time of the Spanish domination) to his signature.

16. Hall, *Africans in Colonial Louisiana,* 103.

17. Usner, *Indians, Settlers, & Slaves,* Chap. 2.

privileged position of free blacks under the Spanish regime reflected a colonial policy designed to impose a corporate authority over competing and consequently more manageable social classes. Spanish administrators conceived of the colonists as distinct elements in a hierarchical social order composed of whites, free blacks, and slaves. Confronted with a recalcitrant and potentially treasonous class of French-speaking whites, the Spaniards enforced measures that undermined planter autonomy. In 1768, when prominent Louisianians organized an ill-fated revolt against Spanish rule, rebellious French planters and merchants charged that Governor Antonio de Ulloa had "supported the negroes dissatisfied with their masters" and had "forbidden slaves to be whipped in New Orleans, in order to please his wife, whose humanity was shocked by their cries, so that the inhabitants, much to their prejudice, were obliged to go six miles out of the town to have their slaves punished." The angry colonists accused the Spaniards of elevating the blacks to the status of freemen while reducing the French to a state of slavery.[18]

In some cases, Spanish policies did elevate slaves to the status of free people of color. Colonial administrators viewed the presence of a free black class as a key element in their strategy of control. The Spanish slave code, Las Siete Partidas, which provided for slave self-purchase (*coartación*), became the most important means of manumission. The new measure permitted slaves to accumulate personal funds by selling their extra labor to their masters or other people in need of their services. This source of income enabled slaves to purchase their freedom. An accompanying measure required the slaveholder to set a fair purchase price. If the slave considered the cost of self-purchase excessive, the bondsman could appeal to Spanish authorities for the imposition of a just value. When his mistress refused to set a price for his self-purchase, for example, the slave Miguel petitioned the court. Judicial officials set a price of five hundred pesos and ordered the slaveholder to draw up manumission papers. Spanish court records show that slaves were often purchased by family members who had already obtained their freedom.[19]

18. Fiehrer, "The African Presence," in *Louisiana's Black Heritage,* ed. MacDonald, Kemp, and Haas, 18–25; Paul F. Lachance, "The Politics of Fear: French Louisianians and the Slave Trade, 1786–1809," *Plantation Society,* I (June, 1979), 173–75; Foner, "Free People of Color," 415–19; Gayarré, *History of Louisiana,* II, 200–22.

19. Fiehrer, "The African Presence," 23–25; Foner, "Free People of Color," 410.

The process of amelioration, once set in motion, could not be effectively controlled. The Spanish had created not so much a new fixed racial order as an unsettled racial and social flux. Angered in 1786 by the lax social regimen and alarmed by the growing numbers of free people of color, Governor Esteban Miró attempted to counteract long-standing practices. On June 2 in his *bando de buen gobierno* (proclamation for good government), the governor restricted assemblages of free blacks, forbade concubinage, and attacked free black women for their "idleness," "incontinence," and "libertinism." Demanding that they renounce their "mode of living," Miró threatened to punish any free black woman wearing feathers, jewels, or silks. The new proclamation prohibited all headdresses and required free women of color to wear their hair bound in a *tignon* (kerchief) as a sign of their inferior status.

Miró also attempted to restrict the activities of the slave population. The governor prohibited slaves from renting apartments or houses, buying "spirituous liquors," or dancing in public squares on days of religious obligation. In spite of the new regulations, long-standing practices persisted.[20]

After 1789, Spain's ameliorative policies and the spread of revolution to France's New World colonies contributed to tumultuous conditions in Louisiana. In Europe and America between 1760 and 1800, widespread discontent with unrepresentative political institutions and privileged elites produced an era of revolutionary upheaval. In the New World, the enormous sweep of revolutionary agitation resulted in the establishment of independent republics in North America and the Caribbean. During the nineteenth century, continuing turmoil in Europe contributed to the emergence of autonomous republics throughout Latin America. As the spread of revolution convulsed eighteenth-century society, the concept of equality became closely linked to the spread of liberty.

In August, 1789, in France, the ideal of equality was intimately bound to the concept of liberty in the Declaration of the Rights of Man and Citizen. In the Declaration, the French National Assembly emphasized man's natural rights, which included "liberty, property, security, and resistance

20. Christian, "A Black History," Chap. XVI, 7; Annie Lee West Stahl, "The Free Negro in Ante-Bellum Louisiana," *Louisiana Historical Quarterly,* XXV (April, 1942), 307; quotations from Gayarré, *History of Louisiana,* III, 179–80.

to oppression." Article I declared, "Men are born and remain free and equal in rights." The concepts of freedom and equality generated a feeling of solidarity, a sense of fraternity. In the new world order, differences would be reconciled. In such a spirit, the principles of *liberté, égalité, fraternité* were proclaimed. In Western Europe and colonial America, revolutionaries insisted on equality in a wide variety of sociopolitical relationships. For a few, this demand meant racial equality.[21]

In the French Caribbean, the struggle for racial equality triggered a fateful chain of events. In Paris in October, 1789, free men of color from Saint Domingue demanded that the French Assembly grant them equal citizenship on the basis of the Declaration of the Rights of Man. Slave uprisings spread through Saint Domingue, Guadeloupe, and Martinique. In St. Marc, Saint Domingue, planters launched a campaign of terror against free blacks and swore that they would recognize neither the rights of the mulattoes, a "bastard and degenerate race," nor those of blacks, a "species of orangutan."[22]

Frustrated in their demands for equal rights, Vincent Ogé and other free men of color organized a revolt with the aid of antislavery forces in France and England. Before launching an uprising in Saint Domingue in October, 1790, Ogé issued a warning to the colonial assembly. Spurning the derogatory epithet "men of mixed blood," Ogé proclaimed: "A prejudice too long maintained, is about to fall. . . . I require you to promulgate throughout the colony the instructions of the National Assembly of the 8th of March, which gives without distinction to all free citizens the right of admission to all offices and functions. . . . I shall not call the plantations to rise; that means would be unworthy of me . . . but if, contrary to my expectations, you do not satisfy my demand, I am not answerable for the disorder into which my just vengeance may carry me."[23]

21. R. R. Palmer, *The Age of Democratic Revolution: A Political History of Europe and America, 1760–1800* (Princeton, 1959, 1964), I, 4–7, II, 572–73; Georges Lefebvre, *The French Revolution,* trans. Elizabeth M. Evanson (1951; New York, 1969), I, 145–52.

22. Shelby T. McCloy, *The Negro in the French West Indies* (Lexington, Ky., 1966), 74–209; James, *The Black Jacobins,* 72–82; Jan Pachonski and Reuel K. Wilson, *Poland's Caribbean Tragedy: A Study of Polish Legions in the Haitian War of Independence, 1802–1803* (New York, 1986), 33.

23. James, *The Black Jacobins,* 73; Rev. John R. Beard, *The Life of Toussaint L'Ouverture, the Negro Patriot of Hayti: Comprising an Account of the Struggle for Liberty in the Island, and a Sketch of Its History to the Present Period* (1853; rpr. Westport, Conn., 1970), 57.

Planters suppressed the insurrection. Defeated, Ogé and his chief lieutenant, Jean-Baptiste Chavannes, were condemned "whilst alive to have their arms, legs, thighs and spine broken; and afterward to be placed on a wheel, their faces toward Heaven, and there to stay as long as it would please God to preserve their lives; and when dead, their heads were to be cut off and exposed on poles."[24]

The swiftness and barbarism with which the uprising was put down did not diminish black aspirations. The following spring, a fratricidal conflict among white colonists heightened their expectations. When France's Constituent Assembly dispatched troops to Saint Domingue to restore order in March, 1791, French soldiers landing in Port-au-Prince fueled the mounting revolutionary fervor. They proclaimed that the French Assembly had declared all men free and equal and greeted mulattoes and blacks in the fraternal embrace. In August, 1791, slaves near Cap Français in the North Province and men of color in the West Province rose up in almost simultaneous revolts against Saint Domingue's white, slaveholding elite. The rebellions dealt a crushing blow to the planter regime.[25]

As events unfolded in Saint Domingue, the revolutionary government in France responded haltingly. Unable to control the rebellious white colonists, the French Assembly accorded full citizenship rights to free people of color on March 28, 1792, in an attempt to win their allegiance. On August 29, 1793, in continued fighting in Saint Domingue, Jacobin emissaries of the French government promised freedom to all slaves in return for their support. Finally, on February 4, 1794, the National Convention abolished slavery outright. In Paris, Deputy Camboulas addressed the assembled representatives: "Since 1789 the aristocracy of birth and the aristocracy of religion have been destroyed; but the aristocracy of the skin still remains. That too is now at its last gasp, and equality has been consecrated. A black man, a yellow man, are about to join this Convention in the name of the free citizens of San Domingo." The hall burst into applause as the new representatives entered.[26]

24. Earl Leslie Griggs and Clifford H. Prator, eds., *Henry Christophe and Thomas Clarkson: A Correspondence* (New York, 1968), 12.

25. James, *The Black Jacobins,* 72–86.

26. Lefebvre, *The French Revolution,* II, 130; James, *The Black Jacobins,* 139–40. Established in 1789, the French National Assembly became the National Convention in 1792.

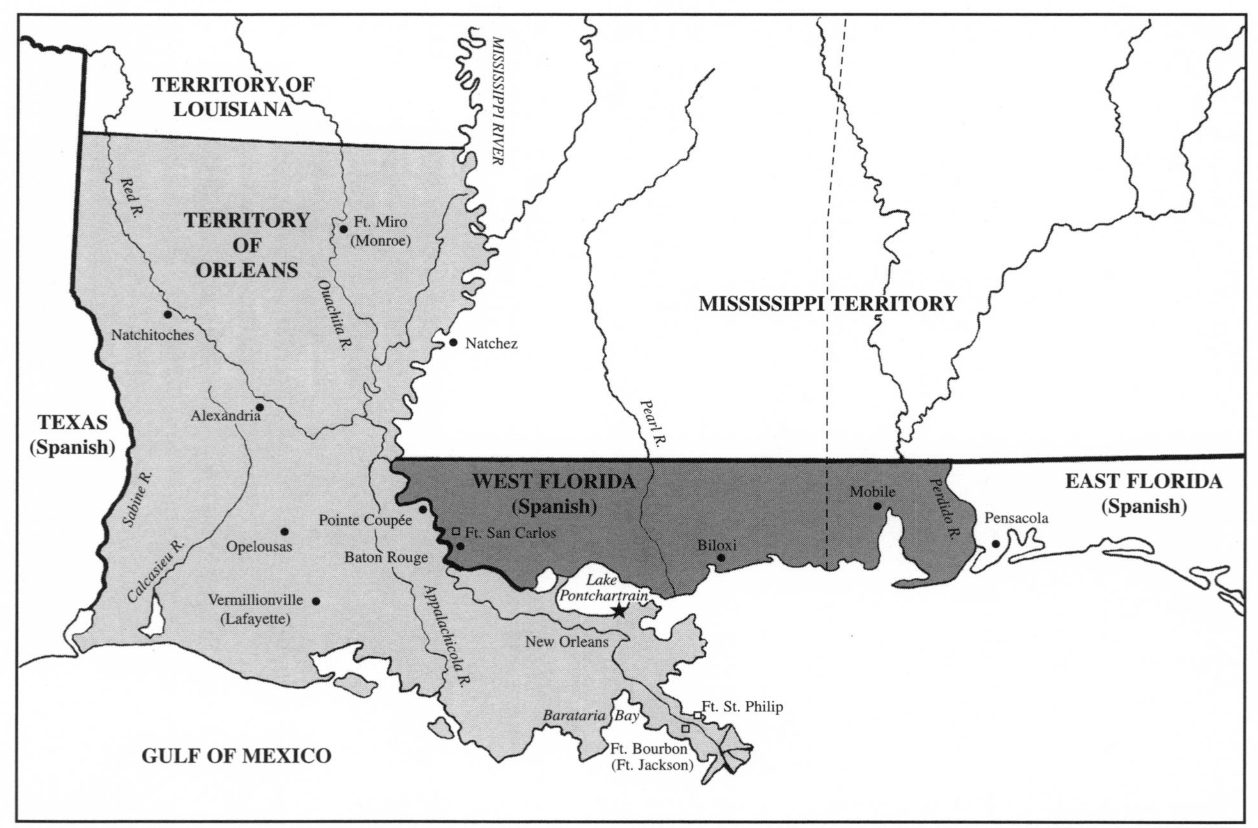

Louisiana During the Territorial Period, 1803–1812

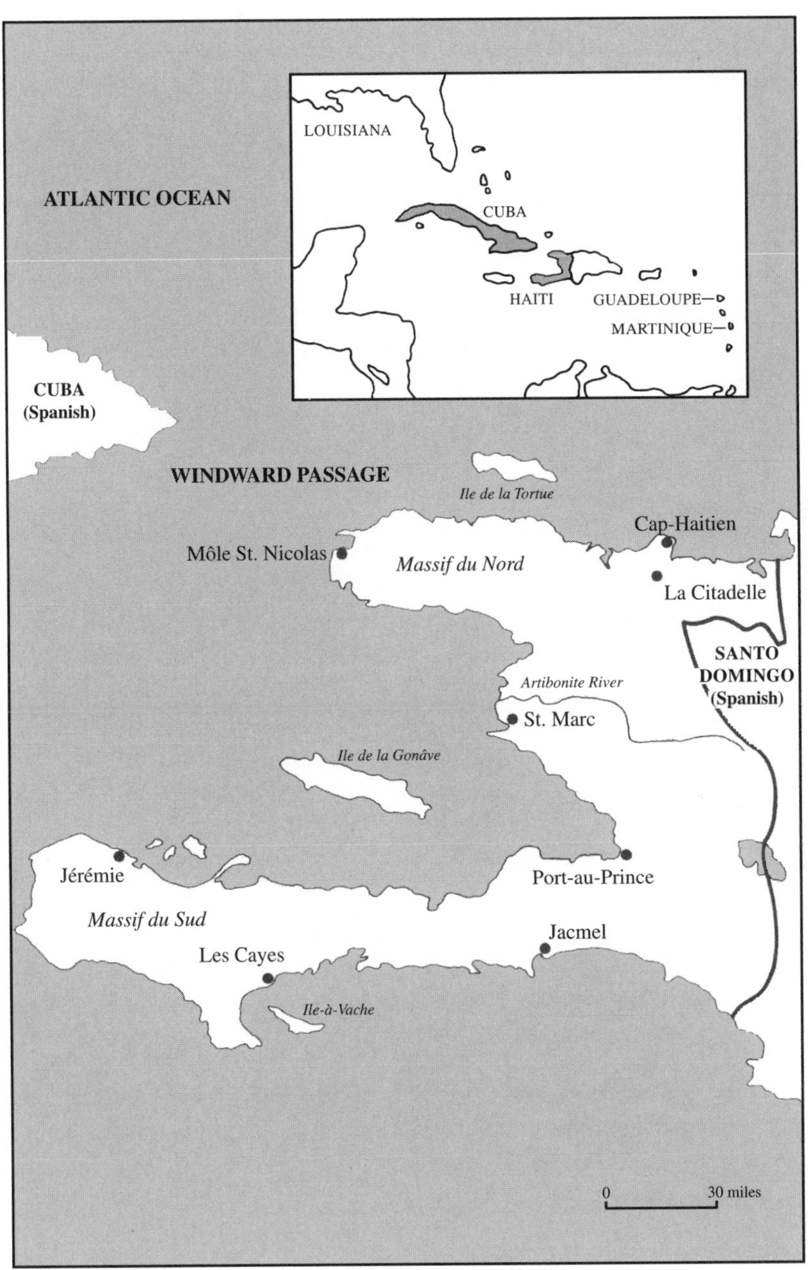

LOUISIANA
CUBA
HAITI
GUADELOUPE
MARTINIQUE
ATLANTIC OCEAN
CUBA
(Spanish)
WINDWARD PASSAGE
Ile de la Tortue
Cap-Haitien
Môle St. Nicolas
Massif du Nord
La Citadelle
SANTO
DOMINGO
(Spanish)
Artibonite River
St. Marc
Ile de la Gonâve
Jérémie
Port-au-Prince
Massif du Sud
Jacmel
Les Cayes
Ile-à-Vache
0
30 miles

Haiti in 1804

The outbreak of revolution in Europe and the French Caribbean produced considerable repercussions in Spanish Louisiana. Spanish authorities could not insulate free people of color and slaves from events underway in France and the Antilles. The ideal of racial equality, given political expression in the French Convention of 1794, and the realization of national independence in Haiti in January, 1804, presented a radical challenge to slavery and racial oppression. While the ideals of the French Revolution formed the theoretical basis for the continuing struggle against racial injustice, Haiti became a symbol of freedom and racial equality.[27]

After 1789, Spanish attempts to maintain control of slaves and free blacks in Louisiana became increasingly difficult. French-speaking people of color seized upon French revolutionary ideals and the images of revolutionary events in the French Caribbean to obtain equal status. Disturbances in the slave population signaled the onset of widespread disorders. Beginning in 1791, a series of plots and slave conspiracies alerted colonial officials to the danger of black insurrection. During the summer, planters uncovered an extensive slave plot in Pointe Coupée, a fertile agricultural district 150 miles upriver from New Orleans. It was quickly suppressed.[28]

In October, authorities investigated charges against Pierre Bailly, an officer in the pardo militia. Manumitted in 1776 at the age of twenty-five, Bailly had distinguished himself in military expeditions against the British during the American Revolution. Between 1779 and 1793, he rose to the rank of first lieutenant in the free pardo militia company. At the same time, he acquired considerable economic security through a variety of successful business ventures. An astute and aggressive soldier and businessman, Bailly resented the discriminatory barriers that blocked the political and social aspirations of free people of color and prevented their assimilation on an equal basis.

In 1791, a white business rival, Luis de Lalande Dapremont, presented evidence to authorities accusing Bailly of conspiring against the Spanish government. Dapremont implicated three other free pardo militiamen, Estaban Lalande, Carlos Brulé, and Roberto Monplaisir, when he recounted

27. David Nicholls, *From Dessalines to Duvalier: Race, Colour and National Independence in Haiti* (Cambridge, Eng., 1979), 3–4; Alfred N. Hunt, *Haiti's Influence on Antebellum America: Slumbering Volcano in the Caribbean* (Baton Rouge, 1988), 3–4.

28. Hall, *Africans in Colonial Louisiana,* Chap. 10.

a conversation at an interracial dance at Lalande's home in which Bailly praised black revolutionaries in the French Caribbean and urged his fellow militiamen to take up arms against white Louisianians. According to the allegations, Bailly had announced that he and his colleagues were only awaiting word from Saint Domingue to "strike a blow like at the Cap [Cap Français]." When the free pardo militiamen refused to corroborate Dapremont's hearsay evidence, Governor Miró acquitted Bailly.[29]

Excitement in New Orleans reached a fever pitch when revolutionaries in France proclaimed the French Republic in 1792 and guillotined the French monarch. In 1793, emotions in the city overflowed when Spain joined the First Coalition against France. Theatergoers insisted that orchestras play "La Marseillaise" and French partisans boldly sang the Jacobin song "Ça ira—ça ira, les aristocrates à la lanterne" ("Hang the aristocrats on the lamppost") in the streets of the city.[30]

Earlier in 1793, the French revolutionary government had dispatched Jacobin agents to the New World to spread the ideals of the revolution. Having declared war on England and Spain, the Convention endeavored to inspire rebellions in enemy territories. At the same time that French Jacobins plotted to invade Louisiana, they urged white Creole Louisianians to "cease being the slaves of a government to which you were shamefully sold." From within the colony, 150 inhabitants signed a petition pleading with the new republic for protection.[31]

Thoroughly alarmed, Spanish authorities responded decisively. Colonial officials arrested six of the most outspoken republicans and dispatched them to the castle fortress at Havana to serve twelve-month prison sentences. Governor Miró's successor, Baron Hector de Carondelet,

29. Kimberly Hanger, "Conflicting Loyalties: The French Revolution and Free People of Color in Spanish New Orleans," *Louisiana History,* XXXIV (Winter, 1993), 12–23; Lachance, "The Politics of Fear," 168*n*17.

30. Alcée Fortier, *A History of Louisiana* (New York, 1904), II, 152; Grace King, *New Orleans, the Place and the People* (1896; rpr. New York, 1926), 142–43. France declared war on England February 1, 1793, and on Spain March 7. See Lefebvre, *The French Revolution,* I, 283; Baudier, *The Catholic Church,* 218; Gayarré, *History of Louisiana,* III, 327.

31. Anne Pérotin-Dumon, "Les Corsaires de la liberté," *L'Histoire,* XLIII (March, 1982), 25; King, *New Orleans,* 142–43; Ernest R. Liljegren, "Jacobinism in Spanish Louisiana, 1792–1797," *Louisiana Historical Quarterly,* XXII (January, 1939), 48; quotation in Gayarré, *History of Louisiana,* III, 337–38.

fortified the city, demanded strict curfews, and prohibited revolutionary songs. By July, 1793, Governor Carondelet had banished sixty-eight suspected French agents from Louisiana.[32]

Despite attempts to suppress dissent, radical influences from France spread through the city. New Orleanians sang Jacobin songs to celebrate the day when they would be republicans and free men. In one of these popular songs, they threatened to guillotine the "swine governor" and send the treasurer and the auditor to the gallows. Under such circumstances, Governor Carondelet viewed the actions of free blacks and slaves with great concern. Colonial officials must, he wrote, "always fear that the free men of color and the slaves will allow themselves to be tempted by the corruption of the French government," and that blacks who joined with the French "do so mostly with the one desire which they so much value: to possess liberty, for which I believe we have more reason to fear these than the whites."[33]

In one instance in which the governor expelled a Saint Dominguan free black, he explained his action: "He is a native of the part of Santo Domingo that belongs to the French and is mixed up in all the intrigues and harassments of the French colony, besides being ungovernable and audacious. Having such a character around under the present circumstances in which I am placed, might produce bad results." Reports of the seditious activities of rebellious militiaman Pierre Bailly also alarmed Carondelet.[34]

In November, 1793, in anticipation of an attack by French forces, Carondelet dispatched reinforcements, including the free pardo militia company, to Fort Saint Philip at Plaquemines near the mouth of the Mississippi River. When military officials at the fort commanded the pardo company to perform manual labor on the fortifications, Bailly, who considered the work demeaning, challenged the authority of his free pardo commander, Francisco Dorville, feigned illness, and remained in his tent. He resented the Spanish regime's discriminatory treatment of the free black soldiers, and he urged his comrades to join him in his boycott.

32. Gayarré, *History of Louisiana,* III, 350–56; Hunt, *Haiti's Influence,* 25.

33. McConnell, *Negro Troops,* 27; Messages of Francisco Luis Hector, El Baron de Carondelet, Sixth Governor of Louisiana, 1792–97 (translation), in Louisiana State Works Progress Administration Project, 1937–41, Vol. 9, p. 214, National Archives.

34. Hunt, *Haiti's Influence,* 26–27.

Not content with inciting his fellow free black soldiers to insubordinate behavior, he voiced his grievances and seditious political views to white officers. In a confrontation with Don Luis Declouet, second lieutenant of the Louisiana regiment, he deplored the regime's color-conscious social hierarchy and praised the French revolutionary government for having introduced "universal equality among men." In Saint Domingue and elsewhere in the French Caribbean, Bailly defiantly declared to his superior officer, the French republic had extended equal citizenship to free men of color.

Determined to restore order to the garrison, the commanding officer, Colonel Gilbert Antoine de St. Maxent, arranged to remove the free black agitator. When Bailly returned to New Orleans, he was charged with defaming the Spanish government and espousing revolutionary ideas. In March, 1794, Governor Carondelet found the irrepressible officer guilty of "having burst into tirades against the Spanish government and of being a manifest follower of the maxims of the French rebels." Carondelet sent Bailly to Morro Castle in Havana, where he remained imprisoned until 1796.[35]

In May, 1795, in another incident involving free black militiamen, Carondelet complained to the Cabildo of "an unlawful meeting, comprised of fifteen mulattoes, intended to induce them to revolt against the white people."[36] The governor noted the participation of Captain Charles Simon and Captain Francisco Dorville, free black militia officers and accused them of conspiring with the French. Although an inquiry cleared the officers of the charges, another reported conspiracy involving the free black militia disturbed colonial officials.

An investigation into more charges of conspiracy among members of the free black militia disclosed that in 1793, a French soldier had approached a free black militiaman with a plot to overthrow the Spanish regime. The French soldier proclaimed to the free black militiaman, Charles Joseph Lange, that all Frenchmen were brothers and invited black militiamen to join the plot. When officials discovered the conspiracy, Lange's commanding officer advised him to testify against the French

35. Hanger, "Conflicting Loyalties," 13, 26.

36. Minutes for May 2, 1795, in Records and Deliberations of the Cabildo, New Orleans Public Library (translation), hereinafter cited as Cabildo Books, NOPL.

soldier. On the basis of his testimony and that of a slave, Noel Trudeau, who had drunk with the men in a tavern, the Frenchman was found guilty and deported to Pensacola.[37]

In spite of Carondelet's precautions, the governor complained to Cabildo officials in May, 1795, that "the colony, by means of secret and undercover plots, is on the verge of being submerged in the horrors which have ruined the French colonies." Carondelet described the activities of French agents who "incessantly worked secretly" with the aim of "procuring to have me hated, by means of the most outrageous calumnies." At the same time, the governor attempted to impress upon Cabildo members his role in maintaining order. He boasted that if "the General of Cap Français had taken these same precautions, its citizens would not have been furiously assassinated."[38]

Meanwhile in the spring of 1795, in an attempted slave insurrection on the plantation of Julian Poydras in Pointe Coupée, colonial officials blamed Jacobin provocateurs for inciting the slaves to set fire to their masters' homes. A subsequent investigation revealed that outside agitators had fueled the unrest with inflammatory propaganda from France and Saint Domingue. Two white insurrectionists were sent to Havana to serve six-year prison sentences, and another white, two Saint Dominguan free blacks, and a slave were banished from the colony. The incident caused planter Joseph Pontalba to take "heed of the dreadful calamities of Saint Domingue, and of the germ of revolt only too widespread among our own slaves." Continued slave unrest in Pointe Coupée and on the German Coast contributed to a decision to shut down the entire slave trade in the spring of 1796.[39]

In 1800, during debates about reopening the African slave trade, Cabildo members agreed to exclude Saint Domingue blacks and noted the presence of black and white insurgents from the French West Indies who were "propagating dangerous doctrines among our Negroes." One angry participant observed: "In our bosom we have a number of Negrophiles who blow the seductive venom into the hearts of Negroes and Mulattoes and place in their hands iron and fire with which to destroy the Whites."

37. McConnell, *Negro Troops,* 27–28.

38. Minutes for May 2, 1795, Cabildo Books, NOPL.

39. McConnell, *Negro Troops,* 26–27; Lachance, "The Politics of Fear," 168.

One Cabildo official noted "the insolent anger of slaves toward their masters and other white people," and another observed that the slaves seemed more "insolent," "ungovernable," and "insubordinate" than in 1795.[40]

Spain's cession of Louisiana to France in 1800 did not quell the fear of slave insurrection among white inhabitants of the Gulf coast settlement. After Napoleon sold the colony to the United States in 1803, American officials were similarly alarmed by the spectacle of armed free black militia units and the aggressive actions of free men of color in demanding their rights. The peculiar problems the Americans encountered stemmed in part from failed colonial policies. Spain's attempts to counteract planter power by establishing a tri-caste racial order had resulted in unstable conditions. As free blacks and mulattoes assumed positions of power and authority within the colony, the ability to equate skin color with servility became more difficult. The practice of race mixing, another by-product of Latin European rule, complicated matters. The inability to make racial distinctions on the basis of skin color contributed to the instability. Just as important, Spanish policies that advanced the interests of free people of color inevitably heightened their expectations; the outbreak of revolution in Europe raised them even further. In such circumstances, the task of imposing the American ideal of a dual racial order was indeed formidable.

In December, 1803, territorial officials feared the reaction of the black militia as the United States assumed formal control of Louisiana. Both Claiborne and co-commissioner General James Wilkinson urged the president and secretary of war to send arms and troops to New Orleans. The appearance of the black corps on parade at the formal ceremonies in December thoroughly frightened white officials. The day after the public gathering, Wilkinson dashed off a request to Washington for reinforcements. The general found that the "formidable aspect of the armed Blacks & Malattoes [*sic*], officered and organized, is painful and perplexing."[41]

Within days of the ceremony, Claiborne also issued an urgent appeal to the State Department for guidance as he confronted his "principal difficulty."

40. Lachance, "The Politics of Fear," 169–75.

41. Donald E. Everett, "Emigres and Militiamen: Free Persons of Color in New Orleans, 1803–1815," *Journal of Negro History,* XXXVIII (October, 1953), 378–79; James Wilkinson to the Secretary of War, December 21, 1803, in *The Territory of Orleans, 1803–1812,* ed. Clarence Edwin Carter (Washington, 1940), 139, Vol. IX of Carter, ed., *The Territorial Papers of the United States.*

Claiborne feared that recommissioning the black militia "might be considered as an outrage on the feelings of a part of the Nation, and as opposed to those principles of Policy which the Safety of the Southern States has necessarily established; on the other hand not to be recommissioned, would disgust them" and have the effect of raising "an armed enemy in the very heart of the Country." The governor proceeded very cautiously.[42]

Although free blacks, having "universally mounted the Eagle in their Hats," appeared reconciled to the new order by the middle of January, General Wilkinson continued to express grave concerns. He warned: "The People of Colour are all armed, and it is my Opinion a single envious artful bold incendiary, by rousing their fears & exciting their Hopes, might produce those Horrible Scenes of Bloodshed & rapine, which have been so frequently noticed in St. Domingo." Other observers shared Wilkinson's sense of unease. Benjamin Morgan pointed out Spain's willingness to accord free blacks "rights in common with other subjects." Moreover, an open invitation to the black militia to remain in the service of Spain intensified American anxieties. Bounded on the east and west by Spanish possessions, American officials could not afford to underestimate Spanish influence.[43]

In January, as Claiborne waited for instructions from Washington, members of the black militia extended their loyalty and services to the "American Republic." In the formal petition signed by fifty-five members of the militia, including the redoubtable Pierre Bailly, the soldiers expressed their confidence in the new government: "We are duly sensible that our personal and political freedom is thereby assured to us for ever, and we are also impressed with the fullest confidence in the Justice and Liberality of the Government toward every Class of Citizens which they have here taken under their Protection." As the document clearly indicated, the petitioners expected to acquire full citizenship rights according

42. Claiborne to James Madison, December 27, 1803, in Rowland, ed., *Official Letter Books,* I, 314.

43. James Wilkinson to Secretary of War, January 11, 1804, in Carter, ed., *Territorial Papers,* IX, 34; McConnell, *Negro Troops,* 42; Christian, "Demand by Men of Color," 56; David C. Rankin, "The Tannenbaum Thesis Reconsidered: Slavery and Race Relations in Antebellum Louisiana," *Southern Studies,* XVIII (Spring, 1979), 33. Benjamin Morgan, a prominent American businessman and politician, is quoted in Everett, "Emigres and Militiamen," 377.

to the terms set forth in the 1803 treaty of cession. Article 3 of the act entitled all the inhabitants of the colony to "the enjoyment of all rights, advantages and immunities of citizens of the United States."[44]

Under the Americans, free people of color in New Orleans felt justified in claiming equal status. They had fought on the side of the colonists in the American Revolutionary War. In highly successful offensives against British garrisons on the Mississippi River and the Gulf of Mexico at Mobile and Pensacola, Governor Bernardo de Gálvez had deployed black soldiers. "No less deserving of eulogy are the companies of Negroes and free Mulattoes," Gálvez wrote in a 1780 account of the campaigns. They had been "continually occupied in the outposts, in false attacks, and discoveries, exchanging shots with the enemy" and had performed with as much courage and vigor as the white soldiers.[45]

Anxious to pacify the militiamen, Claiborne responded promptly to their address. While sidestepping the question of citizenship and the matter of recommissioning the militia, he assured the men that the United States intended to protect their freedom and their property. Anticipating instructions from Washington, Claiborne took no immediate steps to disband the organization.[46]

In Washington, during deliberations early in October, 1803, President Thomas Jefferson had anticipated difficulties with the black militia. The president determined in a cabinet meeting that "the militia of colour shall be confirmed in their posts, and treated favorably, till a better settled state of things shall permit us to let them neglect themselves." In February, upon the advice of Secretary of War Henry Dearborn, Claiborne decided to present the black militia with a regimental banner.[47]

During the summer of 1804, racial tensions mounted over the status of the militia. In early June, as Claiborne reorganized the military forces, he appointed white officers to the black militia. Although black militiamen

44. "Address from the Free People of Color," January, 1804, in Carter, ed., *Territorial Papers,* IX, 174–75.

45. McConnell, *Negro Troops,* 18.

46. Claiborne to Madison, January 17, 1804, in Rowland, ed., *Official Letter Books,* I, 339–40; McConnell, *Negro Troops,* 38–39.

47. Jefferson's notes on a cabinet meeting, October 4, 1803, in Thomas Jefferson Papers, Library of Congress.

raised objections to the dismissal of their officers and expressed a particular aversion to their new commander, Michel Fortier, a wealthy white Creole merchant, Claiborne persuaded them to accept the appointments.

On June 21, Claiborne presented a stand of colors to the black battalion. Fearful of an attack by angry whites, the governor posted a guard around the parade ground to protect the corps. In a related incident, a prominent citizen accused a black militiaman of striking him with his musket. In July, Claiborne faced another crisis when free black leaders challenged their exclusion from a white citizens' meeting.[48]

Led by Edward Livingston, French-speaking whites had gathered to draft a memorial to Congress to air their grievances and assert their rights. Angry free black leaders prepared to hold a similar public meeting so that "they might consult as to *their* rights" and draft their own petition to Congress. One of the men even attempted to publicize a memorial along with details of the anticipated meeting. Certain of violence if the gathering took place, Claiborne was prepared to use force to prevent free blacks from assembling.[49]

The governor convened a meeting with the mayor of the city, Etienne de Boré, and nine influential black leaders. He insisted that they abandon their plans. Assured of their cooperation, Claiborne refused white demands to reveal the identity of the prominent free black leader who had attempted to publicize the memorial. Infuriated by the appeal, native whites were determined to punish the individual responsible for the petition. Claiborne, ever mindful of events in Saint Domingue, was just as determined not to provoke the city's black majority, for at about this time the total urban population of 8,475 residents included 3,105 slaves and 1,556 people of color.

The incident contributed to a decision by whites to discontinue their public meetings. While the governor had managed to calm the situation, white Louisianians continued to fume over Claiborne's recognition of the

48. McConnell, *Negro Troops,* 38–40; Everett, "Emigres and Militiamen," 390–92; Christian, "Demand by Men of Color," 57. See James Wilkinson to the Secretary of War, January 11, 1804, in Carter, ed., *Territorial Papers,* IX, 160, for Wilkinson's assessment of mounting racial hostilities.

49. Claiborne to Madison, July 3, 1804, in Rowland, ed., *Official Letter Books,* II, 234–35.

black militia. In October, 1804, with the establishment of the first territorial legislature, white leaders took their revenge. Territorial legislators forced the inactivation of the unit. In January, 1805, in the *Louisiana Gazette* a "Louisianian" expressed continuing resentment over Claiborne's presentation to the black corps of a banner similar to that of the white militia. The writer also criticized the governor for "putting up with their [the free black militiamen's] disrespectful refusal of the officers whom he had appointed as their adjutants." On April 10, 1805, the legislature again omitted the battalion from the militia law.[50]

After 1803, Claiborne's dismissal of black officers and his failure to incorporate the corps into the territory's military forces had undoubtedly encouraged white opponents of the black militia. With planter dominance assured in the American takeover, the territorial legislature immediately suppressed the military unit. The black militia, a major vehicle of free black advancement and an esteemed social institution within the black community, was one of the earliest casualties of the new regime. Still, spirited free black leadership and intervening events prevented the dispersal of the militia units.

Hardly had Claiborne dealt with the bold demands of free black leaders for political equality when the victory of Haitian revolutionaries in January, 1804, sparked another series of confrontations in Louisiana. In February, the inhabitants of Bayou La Fourche complained of a visit by twelve black Haitians from a passing vessel who threatened them with "many insulting and menacing expressions" and "spoke of eating human flesh, and in general demonstrated great Savageness of character, boasting of what they had seen and done in the horrors of St. Domingo." Other events alarmed officials, and in Pointe Coupée planters warned Claiborne that their slaves were exhibiting a "spirit of Revolt and mutyny [*sic*]."[51]

The behavior of white French emigrés also concerned territorial officials. In January, 1804, Claiborne had complained of the presence in New Orleans of white malcontents from Saint Domingue and Bordeaux.

50. Everett, "Emigres and Militiamen," 379–80; Christian, "Demand by Men of Color," 57; the 1805 population figures cited in the text are from Fiehrer, "The African Presence," in *Louisiana's Black Heritage,* 19; McConnell, *Negro Troops,* 41.

51. Lachance, "The Politics of Fear," 183; John Watkins to Claiborne, February, 1804, in Robertson, ed., *Louisiana Under the Rule,* II, 313–14.

Humiliated by the American takeover, the French partisans agitated against the new government. Although few in number, the handful of French loyalists effectively exploited ethnic divisions. In September, American attorney James Brown bitterly denounced the establishment of a municipal police force by the city council; the "French *Maréchaussée*" (police force), composed of "St. Domingo cut-throats," Brown wrote, "frequent at all hours of the night . . . the tabarets [*sic*] or little Tipling houses and drink with free negroes or slaves, who appear to be their principal associates." The three "disaffected" French commanding officers recruited many of their "*Gendarmerie*" from the "renegado's of St. Domingo . . . these wretches who have sucked the blood of the ill-fated inhabitants" of the island. Within days of Brown's attack, city officials arrested a white Saint Domingue refugee for fomenting revolution among free blacks and slaves.[52]

In August, a slave had informed American authorities of the activities of a white Frenchman named Grandjean. In an incendiary proclamation, "Le Jugement de la raison humaine," and in placards posted in the marketplace and around the city, Grandjean appealed to free blacks and slaves. Unsuspectingly confiding in informants, the refugee described his involvement in a similar plot in Saint Domingue.[53]

Thoroughly alarmed by Grandjean's plans to massacre whites and burn the city, Mayor John Watkins pleaded with territorial officials for armed reinforcements: "But, Sir, from our contiguity to the West India Islands, from the great number of Slaves and free people of color as well as bad disposed white people now among us who have been conversant with the crimes that have disgraced and the innocent blood which encrimsoned the plains of St. Domingo and other countries we shall ever be in danger while the protecting Arm of our country is so feeble."

In the same dispatch the mayor viewed the city's black majority with considerable alarm: "In limits of the City of New Orleans there are in-

52. Claiborne to James Madison, January 24, 1804, in Rowland, ed., *Official Letter Books,* I, 345; James Brown to John Breckinridge, September 17, 1805, in Carter, ed., *Territorial Papers,* IX, 510-12. *Maréchaussée* refers to a rural police force. In Saint Domingue, free men of color and whites were enlisted in the militia and the maréchaussée to hunt runaway slaves, patrol the highways, and suppress maroon colonies (Foner, "Free People of Color," 418).

53. John Watkins to Secretary to the Territory of Orleans John Graham, September 6, 1805, in Carter, ed., *Territorial Papers,* IX, 500–504.

cluding negroes and people of colour . . . nearly twelve thousand souls, and not above four thousand whites of all ages & sexes. The numbers of the former are increasing in a much greater proportion than those of the latter, and that increase is much more dangerous in quality than in quantity. Many worthless free people of colour or persons calling themselves free arrive here daily without our being able to prevent it, or to drive them away after they have come."[54]

As early as May, 1790, a Spanish decree ordered royal officials to prohibit the entry of slaves and free blacks from the French West Indies. After the American takeover, continuing fears of a slave revolt and the city's growing black majority inspired a similar series of restrictive enactments. Territorial officials continued the ban on West Indian slaves, and on June 7, 1806, the territorial legislature barred the entry of free black males from the French Caribbean over fourteen years of age. Subsequent legislation on April 14, 1807, prohibited all free black adult males from entering, regardless of their nationality. Severe penalties, including enslavement, accompanied the statutes.[55]

The suppression of free black aspirations—aspirations heightened by events in Haiti and the spread of revolutionary ideals—and the official abandonment of the militia alienated Creoles of color. In early January, 1806, Claiborne concluded that the legislature's refusal to recognize the free black corps "has soured them considerably with the American Government, and it is questionable how far they would, in the hour of danger, prove faithful to the American Standard." Within weeks of Claiborne's pronouncement, the revelations of a free black named Stephen indicated the extent of their resentment.[56]

According to Stephen, a far-reaching plot existed among armed "Creoles of color" in New Orleans. With few exceptions, the city's "people of color" awaited the arrival of a large Spanish force headed by the Marquis

54. *Ibid.*, 503. For the estimated numbers of Haitian immigrants entering Louisiana between 1792 and 1809, see Paul F. Lachance, "The 1809 Immigration of Saint-Domingue Refugees to New Orleans: Reception, Integration and Impact," *Louisiana History,* XXIX (Spring, 1988), 110–11.

55. Lachance, "The Politics of Fear," 165–84; Sterkx, *The Free Negro,* 93.

56. Claiborne to Secretary of State James Madison, January 8, 1806, in Carter, ed., *Territorial Papers,* IX, 561.

de Casa Calvo to begin an uprising in which they would free slaves and overthrow the Americans. The informant named Spanish agents and their free black accomplices, including "Charles Brulet a yellow man called Captain of the Granadies" and "Landau . . . the person who carries about the paper to ascertain those who are friendly to the Spaniards." Although somewhat skeptical of Stephen's testimony, Claiborne was nevertheless convinced that "the free people of colour have been tamper'd with, and that some are devoted to the Spanish Interest." He ordered a militia company to stand guard every night. In May, territorial legislators once again excluded the free black corps from the militia act.[57]

The suppression of the free black militia pointed to broader changes underway after the American occupation. Stricter controls over free people of color and slaves accompanied Louisiana's transfer to the United States. In December, during the brief period of French rule, colonial officials bowed to the demands of planters and merchants. The colonial prefect, Pierre Clément de Laussat, supported the free importation of slaves and ordered strict enforcement of the Code Noir of 1724. Clearly signaling an end to Spanish policies that diminished planter authority, the directives represented a new departure in race relations. After Louisianians acquired a territorial legislature in 1806, they enacted one of the harshest and most sweeping slave codes in the American South. In declaring that the slave's "subordination to his master and to all who represent him is not susceptible to any modification or restriction," the codes heralded a new order. But American repression could not eliminate the presence of a free black caste unique in southern slave society.[58]

By the turn of the century, Spanish policies had contributed to the emergence of a proud and aspiring class of Creoles of color. For the Spaniards, the free black class had served as a crucial counterweight to planter ambitions. Lenient manumission practices, a lax social regimen, and the exigencies of colonial management promoted economic and social mobility for the free black population. Events in Saint Domingue and rev-

57. "Statement of Stephen, a Free Negro, to Governor Claiborne," January 23, 1806, in Carter, ed., *Territorial Papers,* IX, 575–76; Marcus Christian, *The Battle of New Orleans: Negro Soldiers in the Battle of New Orleans* (New Orleans, 1965), 10; McConnell, *Negro Troops,* 42.

58. Lachance, "The Politics of Fear," 178–84.

olutionary France inspired free blacks to assert their rights. The presence, however, of a class of free people of color proved inimical to the interests of the emergent planter elite. As events in Saint Domingue had shown, free blacks could pose a serious threat to slave society. Under the new authority, Creoles of color would suffer an unprecedented and sustained attack upon their rights.

After 1803, exclusionary emigration laws and restrictive manumission policies threatened to retard the growth of the free black population in Louisiana. At the same time that the territorial legislature prohibited the entry of any free black adult males in 1807, lawmakers also forbade the emancipation of any slave under thirty unless the slave had performed some act of extraordinary heroism. The age restriction prevented a free black husband from purchasing the freedom of his underage slave wife. The children of the couple, following the status of the mother, were destined to remain slaves until the age of thirty.

In spite of the prohibitively harsh legislation that accompanied the American occupation, the free black population grew dramatically during the territorial period. Significantly, a sharp increase in the numbers of free people of color occurred between May, 1809, and January, 1810, when the Spanish government expelled thousands of Saint Domingue refugees from Cuba. Forced to seek asylum in New Orleans, over ten thousand white, free black, and slave exiles nearly doubled the size of the urban population.[59]

Earlier, the Haitian Revolution had forced scores of Saint Dominguans into exile. One hundred of these refugees arrived in New Orleans between 1791 and 1797, two hundred entered between 1797 and 1802, and over a thousand disembarked at the time of the Louisiana Purchase. Partly as a consequence of these in-migrations, the city's urban population of 2,370 whites, 823 free people of color, and 2,126 slaves grew from 5,319 in 1788 to 8,475 in 1805, with 3,804 whites, 1,566 free people of color, and 3,105 slaves. In 1810, after the 1809 entry of 2,731 whites, 3,102 free people of color, and 3,226 slaves, the city's total population jumped to 17,242, with

59. Joe Gray Taylor, *Negro Slavery in Louisiana* (Baton Rouge, 1963), 154; Judith K. Schafer, " 'Open and Notorious Concubinage': The Emancipation of Slave Mistresses by Will and the Supreme Court in Antebellum Louisiana," *Louisiana History,* XXVIII (Spring, 1987), 166; Lachance, "The 1809 Immigration," 110–12.

6,331 whites, 4,950 free people of color, and 5,961 slaves. While city officials counted more refugees than the total increase in the white and slave populations from 1806 to 1810, free black refugees accounted for 90 percent of the increase in the city's free black population. Just as significant, the influx of free blacks and slaves increased the city's black majority from 56.8 percent of the total population in 1805 to 63.3 percent in 1810. The large, multiracial refugee movement reinforced the city's Latin European racial order and revitalized Gallic culture and institutions. Antebellum New Orleans, with the largest concentration of Saint Dominguan refugees in the country, acquired a reputation as the nation's "Creole Capital."[60]

In the 1809 movement, French-speaking whites in New Orleans clamored for the entry of the refugees with their slaves. The city's Gallic community, anxious to persuade white immigrants to remain in the state, set aside their chronic fears of Saint Dominguan slaves and petitioned Congress to suspend the 1808 federal law that forbade the entry of foreign slaves. In a declining majority and eager for an opportunity to offset American influence, French-speaking whites hoped to strengthen Louisiana's French community. The ever-increasing American presence represented a greater immediate threat to French interests than the admission of a large and potentially dangerous class of West Indian slaves.

Creole whites manifested no corresponding interest in the plight of free people of color, although the large number of free black immigrants strengthened the French presence in the city. By the late eighteenth century, the view prevailed among white Creoles that free blacks sympathized with slaves and were likely to foment rebellion. In the aftermath of the Haitian Revolution, they feared and distrusted free people of color. To some extent, social ties rooted in an intense loyalty to a shared French heritage and a long-standing tradition of interracial intimacy mediated relations between the two racial groups. Still, the city's increasingly polarized Anglo-American racial order accelerated a general deterioration in paternalistic social relations between Creole whites and free people of color.[61]

60. Lachance, "The 1809 Immigration," 110*n*5, 111–12; Hunt, *Haiti's Influence,* 4. See also table of population figures in Chap. 3.

61. Lachance, "The Politics of Fear," 186–93; Fiehrer, "The African Presence," in *Louisiana's Black Heritage,* 23–24.

Generally opposed to the entry of any French-speaking immigrants, American officials reluctantly allowed white emigrés to enter the city. At the same time, however, Governor Claiborne attempted to halt the migration of free people of color. He authorized the city council to inspect all arriving vessels for the presence of free black passengers. Under the threat of a fine or deportation, city authorities required free black emigrés to register their entry with city officials. Authorities also required free black males over the age of fifteen to post a bond guaranteeing their good behavior and prompt departure. Under such conditions, only sixty-four men registered with city officials. Claiborne advised the American consul at Santiago de Cuba: "Males above the age of fifteen, have in pursuance to a Territorial Law been ordered to depart.—I must request you, Sir, to make known this circumstance, and also to discourage free people of Colour of every description from emigrating to the Territory of Orleans;—We have already a much greater proportion of that population, than comports with the general Interest."[62]

Claiborne insisted on strict enforcement of the ban on free black males. On August 4, 1809, he asked Mayor James Mather of New Orleans, "Have you been enabled to execute the Law of the Territory as relates to the freemen of Colour?—Are they retiring from the Territory, and to what place, do they seem to give a preference?" The mayor had knowledge "but of few men of color who had left this place." Hundreds of free men of color, although expressly prohibited by the state legislature from entering the region, nevertheless remained in the Louisiana territory. Given the turmoil surrounding the massive influx of refugees, territorial officials could not prevent their entry. On January 27, 1810, estimating that 428 free men of color had entered the city, the mayor complained of his inability to expel them. In November, 1813, the French consul noted the presence of at least five hundred Saint Dominguan free men of color. Like it or not, Louisiana officials faced a larger and even more assertive population of French-speaking people of color after the entry of the emigrés.[63]

By more than doubling the population of French-speaking free people of color, the approximately three thousand men, women, and children

62. Sterkx, *The Free Negro,* 92–94; Lachance, "The Politics of Fear," 193*n*121.

63. Claiborne to Mayor James Mather, August 4, 1809, and Mather to Claiborne, August 7, 1809, in Rowland, ed., *Official Letter Books,* IV, 404, 407.

strengthened the existing three-caste society developed under French and Spanish rule. This reinforcement of the tri-caste racial order ran counter to planter interests. American slaveholders did not require an intermediate class to maintain control. Southern political realities necessitated the cross-class unity of all whites and the immersion of all blacks into a single and subservient racial caste. In bolstering the Latin European hierarchical racial order, the refugees affected the future course of race relations in nineteenth-century New Orleans. In the city, the refugee movement dealt a serious blow to efforts to undermine the presence and status of free people of color.[64]

Even though lawmakers attempted to retard the growth of the free black population by devising exclusionary policies, restrictive manumission laws, and deportation procedures, the free black population continued to grow and prosper during the early decades of the nineteenth century. Other tendencies served to offset, to some extent, restrictions on free black mobility. American adaptations to prevailing economic conditions, Louisiana's proximity to other Latin European regions of the New World, the persistence of French and Spanish institutions, and continuing revolutionary upheaval in Europe and the New World redounded to the benefit of free black society. In New Orleans at the turn of the century, a well-established free black community, reinforced by thousands of Saint Dominguan refugees, formed the basis for the emergence of one of the most advanced free black societies in North America. In the nineteenth century, continued migration and key French institutions assured the survival of its intellectual, social, and revolutionary heritage.

64. Lachance, "The 1809 Immigration," 111–24.

2

The Republican Cause and the Afro-Creole Militia

In February, 1810, in the aftermath of the Saint Domingue refugee movement, American attorney James Brown deplored conditions in Louisiana, where, he complained, "we are at this moment a French province." Brown distrusted the French refugees who "have collected in this City & Territory where they find their own manners, laws, and I may add government." He described the refugees as "the forces of Bonaparte" and associated them with the revolutionary upheaval that had toppled the Saint Domingue slave regime. As he suspected, radical elements accompanied the Saint Domingue exiles into Louisiana.[1]

To the dismay of Attorney Brown and other Anglo-Americans, Louisiana remained at the crossroads of New World revolutionary activity for over a decade after the treaty of cession. In Europe, militant republicanism survived the collapse of the French Republic. Its proponents favored representative government based on political equality and universal male suffrage. Opposed to monarchical regimes of any kind and fiercely anticlerical, they aspired to advance the cause of liberty, equality, and fraternity. In Louisiana, free black veterans of the French republican army, Mexican insurgents, Jacobin corsairs, and other revolutionary agents sustained this spirit of democratic idealism. They established a base of operations in New Orleans and plotted an armed expedition to Spanish America. Their activities profoundly affected the thinking and aspirations of the city's Afro-Creole leaders.

Before their banishment from Cuba, some Saint Domingue refugees operated key privateering bases in Santiago de Cuba and Baracoa under

1. James Brown to Henry Clay, February 26, 1810, cited in Lachance, "The 1809 Immigration," 117–18.

Guadeloupe commissions. Between 1794 and 1810 in Guadeloupe, the Jacobin revolutionary Victor Hugues and subsequent island rulers presided over a short-lived but prosperous corsair economy. Under the Republic and Napoleon, Jacobin filibusters fomented revolution, attacked enemy shipping, and issued French privateer commissions. By February, 1810, when British forces occupied the French-controlled island, Antillean *corsaires de la liberté,* including Louis Aury and Renato Beluche, had shifted their privateering activities to Barataria, a Louisiana settlement just west of the mouth of the Mississippi River.

In 1809, Saint Domingue privateers ousted from Cuba joined the growing numbers of French-speaking smugglers and adventurers in Barataria. The coastal colony, surrounded by marshland and a maze of waterways, served as an effective staging area for depredations on Gulf shipping. The slaves and merchandise seized by Barataria contrabandists produced considerable profits. Smugglers Jean and Pierre Lafitte, refugees of the Saint Domingue revolution, dominated the thriving black market economy. But piracy and contraband profits were not the only concern of some of the island's fugitive inhabitants. *Corsaires-jacobin* remained committed to the revolutionary cause and continued to aid insurgents attempting to establish independent republics in Latin America.

Saint Domingue free men of color who had fought in the Haitian Revolution under the French Republic also frequented the Barataria colony. At least two hundred free black veterans of the conflict, including Lieutenant Colonel Joseph Savary, a former French republican officer, arrived in Louisiana during the immigrant movement. Forbidden by territorial law from entering the region, some of these men found temporary refuge in the privateer settlement. Like the corsaires-jacobin with whom they mingled in Barataria, the free black veterans of the Haitian Revolution preserved their republican idealism. To some extent, their status and background resembled the historical experience of Louisiana's free black militiamen.[2]

2. Lachance, "The 1809 Immigration," 116–25; Stanley Faye, "Privateers of Guadeloupe and Their Establishment in Barataria," *Louisiana Historical Quarterly,* XXIII (April, 1940), 431–34; Pérotin-Dumon, "Les Corsaires," 25–26. There can be little doubt that the Louis Beluche referred to in the Pérotin-Dumon article is Renato Beluche; see Jane Lucas de Grummond, *Renato Beluche: Smuggler, Privateer and Patriot, 1780–1860* (Baton Rouge, 1983), Chap. 5, and Jane Lucas de Grummond, *The Baratarians and the Battle of New Or-*

In the former French colony of Saint Domingue, free men of color had played a crucial role in the Haitian Revolution as soldiers in the French republican army. In Saint Domingue in the 1760s, colonial ordinances had mandated the establishment of a permanent militia composed of free men of çolor. While the ordinances exempted whites from militia duty, they made service compulsory for all free blacks between the ages of fifteen and fifty-five. Led by white officers, free black soldiers played a major role in the defenses of the colony. By the 1780s, free blacks made up the entire rural police force (maréchaussée) and most of the colony's militia. The role of free men of color in the colony's security forces contributed to the view that free blacks represented a relatively stable and well-defined stratum in Saint Domingue's three-tiered slave society. During the eighteenth century, however, free black militiamen became an increasingly volatile element in the colony's social hierarchy.[3]

Between 1730 and 1780, mounting legal restrictions excluded free blacks from the professions and the naval and military departments while compelling them to provide for the security of the colony. In the maréchaussée, free blacks performed the arduous and dangerous tasks of repairing and patrolling the rural roadways, tracking down runaway slaves, and fighting maroons. After three years of duty in the maréchaussée, free men of color were assigned to local militia units, where they were required to arm and supply themselves without reimbursement or pay.

The role of free men of color in Saint Domingue's security forces undoubtedly provoked the resentment of the slave population. Still, the relationship between free blacks and slaves remained exceedingly complex up to the outbreak of revolution. Although the maréchaussée policed the slave population, nearly all free blacks had slave relatives or kinsmen who

---

leans (1961; rpr. Baton Rouge, 1968), 4–26; Christian, *Battle of New Orleans,* 20–27. The exact number of free black Saint Dominguan soldiers who emigrated to Louisiana has not been established; the estimate of two hundred is based on Roland McConnell's assertion that Colonel Savary raised a battalion of 256 free men of color in 1814, most of them veterans of the French republican army (McConnell, *Negro Troops,* 70). The comments of contemporary observers suggest that the number of such emigrés was higher; see the remarks of Governor Claiborne and French consul Louis Tousard cited in Lachance, "The 1809 Immigration," 120–21, 124.

3. McCloy, *The Negro in the French West Indies,* 61–62; David P. Geggus, *Slavery, War, and Revolution: The British Occupation of Saint Domingue, 1793–1798* (Oxford, Eng., 1982), 22.

had been slaves. Many free black men married slave women, and though free blacks served in the militia and owned slaves, free black employers and planters often harbored slave runaways.[4]

As repression increased in eighteenth-century Saint Domingue, free blacks acquired crucial military experience in the French colonial security forces. In September, 1779, the Paris *Gazette* reported that 545 "colored" troops including "Chasseurs, Mulattoes, and Negroes, newly raised at St. Domingo" had volunteered for service in the American Revolution. The volunteer troops sent to North America to oust the British from Savannah, Georgia, included some of the most important military and political leaders of the Haitian Revolution. The French expeditionary army included André Rigaud, Louis-Jacques Beauvais, and Martial Besse, all generals under the French Republic; Jean-Baptiste Villate, republican commandant of Cap Français during the revolution; Alexandre Pétion, a French general and president of the southern republic of Haiti from 1807 to 1818; Henri Christophe, a former slave who became King Henry I of the northern state of Haiti from 1811 until 1820; Julien Raimond, a commissioner to Saint Domingue in 1796 under the French Republic; and Jean-Baptiste Mars Belley, a Senegalese and former slave who joined the French Convention as a deputy of the colony. After Belley pledged Saint Dominguan blacks to the cause of the revolution in a fiery speech to the assembly on February 4, 1794, the Convention abolished slavery. The historic decree cemented a black/republican alliance.[5]

As may be observed from the formidable contingent of free men of color who participated in the French campaign in North America, colonial security forces formed the basis for the emergence of a body of free black soldiers of superior political and military skills. Fighting on the side of rebellious colonists who based their demands for liberty and independence on the principle that "all men are created equal" could only have heightened the aspirations of soldiers of such ability and ambition.[6]

4. Geggus, *Slavery, War, and Revolution,* 20–21; James, *The Black Jacobins,* 37–39.

5. Sidney Kaplan, *The Black Presence in the Era of the American Revolution, 1770–1800* (New York, 1973), 59; Saint-Victor Jean-Baptiste, *Haiti: Sa Lutte pour l'emancipation* (Paris, 1957), 84–85; Shelby T. McCloy, *The Negro in France,* (Lexington, Ky., 1961), 99; Nicholls, *From Dessalines to Duvalier,* 33–34; James, *The Black Jacobins,* 139–40; Geggus, *Slavery, War, and Revolution,* 118–19.

6. Jean-Baptiste, *Haiti,* 91–92.

In terms of their own security, Saint Domingue's provincial authorities had inadvertently created an unwieldy and potentially dangerous instrument of control. Though free blacks had traditionally provided for the defenses of the colony, the democratic revolution in North America signaled a new era. Conditions in the New World and France played into the hands of the regime's enemies. Veterans of the North American campaign and other free black soldiers of the maréchaussée and militia would play a crucial role in the successful overthrow of Saint Domingue's slave society.

As proponents of the republican cause, Rigaud, Raimond, Beauvais, Belley, Villate, and Pétion held key military and political positions under the French revolutionary government. Their brand of Jacobin republicanism demanded the abolition of slavery and the political equality of all men regardless of race. In the early nineteenth century, Haiti's republican leaders continued to support the revolutionary cause in other New World regions. During the revolution, however, the decline of the republican position in Haiti forced leading radicals into exile.

When André Rigaud rejected Toussaint Louverture's leadership in 1799, seven hundred of Rigaud's best soldiers fled to Cuba to escape Toussaint's conquering army. The rupture stemmed in part from a trade agreement Toussaint had negotiated with the British. In 1799, France and Britain were at war, and Rigaud viewed Toussaint's actions as traitorous.

Napoleon Bonaparte's treachery also undermined the republican position in Saint Domingue. Whereas the proclamation of 1794 had produced a black/republican alliance under the French revolutionary government, Napoleon's efforts to reimpose slavery and reassert French authority over Saint Domingue in 1802 fueled a fratricidal conflict. The civil war forced prominent republicans into flight or exile. Under Napoleon, the French deported or imprisoned hundreds of blacks and whites whom they viewed as troublemakers. In Paris in January, 1805, the Spanish chargé d'affaires estimated that 18,213 Saint Domingue deportees of both races had taken refuge in Cuba.[7]

When the movement of refugees from Cuba resulted in ethnic tensions and an increased free black military presence in Louisiana, Governor Claiborne's anxieties mounted. In January, 1810, in a dispatch to General

7. James, *The Black Jacobins,* 227–35; McCloy, *The Negro in the French West Indies,* 101–106.

Wade Hampton, commander in chief of U.S. troops in the Southern Division, the governor requested a garrison of soldiers and expressed alarm over the growing free black military presence. He estimated that the number of free men of color "in and near New Orleans (including those recently arrived from Cuba), capable of carrying arms, cannot be less than eight hundred." Their conduct, he continued, "has hitherto been correct. But in a country like this, where the negro population is so considerable, they should be carefully watched."[8]

As Claiborne's communication to Wade Hampton indicated, the governor, like most other white Louisianians, viewed free blacks as a volatile and potentially dangerous element. Claiborne was no doubt aware that free black soldiers had fought against the colonial planter class in the Haitian Revolution and that free men of color had played a prominent role in slave rebellions in the Americas during the 1790s and early 1800s. When revolutionary upheaval threatened Louisiana's slave regime, the governor resumed his efforts to win the loyalty of the free black soldiers.[9]

In January, 1811, a slave rebellion sent shock waves through the city. "We began on Wednesday last," wrote a New Orleanian, "to have a miniature representation of the horrors of St. Domingo." On January 8, slaves in St. John Parish rose up in a revolt led by the Saint Domingue man of color and slave driver, Charles Deslonde. In New Orleans, the uprising caused chaos "beyond description." The governor imposed martial law and readily accepted the services of free men of color in the defenses of the city. Still, he exercised caution in deploying the free black soldiers, assigning the men to white officers who used them to relieve American troops. Under the command of General Hampton, federal troops and local militia companies quickly crushed the army of over three hundred defiant, though poorly armed, slave rebels.[10]

8. Claiborne to General Wade Hampton, January 27, 1810, cited in Gayarré, *History of Louisiana,* IV, 226–27.

9. David P. Geggus, "The French and Haitian Revolutions and Resistance to Slavery in the Americas," *Revue française d'histoire d'Outre-Mer,* LXXVI (1989), 108–24.

10. Geggus, "The French and Haitian Revolutions," 115; McConnell, *Negro Troops,* 49; Berlin, *Slaves Without Masters,* 124; for quotations see letter from "A Gentleman at New-Orleans," January 11, 1811, cited in James H. Dorman, "The Persistent Specter: Slave Rebellion in Territorial Louisiana," *Louisiana History,* XVIII (Fall, 1977), 393, and Hampton to Secretary of War William Eustis, January 16, 1811, in Carter, ed., *Territorial Papers,* IX, 917.

Some participants in the subsequent investigation believed that the instigators of the uprising had infiltrated the region through Jean Lafitte's Barataria colony. Indeed, conditions along the Gulf coast region represented another major threat to the territory's stability. Revolutionary upheaval in Latin America contributed to the turmoil.[11]

When a republican junta in the city of Cartagena declared the independence of the Province of Cartagena [Colombia] in November, 1811, the president of the revolutionary government, Manuel Rodriguez Torices, dispatched representatives to Louisiana to recruit new citizens. Cartagena agents sought especially to issue privateer commissions against Spanish shipping. In Barataria, Saint Domingue free men of color, the displaced French corsairs of Guadeloupe, and French and Creole speculators and contrabandists professed their support for the new regime. French Jacobins of the most radical stamp, including Louis Aury and Renato Beluche, joined the hundreds of French privateers congregated in Cartagena. French corsairs plundered Spanish shipping until 1815, when royalist forces drove the rebels from the Caribbean port city.[12]

From Barataria, privateers carrying Cartagena commissions attacked Spanish ships as well as those of the United States and other nations. "The whole adjacent coast," New Orleans merchant Vincent Nolte later wrote, "was disquieted and kept in terror by pirates." Despite such complaints, the Lafitte brothers and other contrabandists "were time and again, seen walking about, publicly, in the streets of New Orleans." Among the territory's French-speaking inhabitants, the privateers were popular. In the legislature, Louisiana lawmakers refused to adopt measures to oust the men from their coastal stronghold.[13]

For Governor Claiborne, the necessity of pacifying the increasing number of free black soldiers seemed more urgent than ever. In 1810, in a city with a majority of 10,911 nonwhite residents in a total population of 17,242 inhabitants, the actions of several hundred free black soldiers could prove decisive in the event of civil unrest. Confronted with slave rebellion,

11. Dorman, "The Persistent Specter," 401.

12. Grummond, *Renato Beluche,* Chap. 5; Faye, "Privateers of Guadeloupe," 443–44; Pérotin-Dumon, "Les Corsaires," 28; Grummond, *The Baratarians,* 23–24; Gerhard Masur, *Simon Bolivar* (Albuquerque, N.M., 1948), 244–45.

13. Vincent Nolte, *Fifty Years in Both Hemispheres, or Reminiscences of the Life of a Former Merchant* (New York, 1854), 189; Gayarré, *History of Louisiana,* IV, 304–14.

piracy along the Gulf coast, and revolutionary upheaval in Spanish America, he pressed for authorization of a free Negro militia corps.[14]

Claiborne planned to pacify the free black soldiers by integrating them into the territory's security forces. Even though the territorial legislature had excluded the black battalion from the militia act of May, 1806, Claiborne proposed that lawmakers provide for the establishment of a permanent free black corps in January, 1807, in his annual address to the legislature. The governor's proposal notwithstanding, state officials refused to acknowledge the military unit. In 1809, they again excluded the corps from the militia law.

Still, Claiborne pressed for authorization of the free black militia corps. In the aftermath of the 1811 slave revolt, he presented testimonials in behalf of the soldiers to the territorial legislature and reported that they had "performed with great exactitude and propriety" during the slave uprising. Finally in September, 1812, after the outbreak of war with Great Britain in June, state legislators relented and authorized the organization of the free black corps.[15]

"An Act to Organize in a corps of Militia for the service of the State of Louisiana, as well as for its defense as for its police a certain portion of chosen men from among the free men of colour" permitted the establishment of the militia corps upon a restricted basis. Soldiers were to be selected from among Creoles of color who paid taxes and owned or were the sons of owners of "a landed estate of the value of three hundred dollars" two years prior to their enlistment. Although the bill permitted the governor to issue junior officer commissions to men of color, the commander of the corps was to be white. Furthermore, the bill limited the unit to four companies of sixty-four men each. Subsequent events, however, rendered the new militia law superfluous.[16]

In 1813, Colonel Joseph Savary and other Saint Domingue free men of color, having ignored the prohibition against their entry into Louisiana in

14. See table of population figures in Chap. 3.

15. Berlin, *Slaves Without Masters,* 121–22; McConnell, *Negro Troops,* 42–45; Claiborne to Secretary of State Robert Smith, January 14, 1811, in Rowland, ed., *Official Letter Books,* V, 100.

16. Everett, "Emigres and Militiamen," 394–95; quotations are in McConnell, *Negro Troops,* 52–53.

the 1809 refugee movement, boldly announced their presence. After arriving in the region, Saint Domingue men of color maintained a shadowy existence. For a while, Savary found safe haven in the Attakapas region, an area linked commercially and geographically to the Barataria settlement. In November, 1813, however, he offered to put a force of five hundred Saint Domingue free men of color in the service of Mexico's republican revolutionaries under the command of a former French officer, General Jean-Joseph Humbert.[17]

Both Savary and Humbert had served in the French republican army in Saint Domingue. In 1801, Napoleon Bonaparte had dispatched a number of radical republican generals and pro-republican military units to Saint Domingue with a view toward restoring French authority over the colony while purging his regime of politically undesirable elements. Under such circumstances, the French military command assigned the radical Humbert to the Saint Domingue army. In 1802, after General Victor Emanuel Leclerc, commander in chief of the Caribbean expedition, accused the headstrong Humbert of consorting with subversive elements in the rebellious colony, the general was relieved of his command. Distrusted by Bonaparte for his republican extremism, Humbert left France, and in 1812 he entered the United States.[18]

In August, 1813, General Humbert traveled to New Orleans to organize an expedition in support of the defeated republican army in Spanish Texas led by General José Alvarez de Toledo. Upon his arrival in the city, Humbert met with other sympathizers of the Mexican Revolution. In October, he traveled through Louisiana's border region soliciting support for an invasion of Spanish Texas. Confident that he had raised a force of fifteen hundred men, Humbert returned to the city. Back in New Orleans in November, the general espoused the cause of republican insurgents in Caracas, Cartagena, and Mexico. From the Louisiana frontier, Humbert planned to launch an expedition against royalists in San Antonio. Colonel Savary and

17. Roussève, *Negro in Louisiana,* 28; François-Xavier Martin, *The History of Louisiana from the Earliest Period* (New Orleans, 1882), 362. The Attakapas region included the present-day parishes of St. Landry, Calcasieu, St. Martin, St. Mary, Lafayette, and Vermillion; Louis Tousard to Sérurier (French *ministre plénipotenitaire* to the United States), November 8, 1813, cited in Lachance, "The 1809 Immigration," 124.

18. Pachonski and Wilson, *Poland's Caribbean Tragedy,* 46–48; Gayarré, *History of Louisiana,* IV, 493.

other Saint Dominguan free men of color responded enthusiastically to the general's plan. Savary promised to march with Humbert as soon as he obtained the means to arm, equip, and maintain his men.[19]

The city's immigrant Irish population also responded enthusiastically to the general's call. A spokesman for the Irish immigrants, Theobald Wolfe Tone, applauded the "intrepid and magnanimous Humbert," whose "name is dear to Ireland." Tone invited his fellow Irishmen to honor the hero of Castlebar, who had landed an army of French soldiers in Ireland in August, 1798, in support of the United Irish uprising; Humbert's undermanned army of Franco-Irish soldiers advanced fifty miles before British troops forced their surrender on September 8. The delegation of New Orleans admirers included Tone, Jean Blanque, a former official of the French Republic, and Dr. William Flood, a "severe republican." On November 3, the men proposed to honor Humbert at a public dinner for "those of all countries who honour the brave, and who sympathize in the feelings of a people struggling against their oppressors."[20]

Within weeks of his enthusiastic reception, the impetuous Humbert led a group of filibusters across the Sabine River into Spanish territory. On November 25, 1813, he established a Mexican republican government in exile on Texas soil. Humbert and his followers elected a president, Juan Mariano Picornell, an associate of Toledo's with a long history of support for republican causes. The new republic lacked financial and military support, however, and in early January, 1814, Humbert, Picornell, and their supporters returned to New Orleans. Though Picornell announced his resignation the following month, Humbert and other backers of the Mexican cause continued to devise schemes for an invasion of Spanish territory. Within the year, however, republican militants Humbert, Savary, Flood, and Blanque and their Mexican associates would be ral-

19. Harris Gaylord Warren, "Southern Filibusters in the War of 1812," *Louisiana Historical Quarterly,* XXV (April, 1942), 298–99; Stanley Faye, "The Great Stroke of Pierre Laffite [*sic*]," *Louisiana Historical Quarterly,* XXIII (July, 1940), 734. In September, 1810, Mexican insurgents had proclaimed their independence from Spain.

20. Palmer, *The Age of Democratic Revolution,* II, 499–500; Bernard Marigny, "Reflections on the Campaign of General Andrew Jackson in Louisiana in 1814 and '15," *Louisiana Historical Quarterly,* VI (January, 1923), 67–80; quotations from *Le Courrier de la Louisiane,* November 3, 1813.

lying against another archenemy, the British, in the defenses of New Orleans.[21]

Faced with the prospect of a British invasion in the summer of 1814, Governor Claiborne apprised General Andrew Jackson, the U.S. commander in the Southwest, of the state of military preparedness in the city. In a letter on August 12, Claiborne described the city militia's battalion of free men of color. Only the day before, the governor wrote, battalion leaders had assured him of their loyalty to the United States. In the interview, the militiamen requested that all free men of color residing in the vicinity of the city be enlisted. The men estimated that a force of six hundred men could be raised and led Claiborne to understand that "such a measure would afford much satisfaction, and excite their greatest zeal in the cause of the United States." The governor evaded their request and immediately ordered a census of free black men. He advised Jackson: "If we give them not our confidence, the enemy will be encouraged to intrigue and corrupt them." The governor suggested the recruitment of three or four hundred more free men of color. General Jackson readily agreed. He recommended that four hundred men be added to the corps.[22]

The creation of a battalion of four hundred reliable soldiers represented a significant addition to the region's security forces, for Claiborne doubted the reliability of the state's inhabitants. He expressed his fears to Jackson: "With a population differing in language, customs, manners, and *sentiments,* you need not be surprised if I should not with entire certainty calculate on the support of the people."[23]

Within two weeks of his meeting with the free black officers, however, Claiborne's negotiations with the men appeared to collapse. The governor suspected English or Spanish agents of influencing the men. He described events to Jackson: "Contrary to what I had anticipated, the battalion of freemen of color have not acted *to-day* with their accustomed propriety.

21. J. Villansana Haggard, "The Neutral Ground Between Louisiana and Texas, 1806–1821," *Louisiana Historical Quarterly,* XXVIII (October, 1945), 1056; Faye, "The Great Stroke," 733–35.

22. McConnell, *Negro Troops,* 60; quotations from Gayarré, *History of Louisiana,* IV, 336.

23. Gayarré, *History of Louisiana,* IV, 341.

The great majority were absent from parade, and much discontent is said to prevail."[24]

Although officers of the battalion had assured the governor of the loyalty of their troops, the soldiers' actions represented a serious breach of conduct. The Militia General Order of August 18, 1814, required the muster of the troops twice a month.[25]

On September 21, Jackson rushed a series of dispatches to New Orleans. The correspondence included public addresses designed to mobilize Louisianians against the British. In a letter to the governor, Jackson agreed that free men of color "will not remain quiet spec[ta]tors of the interesting contest. They must be for, or against us." By distrusting the men, Jackson continued, "you make them your enemies, place confidence in them, and you engage them by every dear and honorable tie to the interest of the country who extends to them equal rights and priviledges [*sic*] with white men." Jackson included an appeal to free men of color. Though Claiborne promptly published Jackson's address to white Louisianians, he withheld the message to free men of color.[26]

In October, hostility toward the free Negro militia intensified. A dispute among officers of the black battalion erupted into a public debate. As distrust of the militia escalated, Claiborne anticipated a legislative attempt to abolish the existing battalion. The governor agreed with Jackson that free men of color would not remain sideline observers in the approaching hostilities, especially "if the war (as is apprehended) *should be brought into the bosom of Louisiana*." A number of influential Louisianians, however, rejected their views. They completely opposed the presence of the militia unit. The governor explained their reasoning: "They think that, in putting arms in the hands of men of color, we only add to the force of the enemy, and that nothing short of placing them in every respect upon a footing of equality with white citizens (which our Constitution forbids) could conciliate their affections."[27]

24. *Ibid.*, 342.

25. McConnell, *Negro Troops,* 60.

26. Jackson to Claiborne, September 21, 1814, in John Spencer Bassett, ed., *Correspondence of Andrew Jackson,* (Washington, D.C., 1926–33), II, 56–57.

27. Claiborne to Jackson, October 17, 1814, in Bassett, ed., *Correspondence of Andrew Jackson,* II, 76–77.

In New Orleans, members of the Committee of Defense agreed to the presence of the soldiers on condition that the men be banned from entering the state when the war ended. If the soldiers remained in Louisiana, committee members argued, with their "Knowledge of the use of Arms, and *that pride of Distinction,* which a soldiers pursuits so naturally inspires, they would prove dangerous."[28]

Privately, Jackson scoffed at the notion that armed black soldiers represented an internal threat: "No objections can be raised by the citizens of Norleans [*sic*] on account of their engagement, as they will be removed from amongst them, if fears of their fidelity are entertained."[29]

On October 24, as tensions subsided, Claiborne published Jackson's appeal to free men of color. In the stirring and provocative address, Jackson called on free men of color as "sons of freedom" and Americans to "defend all which is dear in existence." He urged the men to ignore enemy propaganda: "Your intelligent minds are not to be led away by false representations. Your love of honor would cause you to despise the Man who should attempt to deceive you."[30]

In return for their service, Jackson promised them the same compensation in pay and land as white soldiers—$124 in cash and 160 acres of land. On October 31, in another private communication to Claiborne, Jackson explained his seemingly magnanimous approach to free black soldiers: "As to the free people of Colour I have remarked the policy that directed the address. I was aware of the jealousy of the Citizens toward them. This was an actuating motive for the address." By putting the men upon an equal footing, Jackson hoped to spark a rivalry between the militia corps while attempting to evoke a patriotic and prideful response from free black soldiers. He apparently felt he could strengthen the American position in New Orleans by exploiting existing caste antagonisms. If the policy failed, however, the general again assured Claiborne that the soldiers could be "moved in the rear to some point where they will be kept from doing us an injury." Jackson continued: "If their pride and merit entitle

28. Ibid., 77.

29. Jackson to Claiborne, September 21, 1814, in Bassett, ed., *Correspondence of Andrew Jackson,* II, 57.

30. Jackson's address "To the Free Coloured Inhabitants of Louisiana," September 21, 1814, *ibid.*, 58–59.

them to confidence, they can be employed against the Enemy. If not they can be kept from uniting with him."[31]

Predictably, white Louisianians reacted angrily to Jackson's address. They objected strenuously to characterizations of black Louisianians and Saint Dominguan men of color as "fellow Citizens," "sons of freedom," "Americans," and "adopted Children" of Louisiana. Such references suggested notions of equality that most white residents found highly objectionable.

In view of such hostility, many free people of color remained thoroughly alienated. Despite Jackson's flattering language and promises of equal treatment, the climate of race relations in the city and the threat of an imminent British invasion prompted some free blacks to leave the country. On October 28, Claiborne noted the departure of large numbers of free persons of color for Cuba. According to rumor, many others also planned to emigrate to the Spanish colony. Apparently, Spain had extended an invitation to free blacks to enter Cuba.[32]

Despite the evident persistence of discontent within the free Negro community, many free men of color responded enthusiastically to Andrew Jackson's call to arms. Free black soldiers welcomed the general's assurances of equal treatment in the army. Jackson's personal invitation to his "brave fellow Citizens" to defend *their* country unquestionably pleased men whose collective identity included a proud military heritage. In fact, former colonial militiamen and their relatives formed the basis for the first battalion of "chosen men of color."

Lieutenant Noel Carrière's father, a decorated officer under the Spanish, fought in the American Revolution under Galvez and distinguished himself in 1779 against the British. Captains Louis Simon and Charles Porée, first lieutenants Maurice Populus and Baltazare Demozeillier, and privates Jean Dolliole, Voltaire Auguste, Louis Daunoy, Pierre Bailly, and his son of the same name also served in the Spanish militia. Moreover, in the petition to Claiborne in 1804, Simon, Porée, Populus, Demozeillier,

31. *Ibid.*; Jackson to Claiborne, October 31, 1812, in Bassett, ed., *Correspondence of Andrew Jackson,* 88.

32. Gayarré, *History of Louisiana,* IV, 356; Claiborne to Jackson, October 28, 1814, in Rowland, ed., *Official Letter Books,* VI, 294; quotations from Bassett, ed., *Correspondence of Andrew Jackson,* II, 58.

Dolliole, Auguste, Daunoy, and the Baillys had extended their services to the Americans and expressed their confidence that the new government would assure their "personal and political freedom." The general's glowing pronouncements no doubt encouraged the men to believe that by participating in the "Glorious struggle for National Rights" they might expect to enhance their own rights and status.[33]

On December 2, the general arrived in New Orleans. After an inspection tour of the city's defenses, he immediately mustered the existing battalion of approximately 350 free men of color into the service of the United States Army. Brushing aside white objections, Jackson hurriedly dispatched the men to Chef Menteur Pass, a major inlet in the east connecting the city with Lake Borgne, and promptly called for the organization of another such battalion. Colonel Joseph Savary responded immediately to the general's request. Within three days of the first battalion's muster, Savary raised a second military unit of approximately 250 Saint Dominguan refugees.

On December 18, the general's aide, Edward Livingston, read another laudatory address to the men. "Soldiers," Jackson declared: "I invited you to share in the perils and to divide the glory of your white countrymen. . . . You surpass my hopes. . . . The President of the United States shall be informed of your conduct on the present occasion, and the voice of the Representatives of the American Nation shall applaud your valor, as your General now praises your ardor."[34]

As with the general's first message, white Louisianians reacted angrily. In their view, the address placed free blacks upon an equal footing with white soldiers, and such language would foster dangerous attitudes. The day before Jackson's speech, white fears manifested; as the second battalion was being organized, the New Orleans city council restricted the activities of free people of color with a new ordinance prohibiting free blacks from moving about the city after dark.

Seemingly indifferent to white anxieties, Jackson inducted the men into the United States Army. Recognizing Savary's considerable influence and aware of his reputation as "a man of great courage," Jackson personally

33. McConnell, *Negro Troops,* 65–68; quotations from Bassett, ed., *Correspondence of Andrew Jackson,* II, 58, and "Address from the Free People of Color," January, 1804, in Carter, ed., *Territorial Papers,* IX, 174–75.

34. McConnell, *Negro Troops,* 66–70; Gayarré, *History of Louisiana,* IV, 408.

assigned him to the rank of second major of the volunteer battalion. The former French officer became the first Negro in the United States to achieve that military office.[35]

Military authorities again assigned white commanding officers to the second battalion's four companies. In this instance, however, General Jackson acceded to a request by the men to name Major Louis Daquin the commander of their battalion. The earlier dispute involving the officers of the first battalion apparently prompted the Saint Dominguan soldiers to request Daquin as leader. Like Savary, Major Daquin was also a Saint Domingue refugee and a former officer under the French Republic. Though white in appearance, he was reputed to be a quadroon of mixed racial ancestry.[36]

Another contingent of Saint Dominguan free men of color from Barataria also fought in the battle of New Orleans. Whereas American officials had moved diplomatically to obtain the support of the free black militia, they adopted a much harsher policy toward the renegade Baratarians. In September, 1814, at the urging of Governor Claiborne, federal troops invaded Barataria, arrested some of the inhabitants, and dispersed the Lafittes and their followers. Hundreds of refugees from the settlement poured into the city. Claiborne noted the presence among the refugees of "St. Domingo negro's of the most desperate characters." Still, he concluded, they were "probably no worse than most of their white associates."[37]

At the time of the federal invasion of the smuggling entrepôt, Jackson threatened to have the Baratarians arrested and hanged. Jean Lafitte had met with the British in Barataria the summer before the American invasion. Referring to these negotiations, the general declared that he, unlike the British, would not call upon "either Pirates or Robbers to join him in the glorious career [of defending the country]." Once in the city, however, Edward Livingston explained the advantages of enlisting the men. Recognizing the Baratarians would win support for the American cause. Liv-

35. Berlin, *Slaves Without Masters,* 128; Gayarré, *History of Louisiana,* IV, 409; McConnell, *Negro Troops,* 70; quotation from Marigny, "Reflections," 74.

36. Christian, *Battle of New Orleans,* 29; Alice Dunbar-Nelson, "People of Color of Louisiana," part 2, *Journal of Negro History,* II (January, 1917), 59.

37. Claiborne to Jackson, September 20, 1814, in Bassett, ed., *Correspondence of Andrew Jackson,* II, 56.

ingston noted the popularity of the smugglers among the lower classes of French-speaking Louisianians.[38]

Livingston also described the advantage of recruiting approximately five hundred experienced fighting men skilled in the use of heavy artillery. Moreover, the Lafitte brothers offered to provide desperately needed arms and ammunition. Acting as an intermediary, Livingston arranged an agreement. The general offered to pardon the men on evidence of good conduct. According to Livingston's colleague, Vincent Nolte, Jackson found in Livingston "a man who was not troubled by any scruples of conscience, and to whom, as to himself, all means were good that led to the accomplishment of an object."[39]

The two battalions of free men of color, the Baratarians, and proponents of the republican cause in Mexico distinguished themselves in the battle of New Orleans. The presence of the two battalions of approximately six hundred in a force of three thousand soldiers proved decisive. After the victorious battle, Jackson commended the men. On January 21, 1815, the general noted that the two corps of black volunteers had "not disappointed the hopes that were formed of their courage and perseverance in the performance of their duty" and that "Captain Savary continued to merit the highest praise." In the last significant skirmish of the battle, Savary and a detachment of his men had volunteered to clear the field of a detail of British sharpshooters. Though suffering heavy casualties, Savary succeeded in his mission. On February 1, the Louisiana legislature also acknowledged the conduct of the black soldiers. In a joint resolution, lawmakers praised the two battalions of free men of color and, like Jackson, singled out "the brave Savary" who had organized a battalion of men and taken the field "to face the enemy a few hours after its formation."[40]

In his January address, Jackson had also noted that the "privateers and gentlemen" of Barataria had, through their loyalty and courage, "redeemed the pledge they gave at the opening of the campaign to defend the country." The Louisiana legislator Bernard Marigny later described the men and boasted of their role in the battle: "Lafitte and the Baratarians, among whom were found some men of color from San Domingo, though they

38. "Jackson's Proclamation to the People of Louisiana," September 21, 1814, *ibid.*, 58.

39. Nolte, *Fifty Years,* 208.

40. McConnell, *Negro Troops,* 91; Everett, "Emigres and Militiamen," 397–98.

had no property nor family in Louisiana and gold alone was their religion, their god, men who therefore were called pirates. Lafitte and his companions to the number of more than 800, refused the gold of England and remembering only that they were nearly all Frenchmen, they came and fought valiantly against the English, the eternal enemies of France."[41]

"Finally," Marigny continued, "the intrepid Humbert, an old general of the French Republic, sought death everywhere on the battlefield and found it nowhere." Jackson also applauded the actions of Humbert and his associate, Juan Pablo Anaya, a representative of the Mexican revolutionary government: "General Humbert, who offered his services as a volunteer, has continually exposed himself to the greatest dangers with his characteristic bravery, as has also the Mexican field marshal, Don Juan de Anaya, who acted in the same capacity." Other prominent Mexican revolutionaries also participated in the battle of New Orleans. General Toledo and José Bernardo Gutiérrez, an early adherent of the Mexican Revolution and future governor of the Republic of Texas, both volunteered their services. General Toledo was "faultless as a volunteer aid of Governour [*sic*] Claiborne." Mexican leaders no doubt hoped to gain support for their cause by contributing to the American war effort.[42]

Indeed, sympathy for the Latin insurgents ran high in the city. Spanish envoy Don Luis de Onis noted that in New Orleans "the revolutionary flags of Cartagena of the Indies and of the Mexican Republic" appeared alongside "those of European Powers on the occasion of the fiestas to celebrate the peace concluded between England and these States."[43]

The heterogeneous coalition so skillfully forged by Jackson, Claiborne, and their advisers barely survived the battle of New Orleans. During the fighting of January 8, British troops overran the American position on the west bank of the Mississippi River. Jackson ordered the veteran Humbert to assume command of the disorganized troops. "I expect you, General," said Jackson, "to repulse the enemy, cost what it may." The intrepid Humbert replied, "I will; you may rely on it." On the west bank, however,

41. Gayarré, *History of Louisiana,* IV, 504; Marigny, "Reflections," 73–74.

42. Marigny, "Reflections," 75; Gayarré, *History of Louisiana,* IV, 505; John Dick to Richard Rush, August 25, 1815, cited in Harris Gaylord Warren, *The Sword Was Their Passport: A History of American Filibustering in the Mexican Revolution* (Baton Rouge, 1943), 116.

43. Onis to the Viceroy, May 1, 1815, cited in Warren, *The Sword,* 119.

American officers refused to recognize the French general's authority; Humbert was "an unnaturalized foreigner" and only "an American should command Americans." His appointment, which they questioned, was degrading to their "national character" and a personal insult to their acting commander. General Humbert was "displeased and went off." Ultimately, the British retired from the position and withdrew to the east bank. The behavior of the American officers incensed Humbert's allies. Other measures angered the battalions of free men of color. Within weeks of the British departure from Louisiana, ethnic tensions flared.[44]

On February 15, when their American military commander ordered Captain Savary's unit to proceed to Chef Menteur Pass to repair the fortifications at the post, the men refused to obey. Instead of joining a detachment of the first battalion's free men of color already stationed at the pass, the men refused to perform servile labor. Offended by the order, Savary asked his commanding officer, Major Louis Daquin, to tell the general that his men "would always be willing to sacrifice their lives in combat in defense of their country as had been demonstrated but preferred death to the performance of work of laborers." Daquin relayed Savary's message and offered an apology to Jackson: "I am very sorry, *mon Général,* for being unable upon this occasion to carry out the wishes of the government."[45]

Within a week of Savary's defiant refusal to lead his men out of the city, Major Daquin reported that 144 men from both battalions had left their posts. On February 24, Daquin reported that if steps were not taken, there would be no privates at the military outpost. Jackson noted the "mutiny and desertion from Chef Menteur" and the refusal of Savary's corps "to march out of the city agreeable to my order." He refrained, however, from taking action against the soldiers and their insubordinate officer.[46]

44. Gayarré, *History of Louisiana,* IV, 492–94. The British withdrew from Louisiana on January 27, 1815.

45. Major Louis Daquin to Brigadier General Robert McCausland, February 15, 1815, in Andrew Jackson Papers, Library of Congress, Washington, D.C.

46. McConnell, *Negro Troops,* 94; Jackson to Lieutenant Colonel Arbuckle, March 5, 1815, in Bassett, ed., *Correspondence of Andrew Jackson,* II, 183. Marcus Christian speculates that in ordering the men to the Chef Menteur outpost, Jackson yielded to white pressure to remove the black soldiers from the city (Christian, *Battle of New Orleans,* 42).

Though Jackson sought to maintain martial law and military discipline after the battle, absenteeism and mass desertions ensued. At the end of February, the general expelled French consul Louis Tousard from the city after he issued an excessive number of certificates of French citizenship; such citizenship automatically exempted the soldiers from continued militia service. Accordingly, Jackson also ordered all French citizens to leave the city within three days. The general's actions infuriated the city's Gallic community.

While large numbers of French-speaking militiamen abandoned their posts, some joined a new military unit being organized by General Humbert. After the battle of New Orleans, Humbert, General Toledo, and their associates resumed plans to assist republican insurgents in Mexico. In early February, Jackson authorized Humbert to organize a military corps. Within a week, Humbert announced the establishment of a unit of soldiers reminiscent of the French Légion des Francs, a small fighting force designed to wage guerrilla warfare. By March, approximately one hundred whites of French and Spanish descent had joined the corps to participate in an overland attack on royalists in Texas.[47]

Thirty-one free men of color from Daquin's former battalion also joined Humbert's fighting force. Both before and after the battle of New Orleans, free black veterans of the French republican army identified with the independence movement in Mexico. They, like their counterparts in the Republic of Haiti, supported democratic change in Latin America. In this respect, Colonel Savary and his soldiers nourished a republican revolutionary tradition within the black Creole community.[48]

In New Orleans, the movement to assist Mexican revolutionaries remained at a standstill until the arrival in the fall of the Mexican republic's ambassador to the United States, José Manuel de Herrera. Undeterred by the increasingly precarious status of his government, the Mexican con-

47. For mention of the French Légion des Francs, see Marianne Elliott, "The Role of Ireland in French War Strategy, 1796–1798," in *Ireland and the French Revolution,* ed. Hugh Gough and David Dickson (Dublin, 1990), 204–209; Gayarré, *History of Louisiana*, IV, 580–82; Warren, *The Sword,* 119–20; McConnell, *Negro Troops,* 93–94; Faye, "The Great Stroke," 753–54.

48. Warren, *The Sword,* 120–21; Claiborne to Brigadier General Edmund P. Gaines, in Rowland, ed., *Official Letter Books,* VI, 357–58.

gress, Ambassador Herrera proceeded with plans for an attack on the royalist army. In March, 1816, he received favorable news from Haiti.[49]

In Haiti, freedom and racial equality, the cornerstones of the nation, remained primary concerns of Haitian leaders after the establishment of national independence. In the Republic of Haiti, President Alexandre Pétion opened the sheltered harbor of Les Cayes on the island's southern coast to republican revolutionaries in Spanish America. As early as 1806, in the southern city of Jacmel, the Haitian government offered refuge and aid to the Spanish-American revolutionist Francisco de Miranda in his ill-fated attempt to liberate Venezuela. Later, under Pétion, the Haitian republic supplied troops, arms, provisions, and munitions to Simón Bolivar on the condition that he end slavery in liberated territories. Haiti's assistance to the Spanish-American insurgency contributed to the independence of Venezuela, Colombia, Peru, Ecuador, and Bolivia. The role of Haiti and Haitian soldiers in republican insurgencies represented a major contribution to the progress of democratic revolutions.[50]

As events in Louisiana demonstrated, the United States government also befriended republican rebels in the Spanish colonies during the early years of revolutionary upheaval. Yet relations between the Republic of Haiti and the United States remained tense. From the outset, southern slaveholders deplored contact with the black nation. Haiti, the product of a successful slave revolt, represented a fearsome specter to the slaveholding South. Haiti's support of liberation movements in Latin America heightened southern fears. Antebellum South Carolina senator Robert Y. Hayne voiced such concerns in 1825: "Those governments [Latin republics] have proclaimed the principles of 'liberty and equality,' and have marched to victory under the banner of 'universal emancipation.' You find

49. Faye, "The Great Stroke," 754; Harris Gaylord Warren, ed. and trans., "Documents Relating to the Establishment of Privateers at Galveston, 1816–1817," *Louisiana Historical Quarterly,* XXI (October, 1938), 1086–88.

50. In 1807, Haiti split into two competing states headed by Henri Christophe in the north and Pétion in the south. Although he condemned slavery, Christophe, who was crowned King Henry I in 1816, feared foreign intervention and refused to actively promote abolitionism in neighboring countries. See Nicholls, *From Dessalines to Duvalier,* 46–47; Robert Debs Heinl and Nancy Gordon Heinl, *Written in Blood: The Story of the Haitian People, 1492–1971* (Boston, 1978), 157-59; Rayford W. Logan, *Haiti and the Dominican Republic* (New York, 1968), 100.

men of color at the head of their armies, in their Legislative Halls, and in their Executive Departments. They are looking to Hayti, even now, with feelings of the strongest confraternity." Owing to southern influence, the United States withheld political recognition of the Haitian nation until the Civil War.[51]

In March, 1816, an offer of aid from President Pétion and news of the enlistment of a radical Jacobin privateer, Louis Aury, reinvigorated the insurgent movement in Louisiana. In New Orleans, the audacious Colonel Savary boarded the *General Morelos,* a schooner commissioned by Minister Herrera to transport messages to Aury in Haiti. Savary carried Herrera's dispatches, including at least a dozen Mexican privateer commissions and a Mexican republican flag.

After his ouster from Guadeloupe by the British in 1810, the Parisian-born Aury frequented the Barataria colony. In 1813, the republican privateer hoisted the revolutionary flag of Cartagena and sailed south to the Spanish Main, where he headed Cartagena's naval fleet. In January, 1816, after Spanish forces invaded the republican stronghold, Aury's severely battered ships, manned by veteran Haitian sailors, limped into port in Haiti.

In Les Cayes, a Mexican emissary invited Aury to take command of a naval squadron under the authority of the Mexican Republic and promised Aury privateer commissions, arms, money, and an army of Louisiana volunteers. Under the terms of the agreement, Aury would attack royalist ports along the coast of Mexico. The Jacobin corsair accepted the offer.[52]

In June, Savary accompanied Aury from Les Cayes to New Orleans on board the commodore's flagship, the *Belona*. Aury's quadroon mistress and her maid also joined the expedition to the Gulf of Mexico. En route, Savary and Aury developed a close association, and the two men were

51. Warren, "Southern Filibusters," 293; Heinl and Heinl, *Written in Blood,* 156–57; Patrick Bellegarde-Smith, *In the Shadow of Powers: Dantes Bellegarde in Haitian Social Thought* (Atlantic Highlands, N.J., 1985), 9.

52. Harris Gaylord Warren, "José Alvarez de Toledo's Reconciliation with Spain and Projects for Suppressing Rebellion in the Spanish Colonies," *Louisiana Historical Quarterly,* XXIII (July, 1940), 851; Stanley Faye, "Commodore Aury," *Louisiana Historical Quarterly,* XXIV (July, 1941), 611–28; Warren, *The Sword,* 130; Faye, "The Great Stroke," 758; François Dalencour, *Alexandre Pétion devant l'humanité: Alexandre Pétion et Simon Bolivar, Haiti et l'Amérique Latine* (Port-au-Prince, 1928), 14.

loyal allies in the Gulf coast expedition. In early July, Colonel Savary disembarked in New Orleans and presented Herrera with Aury's plans to establish a base of operations at Galveston Bay. The proposed offensive involved an attack on Tampico from a temporary port at Galveston. An army, disembarking on transport vessels, would launch a land-based attack on the city. Savary, Humbert, and other supporters of Mexican independence prepared to rendezvous with Aury at Galveston.[53]

On the Texas coast, the *Belona* and several other vessels ran aground attempting to enter Galveston Bay; in view of the tortuous entrance to the bay, Aury decided to relocate his headquarters. As he prepared to leave, Herrera arrived with reinforcements, including a contingent of forty free men of color commanded by Savary. On September 12, Herrera took formal possession of Galveston in the name of the Republic of Mexico. The men raised the red-bordered, blue-and-white-checked flag of the Republic of Mexico and swore to defend it "unto death."[54]

Early in May, Aury proposed to move the new provisional government of Texas to Matagorda Bay. The convoy included three armed schooners and eleven prize vessels carrying a force of 250 men. Unfortunately, conditions at the new Texas base proved as inhospitable as at Galveston. Aury lost almost all his ships in Matagorda's shallow harbor. In June, short on provisions, he led his half-starved men back to Galveston Bay. Despite their severe losses and their failure to further the republican cause in Mexico, Aury and Savary remained close allies, as Pierre Lafitte noted at the time. Savary, Lafitte wrote, is "a man in whom Mr. Aury has much confidence."[55]

Overcome by his losses in the Mexican expedition, the French commander addressed a letter of farewell to Ambassador Herrera. On July 21, he left Texas and sailed for the new privateering republic proclaimed on Amelia Island. Whether or not Colonel Savary and his men remained with Aury on his journey to Florida's Atlantic coast is unclear. At some point within the next two years, Savary returned to New Orleans.[56]

53. Faye, "Commodore Aury," 628–29.

54. *Ibid.*, 632–33; Warren, ed., "Documents Relating to the Establishment of Privateers," 1091–93; Warren, *The Sword*, 143–44.

55. Warren, *The Sword*, 178–83; Faye, "Commodore Aury," 643; Faye, "The Great Stroke," 774.

56. Faye, "Commodore Aury," 643–44.

Among the city's Creoles of color, the "celebrated Savary" enjoyed an esteemed position. Even white Louisianians acknowledged the former French officer's extraordinary accomplishments. In 1819, the state legislature awarded Savary one of the highest pensions granted to any of the veterans of the War of 1812. The $30-a-month allotment covered a period of five years; in December, 1823, the legislature extended the pension for another four years.[57]

In New Orleans, the entry of Colonel Savary and other Saint Dominguan free black soldiers in the 1809 refugee movement strengthened the city's community of free people of color. Above all, they introduced the city's Afro-Creole leaders to a strain of radical republicanism that had triumphed over slavery and racial oppression in Saint Domingue/Haiti. Their assimilation into the free black population broadened and deepened the historical and cultural identity of the city's Afro-Creole community.

After the battle of New Orleans, support for the black militia declined among free men of color. For both free blacks and slaves, military service had functioned as a crucial means of advancement during the colonial era. The soldiers' humiliating treatment after the battle and their disappointment at not receiving some measure of political recognition contributed to their sense of disillusionment. In 1816, Claiborne ordered officers of the free black battalion to muster their troops twice a month and bring the corps to full strength with volunteer enlistments. Although officers of the corps often attempted to complete the unit, they failed repeatedly to muster a full battalion. Between 1816 and 1828, the men's lack of interest in the militia became increasingly evident. Still, the soldiers and their supporters attached crucial significance to the historic legacy of black men-at-arms.[58]

57. Desdunes, *Our People,* 81; Roussève, *The Negro in Louisiana,* 65; McConnell, *Negro Troops,* 109; Everett, "Emigres and Militiamen," 398.

58. McConnell, *Negro Troops,* 97–100.

3

The New American Racial Order

As the pattern of a dual racial order spread through the South during the opening decades of the nineteenth century, a three-tiered caste system set New Orleans apart. The city's unusual racial pattern contrasted sharply with an Anglo-American order that attempted to confine all persons of color—both slave and free—to a separate and inferior caste. In Creole New Orleans, an intermediate class of free people of color had gained a measure of social acceptance under Latin European influences. Until the 1830s, the city's liberal religious culture helped to delay the imposition of a sharply defined, two-tiered racial hierarchy.

Louisiana's Catholic Church never achieved the institutional strength to impose a strict code of morality upon masters and slaves. Still, Catholicism exerted a considerable influence on race relations. Under the French colonial regime, the church's efforts to incorporate free blacks and slaves into the religious life of the community contributed to a state of racial flux. After the Spanish takeover, the church's integrative policies acquired new momentum and produced an important alliance between black New Orleanians and the Spanish clergy.

In the 1770s, under instructions from metropolitan authorities, Spanish Capuchins began demanding adherence to provisions of the Spanish slave code that prohibited miscegenation, banned labor on Sundays, regularized slave marriages, and required the religious instruction of slaves. Opposed to interference in the master-slave relationship, white Creole planters withdrew from active participation in the church and generally refused to comply with statutes designed to protect their slaves' spirituality and religious obligations. Free blacks and slaves, perceiving the Spanish clergy as a useful ally, filled the resulting vacuum by taking the place of whites as godparents for unbaptized African and Creole slaves.

The church reciprocated with its legally sanctioned policy of religious protectionism. In an incident in 1784, the Capuchin friars clashed openly with Spanish officials over the treatment of one of their slaves.[1]

In June, Bishop Cirilo threatened to report the *alcalde* (provincial magistrate) Francisco Maria de Reggio to the crown for his treatment of Batista, a slave of the Capuchin household. Earlier in the month, Spanish troops captured sixty *cimarrones* (runaway slaves) led by the daring San Malo. In the ensuing inquiry, San Malo testified that he, Batista, and two of their companions were captured in May by a group of Americans. The cimarrones freed themselves, except for Batista, and murdered the three men, a woman, and a boy. San Malo described Batista's role: "You, Batista, you could do nothing because the English (Americans) distrusting you more than anyone else tied your hands more carefully than the others."[2]

The alcalde sentenced Batista to receive one hundred lashes at the foot of the gallows where San Malo and three of his followers were to be hanged. The Capuchin priests criticized the hastily convened legal proceedings and argued that Batista had been denied due process of law. When the bishop threatened to lay the matter before the crown, the alcalde retorted that he would be pleased to give an account of the incident to the king. Testimony revealed that Batista had been illegally hired out to work two miles from the Capuchin residence. Nevertheless, in an act of defiance, the priests refused to accompany the accused men to the scaffold. They protested to the alcalde's emissary that "their hearts could not endure to see an innocent creature, 'a child of their very house,' suffer unjustly." On the day of the public executions, Reggio delayed the hangings in an attempt to persuade a priest to accompany the cimarrones to the gallows. Father Antonio de Sedella, the vicar of St. Louis Church, confronted

1. George M. Fredrickson, *White Supremacy: A Comparative Study in American and South African History* (New York, 1981), 94–99, 129–30; Foner, "Free People of Color," 406–407; McGowan, "Creation of a Slave Society," 50–275.

2. Baudier, *The Catholic Church,* 201–202. Father Cirilo de Barcelona replaced Father Dagobert de Longuory as pastor of St. Louis Church and the head of the Capuchin mission in Louisiana with the latter's death in 1776. In 1782, Cirilo was appointed auxiliary bishop by the Bishop of Cuba, with authority over Louisiana (Baudier, *The Catholic Church,* 187–200). Quotation from Gilbert C. Din, "*Cimarrones* and the San Malo Band in Spanish Louisiana," *Louisiana History,* XXI (Summer, 1980), 256*n*58.

Spanish authorities and refused Reggio's request, declaring that the condemned men had already been shriven and that "anyone could help them to die."[3]

When Bishop Cirilo, Sedella, and their supporters appeared on the gallery of the church residence on the Plaza de Armas (Jackson Square) to witness the executions, they cried out against the injustice of the punishment. Reggio described Cirilo's violent public attack when the sentence was passed, declaring that the bishop behaved in a way "not at all becoming to his elevated and respectable character."[4]

During the 1780s, Cirilo continued his campaign to ensure the humane treatment and spiritual well-being of the slaves. He complained repeatedly to his superiors of the extent to which planters neglected their slaves' spiritual welfare. In June, 1791, a fellow Capuchin, Father Joaquin de Portillo, criticized Governor Esteban Miró in an incident involving the illegal burial of a four-year-old slave girl. A black woman with "more religion than many whites," Portillo pointed out, had informed him of the unlawful interment of the child in the private garden of Monsieur Segui. The woman had also offered to pay for a burial in consecrated ground. Although many slaveholders reaped the benefits of slave labor, Portillo charged, they refused to provide their slaves with a Christian burial; the governor ignored such abuses, though he was well aware of the problem. Stung by Portillo's accusation, Miró demanded that Segui exhume the child's body, provide for the cost of a Christian burial, and pay a fine of ten pesos.[5]

In July, Portillo encountered slaves working near St. Louis Cathedral on a holy day of obligation. When the priest ordered the slaves to stop, they replied that their master would simply make them work elsewhere. Infuriated, Portillo notified Miró. The governor halted the work and warned that such violations of church law would be severely punished. In January, 1792, Governor Carondelet upheld Miró's threat and affirmed his intention to ensure humane treatment of the slaves. Determined to

3. Din, "*Cimarrones,*" 257; Caroline Maude Burson, *The Stewardship of Don Esteban Miró 1782–1792: A Study of Louisiana Based Largely on the Documents in New Orleans* (New Orleans, 1940), 117.

4. Baudier, *The Catholic Church,* 202.

5. Ibid., 205–206, 213.

counteract planter power and dissipate the threat of slave rebellion, Carondelet enforced provisions of the Spanish slave code that prohibited excessive brutality and permitted slaves to file complaints against their masters.[6]

The transfer of Louisiana to the United States in 1803 revolutionized church/state relations. Governmental support for religious policies designed to ensure the slave's moral and physical well-being ended. Nonetheless, the new schismatic head of the Catholic Church, Antonio de Sedella, continued the Spanish Church's protectionist and assimilationist policies and maintained the loyalty of black New Orleanians.

Sedella, the friar who had confronted Spanish officials over the treatment of the Capuchin slave, was first appointed pastor of St. Louis Parish Church in 1787. Wearing open sandals and a long, brown-hooded robe tied with a thick cord at the waist, the enigmatic clerical leader purported to shun the temporal affairs of the church in observance of his Franciscan vow of poverty. After the Louisiana Purchase, the Spanish crown granted him a pension and invited him to return to Spain. Though he decided to remain in New Orleans, Sedella retained close ties to his superiors in Spain and supplied the Spanish government with intelligence reports.[7]

In the absence of an officially recognized ecclesiastical authority after 1800, a contest for the St. Louis pastorate ensued. In 1805, Sedella was at the center of the controversy. In March, the religious schism resulted in a public confrontation in the cathedral, in which hundreds of Catholics assembled to elect a parish priest. The congregation proclaimed Sedella their pastor and also chose a lay committee of trustees or *marguilliers* (church wardens) to handle cathedral affairs. Sedella's supporters justified their novel selection process on the grounds that the church belonged to the people and not to autocratic ecclesiastics. The Marquis de Casa Calvo, a former Spanish gover-

6. Ibid., 213; Hall, *Africans in Colonial Louisiana,* 323–24; Hans W. Baade, "The Law of Slavery in Spanish Luisiana, 1769–1803," in *Louisiana's Legal Heritage,* ed. Edward F. Haas (Pensacola, Fla., 1983), 52.

7. Baudier, *The Catholic Church,* 275. For a firsthand description of Sedella, see A. Levasseur, *Lafayette en Amérique, 1824–1825, ou journal d'un voyage aux Etats-Unis* (Paris, 1829), II, 232. For evidence of Sedella's intelligence activities, see "Letters of Padre Antonio de Sedella" (typescript translation), Howard-Tilton Memorial Library, Tulane University, New Orleans, 93–145.

nor and supporter of Sedella, sanctioned the action by transferring all church properties to the newly chosen committee of marguilliers.

In September, a papal bull placed the church and the Diocese of Louisiana under the jurisdiction of the Bishop of Baltimore. Ignoring the decree, the lay committee retained control of St. Louis Cathedral and reserved the authority to appoint their own pastors. They based their independence from Rome on French precedents. During the Revolution, the Civil Constitution of the Clergy adopted by the Constituent Assembly in July, 1790, asserted the French nation's independence from Rome and provided for the popular election of the clergy.

Historically, the mendicant nature of Franciscan missions required the establishment of church proprietorships. Lay trustees managed church finances and properties, while the friars devoted their energies to the spiritual and corporal welfare of the congregation. Still, the "election" of Sedella and the church wardens represented a highly irregular break with church practice. The system of church marguilliers underwent a unique transformation in the 1805 schism.[8]

The popularity of Sedella and earlier Capuchin friars with native Louisianians stemmed in large measure from their willingness to adapt to prevailing conditions. Under the French and Spanish regimes, the Catholic Church tolerated practices that had contributed to instability and revolution in France. Near the time of the Louisiana Purchase, the French traveler C. C. Robin described the extraordinary liberality of Sedella and his fellow Capuchins: "Religion in this colony is all in form; there is no longer any of the spirit in it. . . . In the city they are well satisfied with the Capuchins who perform the functions of the parish priests. They leave the conscience free. In no other country in the world is tolerance more extended. Women, negroes, and officers in the governor's suite are almost the only ones who go to church."[9]

After 1803, priests assigned to New Orleans complained bitterly to their American superiors of Jansenist religious practices. Despite their outcries, Sedella condoned the unorthodox religious movement. Jansenism, a dissident and amorphous revival movement in Catholic France, flourished in eighteenth-century Louisiana. Though the French monarchy and Catholic

8. Baudier, *The Catholic Church,* 256–60, 275.

9. Robertson, ed., *Louisiana Under the Rule,* I, 211.

Church leaders made sporadic attempts to suppress the fractious religious movement, Jansenism remained a potent influence in Catholic Louisiana. During the years of Sedella's curacy, Jansenists enjoyed free expression of their religious beliefs; the movement remained influential among the city's French-speaking Catholics into the twentieth century.

Sedella exercised the same spirit of tolerance toward freemasons. Condemned, like Jansenism, by the papacy, freemasonry flourished in New Orleans. During the early decades of the nineteenth century, Sedella welcomed members of the masonic fraternity into the Catholic fold and accorded them all of the church sacraments. He allowed them to display their masonic regalia in the cathedral and insisted that Catholic priests accompany coffins adorned with masonic symbols to the cemetery. In memorial services for Napoleon Bonaparte in December, 1821, Sedella invited the renowned masonic orator Judge J. F. Canonge to deliver the commemorative address.[10]

As may be surmised from his treatment of Jansenists and freemasons, Sedella exercised a remarkable degree of tolerance toward other religious denominations. During the early decades of the 1800s, his broad-mindedness promoted an exceptional spirit of religious ecumenism. Not long after her arrival in the city in May, 1818, the Catholic nun Philippine Duchesne described events on the Sabbath thus: "Protestants stop preaching on Sundays to hear the holy Pastor, who preaches in English. They love him as much as the Catholics do." Only the year before, Sedella had allowed a Protestant minister to address a large Catholic congregation assembled in the cathedral.[11]

The Spanish curé's unorthodox notions of religious tolerance revolutionized the city's Catholic Church. His acceptance of democratizing influences identified with revolutionary France strengthened the city's liberal Latin European religious culture. Under Sedella, the church itself served as a transmitter of liberal social practices and radical French ideas during the early

10. Baudier, *The Catholic Church,* 30, 275–339; Glen Lee Greene, *Masonry in Louisiana: A Sesquicentennial History, 1812–1962* (New York, 1962), 76; Viatte, *Histoire littéraire,* 221.

11. Philippine Duchesne to Louis Barat, June 21, 1818, cited in Louise Callan, *Philippine Duchesne: Frontier Missionary of the Sacred Heart, 1769–1852* (Westminster, Md., 1957) 247. Callan incorrectly identifies the English-speaking pastor as Bishop Louis DuBourg. See Annabelle M. Melville, *Louis William DuBourg: Bishop of Louisiana and the Floridas, Bishop of Montauban, and Archbishop of Besançon, 1766–1833* (Chicago, 1986), II, 518–19; Greene, *Masonry in Louisiana,* 75.

decades of the nineteenth century. His actions delayed the emergence of conservative proslavery forces within the Catholic Church in New Orleans.

Sedella's unconventional practices carried over into his dealings with black Catholics. Disregarding church doctrine and criticism by American Church authorities, he administered Catholic sacraments to slave and free black concubines and their illegitimate children. Newly appointed diocesan priests complained bitterly of having to perform baptisms, marriages, and burials for concubines, prostitutes, divorcées, and freemasons. In 1826, such practices prompted one of Sedella's rivals to describe the city as a "new Babylon," the "sewer of all vice and refuge of all that is worst on earth."[12]

Reminiscent of the Spanish mission's complaints in 1772, Sedella's rivals also criticized living arrangements within the Catholic rectory. Sedella's new contender for control of St. Louis Cathedral in 1815, Louis DuBourg, the recently assigned bishop of New Orleans, informed his superiors in Rome of the excessive influence within the rectory of Sedella's mulatto housekeeper. Some of his informants, DuBourg wrote, believed that a liaison existed between the two. As evidence of such a relationship, Sedella's critics pointed to the young boy who assisted the priest during Mass and performed other duties around the church. Owing to the boy's physical resemblance to the priest and conditions within the church residence, some observers believed Sedella was the child's father.[13]

In all likelihood, the American Church authority also frowned upon Sedella's involvement in two highly controversial court cases brought by slaves. In 1819, Sedella testified in favor of Marie, a slave, and her son by a white man, Erasmus R. Avart. Avart provided for the emancipation of Marie and the boy in his will. Avart's heirs, however, contested the document on the grounds that Marie's lover, "consumed with passion" for the slave woman, was of unsound mind. In spite of the testimony of Sedella and others that Avart was in complete possession of his mental faculties, Marie and her son remained enslaved.[14]

In 1820, Sedella again testified, in behalf of Rose, a freedwoman, and her young child. Although Rose's former master, who was her father, had

12. Baudier, *The Catholic Church,* 275–79; 305.

13. Charles Edwards O'Neill, "'A Quarter Marked by Sundry Peculiarities'": New Orleans, Lay Trustees, and Père Antoine," *Catholic Historical Review,* LXXVI (April, 1990), 272.

14. Schafer, "Open and Notorious Concubinage," 179–82.

signed emancipation papers in Cuba in 1805, he reclaimed the free woman of color and her child after their arrival in New Orleans. Sedella baptized Rose a free person and espoused her cause. In this instance, the court decided in favor of the woman and her offspring.[15]

In opposing orthodox Catholicism and advocating the rights of free blacks and slaves, the Spanish priest maintained the loyalty of the city's free black population. Near the time of Sedella's "election" to the St. Louis pastorate in 1805, Governor Claiborne noted the friar's "great influence with the People of Colour." As their status deteriorated under the American regime, Afro-Creole Catholics recalled the spirit of tolerance fostered by Sedella. Their special rapport with "Père Antoine" remained a powerful source of spiritual inspiration.[16]

When Sedella executed his will in December, 1828, he provided that a sum of five hundred dollars be divided among his *filleule et filleuls* (female and male godchildren) without distinction of color. His death the following year brought the city to a standstill. Edward Livingston adjourned the First District Court with a eulogy. "His holiness and virtues," the city leader declared, "entitled him to canonization." There was not one reason, Livingston continued, "why he should not be received as a saint in heaven" for he had "led the life of one on earth."[17]

Businesses, theaters, newspapers, and city government suspended operations on the day of the funeral. Together with a "vast number of gentlemen of all denominations" and nearly all the city's public officials, a large contingent of freemasons attended the funeral services. Masonic leaders, recalling Sedella's devotion to masonry's founding principles, urged lodge members to attend the services. They reminded their fellow masons that Sedella had "never refused to accompany to their abode the mortal remains of our Brethren."[18]

15. *Ibid.*

16. Claiborne to Secretary of War Henry Dearborn, October 8, 1806, in Rowland, ed., *Official Letter Books,* IV, 25–26. Sedella's close ties to the Afro-Creole community are corroborated by Audrey Marie Detiege, *Henriette Delille, Free Woman of Color: Foundress of the Sisters of the Holy Family* (New Orleans, 1976), 11.

17. Albert A. Fossier, *New Orleans: The Glamour Period, 1800–1840* (New Orleans, 1957), 334; Melville, *Louis William DuBourg,* II, 857–58.

18. Melville, *Louis William DuBourg,* II, 858; Fossier, *New Orleans,* 331, 333.

Thousands of candles flickered in St. Louis Cathedral, where the deceased Sedella "seemed like a saint, rapt in holy meditation." Long lines of mourners of "all ages, sexes and colors flocked to pay their last tribute of respect to him, whom, when alive, they regarded as their guide, their father and friend."[19]

For many years after Sedella's death, St. Louis Cathedral's large, racially mixed congregations attested to the persistence of Latin European racial patterns. Many startled visitors to the city described the diversity of the church's communicants. In 1838, Harriet Martineau wrote that the cathedral was a place where "the European gladly visits, as the only one in the United States where all men meet together as brethren. . . . Within the edifice there is no separation." According to Martineau, all knelt together from the "fair Scotchwoman or German to the jet-black pure African." During the sermon the sight of the "multitude of anxious faces, thus various in tint and expression, turned up towards the pulpit, afforded one of these few spectacles which are apt to haunt the whole future life of the observer like a dream."[20]

In 1833, the British visitor Thomas Hamilton offered a similar observation:

> Both Catholic and Protestant agree in the tenet that all men are equal in the sight of God, but the former alone gives practical exemplification of his creed. In a Catholic Church . . . the slave and the master, kneel before the same altar in temporary oblivion of all worldly distinctions. . . . But in Protestant churches a different rule prevails. People of colour are either excluded altogether or are mewed up in some remote corner, separated by barriers from the body of the church. . . . Can it be wondered, therefore, that the slaves in Louisiana are all Catholics; that while the congregation of the Protestant church consists of a few ladies, arranged in well-cushioned pews, the whole floor of the extensive cathedral should be crowded with worshippers of all colours and classes?[21]

On a visit to the city in 1845, Dr. Thomas L. Nichols, a northern social reformer, noted "something very interesting in the appearance of the

19. Melville, *Louis William DuBourg,* II, 857; Fossier, *New Orleans,* 332.

20. Berlin, *Slaves Without Masters,* 326; Harriet Martineau, *Retrospect of Western Travel* (London, 1838), I, 259.

21. Thomas Hamilton, *Men and Manners in America* (Philadelphia, 1833), 40–41.

worshippers" in St. Louis. Never had he seen such a "mixture of conditions and colours." On the church pavement, "white children and black, with every shade between, knelt side by side" with "no distinction of rank or colour." The most zealous abolitionist, Nichols continued, "could not have desired more perfect equality." Interracial mixing continued in the cathedral throughout the nineteenth century.[22]

Practices in St. Louis Cathedral contrasted sharply with an increasingly prevalent pattern of racial segregation and exclusion in religious institutions elsewhere in the South. The persistence of the city's Latin European religious culture, together with Sedella's radical notions of religious tolerance, forestalled the emergence of a conservative proslavery orthodoxy—an orthodoxy that had engulfed most of the South by 1830.

In 1815, Abbé Henri Baptiste Grégoire, a radical republican bishop and Jansenist sympathizer in France, had forwarded abolitionist tracts to Bishop John Carroll, head of the American Catholic Church. Grégoire urged Carroll to take a stand against slavery. Grégoire's pleas notwithstanding, the South's Catholic Church leaders adopted an aggressively proslavery stance and largely ceased to minister to southern blacks. They affirmed planter dominance by furnishing a scriptural rationale for slavery and the conservative social order.[23]

In New Orleans, although the liberality of the city's religious culture helped delay the erosion of free black status and privilege, the city's Catholic Church gradually succumbed to the forces of racial repression. Still, Sedella's unique philosophy of religious tolerance and his spirit of revolt remained potent forces. Liberal-minded, French-speaking Catholics of both races nurtured his legacy of dissent as conservative church leaders and their supporters rallied to the South's proslavery standard.

In Virginia, in the wake of the Haitian Revolution, the Gabriel Prosser plot of 1800, and a major increase in the size of the free black population, state lawmakers enacted a new body of laws designed to consolidate and

22. Thomas Low Nichols, *Forty Years of American Life* (1864; rpr. New York, 1937), 127–28.

23. Randall M. Miller, "The Failed Mission: The Catholic Church and Black Catholics in the Old South," in *Catholics in the Old South: Essays on Church and Culture,* ed. Randall M. Miller and Jon L. Wakelyn (Macon, Ga., 1983), 157–70; Ruth F. Necheles, *The Abbé Grégoire, 1787–1831: The Odyssey of an Egalitarian* (Westport, Conn., 1971) 251*n*39, 277.

safeguard the slave regime. Following Virginia's lead, other southern states promptly implemented similar laws. While the new codes obligated slaveholders to provide for humane treatment of their bondsmen, the laws also discouraged manumission and restricted free blacks' association with slaves. At the same time, distrust of the free black population inspired widespread efforts to expel them from the region. In Louisiana in 1807, the territorial legislature enacted a restrictive manumission law and a statute prohibiting the entry of free black males, which followed the South's new pattern of social control.[24]

In Louisiana, severe penalties accompanied the exclusionary law. The 1807 statute levied a fine of twenty dollars a week upon free black migrants. If the offender failed either to leave the state or to pay the fine within a two-week period, the statute empowered legal authorities to arrest the violator and hire out his services to cover the costs of his trial and confinement. In New Orleans only two years earlier, city officials had attempted to restrict the movement of free people of color with a residency ordinance. The 1805 regulation required free black inhabitants to present legal proof of their free status at the mayor's office in return for a residency permit. Territorial and municipal laws notwithstanding, large numbers of free blacks migrated into the region from the North and South. In New Orleans, the free black population climbed from 4,950 in 1810 to 11,562 in 1830. Lured by the prospect of economic opportunity during the decades of economic expansion following the War of 1812, the majority of free black immigrants entered Louisiana clandestinely by way of the state's extensive network of waterways.[25]

During the territorial period, measures designed to impose a stricter social regimen accompanied attempts to impede the growth of the free black population. According to territorial legislation of 1806, free blacks must never "conceive themselves equal" to whites. The law prohibited free persons of color from insulting or striking a white person under penalty of fine or imprisonment. The legislature also required free blacks bearing arms to carry freedom papers.[26]

24. Willie Lee Rose, *Slavery and Freedom,* ed. William W. Freehling (New York, 1982), 24–27. For developments in Louisiana along the lines Rose describes, see Taylor, *Negro Slavery,* 223–24.

25. Sterkx, *The Free Negro,* 93–164; see population table in Chap. 3.

26. Sterkx, *The Free Negro,* 161, 240–41.

The Louisiana Civil Code of 1808 required free persons of color to identify themselves on public documents with the initials "f.p.c.," "f.w.c.," or "f.m.c." The code prohibited marriages between free persons of color and whites. The colonial Code Noir had also banned marriages between whites and free people of color, but Spanish authorities were authorized to issue dispensations. In his first year as governor in 1766, Antonio de Ulloa sanctioned the marriage of a white Frenchman and a Negro woman. Under General Alejandro O'Reilly, colonial officials also acknowledged the racially mixed marriage in November, 1769, of Catiche Villeray, a free woman of color, and Jean Paillet, a white native of France. Moreover, Spanish authorities largely ignored the widespread practice of interracial concubinage for almost twenty years. Under American authority, Louisiana prohibitions against interracial marriages were carried to such an extreme that, in at least one instance, the white male partner in an interracial union was required to take an oath that Negro blood flowed in his veins.[27]

Under the Spanish regime, lenient provisions of Las Siete de Partidas had also provided for the legitimation of mixed-blood children born in concubinage. The statutes entitled the offspring of such relationships to become legal heirs. Accordingly, the Spanish official Nicholas Vidal bequeathed "an equal portion of his estate" to his four mixed-blood children, the progeny of his illicit relationship with a free black woman.[28]

Similarly, Andres Juen, a native of France who died in 1784, provided in his will for his three illegitimate, racially mixed children. With plantations on Bayou St. John and in Mandeville, Juen bequeathed large sums of money to his son, Juan Luis, and his two daughters, Roseta and Goton, all of whom he had "fed, educated and maintained in his home, as his own family."[29]

27. Christian, "A Black History," Chap. XVI, 34; Virginia R. Dominguez, *White by Definition: Social Classification in Creole Louisiana* (New Brunswick, N.J., 1986), 24–25; Toledano and Christovich, "The Role of Free People of Color," in *Faubourg Tremé,* ed. Christovich and Toledano, 90; Stahl, "The Free Negro," 309–10.

28. Christian, "A Black History," Chap. XVI, 34; Toledano and Christovich, "The Role of Free People of Color," in *Faubourg Tremé,* ed. Christovich and Toledano, 91.

29. Laura L. Porteous and Walter Prichard, "Index to Spanish Judicial Records of Louisiana, LXXI, September, 1784," *Louisiana Historical Quarterly,* XXIV (October, 1941), 1260.

The Louisiana Code of 1828 strictly prohibited such practices. Under Spanish law and subsequent Louisiana statutes, an illegitimate child could acquire legal status when a parent acknowledged paternity before a notary in the presence of witnesses. By contrast, according to the terms of the new law, legitimation could occur only after the subsequent marriage of the natural parents. Although an 1831 law provided for other means of legal recognition, it likewise prohibited the legitimation, under any circumstances, of a mixed-blood child. Categorized as bastards, such children could not inherit from either parent. The court concluded that the law had placed such persons "under certain disabilities and incapacities, from which it is not the province of the courts of justice to relieve them." Unmoved by a bill in 1857 to legitimize the mixed-blood child of an interracial relationship, state senator H. M. St. Paul of Orleans Parish bitterly condemned the proposed measure: "Oh! but we are told that some of them are rich—some of them are fair, scarce a characteristic of the African origin remaining. What if they Be?... Does it therefore follow that we are to recognize their social equality, invite them to our homes, and give our children to them in marriage? Never! Never!"[30]

After 1812, an array of state and local regulations restricted interracial contact and free black access to public accommodations. A New Orleans ordinance of June, 1816, segregated theaters and public exhibitions. The regulation prohibited whites from occupying "any of the places set apart for people of color; and the latter are likewise forbidden to occupy any of those reserved for white persons." Beginning in the 1820s, omnibus lines either excluded persons of African ancestry altogether or operated separate cars for them as a matter of company policy. During the antebellum period, free blacks and slaves were either completely excluded or assigned to separate and usually inferior facilities in places of public accommodation.[31]

During the 1820s, mounting resentment over more intimate forms of race mixing led to an attempt to halt the infamous quadroon balls. The "Mother of a Family" complained in the *Louisiana Gazette* of the behavior of free women of color. While their insolence drove white women from the

30. Sterkx, *The Free Negro,* 180, 246.

31. Roger A. Fischer, "Racial Segregation in Ante Bellum New Orleans," *American Historical Review,* LXXIV (February, 1969), 931-33.

walkways, she wrote, their sexual liaisons with white men threatened the racial purity of Louisiana's best families. In June, 1828, city officials bowed to public pressure with an ordinance that prohibited white men from attending "dressed or masked balls composed of men and women of color."[32]

Boom conditions in antebellum Louisiana and a corresponding demand for labor resulted in the growth of slave and free black populations (see table). By 1830, Louisiana's nonwhite majority represented 58.5 percent of the population. The state's black majority, as well as an attempted slave revolt in March, 1829, only forty miles north of New Orleans, which left an "insurrectionary spirit" in its aftermath, prompted a reassessment of the state's security system.

Early in 1830, the arrest of Robert Smith, a free black New Orleans merchant, for possession and dissemination of an abolitionist tract added to the frenzied atmosphere. The pamphlet was David Walker's *Appeal . . . to the Colored Citizens of the World,* published in 1829; it condemned slavery and urged blacks to rise up in revolt against white tyranny. Another

WHITES, FREE PEOPLE OF COLOR,
AND SLAVES IN NEW ORLEANS, 1769–1860

Population figures

Year	Whites		Free People of Color		Slaves		Total
1769	1,803	(57.6%)	99	(3.2%)	1,227	(39.2%)	3,129
1788	2,370	(44.6%)	823	(15.5%)	2,126	(39.9%)	5,319
1805	3,804	(43.2%)	1,566	(19.0%)	3,105	(37.8%)	8,475
1810	6,331	(36.7%)	4,950	(28.7%)	5,961	(34.6%)	17,242
1820	13,584	(49.9%)	6,237	(23.0%)	7,355	(27.1%)	27,176
1830	20,047	(43.5%)	11,562	(25.1%)	14,476	(31.4%)	46,085
1840	50,697	(60.4%)	15,072	(18.0%)	18,208	(21.6%)	83,977
1850	89,452	(76.9%)	9,905	(8.5%)	17,011	(14.6%)	116,368
1860	144,601	(85.0%)	10,939	(6.4%)	14,484	(8.5%)	170,024

SOURCE: Adapted from Joseph Logsdon and Caryn Cossé Bell, "The Americanization of Black New Orleans, 1850–1900," in *Creole New Orleans: Race and Americanization,* ed. Arnold R. Hirsch and Joseph Logsdon (Baton Rouge, 1991), 206.

32. *Niles' Weekly Register,* November 5, 1825, p. 160; Fischer, "Racial Segregation," 935.

free black and a number of slaves were also arrested for possessing copies of the pamphlet.

The specter of black rebellion spurred lawmakers into action. The legislature launched another major campaign to restrict the growth and movement of the free black population. In addition to renewed attempts to reduce the size of the state's nonwhite majority, the legislative agenda also included plans to organize a new militia. In the movement to reform the state's security forces, state lawmakers delivered the coup de grace to the free black militia. When the 1834 state militia bill withdrew formal authorization from the "Battalion of Chosen Men of Color," the free black militia came to an official end.[33]

After 1830, continued evidence of discontent in Louisiana, the emergence of an increasingly militant abolitionist movement in the North, and the Nat Turner insurrection of 1831 stiffened planter resolve. The legislative enactments of 1830 contained seventeen sections designed to regulate the activities of free people of color and reaffirmed the 1807 ban on the entry of "free negroes and mulattoes." Another law required slaveholders to ensure the removal of emancipated slaves within thirty days by posting a one-thousand-dollar bond. A modification of this measure in 1831 permitted slaveholders to forego the bond payment by obtaining permission to free a slave from the parish police jury. In this measure the legislature shifted the weight of the decision-making process to planter-dominated police juries. The juries' familiarity with local conditions, it was determined, would serve to curtail the number of domestic emancipations. Under such circumstances, the number of manumissions varied greatly from parish to parish. After 1852, however, no parish police jury approved an emancipation petition; those seeking such permission redirected their appeals to the state legislature.

Free persons of color who had entered Louisiana after 1825 were ordered to leave the state within sixty days. Although the law was modified, governing authorities reserved the right to expel any free black whom they considered undesirable. Free blacks who had entered the state between 1825 and 1830 were allowed to remain only after obtaining a special license. If they left the state, however, they would not be allowed to return, even with the license.

33. McConnell, *Negro Troops,* 102–104; Sterkx, *The Free Negro,* 98.

A subsequent modification of the law the following year permitted free black residents to return to Louisiana provided they did not "go to or return from, the West India Islands" or their absence did not exceed two years. Furthermore, state lawmakers demanded that all free blacks who had entered the state between 1812 and 1825 register their names with the parish judge where they resided or in the New Orleans mayor's office, "setting forth their age, sex, color, trade, or calling, place of nativity, and the time of their arrival in the state."[34]

In 1842, when the earlier statutes forbidding the entry of free blacks were restated, Louisiana lawmakers even anticipated the entry of prospective freedmen by banning a category of slaves referred to as *statu liberi;* the term designated a slave entitled to future emancipation. Anyone found guilty of bringing such a slave into Louisiana was subject to a fine of one thousand dollars and imprisonment.[35]

Ultimately, changing labor patterns in New Orleans also limited free black social and economic mobility. Except for a city resolution of 1822 that instructed municipal managers to hire only white laborers, economic conditions favored the class of free black skilled tradesmen, retailers, and businessmen. Under the French and Spanish, free blacks and slaves had dominated the skilled professions. As the city evolved into one of the nation's largest port cities, free black artisans continued to dominate some skilled trades. By the 1850s, however, most of the city's free black workers were unskilled laborers facing intense competition from European newcomers. During the 1840s, in the wake of a large-scale movement of German and Irish immigrants into the city, free black waiters, hotel workers, peddlers, cabbies, draymen, stevedores, and steamboat roustabouts were almost completely replaced by European workers. Competition from white laborers also contributed to the erosion of the free black property base.[36]

34. *Acts of the State of Louisiana,* 1830, 90; Sterkx, *The Free Negro,* 101, 121–29, 144; Schafer, "Open and Notorious Concubinage," 167; Christian, "A Black History," Chap. VI, 34–37.

35. Stahl, "The Free Negro," 330.

36. Sterkx, *The Free Negro,* 221; Christian, "A Black History," Chap. III, 1; Foner, "Free People of Color," 423–27; Roger W. Shugg, *Origins of Class Struggle in Louisiana: A Social History of White Farmers and Laborers During Slavery and After, 1840–1875* (1939; rpr. Baton Rouge, 1968), 118–19; Robert C. Reinders, "The Free Negro in the New Orleans Economy, 1850–1860," *Louisiana History,* VI (Summer, 1965), 274–85.

Under colonial conditions, white men had often bequeathed land and slaves to their black mistresses and racially mixed children. Interracial relationships had formed the basis for the state's prosperous class of Creoles of color; during the late eighteenth and early nineteenth centuries, free persons of color accumulated considerable wealth and property. After the Louisiana Purchase, free blacks benefited from the boom conditions associated with westward expansion. In 1836 in New Orleans, 855 free persons of color paid taxes on $2,462,470 worth of property (almost $3,000 worth of property per owner). During the 1840s, however, the city's free black property holders suffered a major setback. The decline of Latin European racial patterns, competition from white laborers, a sustained economic depression from 1837 to 1843, and a new array of state and local laws designed to limit their mobility dealt a severe blow to free black property holders in New Orleans. By 1850, their holdings had dropped to $755,765, and in 1852, the total real estate holdings of 234 property owners had declined to $401,300 (an average of $1,715 worth of real estate per owner).[37]

By 1860, free persons of color had recouped some of their losses. In that year, 283 free black property owners possessed $724,290 worth of real estate ($2,559 per property owner). Still, during the antebellum era some militant anti-Negro factions challenged the right of free blacks even to own property. In 1795, Spanish law had affirmed that "free people of color, enjoying by law the same advantages with the other members of the nation with which they are incorporated, may not be molested in the possession of their property, injured, or ill-treated under the penalties provided by laws for the safety and security of the property of white persons." Accordingly, Spanish statutes exempted free people of color from taxation. While American law required free blacks to pay taxes, Louisiana's governing bodies generally upheld colonial precedents touching on property rights. In 1836, the Louisiana Supreme Court decided in favor of François Boisdoré and John Goulé, both free men of color, in a case involving their rights as stockholders. The directors of the Citizen's Bank of

37. Loren Schweninger, "Prosperous Blacks in the South, 1790–1880," *American Historical Review,* XCV (February, 1990), 34–38; Reinders, "The Free Negro in the New Orleans Economy," 280; Richard Tansey, "Out-of-State Free Blacks in Late Antebellum New Orleans," *Louisiana History,* XXII (Fall, 1981), 384–85.

Louisiana had attempted to deprive the men of their bank stock on the grounds that the bank's corporate charter denied stock ownership "either directly or indirectly" to "persons not being a *free white citizen* of the United States." Boisdoré and Goulé won their case on appeal. In 1859, state lawmakers devised an extreme attack on free black property rights with legislation that prohibited them from owning liquor licenses, coffeehouses, and billiard halls.[38]

Free blacks sometimes fought and sometimes evaded the increasingly severe legal restrictions that governed their lives up to the outbreak of the Civil War. In 1833, a group of armed men attacked a segregated streetcar bound for Lake Pontchartrain after the white driver refused to allow them to board. During the summer of 1843, Voltaire Vonvergne, a free man of color, led a group of his friends onto a railway car reserved for whites. When he and his associates refused to leave the coach, railway workers unfastened the car from the train. In the ensuing violent confrontation, Vonvergne fired a shot at the conductor. An angry white mob attacked and nearly beat him to death before New Orleans police arrested him for violating the state's segregation ordinances.[39]

Separate institutions created by the city's Anglo-Protestant free black community evoked a similarly harsh reaction. After the Louisiana Purchase, free blacks who migrated to New Orleans from other areas of the United States gravitated to the city's American section, the Faubourg St. Marie or Second Municipality, which stretched from Canal to DeLord Street (present-day Howard Avenue). Protestant and English-speaking, they introduced their own distinctive blend of African and North American culture into Creole New Orleans. In response to the rising tide of race discrimination, they established two historically autonomous black institutions, the African Methodist Episcopal (AME) Church and Prince Hall freemasonry.[40]

38. Christian, "A Black History," Chap. XV, 13; Reinders, "The Free Negro in the New Orleans Economy," 283; quotations from Rankin, "The Tannenbaum Thesis Reconsidered," 25, and *Boisdoré and Goulé, f.p.c.* v. *Citizen's Bank of Louisiana,* No. 2956, 9 La. Ann. 506 (1836).

39. Fischer, "Racial Segregation," 936; Sterkx, *The Free Negro,* 245.

40. Joseph G. Tregle, Jr., "Creoles and Americans," in *Creole New Orleans,* ed. Hirsch and Logsdon, 154–56; Logsdon and Bell, "The Americanization of Black New Orleans," *ibid.*, 208.

Anglo-Protestant free black leaders had founded the AME Church and Prince Hall freemasonry in the North during the revolutionary era. At the outset, they condemned slavery and demanded equal rights. Even though they assumed a much less militant demeanor in creating churches and lodges in the antebellum South, the church suffered a major setback in 1822, when South Carolina suppressed the large AME congregation in Charleston as a consequence of the Denmark Vesey conspiracy. In New Orleans, despite repeated raids and arrests, the free black church, in tandem with the Prince Hall masonic lodges, flourished as a separate black institution until the late 1850s, when city authorities forced the church to close.[41]

Although conditions worsened in the South during the 1830s, an AME organizer planned for the establishment of a church in New Orleans. Early in the 1840s, local Prince Hall freemasons established contact with a Missouri AME minister working on a steamboat shuttle from St. Louis to New Orleans. In 1844, when white leaders of St. Paul's Methodist Episcopal Church introduced segregated seating and other discriminatory measures, free black leaders withdrew from St. Paul's and established their own church under AME auspices—St. James AME Church. In 1848, the burgeoning congregation acquired legal authorization from the state legislature with an act of incorporation. The church's existence as a corporate entity, however, was short-lived.

From the outset, city officials harassed and arrested church members. In 1848, surveillance of St. James produced evidence of white participation in religious services. Suspecting the whites of seditious activities, police raided the church and arrested over fifty free blacks and slaves and four whites (three men and a woman). A city official forwarded details of the incident to the state attorney general with a recommendation for legislative action. In 1850, lawmakers adopted an enactment that revoked the church's corporate status. Nevertheless, the church and the lodges continued to grow, with overlapping leadership. Within ten years, black leaders established five AME churches and three Prince Hall masonic lodges.

41. Lerone Bennett, Jr., *Before the Mayflower: A History of Black America* (Rev. ed.; New York, 1986), 82–84; Donn A. Cass, *Negro Freemasonry and Segregation: An Historical Study of Prejudice Against American Negroes as Freemasons* (Chicago, 1957), 13; Loretta J. Williams, *Black Freemasonry and Middle-Class Realities* (Columbia, Mo., 1980), 12–14; Charles Spencer Smith, *A History of the A.M.E. Church* (1922; rpr. New York, 1968), 14.

During the 1850s, police continued to harass church and lodge members. The AME minister John M. Brown was arrested five times for refusing to exclude slaves from services. In 1853, in a press account of the church, a New Orleans correspondent for a Mississippi newspaper characterized St. James as one of a number of evils in the city that required a "root and branch" eradication. The writer described the "large brick church . . . which is under the control of a negro Bishop, and where services are performed by a negro minister, in direct violation of the laws of the State." The observer also warned its readers that a "Bishop Allen, of Philadelphia, occasionally visits this city to look after the fortunes of his black flock, and no doubt infuses in them a spirit of hostility to the whites."[42]

Similarly, many whites must also have viewed the unsupervised activities of the city's clandestine masonic lodges with extreme alarm. In February, 1857, police arrested about thirty free blacks and slaves gathered at the Orleans Ballroom for a masonic ceremony. A city magistrate, charging the men with unlawful assembly, fined the free blacks twenty-five dollars and ordered beatings for the slaves.[43]

Finally in 1858, mounting public concern over the increasing size and frequency of gatherings of persons of color led city officials to enact a severe new ordinance. The law prohibited assemblages of either free blacks or slaves for religious services or any other purposes, without white supervision. On the basis of the new regulation, the city immediately closed St. James and seized control of church property.

In subsequent legal proceedings, attorney J. J. Michel defended the city's action on the grounds that the assemblage of free persons of color in St. James represented a threat to the institution of slavery. Such gatherings afforded free blacks an opportunity to "excite to rebellion and crime, the slaves of the country; among whom may be found their kindred and friends." Furthermore, the boldness of St. James leaders in expanding their churches demonstrated "the encroaching disposition of these free

42. Smith, *A History of the A.M.E.,* 33–36; for the act of incorporation, see 430–31. Joseph A. Thornton, "A History of St. James A.M.E. Church," in *The Jubilee Anniversary Program, St. James A.M.E. Church* (New Orleans, 1945), 18–20; Joseph A. Walkes, Jr., *The History of the Prince Hall Grand Lodge of Louisiana, 1842–1979,* (N.p., 1986), 17–19; New Orleans *Daily Crescent,* October 2 and 3, 1848; *Acts of the State of Louisiana,* 1850, 179; quotations from Boston *Liberator,* September 16, 1853.

43. New Orleans *Daily Delta,* February 22, 1857.

negroes. If this course were allowed to go on, in a very few years the white population would really be unsafe from their aggressions." The Louisiana Supreme Court upheld the city attorney's views, concluding that the "African race are strangers to our Constitution, and are the subjects of special and exceptional legislation."[44]

In outlying areas of the state, free blacks suffered more violent forms of repression and persecution. The Attakapas region, with the largest concentration of free blacks outside of New Orleans, became the scene of a virtual reign of terror. One contributor to a St. Landry Parish newspaper, the Opelousas *Patriot,* characterized free persons of color as a "cancer upon society." Another St. Landry resident urged the expulsion "from among us [of] all free Negroes or people of mixed blood." The editor of the *Patriot* warned free black residents of the region to "flee the society of the white man voluntarily before you are compelled to do so by his irrevocable decrees."[45]

Finally in 1859, white militants in the Attakapas parishes organized vigilante committees and launched a violent campaign to drive free blacks and "suspicious" whites from the area. After a particularly bloody attack on a racially mixed colony near Bayou Queue Tortue in Lafayette Parish, Governor Robert Wickliffe ordered the committees to disband. Continued forays by the marauders, however, persuaded many free black residents of southwest Louisiana to leave the region.[46]

Beginning in New Orleans in 1855, Lucien Mansion and other Afro-Creole leaders mobilized to assist the evacuees. Mansion, a wealthy black philanthropist, Romantic writer, and cigar manufacturer, contributed large sums of money to the migration movement. Louis Nelson Fouché, a highly educated Afro-Creole activist, also attempted to assist the refugees in the crisis. Fouché undertook plans for resettling the migrants in a proposed colony in Mexico.[47]

In July, 1857, Fouché entered into an agreement with the Propriétaires-Associés de l'Habitation de la Confrérie de St. Pierre (Proprietor-Members of the Dwelling Place of the Brotherhood of St. Peter). With the sanction of the Mexican government, Fouché and his associates planned to

44. *A.M.E. Church* v. *City of New Orleans,* No. 6291, 15 La. Ann. 441 (1858).

45. Sterkx, *The Free Negro,* 111, 113, 298.

46. *Ibid.*, 297–301.

47. Desdunes, *Our People,* 65, 112–13, 133; Roussève, *The Negro in Louisiana,* 48, 66–67.

organize a colony, Eureka, for foreign emigrés and Mexican nationals in the state of Veracruz. The contract required Fouché to transport one hundred families of no fewer than four hundred persons by ship from New Orleans over a period of two to four years. In return for renouncing their American citizenship, the settlers would be assured of all the rights of Mexican citizens. Mexican President Ignacio Comonfort expressed confidence that the undertaking "will yield great good for the Republic."[48]

During the summer, another small group of St. Landry Parish refugees settled on the banks of the Popolopan River in the state of Veracruz. Their encouraging reports of the absence of caste distinctions and their success with corn cultivation prompted others to migrate. A number of St. Landry families, including members of the prosperous Donatto family, joined the Louisiana exiles.

In 1858, Emile Desdunes, a Haitian-educated native New Orleanian and an associate of Fouché, acted as an agent for Emperor Faustian Soulouque after the Haitian ruler invited the refugees to immigrate to Haiti. Desdunes offered the desperate evacuees free transportation to the island nation and assured them of political and social equality. In May, 1859, 150 free people of color departed New Orleans for Haiti. One newspaper report estimated that nearly two hundred free black residents left for the Caribbean island the following month from East Baton Rouge and St. Landry Parishes. As a consequence of the turmoil surrounding Soulouque's overthrow and the reestablishment of the republic in 1859, a large number of emigrés returned to Louisiana by the end of the summer. Still, Haiti's new president, Fabre Geffrard, continued Soulouque's policy of encouraging emigration from Louisiana, and in early 1860, a group of eighty-one refugees from the Attakapas region left for Port-au-Prince.[49]

Some New Orleans newspapers also clamored for the expulsion of free people of color from the state. The New Orleans *Bee* (*L'Abeille*) claimed that without guidance from the "superior [white] race" free blacks would "lapse into a state of barbarism and crime." Such a class of persons, the *Bee* maintained, should be expelled since they were "dangerous companions to the slaves." The New Orleans *Daily Picayune* advocated their expulsion on

48. *Documens relatifs à la colonie d'Eureka, dans l'état de Veracruz* (New Orleans, 1857), 11.
49. Desdunes, *Our People,* 112–13; Sterkx, *The Free Negro,* 296–97, 302–303.

the grounds that free blacks were a "debauching, drunken, insolent group whose main object was to tamper with slaves and thereby make them discontented." In 1859, the paper urged Louisiana legislators to follow the example of Mississippi, where lawmakers had enacted a measure requiring all free blacks to leave within a specified period of time.[50]

Though Louisiana did not banish free blacks from the state, laws designed to suppress the growth of the free black population reached a climax during the 1850s. An 1852 state law required emancipated slaves to leave the United States within twelve months. The master of the manumitted slave was required to provide $150 for deportation costs, and if the slave's departure was delayed beyond the twelve-month limit, the freedman was subject to reenslavement. Although the legislature modified the law in 1855 because of a flood of petitions, the new restrictions were equally stringent. Finally in 1857, slave emancipations were entirely prohibited, and two years later, the legislature admonished "free persons of African descent to choose their own masters and become slaves for life."[51]

After 1840, exclusionary measures and the campaigns of intimidation and violence produced the desired results. While the number of free blacks in New Orleans increased steadily between 1810 and 1840, the size of the population dropped significantly after that, from 15,072 in 1840, to 10,939 in 1860. During the same period, the population of free persons of color for the entire state dropped from 25,502 to 18,647.[52]

In 1856, the state supreme court boasted that "in the eye of the Louisiana law, there is (with the exception of political rights, of certain social privileges, and of the obligations of jury and militia service,) all the difference between a free man of color and a slave, that there is between a white man and a slave." A dissenting opinion, however, revealed a harsher reality. Slaves and free people of color, the opposing minority declared,

50. New Orleans *Bee,* February 9, 1856, and New Orleans *Daily Picayune,* January 17, 1859, cited in Sterkx, *The Free Negro,* 308–309.

51. Schafer, "Open and Notorious Concubinage," 167–68; Christian, "A Black History," Chap. XVI, 40.

52. The statewide population figures for 1860 are taken from U.S. Bureau of the Census, Eighth Census, 1860, 194–96. Berlin, *Slaves Without Masters,* 136. The decline of the free black population in Louisiana was not an isolated phenomenon; in the South, the free black population dropped from 8.1 percent of the total black population in 1840, to 6.1 percent in 1860 (Fredrickson, *White Supremacy,* 86).

made up "a single, homogenous class of beings, distinguished from all others by nature, custom and law and never confounded with citizens of the State. No white person can be a slave; no colored person can be a citizen."[53]

Latin European influences and economic and military necessities favored the perpetuation in New Orleans of an intermediate class of free persons of color during the early decades of the nineteenth century. Ultimately, however, the decline of Latin European institutions and the inmigration of white European laborers eroded the social and economic status of the free black class. In Louisiana, as elsewhere in the South, segregation, anti-miscegenation laws, and the legal ostracism of racially mixed children signified the imposition of a two-category pattern of racial classification. While increasingly restrictive manumission laws and exclusionary measures curtailed the size and mobility of the free black population, the movement toward a dual racial order reduced all free persons of African ancestry to a degraded status.[54]

Relegated to a debased status, deprived of citizenship, denied free movement, and threatened with violence, free blacks evaded, resisted, or fled the rising tide of white oppression. In New Orleans, some French-speaking intellectuals chose to remain in the city. Like intellectuals in France and the Caribbean, they channeled some of their discontent into a new mode of artistic expression influenced by European models.

53. Judith K. Schafer, "The Long Arm of the Law: Slavery and the Supreme Court in Antebellum Louisiana, 1809–1862" (Ph.D. dissertation, Tulane University, 1987), 9.

54. Fredrickson, *White Supremacy,* 94–99, 129–30.

4

Romanticism, Social Protest, and Reform

In a French-language literary work written before 1840, a War of 1812 veteran protested the treatment of black soldiers in the aftermath of the battle of New Orleans. The poem, titled "The Campaign of 1814–15" and attributed to Creole of color Hippolyte Castra, also dramatized the plight of Louisiana's free black population:

I remember that, one day, during my childhood,
A beautiful morning, my mother, while sighing,
Said to me: "Child, emblem of innocence,
You do not know the future that awaits thee.
You believe that you see your country under this beautiful sky
Renounce thy error, my tender child,
And believe above all your beloved mother . . .
Here, thou art but an object of scorn."

Ten years later, upon our vast frontiers,
One heard the English cannon,
And then these words: "Come, let us conquer, my brothers,
We were all born of Louisiana blood."
At these sweet words, and embracing my mother,
I followed you, repeating your cries,
Not thinking, in my pursuit of battle,
That I was but an object of scorn.

Arriving upon the field of battle,
I fought like a brave warrior;
Neither the bullets nor the shrapnel,
Could ever fill me with fear.
I fought with great valor
With the hope of serving my country,
Not thinking that for recompense
I would be the object of scorn.

After having gained the victory,
In this terrible and glorious combat,
All of you shared a drink with me
And called me a valiant soldier.
And I, without regret, and with a sincere heart,
Helas! I drank, believing you to be my friends,
Not thinking, in my fleeting joy
That I was but an object of scorn.

But today I sigh sadly
Because I perceive a change in you;
I no longer see that gracious smile
Which showed itself, in other times, so often
Upon your honeyed lips.
Have you become my enemies?
Ah! I see it in your fierce looks,
I am but an object of scorn.[1]

Castra no doubt read his poem to members of La Société des Artisans, an organization created by free black artisans and veterans of the war. With the demise of the militia, former members of the military organized a number of such benevolent and social organizations. Louis Victor Séjour, a quartermaster in Daquin's battalion and a native of Saint Domingue, also joined La Société. Séjour's teenaged son, Victor Séjour, made his literary debut before its members. Reputed to have included white members as well as free men of color, La Société provided a forum for the numerous literary works that circulated in New Orleans during the 1830s. The protest nature of works such as Castra's, the popularity of the French Romantic literary style, and the presence of an interracial social organization indicated the considerable impact in the city of events in France. Revolutionary upheaval in post-Napoleonic France sent large contingents of proscribed republicans, journalists, and other political dissidents fleeing to Louisiana.[2]

Between 1830 and 1850, the influx of emigrés strengthened an existing cluster of French-speaking free thinkers and political liberals. Resident in-

1. McConnell, *Negro Troops,* 107–108.

2. *Ibid.*, 106; Roussève, *The Negro in Louisiana,* 82.

tellectuals joined with the newly arrived refugees to establish a remarkably productive French-language literary community. In Louisiana, in resuming their attacks on religious and political oppression, many French-speaking writers commonly expressed their views in literary works. In 1849, in the *Courrier de la Louisiane,* an ardent republican set his radical beliefs to verse:

Ah! that you might allow Democracy
To overthrow hideous tyranny everywhere!
And that, expelling kings, majestic Liberty
From the scepters make an auto-da-fé!
Let it come to pass that the Pope accepts republicanism
And of the different religions makes only one Church![3]

Predictably, the revival of egalitarian principles clashed with prevailing social and political realities. Coinciding with turmoil in France, the Louisiana legislature's 1830 campaign to impose a stricter racial regimen did not go unchallenged. French-speaking intellectuals in New Orleans attacked the legislative agenda on the basis of the democratic ideals of the revolutionary era.

In February, 1830, Milo Mower, a French emigré and possibly one of a number of journalists fleeing France as a result of events surrounding the revolution of 1830, began publication of *Le Libéral.* Efforts were underway in the state capital in Donaldsonville to expel free blacks who had entered Louisiana in contravention of the 1807 statute that banned the entry of free men of color. In one of the earliest issues of the newspaper, Mower and his associates attacked "the friends of ignorance, of prejudice, and oppression" and set out to "unmask hypocrisy and defend the rights of man."[4]

3. Tinker, *Les Ecrits,* 5; quotation from Viatte, *Histoire littéraire,* 243–44.

4. Timothy F. Reilly, "*Le Liberateur*: New Orleans' Free Negro Newspaper," *Gulf Coast Historical Review,* II (Fall, 1986), 5–24. Unable to locate existing copies of *Le Liberateur,* Reilly accepted Tinker's speculative conclusion regarding the paper's title, but extracts from it published in the *Genius of Universal Emancipation* indicate that it was called *Le Libéral,* not *Le Liberateur*. Also, Reilly surmised that Mower was either a free man of color or an Alsatian immigrant. It is unlikely, however, that city authorities would have allowed a person of African descent to publish such a highly provocative newspaper for such an extended period of time; in view of Reilly's findings, it is more likely that Mower was white. Quotation is from *Le Libéral,* March 19, cited in *Genius of Universal Emancipation,* May, 1830.

In attempts to justify the legislative movement, Louisiana newspapers depicted gruesome images of the slave revolution in Saint Domingue. Proponents also attacked *Le Libéral* and accused the paper of advocating the abolition of slavery. The paper's enemies angrily challenged the newspaper's attempt to defend people of color: "What . . . they tell us [is] that we don't have the right to oppress this element of the population. How dare they? . . . Death is too kind a punishment for such a villain." In response to such charges and threats, Mower and his colleagues claimed they were opposed to general emancipation or the violent overthrow of slavery. The paper sought only to protect the rights of free blacks who, it claimed, had done nothing to warrant their removal.[5]

While state legislators devised new expulsion decrees and emigration restrictions, they also undertook efforts to suppress *Le Libéral,* a "seditious newspaper." In March, the paper lashed out at its opponents. Expressing confidence that the courts would uphold provisions in the state constitution providing for a free press, *Le Libéral* swore to "revile the blindfold of error" and "break the chains of oppression." The paper went even further: "The more that they try to force us to yield to their despotism, the greater will be our resistance and we will defy tyranny and oppression until our last breath."

An anonymous contributor applauded the editor for his "truly republican" views and attacked state legislators for disregarding the constitution and committing "intolerable abuses" against free people of color. In his letter to the editor, the reader warned that a great number of free blacks were preparing to leave the country in an effort to "flee these new laws, one more arbitrary than the other." Free people of color, the writer continued, although a prosperous and law-abiding people, "see themselves more persecuted (though in a free country) than they would be in a monarchy governed by one of the descendants of Tarquin, Nero or Caligula."[6]

In a subsequent issue, *Le Libéral* celebrated a partial victory. A modified version of the expulsion bill provided that only those who had arrived in the state since 1825 would be subject to removal. While state authorities reserved the right to expel any undesirable person of color, an accompanying modification narrowed the law's applicability considerably. The statute

5. *Le Libéral,* February 24, cited in *Genius,* April, 1830.

6. *Le Libéral,* March 19, 1830, *ibid.*, May, 1830.

was not to be applied to free persons of color who were married, who had children born in the state, or who could "give security for their good conduct." *Le Libéral* took credit for the change, for if "we had remained silent and passive spectators . . . the enemies of tolerance and humanity . . . would have met with complete success." The paper continued: "The first good with which God endows man . . . is Liberty, its enjoyment by consequence must be of the utmost necessity." Some lawmakers, however, "would like to preserve, upon a republican basis, laws created for a despotic government." In a lengthy poem titled "Address to the Louisiana Legislators," a contributor to the newspaper admonished the "despotic" senate. The paper continued: "The good of all, you say: Hush up your hatred."[7]

At the end of May, 1830, *Le Libéral* took a more radical position. On the basis of natural rights and representative government, the paper argued in favor of voting rights for free men of color. As a productive, talented, and industrious element in society, as property holders, and as public defenders in the War of 1812, free men of color were entitled to suffrage. In the same issue, *Le Libéral*'s editors applauded a letter from a slaveholder in Florida. The slaveholder, comparing Brazilian slavery with slavery in the American South, pointed to the beneficial effects of lax manumission laws and the right of slaves to own property. In Brazil, property rights and the prospect of freedom promoted loyalty and industry among the slaves. The letter, the editors observed, contained "much sound reasoning."

Le Libéral refrained from a direct attack on slavery. Instead, the newspaper offered a sweeping and provocative denunciation of race relations under slavery. Referring to men of mixed racial ancestry, men "who are our work, since we are their fathers," the paper observed: "But how can we treat men like ourselves in this way, men who live on the same soil, often share the same roof, who must live with us and often close our eyes? We ought to call ourselves tyrants."[8]

Le Libéral's days were numbered. The newspaper clearly violated a new state law, enacted in March, that overrode the state constitution's guarantee of a free press and represented a grave assault upon liberties provided for in the nation's Constitution. It stated that "whosoever shall

7. *Le Libéral,* n.d., *ibid.*, June, 1830.

8. *Le Libéral,* May 27, 1830, *ibid.*, July, 1830.

make use of language, in any public discourse . . . having a tendency to produce discontent among the free coloured population of this state, or to excite insubordination among the slaves therein, or whosoever shall knowingly be instrumental in bringing into this state, any paper, pamphlet or book, having such tendency as aforesaid, shall on conviction thereof, before any court of competent jurisdiction, suffer imprisonment at hard labour, not less than three years, nor more than twenty-one years, or death, at the discretion of the court."[9]

City authorities arrested Mower in August, 1830, for passing out allegedly inflammatory literature. The Baltimore editors of the antislavery tract *Genius of Universal Emancipation,* who had established contact with Mower not long after *Le Libéral* appeared, reported that the French editor lacked funds to continue publication. According to them, the so-called incendiary pamphlet was merely a solicitation for support, and they denounced New Orleans officials for arresting Mower on false charges. The fate of *Le Libéral* and the severity of the 1830 state law, however, did not silence French-speaking critics of race relations in nineteenth-century New Orleans. Instead, attacks on racial oppression appeared in the guise of literary works. The intellectual excitement that accompanied the French Romantic literary movement enabled French-speaking writers like Castra and others to protest existing social evils during the antebellum era.[10]

In meetings of La Société des Artisans and other such organizations, Creole writers exchanged views and presented their artistic works in a favorable setting. Still, the climate of race relations in the city and the 1830 state law restricting written materials represented insurmountable obstacles to the literary careers of free black artists. Under such circumstances, one member of La Société, the elder Séjour, encouraged his son to pursue his vocation in France; Séjour had fled his native city of Saint Marc in Saint Domingue and was determined to see his son succeed. Convinced that the teenager possessed exceptional writing ability and anxious that he escape the onus of race prejudice in Louisiana, Séjour dispatched the young man to France in the mid-1830s to continue his studies. He funded

9. Clement Eaton, *Freedom of Thought in the Old South* (Durham, N.C., 1940), 129–30; *Acts of the State of Louisiana,* 1830, 96.

10. *Genius,* September, 1830. According to Reilly, Mower disappeared from the public record after his arrest, and he speculates that he was deported to Europe (Reilly, "Le Liberateur," 20–21).

his son's education at a college in Paris with profits from his successful dry goods store in New Orleans.

When Victor Séjour arrived in France, he was already well educated. Having studied in New Orleans under Michel Séligny, a skilled writer and Creole of color, Séjour was also well versed in the Romantic literary style. The young writer quickly attracted the attention of another writer of African descent, the French novelist Alexandre Dumas. Under the influence of Dumas and other French literary artists, Séjour eventually enjoyed remarkable success in Parisian theaters.[11]

Soon after his arrival in Paris, the New Orleans writer encountered the fiery antislavery journalist Cyril Bissette. A free man of color from Martinique, Bissette had already won a legendary reputation in the French abolitionist movement. Arrested in 1822 in his home in Martinique for disseminating seditious literature, the well-to-do Bissette was stripped of his possessions, sentenced to the galleys for life, and branded with the letters *GAL* for galley slave. In France, Bissette's case became a cause célèbre.

Freed from prison in 1827, the embittered exile became an impassioned enemy of slavery. In 1834, Bissette launched an abolitionist tract titled *Revue des Colonies*. While demanding that slavery be abolished, Bissette also publicized the accomplishments of men of African descent. Eulogies of the Haitian Revolution and portraits of successful men of color contrasted sharply with news items depicting the horrors of slavery.[12]

In one instance, Bissette noted the success of Dr. Jacques Derham, a New Orleans physician and former slave from Philadelphia who had purchased his freedom at the end of the American Revolution. By 1788, Derham had established a large medical practice in New Orleans, where, according to the *Revue,* he treated both blacks and whites. In 1836, in other news from New Orleans, editor Bissette summarized his survey of the city's newspapers. In an article titled "The Sale of Slaves and Beasts," he noted that the papers were full of advertisements for the "sale of male

11. McConnell, *Negro Troops,* 105–106; J. John Perret, "Victor Séjour, Black French Playwright from Louisiana," *French Review,* LVII (December, 1983), 187; Charles Edwards O'Neill, *Séjour: Parisian Playwright from Louisiana* (Lafayette, La., 1996), Chap. 1; Roussève, *The Negro in Louisiana,* 66–83; McCloy, *The Negro in France,* 165; Viatte, *Histoire littéraire,* 265; Hunt, *Haiti's Influence,* 74.

12. David O'Connell, "Victor Séjour: Ecrivain américain de langue française," *Revue de Louisiane,* I (Winter, 1972), 60–61; McCloy, *The Negro in the French West Indies,* 135–212.

and female slaves, that they offer to sell pell-mell with donkeys, mules, mares and other beasts of burden." Although the monthly *Revue* suspended publication in 1842, the resourceful Bissette kept his cause before the French parliament in his writings and public statements. Bissette's unrelenting struggle in the 1840s helped pave the way in France for the abolition of slavery in 1848.[13]

In March, 1837, Bissette published one of Séjour's short stories, "Le Mulatre," in his *Revue*. Like so many of his literary colleagues, the New Orleans writer set his antislavery story in Saint Domingue, "today the republic of Haiti." The setting had more than symbolic relevance; Séjour's father was a native of Saint Marc, the city in which the story takes place. Some of the writer's relatives still lived in Haiti, and Séjour's nephew, Frédéric Marcelin, became a noted political activist and renowned Romantic writer. Séjour possibly was relating some of his family's experiences in their Caribbean homeland. Séjour's convincing and vivid descriptions of black culture suggest that the writer visited the island himself.[14]

The story of the mulatto Georges is told to a white visitor by a white-haired, elderly Negro named Antoine. His listener then relates Séjour's story to the reader. When the white traveler arrived in the Saint Domingue city and greeted Antoine with a handshake, the older man chastised him: "Master . . . it is a noble heart that makes you do that . . . but don't you know that a Negro is as lowly as a dog? . . . Society rejects him; men detest him; the laws censure him."[15]

Although the central character of the story is Georges, he is not the hero, for, as Antoine explains in relating Georges' story, slavery transforms everyone, even children, into brutish creatures. The only heroes of the story were the black maroons who had "escaped the tyranny of their masters." Initially, Georges sided with Alfred, his master, whose life Georges had saved. Ultimately, however, Alfred betrayed Georges, and the deceived slave turned on his master. In the course of events, Georges wholly identified with the "enemy" and joined the black maroons. When

13. *Revue des Colonies,* April, 1837, p. 432; October, 1836, p. 180; McCloy, *The Negro in the French West Indies,* 136.

14. O'Connell, "Victor Séjour," 62; Viatte, *Histoire littéraire,* 403–405.

15. O'Connell, "Victor Séjour," 62.

the mulatto approached their forest hideaway, he greeted them with the passwords "Africa and freedom."[16]

Antoine described how, because of slavery, Africans were "torn away by deception or by force from their country," and in "becoming, through violence, the goods, the property of their fellowmen," were deprived of elemental human traits: "Though he [the slave] may be born good, noble, generous; though God gives him a loyal and great spirit; despite that, very often he goes to his grave with hands stained with blood, and his heart still greedy for vengeance; because experience has taught him that his good actions were of no account and that he must love neither his wife, nor his offspring; for one day the first will be seduced by the master and his children sold away regardless of his grief." How, Antoine asked his friend, "can the human heart be cultivated in the midst of such misfortunes?" Antoine's characterization of slave society forms the basis for the story. The old slave went on to describe Georges' ill-fated destiny.[17]

In surprisingly explicit language, Séjour described the lurid events surrounding the sale of a beautiful Senegalese woman, Georges' mother, and the sexual assaults that both Georges' mother and his wife suffered at the hands of their master, Alfred. Surmising that the slaveholder was "perhaps good, humane, loyal with his peers," Antoine nevertheless made clear that Alfred "was a hard, evil man towards his slaves." When Alfred insisted that Georges' wife be hanged for having forcefully resisted his sexual advances, Georges escaped and could think of nothing but revenge. In the end, Georges murdered Alfred and the slaveholder's wife. As he killed them, however, he discovered that Alfred was his father, and then he committed suicide.[18]

Although Séjour's short story may have circulated among black families, it was never published in New Orleans. The state law of 1830 dealing with the dissemination of seditious publications was clearly designed to prevent the spread of reading materials as inflammatory as Séjour's "Le Mulatre."

Despite these severe restrictions, the city's free people of color still managed to fashion a vibrant literary movement. The considerable talents of

16. *Ibid.*, 71.
17. *Ibid.*, 62–63.
18. *Ibid.*, 65.

Séjour, himself the product of a free black school, testified to the presence of a highly sophisticated literary community. Although Creoles of color did not enjoy the privilege of freely expressing themselves until the early 1860s, the French Romantic literary movement served as a vehicle for the expression of some of their feelings and attitudes during the antebellum period.

Séjour's short story, written in the same Romantic style as that of his contemporaries in France and the Caribbean, appeared in *Revue des Colonies* alongside the works of leading writers of Haiti, Guadeloupe, and Martinique. Besides calling for the abolition of slavery and publicizing the achievements of men of color, Bissette encouraged the literary careers of black intellectuals. Issues of the *Revue* included the works of Haitian authors Ignace Nau and Beauvais Lespinasse. Pierre Marie Pory-Papy of Martinique, destined to join Bissette, Alphonse de Lamartine, Félicité de Lamennais, and Victor Hugo in the French National Assembly of 1848, contributed his poetry to the *Revue*. Joseph Saint-Rémy, a native of Guadeloupe and a devotee of Lamartine, sketched the lives of the Haitian Republic's leading men of letters.[19]

Séjour's short story and the contributions of other black writers to Bissette's journal clearly demonstrated the enormous impact on black intellectuals of events in Haiti. Images of Saint Domingue, the Haitian Revolution, and the establishment of the black republic inspired a generation of Romantic writers. In France, Victor Hugo and Alphonse de Lamartine dramatized events in revolutionary Haiti in launching a campaign of literary emancipation. Whereas the classical French tradition of the eighteenth century had viewed non-European cultures as barbaric and unworthy of literary treatment, a new generation of Romantic writers defied Classicism's ethnocentric assumptions.

In 1818, Hugo, a leading figure in the Romantic movement in France, based one of his earliest novels on the black revolution in Saint Domingue. In *Bug-Jargal,* tragic consequences followed the mistaken execution of a black rebel leader. Although the noble revolutionary, an African king in his native land, saves the life of a young French soldier, the black leader is

19. McCloy, *The Negro in France,* 160–61. For examples of Caribbean writers' contributions to *La Revue,* see issues from July, 1835, November, 1836, and March–May, 1837.

condemned to death through a misunderstanding; the fatal injustice casts a shadow over the soldier's life.

Like Hugo, the Romantic writer Lamartine, another transitional figure in the history of French literature, dramatized the slave uprising in his depiction of the Haitian Revolution in *Toussaint Louverture,* written between 1839 and 1842. Inspired by his involvement in the Société Française pour l'Abolition de l'Esclavage after 1834, the French writer idealized the revolutionary leader in his play. In eulogizing the "hero of the blacks," Lamartine portrayed Louverture as the embodiment of Haiti: "This man is a nation."[20]

Such themes in Romantic literature and the inclination of leading French writers to infuse their works with social and political commentary revealed the persistence of the ideals of the eighteenth-century democratic revolutions. Many of the most important French Romantics viewed their art form as a device for bringing about change.

The French Revolution had proclaimed the gospel of equality. In revolutionary ideology, human beings interacted peacefully and cooperatively with one another under natural conditions. The inability of humanity to achieve freedom and universal brotherhood was the consequence of oppressive, greedy, and bloodthirsty tyrants who set individuals against one another. In this view, harmonious human relations followed naturally from freedom. The mission of the revolutionaries became the liberation of enslaved peoples. A deep faith in a universal brotherhood of free men and a missionary-like zeal to spread the ideal of social justice reappeared in post-Napoleonic France.[21]

European Romanticism contributed to the renewed desire for change, and German philosophers gave crucial impetus to the movement. After the turn of the century, German thought produced a revolution in philosophy comparable in significance to the French Revolution. And like the

20. George Saintsbury, *A Short History of French Literature* (Oxford, Eng., 1901), 498. *Bug-Jargal* was written in 1818, then revised, and finally published in 1826 (Sir Paul Harvey and J. E. Heseltine, comps. and eds., *The Oxford Companion to French Literature* [Oxford, 1959], 93). William Fortescue, *Alphonse de Lamartine: A Political Biography* (New York, 1983), 82-83; Alphonse de Lamartine, *Toussaint Louverture* in *Collection Michel Lévy,* ed. Michel Lévy Frères (Paris, 1870), viii, xiv.

21. J. L. Talmon, *The Unique and the Universal: Some Historical Reflections* (New York, 1965), 25–35; Lefebvre, *The French Revolution,* I, 149.

cataclysm in France, the revolution in thought embodied a fundamental faith in individual freedom. Believing that the age of democratic revolution would produce the final stage in history when the ideal of freedom would be realized, German philosopher G.W.F. Hegel challenged previously held notions about the nature of human relations. Only by interacting from an equal and autonomous basis could individuals be truly free. For both the oppressed and the oppressor, self-realization could occur only within the context of individual liberty. The Hegelian concept of freedom and the works of other German philosophers gave crucial impetus to European Romanticism. German ideas spread through Europe and across the Atlantic as an aspect of the Romantic movement.[22]

In France, leading intellectuals drew heavily upon Hegel and other German philosophers, including Johann Gottfried Herder. Herder advanced the view in *Ideas on the Philosophy of the History of Mankind,* published between 1784 and 1791, and other works that a purposeful, natural, and harmonious social order existed as part of God's design. This natural order, he explained, operated "not through the will of a sovereign, or the persuasive power of tradition, but through natural laws on which the essence of man reposes." Natural laws were a function of human reason. Since God had bestowed the power of reason upon all men, "every good employment of the human understanding necessarily must and will, at some time or other, promote humanity." Reasonable conduct produced equity and happiness. Ultimately, humanity would achieve a state of benevolence and harmony.[23]

The institutions of class, church, and the dynastic state were artificial creations imposed upon society by usurpers. Such contrivances ran counter to the organically evolving nation and had no place in the natural order. Though irrational behavior and uncontrolled passion often disrupted the social balance, every illogical action produced its nemesis. Conflict ensued. With the return of balance and order, the struggle became a lesson and a stimulus for self-improvement. The dialectic produced progress and social regeneration. This historical process operated at

22. J. L. Talmon, *Romanticism and Revolt: Europe, 1815–1848* (New York, 1967), 82; David Brion Davis, *The Problem of Slavery in the Age of Revolution, 1770–1823* (Ithaca, N.Y., 1975), Epilogue.

23. Talmon, *The Unique and the Universal,* 109; Roland N. Stromberg, *An Intellectual History of Modern Europe* (New York, 1966), 198.

every level of civilization since all men shared the same humanity. In the new view of history, the inherent genius of all peoples and all nations contributed to the advancement of civilization.

Both civilization and the nation arose from the inner genius and collective consciousness of the common people. Herder reveled in the uniqueness of every age and every nation. He glorified the songs, literature, art, and folkways of ordinary people as expressions of a culture's authentic wisdom. Through the realization of their native genius, all peoples contributed to the brotherhood of humanity and God's universal design. From the tribal society to the nation-state, the unfolding of history represented God's will at work.[24]

German philosophy's "romanticized" view of an organically evolving society generated cultural pride and an intense interest in the study of history. In the early nineteenth century, French intellectuals drew upon German concepts to promote democratic ideas. The influential historians Edgar Quinet and Jules Michelet popularized the new philosophy in their books and public addresses. In Quinet's lectures at the Collège de France, the ardent republican portrayed the French nation as the leader in the movement toward democracy. He advocated establishing a humanitarian republic in France, which would hold out the hope of liberty and justice for oppressed nations.

Beginning in the 1830s, in his *History of France* and *History of the French Revolution,* Michelet applauded the inner genius of the French people and glorified the French Revolution. "Frenchmen," he wrote in 1846, in the view of "the ever-enduring coalition of aristocracies, you will always be guilty of one crime,—to have wished, fifty years ago, to deliver the world." In 1831, in his *Introduction à l'histoire universelle,* Michelet drew upon German historicism to form the basis for his analysis of the past: "With the world began a struggle which shall end with the world, and not sooner—the struggle of man against nature, of mind against matter, of freedom against fate. History is nothing other than the relation of that interminable warfare. . . . Freedom doubtless has its limitations, *and yet it moves*."[25]

24. Talmon, *The Unique and the Universal,* 104–10.

25. C.H.C. Wright, *The Background of Modern French Literature* (Boston, 1926), 86–87; Fritz Stern, ed., *The Varieties of History: From Voltaire to the Present* (1956; rpr. New York, 1973), 118; David Owens Evans, *Social Romanticism in France, 1830–1848* (London, 1951), 2.

By stressing the superior virtue of the common people and characterizing their art as an expression of an inner spirit or native genius, German thought also overturned traditional standards of artistic expression. Under the influence of German ideas, Romantic artists rejected the philosophical underpinnings of eighteenth-century Classicism. A craving to rediscover nature, the natural, and native genius replaced the taste for the grandiose, sophisticated, and conventional. In the sociopolitical sphere, Romanticism's emphasis on unrestricted self-expression bred a desire for freedom from religious mores, political despotism, and a hierarchical social order.[26]

In France, the Romantic notion of the artist-seer coalesced with socialist thought to produce a new concept of the artist's role in society. One of the earliest socialist thinkers, the Comte de Saint-Simon, proposed a planned society managed by experts in the fields of science, art, and industry. Beginning in the 1820s in France, followers of Saint-Simon proposed to "foster the union of scientists, industrialists, and artists, as the only means of rescuing society from its present state of crisis." For Saint-Simon, the intelligentsia represented the spiritual authority in modern society. In this view, the role of the literary artist became paramount since literature was "the living expression of the forms and needs of society" and a "powerful lever for the development of moral energies."[27]

Saint-Simonians sought to attract contemporary writers and other artists to their movement, for the arts must "serve the common cause by propagating generous ideas" and by promoting "the general movement of the human intelligence." The artist was to enlighten and educate the masses: "Art today must have social usefulness. It must appeal to the people." In 1826, the Saint-Simonian physiologist Philippe Buchez wrote: "Literature and the fine arts are not the works of idleness and dissipation; they are the creations of passionate sentiments, that is to say, of all that is least individualistic in Man." The collectivist spirit was "the sense of social purpose which becomes the motive of the artist's every act and the source of all his passionate inspirations."[28]

26. Talmon, *Romanticism and Revolt,* 136–41.

27. Evans, *Social Romanticism,* 27–28.

28. *Ibid.*, 28.

French socialists also maintained that human beings would be more receptive to needed reforms once their emotions were softened by evocative scenes of human misery and suffering. As the reading audience empathized with the victims of injustice, their aroused emotions would culminate in a feeling of social solidarity. In compelling portrayals of the weak and disinherited, Félicité Robert de Lamennais, Alphonse de Lamartine, Pierre-Jean de Béranger, Victor Hugo, and others sought to sensitize their readers to the plight of society's outcasts. By stressing the value of social unity, Romantic writers popularized the theories of early French socialists. In France, the social novels that proliferated from 1830 to 1848 became a powerful force for diffusing democratic principles.[29]

Spurred on, like French socialists, by the sense of an unfinished revolution, a generation of Romantic poets, novelists, and dramatists became active agents of social and political change. Victor Hugo and other Romantics saw their art form as a "force for civilization" growing out of the revolutionary heritage. In 1830, the historic phrase, *la liberté dans l'art, la liberté dans la société,* appeared in the preface to Hugo's *Hernani.* A production of the drama at the Comédie Française in Paris turned to chaos when Classicists attempted to drive the play from the stage.[30]

For some of the most outstanding French writers, literary Romanticism led to political activism and revolt. Lamartine, one of the most politically active Romantic writers, advocated universal suffrage, freedom of the press, freedom of conscience, and the abolition of slavery. When he entered the Chamber of Deputies in 1833, he devoted himself to humanitarian reforms, opposing capital punishment and slavery and defending the interests of the working class and the dispossessed. In 1848, Lamartine headed the revolutionary provisional government in France. French Romanticism produced equally significant social and political results in French-speaking regions of the New World.[31]

In Haiti, political Romanticism gained momentum with the establishment in 1835 of a *cénacle* (literary society) in Port-au-Prince. An influential circle of leading Haitian writers—the Nau brothers Ignace and Emile,

29. *Ibid.*, 28–37.

30. Frederick B. Artz, *Reaction and Revolution* (New York, 1934), 196; Evans, *Social Romanticism,* 29–30.

31. Evans, *Social Romanticism,* 82–83.

the Ardouin brothers Coriolan and Beaubrun, Beauvais Lespinasse, and others—modeled their society after the Cénacle de l'Arsenal in Paris. The Parisian cénacle was an inner circle of leading Romantic writers, including Lamartine, Hugo, and Dumas. Combining literary and political themes, Haitian writers introduced the concepts of Lamartine and other Romantics while expressing concerns for the welfare of their nation and the aspirations of people of African ancestry. Romantic writers in Haiti published their views in their journals, *Le Républicain,* founded and suppressed in 1836, and its immediate successor, *L'Union*. The cénacle quickly assumed a key political role in Haitian affairs.

As opponents of the government, the republican contributors to the newspapers attacked the authoritarian presidency of Jean-Pierre Boyer and the self-serving political and military elite that surrounded him. They demanded freedom of the press and speech, representative government, and economic independence. Members of the cénacle and their supporters laid the intellectual groundwork for one of the earliest manifestations of political Romanticism, the Haitian Revolution of 1843.

The theoreticians of *Le Républicain* and *L'Union* revived and popularized the notion of harmony among social classes. In both the Haitian Revolution of 1843 and the French Revolution of 1848, the concept of *fraternité,* as in the spirit of the Revolution of 1789, was to form the basis for societal regeneration. In the view of these nineteenth-century French-speaking intellectuals, social solidarity was considered an essential prerequisite to achieving cultural autonomy, national unity, and the establishment of a viable nation-state.[32]

A great deal hinged on Haiti's effectiveness as an independent nation. The writers of *Le Républicain* and *L'Union* viewed their country as the "cradle of African independence." Haiti's mission was to "carry the torch of civilization into the midst of unfortunate Africa." Beauvais Lespinasse wrote: "But can we speak on the political state of Haiti, on the future of the Antilles and of the black race in America, without pausing to think of Africa? It is to Africa, our mother, that we owe the colour which is still, in the eyes of some nations, the emblem of inferiority. Hence, Africa must be

32. Pradel Pompilus, *Manuel illustré d'histoire de la littérature haitienne* (Port-au-Prince, 1961), 33; Bellegarde-Smith, *In the Shadow of Powers,* 42–43; Nicholls, *From Dessalines to Duvalier,* 73–76.

the object of our wishes, of all our desires, of all our hopes." Destined to lead in the struggle for African independence, Haiti must succeed materially and politically. In succeeding, Haiti and other black nations would destroy the race prejudice that existed against all people of African origin.[33]

The influence of the French Romantic movement among free black intellectuals in New Orleans became more evident in 1843 with the publication of a short-lived, interracial literary journal, *L'Album littéraire: Journal des jeunes gens, amateurs de littérature* (*The Literary Album: A Journal of Young Men, Lovers of Literature*). German historicism, the notion of the artist as seer, the use of artistic media to evoke compassion for victims of injustice, and other aspects of literary Romanticism appeared in the works of Louisiana's Creole writers. And like Romantic writers in France and the Caribbean, many contributors to *L'Album* used their literary skills to challenge existing social evils in nineteenth-century Louisiana.

The works of free men of color Joanni Questy, Armand Lanusse, Camille Thierry, Mirtil-Ferdinand Liotau, and Michel Saint-Pierre dominated the contributions to *L'Album*. Influential Creoles of color Armand Lanusse and Joanni Questy played a leading role in creating and publishing the journal, although Jean-Louis Marciacq, a white, was the actual publisher. Until their deaths in the late 1860s, Questy and Lanusse remained leaders of the Romantic literary movement among free black intellectuals in New Orleans.[34]

Clearly, the 1830 law restricting reading materials, as well as the highly provocative nature of some of the pieces, persuaded a number of artists not to sign their contributions. Other writers used pseudonyms or simply initialed their works. The French-language periodical containing social commentary, poems, and short stories began as a monthly review, but at the request of subscribers, the editors produced a shortened, bimonthly edition. In one of the earliest issues, an essayist described the collection of poems and short stories as the "first songs" of aspiring young writers; he urged his readers to "give them their wings."[35]

33. Nicholls, *From Dessalines to Duvalier,* 75.

34. Viatte, *Histoire littéraire,* 281; New Orleans *Tribune,* May, 1869; Roussève, *The Negro in Louisiana,* 68–69.

35. Tinker, *Les Ecrits,* 297; *L'Album littéraire: Journal des jeunes gens, amateurs de littérature,* July 1, 1843, p. 7, hereafter cited as *L'Album.*

In all likelihood, the publisher Marciacq and the French emigré Eugene Supervielle, a white contributor to *L'Album,* were among those French journalists and political exiles who had fled turmoil and revolution in France and the French Caribbean. As trained newspapermen or college graduates, many of the exiled refugees pursued careers in teaching and journalism to support themselves and their families. They founded the majority of nineteenth-century French-language periodicals in Louisiana. Like many of their fellow emigrés, both Marciacq and Supervielle established newspapers. During the 1840s, Marciacq also directed a school for children of color in New Orleans; his involvement in *L'Album* was probably related to his association with the school. Emigrés and Parisian-educated Creoles transmitted the main currents of Romantic thought to Louisiana. The clarity with which some of the most abstruse aspects of Romantic thought reemerged in the pages of *L'Album* indicated the presence of a highly sophisticated community of French-speaking literati.[36]

A lengthy essay entitled "Philosophy of History" prefaced two of the earliest issues of *L'Album*. It first appeared in early July and demonstrated the influence of German historicism and other Romantic tendencies. Among European intellectuals, the reaction to eighteenth-century rationalism had revived an intense interest in religion and human spirituality. Like many European Romantics, the anonymous essayist attached an overriding importance to a transcendent moral authority.

In history, God's spirit governed human affairs, leading "humanity by the hand" and enlightening mankind. "Without the idea of this liberating action, history would only be a mysterious and endless labyrinth. . . . Society would have no other laws than those of brute force and accident." Organic society was the "coming together of intelligent beings." Social harmony flowed from a belief in and obedience to this divinely inspired rational order.

History taught that "all people are great" in the eyes of God. All human beings are capable of achieving the idealized society, for "if man is united with the one who shaped him, he is within the domain suited to his nature,

36. Edward Larocque Tinker, *Bibliography of the French Newspapers and Periodicals of Louisiana* (Worcester, Mass., 1933), 12–13; Viatte, *Histoire littéraire,* 260; Tinker, *Les Ecrits,* 103, 297–98.

and by consequence in a happy state, because order always produced well-being, happiness." But a "weakening of spiritual ideals" inevitably produced decline. The nineteenth century had made a "profession of every evil," and a slackening of faith had brought about an era of decadence: "In separating himself from God, man betrayed himself. All of a sudden his spirit lost the bright light with which it overflowed, and the darkness of the most deplorable ignorance became his lot. Seeing then nothing more perfect than himself, and deprived of the single object suited to his love, he began to love himself without measure and his brow bowed under the abject empire of lust." Mankind remained estranged from his maker, and "a thousand wild passions bound him in chains and controlled him." Social harmony gave way to chaos and violence, and "the harshest slavery" replaced "gentle liberty."

History taught that war had always raged over "humanity like a continuous fire." In essence, the writer continued, as "we read in the writings of a German philosopher," human existence was an uninterrupted "struggle between good, the divine principle on the one hand, and the evil and adverse principle on the other," making up "the whole of the individual life, from the cradle to the grave, and of history in general, from the creation of man until Judgment Day." Yet redemption was at hand. The carnage of war was the key to humanity's salvation: "Corrupted by all the vices inherent in his state of degradation, man can only be strengthened through bloodshed, and war is the organic means of the regenerative law."

In subsequent issues of *L'Album,* an anonymous essayist discussed the plight of the young men whose literary ambitions the publication was created to promote. Although the series of three articles represented a harsh condemnation of conditions in Louisiana, the author made no overt reference to slavery or race prejudice. Still, in a publication dedicated to the work of young Creoles of color, the author's bitter attacks on contemporary society and his aggressive defense of "Louisiana's youth" represented an unmistakable denunciation of discrimination.

The young men of Louisiana, the writer explained, constituted the main focus of the study. Yet an honest assessment of their prospects for the future required a consideration of present-day conditions. The first commentary, entitled "Horrors of the Day," dealt entirely with the "disasters of the present." The author deplored "the sad and awful condition of Louisiana society," where the state, "in spite of all the proclamations of equality that could be made, in spite of the declarations of the rights of man, is divided into two categories. Money determines whether one is in the privileged classes or under the common law, which is nothing but the absence of all rights." Fortunes were amassed by unprincipled scoundrels: "Oh, my dear friends, for shame! it is precisely these worthless upstarts who are always armed with a fearsome whip to crush one whose station in life is already wretched." For thievery "you will see a Negro subjected to the iron yoke before the entire public," and for vagrancy and beggary "you will also see a white . . . locked up in the horrors of a convict-prison."

The spectacle of rampant greed, unrelieved poverty, and institutionalized injustice "grips our hearts with deep sorrow, showering grief over all our thoughts, filling the soul with terror and despair." What would the great hero of the American Revolution, George Washington, think of such depravity? the writer asked. In the absence of moral fortitude, the nation relied upon the only instinct that indifference had not overcome, the "blind and brute instinct for survival."

If allowed to express himself freely, the writer continued, "how many truths would be revealed!" But he dared not for fear of falling "under the blows of the law." One must "hold one's tongue, one is obliged to fill his heart with grief, one must smother the sighs and the bitterness in the depths of his soul." In concluding the essay, the writer stressed the importance and virtue of Louisiana's youth. Since he had "often seen a man of importance cast him [the youth] a curse," the subject required special attention, and he proposed to resume the topic in a subsequent issue.[37]

In an article entitled "Crime Everywhere" in the August issue of *L'Album,* the writer continued his attack on conditions in Louisiana. He lamented the "British rise, by the triumph of the material, through callous genius," and the decline of the moral legacy of the American revolutionary leaders Benjamin Franklin and George Washington. Crime and atrocities proliferated under British dominance: "Like those executioners who once upon a time killed Christian virgins on the chevalet, they have taken Louisiana's honor, and have bathed it in the sewer and drenched it in the filth of the arenas." In earlier times, voices had arisen to "celebrate the benefits of liberty, this maiden of heaven by which each is a king on

37. *L'Album,* July 1, 1843, pp. 50–51; July, 1843, pp. 75–76, 77-81.

earth." Now, under English influence again, tyranny and chaos prevailed in the name of independence, peace, union, and universal brotherhood.

Change was imminent and Louisiana's youth had a role to play in the impending transformation: "Young Louisianians . . . you will touch with a finger the vice which consumes the heart of this society; and then, young men, capable of creating because you are capable of believing, worthy of liberty, because within you liberty is in no way a selfish motive, but a faith, it will be up to you to give life through your spirit to all of these lifeless remains; it will be up to you to say to the corpses of the nineteenth century: 'Rise and go forward!' "[38]

In the third of the series of essays dealing with Louisiana's youth, the author acknowledged his role as the head of *L'Album*. In an article titled "To Louisianians," he defended himself against the charge that he advocated revolution. To the contrary, the writer maintained, he and his colleagues desired reform, not revolution. The essayist affirmed his commitment to education, defending the "fine minds" of Louisiana's youth and upending the accusations of his critics. Whenever "I hear men in high places recriminate a young man and regard him as a stupid fellow, Oh! then I feel my heart swell under a mountain of indignation." Might not such curses and insults, the author asked, emanate from minds that had "a taste for upheaval, an instinct for anarchy,—crime in them,—failure in them,—corruption in them, fraud in them,—finally, dread in them?" Was contemporary Louisiana so corrupted that "we can hope for nothing" and that present-day society "yields entirely to fear?" The author concluded by urging expanded educational and professional opportunities for "young Louisianians."[39]

In early August, an anonymously written literary essay titled "Scrapbook to Louisiana" prefaced the publication. Like Romantic writers and socialists in France, the author of the work portrayed the literary artist as a seer and agent of change. Immersed in ignorance and hypocrisy, Louisiana drew back in terror from the bearer of truth and knowledge, "the man of letters." The creative writer, condemned to oblivion, remained an object of scorn: "But of the poet, worn and vicious woman

38. *Ibid.*, August 1, 1843, pp. 101–105.

39. *Ibid.*, August 15, 1843, p. 122.

[Louisiana], what have you done with the poet! oh! my God! The one, great by creation and by genius, a patriot in heart and soul, you confine him to a shanty . . . asking for death to relieve him." In the midst of political chaos the essayist, a poet himself, remained unshaken: "I defy you to make me change my countenance and my arms equipped with a sword which promises to come and cut the Gordian knot which holds you captive in the midst of a forest of stupidities."

Future generations would be kind to neither Louisiana as a whole nor to New Orleans, where poets, "the men who should be, oh Louisiana, your models and your symbols," were treated with profound contempt. "New Orleans," the writer continued, "you have embittered the gentlest and sweetest voices, and . . . when posterity pauses to listen to your nineteenth century, it will only hear in your beautiful land an abusive struggle, the raucous roaring of absurdities, a hubbub of frauds and baseness, a tempest of villainies and plunders, whereas, from one end of the earth to the other the great voices of Monsieurs Chateaubriand and Lamartine . . . rising majestically towards heaven like the voices of two angels . . . will be heard.[40]

The poems and short stories of Creoles of color Armand Lanusse, Joanni Questy, Camille Thierry, and others followed the introductory commentary. An angry, embittered, and despairing tone pervades the pieces. The works of two whites—a short story by Eugene Supervielle and a poem by Terence Rouquette—also appeared in the journal. Though a native Louisianian, Rouquette had experienced considerable exposure to the French Romantic literary style. His two older brothers, Parisian-educated writers Adrien and Dominique, exerted a significant influence over the Romantic movement in New Orleans. Beginning in the late 1830s, they helped popularize the philosophy of Alphonse de Lamartine.[41]

Romantic thought favored an idealized view of nature, native wisdom, and simplicity—the genuine—as against the traditional preference for the sophisticated, classical, and conventional—the false. Typical of this Romantic view, Rouquette extols the simple lifestyle of Louisiana's Choctaw Indians in his poem "Disenchantment." Disillusioned in love, he deni-

40. *Ibid.*, August 1, 1843, pp. 13, 98–100.

41. Viatte, *Histoire littéraire*, 252–512 *passim*.

grates contemporary society and craves the consolation of a peaceful existence:

Oh! that I might have lived in my wild forest,
  Like the happy Choctaw,
Yes, sleeping in the wilderness on a bed of leaves,
  Smoking the Bachouctas:
I would have passed days free of anxiety,
  Far from a depraved world
Where I have often dreamed in loneliness
  The oblivion of painful suffering!

He would like, he writes, to be "very far from the cynical crowd . . . To gather strength and lose myself in the forests of America."[42]

Like Rouquette, Creole of color Michel Saint-Pierre also thought of escape. Saint-Pierre, however, contemplated death as a means of release. In a poem dedicated to Auguste Populus entitled "Two Years Later," the writer thanks his friend for sustaining him in his struggle "against cruel fate." The poet writes: "Friend, if hope again dwells in my heart, If sometimes I smile and talk of happiness, If the future pleases me in my new life, I owe it to you alone." Despair had driven Saint-Pierre to the point of suicide, but Populus' steadfast devotion had saved him: "Friendship gives to the soul absolute power to overcome misfortune to soothe suffering."[43]

Saint-Pierre's expressions of hopelessness and despair reverberated in the work of Camille Thierry and other free men of color. In Thierry's poem "Ideas," an obsession with an unfaithful lover leads the artist to entertain thoughts of murder and suicide. Joanni Questy dreamed of vengeance in his poem "Thinking of You in the Night." Forsaken for "a wealthy noble royally dressed," the writer "on a dirty pavement, like a dog without a master . . . thinks of you in his impudence." In his humiliation, the narrator thought of "murder, Oh! but a horrible murder!"[44]

In the poem "A Prayer," Questy depicted himself as God's "poor child in exile" who sought respite from "implacable suffering" that, over time,

42. *L'Album,* July, 1843, p. 86. *Bachouctas* was a type of wild tobacco.

43. *Ibid.*, August 15, 1843, p. 130.

44. *Ibid.*, August 1, 1843, pp. 137–38.

had "crushed his heart!" In another work, a "Poetic Essay," Questy bemoaned the loss of a deceased mate who had given him the only hope and joy he had known in a "hateful world." Before her presence in a life "tortured with torments," the poet confessed, "I slandered God, I cursed life!" With her death, the poet, "broken under an iron fist," despaired of future happiness.[45]

Creole writers also attacked the practice of *plaçage,* or institutionalized concubinage, as a form of human bondage. Miscegenation and interracial cohabitation had proliferated under the French and Spanish. Even though colonial law prohibited interracial marriages, the social practice known as plaçage enabled mixed-race couples to enter into a quasi-legitimate marital arrangement. In plaçage a *représentant* (the young woman's mother or a close relative) would investigate the financial stability and social standing of the white suitor. If the man was found acceptable, the representative would then negotiate a contract with the parents of the young woman of color (the *placée*). In the contract, the prospective "husband" would agree to provide financial support for the young woman and any offspring of the "marriage." Under Latin European influences, Afro-Creole historian Rodolphe Desdunes wrote, such unions often led to stable partnerships and became socially acceptable, since "white persons of Latin extraction, more conscientious of morals and word of honor, contracted religious marriages and thus avoided the stigma of prostitution." Furthermore, the mixed-blood children of such unions "bore the name of their parents . . . and were admitted to the sacraments of the Catholic religion." In some instances, the offspring of the plaçage also inherited considerable wealth upon the death of their white father.[46]

For Creoles of color, the decline of Latin European racial attitudes, the increasing conservatism of the American Catholic Church, and the denial of legal recognition for children of interracial unions undermined plaçage's institutional viability. As portrayed in Creole literary works of the 1840s, plaçage agreements reduced young women of color to the status of prosti-

45. *Ibid.*, pp. 100–101.

46. Foner, "Free People of Color," 409–11; Frederick Law Olmsted, *The Cotton Kingdom: A Traveller's Observations of Cotton and Slavery in the American Slave States,* ed. Arthur M. Schlesinger (New York, 1953), 235–36; quotation from Desdunes, *Our People,* 109.

tutes; these Creole writers saw the practice as a threat to the social fabric of their community.

In his short story, "A Marriage of Conscience," Armand Lanusse dramatized the sordid and ultimately tragic circumstances associated with concubinage. A young woman, raised in a household outside her own in which she was taught to respect "the admirable precepts of the Christian religion," was forced to return home. The young woman's mother insisted that the sixteen-year-old accompany her sisters to the balls the women regularly attended. The gatherings, where unescorted women were prey to a "vulgar herd of brutish youths," made her "tremble with terror." Her fears subsided, however, when she fell in love with the well-mannered and handsome Gustave.

Happiness gave way to sorrow when Gustave proposed to make the young woman his mistress. Horrified, the girl refused. The mother explained that "this young man, occupying a much higher position in society," could not be expected to have a legitimate marriage with a woman of low station; she then proposed an alternative: "But my daughter since a condition that so many young people seek in this country fills you with repugnance, why don't you enter into a *marriage of conscience?*" The young woman agreed, for as she reasoned, "a union made at the foot of the altar should always be enough, it seemed to me; who would dare violate its sanctity?" A priest wed the couple.

Before long, however, the new bride bitterly regretted her decision: "I did not understand that here, [such a marriage] lacked the sanction of law." Within a year, Gustave was frequenting the balls, courting other women, and neglecting his pregnant wife. As Gustave prepared to legally marry a woman of his social standing, his former lover reminded him of their matrimonial oaths. In banishing her from his presence, Gustave coldly replied: "You forget . . . that we are only united in a marriage of conscience." The baby died, and the young woman was trampled to death when she threw herself before the carriage of Gustave and his new wife.[47]

In an unsigned short story entitled "Mary," set in New Orleans during the 1830s, another writer depicted plaçage in similar terms. The story's

47. *L'Album,* August 15, 1843, pp. 132–35.

young heroine of that name, unlike most of her companions who formed a "feminine coterie whose only God is money," refused to compromise her virtue for pleasure and wealth, insisting on an honorable, moral life. Though persecuted by her mother and subjected "to privations of every kind," Mary would not be "handed over to the highest bidder" to become part of the "vast domain of corruption, misery and deprivation." The young woman committed suicide rather than submit. The narrator concluded that God would forgive the noble Mary, a victim of honor, for seeking her salvation in death.[48]

In another anonymous work, "A New Impression," a poet attacked plaçage in harsher language:

> . . . a shameless mother
> Today sells the heart of her grieving daughter;
> And virtue is no more than a useless word which is cast aside,
> . . . again a victim,
> That selfishness overcomes to the cruel extent,
> Again a beauty whose virginal forehead,
> Bows down while blushing at its deadly fate,
> Again hell! again a timid girl,
> At the mercy of a vile heart, greedy for gold,
> Selling all that God in his heavenly abode
> Had without question created out of divine love![49]

With the demise of *L'Album,* Armand Lanusse, one of its creators, conceived of publishing an anthology of poetry by Creoles of color. In 1845, he produced *Les Cenelles,* a work of approximately two hundred pages containing eighty-five poems by seventeen authors. The new book differed markedly from the earlier periodical. Shorn of virtually all social commentary and political content, the contributions to *Les Cenelles* were more subdued in tone. Significantly, however, quotations from Félicité de Lamennais, Victor Hugo, and Alphonse de Lamartine and references to the work of Alexandre Dumas and Pierre-Jean de Béranger indicated the

48. *Ibid.*, July, 1843, pp. 84–85.
49. *Ibid.*, p. 81.

considerable influence of some of the most politicized French Romantic writers. Moreover, a number of the works repeated some of *L'Album*'s concerns and themes.[50]

In the preface to *Les Cenelles,* as in the anonymously written introductory essays to *L'Album,* Armand Lanusse emphasized the value of education as "a shield against the spiteful and calumnious arrows shot at us." Similarly, Lanusse expressed concern for the young men of Louisiana who "we would wish to defend, with all the strength of our souls, against the indifference of some and the maliciousness of others." The editor singled out for praise "the young men whose imagination has been forcefully captured by everything that is great and beautiful in the careers so gloriously pursued by men such as Hugo and Dumas." Although the poet often endured ridicule and impoverishment, Lanusse defended his profession and encouraged young writers. They should pursue their careers even though "beset by all the troubles that those sublime geniuses [Hugo and Dumas] experienced at the beginning of their literary lives." [51]

With eighteen selections, including the introduction and dedication, Lanusse contributed the greatest number of works to *Les Cenelles.* In a few of his poems, he resumed his critical literary treatment of the practice of plaçage. In "Epigram," a sinful mother asks for absolution in the confessional. She assures the priest that she wishes to renounce Satan, but first she cynically queries: "To remove henceforth all incentive to sin, why can't I, father—what?—*establish* my daughter?" Lanusse used the phrase "establish my daughter" in the colloquial sense, referring to the practice of arranging a plaçage. In the short poem, Lanusse picked up on the theme of the conscienceless mother who sought material gain from her daughter's concubinage. The bitterly satirical piece notes the irony in the mother's actions.[52]

In another work, "To Elora," the narrator urges a wavering young woman to honor her engagement vow and marry her fiancé. Avoid the

50. *Les Cenelles,* translated as "Mayhaws," refers to the highly prized fruit of a hawthorn shrub. In choosing this title, Lanusse evoked the image of an indigenous delicacy that thrived in the midst of a harsh environment (Jerah Johnson, "*Les Cenelles:* What's in a Name?" *Louisiana History,* XXXI [Winter, 1990], 407–10); Roussève, *The Negro in Louisiana,* 67–91.

51. Régine Latortue and Gleason R.W. Adams, eds. and trans., *Les Cenelles: A Collection of Poems by Creole Writers of the Early Nineteenth Century* (Boston, 1979), xxxvii.

52. *Ibid.*, xxvi, 95.

fate, he pleads, "of many young girls who form loosely these impure liaisons." He points to the unfortunate example of Noémie, Elora's friend, who was lured by jewels and a new silk dress to enter into an illicit affair. Her mother "without remorse, was an accomplice to the corruption." Soon, Noémie's lover disappears and another affair is quickly arranged. Before long, Noémie succumbs to a life of vice. Lanusse warns Elora:

In vain in palaces displaying their splendor
Would they like to hide this horrible ugliness,
Those who live in the lap of luxury
Have, printed on their forehead: indignity, disgrace![53]

In "The Young Lady at the Ball," Lanusse expresses similar concerns. The narrator warns Emma, the young and beautiful subject of the poem, to control her self-indulgent way of life: "The glitter which surrounds you and charms your eyes is only a deceptive prism which conceals death." But like the attraction of the careless moth to the warmth of the open flame, Emma's recklessness spells her destruction. She yields entirely to pleasure. Consumed by desire, she perishes, and "upon her grave, later, a wailing voice said: Rest in peace, poor child, poor Emma!"[54]

Many of the other poems in *Les Cenelles* deal with love, friendship, and happiness. A considerable number, however, such as several of Lanusse's pieces, address the harsher side of human reality. The plight of an orphan, unfulfilled love, human greed, despair, death, and other tragic themes appear in the poetry. And like the repeated allusions to plaçage, a note of intense anger and frustration reemerges in *Les Cenelles*.

Pierre Dalcour boldly expressed such feelings in a poem dedicated to his friend Constant Reynès, a work entitled "Time of Disillusionment":

The world is a sewer where reign all vices
Where each one basely indulges all his whims,
Where the strong holds the weak, beaten, under his feet
Where men, without shame, still talk of virtue!

Virtue! Virtue! This word, empty but sonorous,
That everyone down here describes differently

53. *Ibid.*, 99–101.
54. *Ibid.*, 109.

Is only a coat which hides shameful vices
For the most hypocritical is the most virtuous![55]

Lanusse chose "Time of Disillusionment" to be the concluding work in *Les Cenelles;* one of Dalcour's poems, "Love Song," opens the book. Interpreted allegorically, the editor's arrangement of these two poems serves as an indictment of the proscriptive environment in which Lanusse and his compatriots lived and worked. In "Love Song," written for the book in November, 1844, the narrator expresses an idealistic faith in the healing qualities of love:

For Love, only the love of a maiden adored
Can console a heart burdened with sorrow;
It is the refreshing oasis, the sacred manna,
The source of pure water in the midst of the desert.[56]

In "Time of Disillusionment," even love is portrayed as an illusion. For the poet, all hope of happiness is lost:

There is barely one lustre beyond my twenty years,
Already the flowers of my springtime have wilted,
Already skepticism has withered my heart,
Already I no longer believe in happiness on this earth![57]

Dalcour, a native New Orleanian living in self-imposed exile in France, also contributed a large number of works to *Les Cenelles*. He composed the twelve poems included during a sojourn in the city. Raised and educated in Paris, Dalcour frequented the French capital's most prominent literary circles and, like Victor Séjour, associated with France's leading Romantic writers. Although he returned to live in New Orleans and achieved considerable prestige within the Creole community, he could

55. *Ibid.*, 57.

56. For Lanusse's editorial decision regarding Dalcour's poems, see Roussève, *The Negro in Louisiana,* 71; Desdunes, *Our People,* 12–13. Armand Lanusse, ed., *Les Cenelles: Choix de Poésies Indigènes* (New Orleans, 1845), 21–22.

57. Lanusse, ed., *Les Cenelles,* 209. A *lustre* is a five-year period.

not adjust to the city's stifling racial environment and went back to France.[58]

Another of the largest contributors to *Les Cenelles,* B. Valcour, was also educated in Paris. One of his eleven pieces, a work written in 1838 titled "Letter to Constant Lépouzé," indicates the close relationship that existed between Creole intellectuals and some of the city's white emigrés. Lépouzé, one of Valcour's teachers and a white native of France, was also a distinguished classical scholar, Romantic poet, and educator. In 1838, he produced a French translation of thirty-three of Horace's Latin satires and odes. The book, *Poésies diverse* (*Sundry Poems*), was published in New Orleans and included thirteen of Lépouzé's poems. When Lépouzé presented his student with a copy of the book, the younger poet composed his eulogistic poem.[59]

Lépouzé, the poem explains, was never an "avaricious master who, ever lacking funds, taught only for his pay." Unlike other instructors, Lépouzé did not "make of us a private monopoly, Did not sell the students' seats, and then the students too." Valcour's poem affectionately describes Lépouzé's considerable influence:

> I've long been out of touch, but never did forget
> That even as a child, I had been formed by you
> Of all your kindnesses, I love the memory;
> Deep within my heart I've kept your valued precepts.
> To you I owe all my poetic tastes.[60]

Lépouzé had settled in New Orleans in 1818. At the time of *Les Cenelles*' appearance, he and another white emigré, Louis Armand Garreau, were two of the most respected white educators within the free black community. Garreau, a native of Cognac, France, immigrated to New Orleans in 1841 and taught in a private boys' school there. During the late 1840s, he assisted his fellow republican partisans, emigrés Prudent de Bautte and Alexandre Barde, with their newspapers. In 1849, he wrote a historical novel titled *Louisiana*. Premised on overtly antislavery opinions, the piece was included in *Veillées Louisianaises* (*Louisiana Evenings*), a two-volume

58. Desdunes, *Our People,* 35; Roussève, *The Negro in Louisiana,* 70–71.

59. Desdunes, *Our People,* 39–40; Viatte, *Histoire littéraire,* 233; Tinker, *Les Ecrits,* 291.

60. Latortue and Adams, eds., *Les Cenelles,* 5–7.

collection of French-language works edited by another white French emigré, Charles Testut. With the appearance of his novel in Testut's publication, the radical Garreau left for Europe, but in France, he became embroiled in politics and suffered political persecution and failure. In 1858, he fled the regime of Napoleon III and returned to New Orleans.[61]

At the time of Garreau's death in 1865, a Creole admirer noted in the obituary that it was to Garreau that "most of our young men owe their instruction." Garreau made no distinctions, the writer noted, when "it was a question of spreading the benefits of education." Of all those who mourned the death of the "eminent writer, none regret it more than the numerous friends that this man of true merit has made in the population of color of this city."[62]

Besides the militant republican Louis Garreau, Creoles of color formed lasting associations with other white literary critics of Louisiana's social order. In 1850, Charles Testut included Creole artists Armand Lanusse, Joanni Questy, and Camille Thierry in his critical study of Louisiana writers entitled *Portraits littéraires de la Nouvelle-Orléans* (*Literary Portraits of New Orleans*). In 1851, Testut also published a poem by Camille Thierry in his book of verse, *Fleurs d'été* (*Flowers of Summer*). In his poem entitled "Thanks," Thierry acknowledged Testut's moral support after the death of his father, a white emigré from France, and related the consequences of his loss:

> Misfortune, I would have conquered it,
> If the one that I love, my father,
> Hell! had lived longer!
> He sleeping . . . farewell to college
> That he had so much dreamed of for me;
> Farewell to France which protects
> Children placed under its law![63]

61. Tinker, *Les Ecrits,* 22–23, 87–88, 214–16, 291; Christian, "A Black History," Chap. XIX, 11–12; Viatte, *Histoire littéraire,* 248; John Maxwell Jones, Jr., *Slavery and Race in Nineteenth-Century Louisiana French Literature* (Camden, N.J., 1978), 53. Also see Armand Garreau, "Louisiana," in *Veillées Louisianaises,* ed. Charles Testut (New Orleans, 1849), I, 159–395.

62. New Orleans *Tribune,* March 30, 1865.

63. "*Portraits littéraires de la Nouvelle-Orléans,* by Charles Testut"(Typescript of 1939 translation by Olivia Blanchard in Howard-Tilton Memorial Library, Tulane University), 90, 95, 100; Charles Testut, *Fleurs d'été* (New Orleans, 1851), 95.

In his response, "Le Poète—Réponse à M. Camille Thierry," Testut alluded to a particularly vicious literary critique and portrayed himself as the defender of his fellow poets, his "forsaken brothers." He deplored those who viewed poets as pariahs, and he struck a more provocative note while describing the poet as the consoler of the poor, sick, orphaned, and enslaved:

> Who knows how to say to the pauper: "Hope!"
> "Persevere!" to those who grieve;
> To the orphan: "Behold your mother!"
> To the sick: "God heals!"
> To those who in chains,
> Victims of human laws,
> Unjustly are cast:
> "Go! let hope sustain you:
> Soon liberté!"

It was, Testut replied, "le poète."[64]

While Lépouzé, Garreau, and Testut collaborated with free black literary artists in New Orleans, American emigré Victor Séjour achieved fame in France. In 1841, the year of Garreau's arrival in New Orleans, the Parisian literati applauded a work by Séjour entitled "Napoleon's Return." This nationalistic ode to Napoleon constituted Séjour's only contribution to *Les Cenelles*. The poem demonstrated another important aspect of French Romanticism: the cult of Napoleon. During the early decades of the nineteenth century, historians like Edgar Quinet, literary artists like Victor Hugo, and songwriters like Pierre-Jean de Béranger portrayed Napoleon as the bearer of France's democratic ideals.

In the popular mind, the economic hardships and political despotism of the Napoleonic years were forgotten, and the former emperor was depicted as the liberator of the common people, the champion of the Republic, the incarnation of the French nation, and the soldier-emissary of the human fraternity. Séjour's poem commemorated the return from St. Helena of Napoleon's remains in 1840 and their ceremonious interment in Paris at the Invalides. In such a setting, the artist's depiction of Napoleon as the em-

64. Testut, *Fleurs d'été,* 103.

bodiment of the French nation achieved popular acclaim. In France, "Napoleon's Return" earned Séjour his earliest literary triumph. Though the nation, like the great Napoleon, had fallen, Séjour expressed confidence:

Courage, noble France.
Your shame, your suffering, cannot long be extended
For on the marble of the tomb,
Reviving in our hearts our truncated hatred,
We will go, young and old, to hone again our swords
Dulled at Waterloo!!![65]

In New Orleans, another contributor to *Les Cenelles,* the Creole poet Manuel Sylva, remained immune to the intense Gallic nostalgia for French ascendancy under the empire. In one of his two contributions to the anthology, Sylva rejected the highly romanticized view of the French emperor and reminded his readers of the harsh conditions that had existed in Napoleonic France. In a work titled "The Dream," Sylva satirizes Louis Napoleon Bonaparte's efforts to follow in the footsteps of his uncle, the great Napoleon. In the thinly disguised character of Melval, the Bonaparte pretender dreams that his name, like Napoleon's, is "praised up to the skies." Under Melval, the empire reemerges and the emperor's reign is a golden age. "Down with Liberty," as Emperor Melval reestablishes feudalism and courts the aristocracy. The "two Napoleons are now at the same level." But at the height of his success, the hapless Melval awakes from his dream and finds "himself once more what he was yesterday." [66]

Several of the poems in *Les Cenelles,* including works by B. Valcour, Pierre Dalcour, and Camille Thierry, reflect the influence of Pierre-Jean de Béranger, the French Romantic songwriter and poet who was a major popularizer of the Napoleonic cult. Rescued from poverty by Lucien Bonaparte, Béranger retained his Bonapartist sympathies, but such sentiments did not define his political outlook. The poet dedicated his talents to the interests of France's laboring classes and remained an ardent advocate of social reform and the republican cause. During the post–Napoleonic

65. Roussève, *The Negro in Louisiana,* 87; Wright, *Background of Modern French Literature,* 96–98; Latortue and Adams, eds., *Les Cenelles,* xxviii, 165.

66. *Ibid.*, 81.

era, French authorities fined and imprisoned him repeatedly for his seditious political writings.[67]

As Creole artists indicated in their works, Béranger enjoyed considerable popularity in New Orleans. Some of his admirers even formed an organization modeled after Béranger clubs in Paris and named themselves "Disciples de Béranger." Around 1850, they invited the highly politicized Romantic writer Charles Testut to write a dedicatory poem to the French poet as an expression of their esteem.[68]

The poet B. Valcour modeled one of his works in *Les Cenelles,* "The Louisiana Laborer," after a Béranger work, "Le Vilain" ("The Peasant"). In the style of the French poet, Valcour expresses a sense of identity with the common people. Through the person of his lover Rose, the artist conveys his attachment to Louisiana's laboring classes. The narrator chooses Rose, a commoner, over a woman of wealth and great beauty because ladies with "lovely hats and gowns of finest silk forever all my pleasures would restrain." Rose, however, is "of the people" and, the poet continues, "there too are my loves." In the final passage, the Parisian-educated writer departs from the lighthearted tone of the preceding stanzas and alludes to the purpose of lyrical poetry and Afro-Creole discontent:

> Then they said to me: you must go to France,
> To see her people, teach yourself their songs.
> To lighten the sufferings of one's brothers
> Never does one need to seek instruction,
> Misunderstood sons of New Orleans,
> Despite her many faults I love her still.
> Faithful to my land I want to remain.[69]

In the introduction to *Les Cenelles,* Armand Lanusse explains the reasons for publishing the book. By including works of amateur artists in a published collection of poems, Lanusse and his colleagues hoped to promote the careers of aspiring young writers. They sought also, the editor wrote, to emphasize the value of learning, because they believed that edu-

67. Wright, *Background of Modern French Literature,* 98; Saintsbury, *A Short History,* 482.

68. Marie L. Lagarde, "Charles Testut: Critic, Journalist and Literary Socialist" (M.A. thesis, Tulane University, 1948), 103.

69. Latortue and Adams, eds., *Les Cenelles,* xxii, 11–13, 22.

cation offered some protection from the harsh realities of life in nineteenth-century Louisiana. The same concerns had animated the founders of *L'Album littéraire*. As the title of *L'Album* indicated, the periodical was dedicated to the literary works of young amateurs. In the introductory essays, as in the introduction to *Les Cenelles,* a contributor had defended "Louisiana's youth" while emphasizing the value of education and the need for educational reform. No doubt aware that literary Romanticism had served as a springboard to other forms of social and political activism in France and Haiti, *L'Album*'s essayist had envisioned a leading role for these "young Louisianians" in his prediction of imminent, cataclysmic change.[70]

In New Orleans, the movement's broader implications became evident during the 1840s, when Lanusse and other Creole leaders undertook concrete measures to promote learning. In their campaign, they sought to assure all free black children of an education. Their efforts addressed one of the most serious abuses of the city's educational system.

A will drawn up in 1832 by a New Orleans widow, Justine Firmin Couvent, provided for the creation of a free school for destitute orphans of color in the city's Faubourg Marigny. The district's orphaned children, many of whom were the illegitimate offspring of interracial liaisons, endured conditions of extreme deprivation. Appalled by their indigence and illiteracy, Madame Couvent, a native of Guinea and former slave, donated land and several buildings to establish an educational facility. Couvent was a devout Catholic and stipulated that the school should be supervised by the Catholic clergy. She named a family friend, free man of color Henry Fletcher, as executor of the will, and a Catholic priest, Constantine Maenhaut or his successor in office, as supervisor. Upon Madame Couvent's death in June, 1837, Fletcher assumed authority over the estate. Public officials, however, opposed expanded educational opportunities for the free black class and discouraged the school's establishment. Fletcher consequently failed to act on the widow's bequest, and the provisions of the will remained null for nearly twelve years.[71]

70. *Ibid.*, xxxvii; *L'Album,* August 1, 1843, p. 105.

71. Rodolphe L. Desdunes, "Mme. Bernard Couvent," trans. Raoul M. Pérez, *Negro History Bulletin,* VII (October, 1943), 7–9; Marcus B. Christian, "Dream of an African Ex-slave," New Orleans *Louisiana Weekly,* February 1, 1938; Nathan Willey, "Education of the Colored Population of Louisiana," *Harper's New Monthly Magazine,* XXXIII (July, 1866), 248; Baudier, *The Catholic Church,* 392.

Although black Creole property taxes contributed in 1841 to the funding of a free public school system in New Orleans, white officials barred free children of color from attending the newly established institutions. Creole families who could afford to send their children to private schools continued to patronize the existing network of religious and secular institutions. Still, poor children remained deprived of educational opportunities, and after 1841, the free black community complained continuously of funding a tax-supported public school system from which their children were excluded.[72]

Father Maenhaut, religious supervisor of the Couvent estate, brought the widow's legacy to the attention of François Lacroix, a prominent Creole of color, who was a slaveholder and a wealthy philanthropist. Described as "an eccentric man, but a person of admirable generosity," Lacroix informed other Creole leaders of the widow's bequest, and in April, 1847, the state legislature passed a law enabling the men to carry out the will's provisions. The new statute provided that six or more persons associating "themselves for any literary, scientific, religious or charitable purpose" could acquire legal recognition as a corporate entity.[73]

Led by Lacroix, Barthélemy Rey, Maximilien "Emilien" Brulé, Armand Lanusse, Louis Nelson Fouché, and Adolphe Duhart, Creole businessmen and intellectuals formed the Société Catholique pour l'Instruction des Orphelins dans l'Indigence (Catholic Society for the Instruction of Indigent Orphans). Ten representatives of the society—François Lacroix, François Escoffié, Martial Dupart, Barthélemy Rey, Chazal Thomas, Joseph Jean Pierre Lanna, Etienne Cordeviolle, Emilien Brulé, Joseph Claude Thomas, and Nelson Fouché—obtained an act of incorporation. "Up to this day," the incorporators disdainfully declared in 1847, "a deplorable indifference has paralysed all means to establish it [the school]." [74]

After achieving corporate status for the institute, the men launched a movement to obtain control of the Couvent estate. In 1848, the society ac-

72. Christian, "A Black History," Chap. XIX, 14–18; Sterkx, *The Free Negro,* 269.

73. Desdunes, "Mme. Bernard Couvent," 7; *Acts of the State of Louisiana,* 1847, 151.

74. Christian, "A Black History," Chap. XIX, 15; Willey, "Education of the Colored Population," 248; Act of Incorporation, April 20, 1847, Notary Octave de Armas, New Orleans Notarial Archives; *Prospectus de l'institution Catholique des orphelins indigents* (New Orleans, 1847), 2.

quired authority to execute the terms of the widow's bequest, after filing suit against the Fletcher succession for thousands of dollars in back rents. Under the auspices of the society's corporate authority, Armand Lanusse assumed leadership of the movement. He solicited support for the school, directed business affairs, devised the school curriculum, and organized the faculty. In 1848, he and his associates opened a temporary facility, with Félicie Callioux, a free woman of color, as principal. Orphaned children attended the school free of charge, while those whose families could afford tuition paid a nominal fee.[75]

Boys and girls from all sections of the city attended the school. At the outset, five teachers, Joseph Bazanac, Ludger B. Boguille, Joseph Vigneaux-Lavigne, Madame Joseph Bazanac, and Madame Adolphe Duhart—all members of the free black community—taught classes in both French and English. Founded under the ostensible patronage of the Catholic Church, the administrators maintained a liberal admissions policy. Significantly, the school accepted children of all religious denominations.[76]

When the permanent facility was completed in 1852, the board of directors made Lanusse the school's principal. Lanusse chose Constant Reynès and Joseph Vigneaux-Lavigne as his chief advisors and named Joanni Questy assistant principal. Either as teachers or administrators, leading Creole literary artists, educators, and artisans played a vital role in the school's survival through the nineteenth century. These included François Escoffié, Noel J. Bacchus, Basile Crokère, Samuel Snaer, Louis Lainez, J. Manuel Camps, William F. Vigers, Louis Nelson Fouché, Nathalie Populus Mello, Paul Trévigne, Armand and Adolphe Duhart, Henry Louis Rey, Aristide Mary and Rodolphe Lucien Desdunes, Eugène Luscy, and Louis A. Martinet.[77]

Evidently alarmed by the spread of free black religious, social, and educational societies like the Société Catholique pour l'Instruction des

75. Christian, "Dream"; Desdunes, *Our People,* 22, 104; Desdunes, "Mme. Bernard Couvent," 8.

76. Desdunes, *Our People,* 104; *Prospectus de l'institution Catholique,* 3; Willey, "Education of the Colored Population," 248.

77. Desdunes, *Our People,* 22, 104–107; Christian, "A Black History," Chap. XIX, 13; "History of the Catholic Indigent Orphan Institute" (Typescript, Marcus B. Christian Collection, Earl K. Long Library, University of New Orleans).

Orphelins dans l'Indigence, state lawmakers modified the 1847 incorporation law. An 1850 amendment to it provided that "in no case shall the provisions of this act be construed to apply to free persons of color in this State incorporated for religious purposes or secret associations, and any corporations that may have been organized by such persons under this act, for religious purposes or secret associations are hereby annulled and revoked." In 1855, a subsequent enactment extended the ban to all charitable, scientific, or literary societies. Designed to suppress the spread of free black institutions, the two measures dealt a severe blow to free black schools. Between 1850 and 1860, student enrollment for children of color in such schools dropped from 1,008 to 275.[78]

One of the most serious assaults upon free black schools occurred in St. Landry Parish. The region possessed the largest population of free persons of color outside of New Orleans. In the decade before the war, white militants of the area conducted a campaign of terror against free black inhabitants. In Washington near Opelousas, the Grimble Bell School, a major educational institution for the region's free black population, operated as a boarding school for many years during the antebellum period. The school averaged an enrollment of 125 students, with four teachers offering classes on the primary and secondary levels. The school charged fifteen dollars a month for board and tuition. During the 1850s, however, white officials closed the facility. Deprived of the school, parents who remained in the region were forced to the send their children to private schools in New Orleans.[79]

The perception that slaves attended free black schools contributed to their unpopularity. State law prohibited the education of slaves under penalty of heavy fines and severe punishment. In 1852, city officials enacted a resolution designed to enforce state law. The new ordinance authorized police to search free black schools for the presence of slaves. Still, whites remained suspicious. Their fears were not unwarranted.[80]

78. *Acts of the State of Louisiana,* 1850, 79; Robert C. Reinders, "The Decline of the New Orleans Free Negro in the Decade Before the Civil War," *Journal of Mississippi History,* XXIV (January–October, 1962), 89.

79. Sterkx, *The Free Negro,* 269–70.

80. Betty Porter, "The History of Negro Education in Louisiana," *Louisiana Historical Quarterly,* XXV (July, 1942), 731; Christian, "A Black History," Chap. XIX, 18.

In some instances, members of the city's free black intelligentsia conducted clandestine "schools" for slaves. Instructors moved their meeting places to different locations every few weeks to escape detection by city authorities. The classes met at night in a room or concealed alleyway, with the students entering and departing either alone or in pairs to avoid attracting attention.

In one instance, Creole of color Ludger B. Boguille, a member of the Couvent school's first teaching staff, permitted a slave child to attend his private school for free children of color. The boy's father, a highly influential New Orleanian, wished to have his son, "a bright-looking boy," educated. Boguille agreed, confident that the father's prominent status would protect him from legal action. When the parents of the other students learned of the child's status, they withdrew their own children, forcing Boguille to dismiss the child. He continued, however, to tutor the boy privately at the slaveholder's residence.[81]

The patronage of the Catholic Church shielded Ecole des Orphelins from public censure. The school remained open through the 1850s, and the board of directors even obtained donations from city officials and the state legislature. In 1854, for instance, the state legislature's Joint Committee on Charitable Institutions recommended a two-thousand-dollar appropriation for the Couvent school. A "careful scrutiny of the establishment" had convinced lawmakers that the school was being conducted properly. Before the war, however, public appropriations remained minimal, with the board of directors relying mainly upon charitable contributions for the school's support. Over the years, wealthy Creoles of color François Lacroix, Aristide Mary, and Thomy Lafon donated thousands of dollars to the institution.[82]

With the passage of the 1847 state law providing for the incorporation of religious, philanthropic, or learned societies, Afro-Creole leaders moved swiftly to obtain recognition for a Catholic convent also. The Sisters of the Holy Family, a small order founded in 1842 by Henriette Delille, a prominent member of the free Creole community, maintained a hospice for the indigent and provided religious instruction and medical

81. Willey, "Education of the Colored Population," 247–49.

82. Sterkx, *The Free Negro,* 269; Christian, "A Black History," Chap. XIX, 15.

care for free blacks and slaves. In a number of important instances, the interests of the Catholic nuns coincided with those of the men who had incorporated and established the Couvent school.

As a girl, Henriette Delille attended a small Catholic school founded by Sister Marthe Fortière, a white emigré and the only member in New Orleans of the Dames Hospitalier (Ladies of Charity), a French religious order. Fortière had opened the girls' school in the French Quarter in 1823, with the financial assistance of the free black community. The school's foundress, however, was interested primarily in charitable work; she aided indigent persons of color and organized classes in religious instruction for slaves. The school became a center of missionary activity, in which Fortière trained Delille and other students to assist her in her work. In 1826, she attempted to found an interracial branch of the Dames Hospitalier with two young women she had prepared for the sisterhood, a white candidate and Juliette Gaudin, a free woman of color and a close friend of Delille. Although Fortière failed to gain the church's authorization for the proposed convent, the setback did not discourage her young protégés. Inspired by the nun's faith and dedication, the young women, including the teenaged Delille, were determined to follow in their mentor's footsteps. In deciding to pursue a religious calling, however, Gaudin, Delille, and other young women of color defied the wishes and traditions of their families.[83]

For three generations, Delille's maternal forebears had entered into extramarital relationships with prosperous white men. Delille's family groomed the light-complexioned young girl for such a liaison. In 1824, Henriette's sister Cecilia contracted a plaçage with a wealthy Austrian emigré whom she had met at a quadroon ball. Henriette, however, had already come under the influence of Fortière; seventeen years old in 1830, she remained adamant in her refusal to attend the balls. Moreover, she openly attacked plaçage liaisons as violations of the Catholic sacrament of marriage. Henriette's arguments encouraged her two quadroon cousins, Marguerite and Minion Ann Boisdoré, to break with the traditions of their caste and

83. Detiege, *Henriette Delille,* 18–20; Charles E. Nolan, *Bayou Carmel: The Sisters of Mount Carmel of Louisiana, 1833–1903* (Ann Arbor, 1977), 18–19; Cyprian Davis, *The History of Black Catholics in the United States* (New York, 1993), 105–107; Toledano and Christovich, "The Role of Free People of Color," in *Faubourg Tremé,* ed. Christovich and Toledano, 99.

marry men of color. Ultimately, under Henriette's influence, Cecilia's daughter Antoinette also married a free Creole of color.

Delille's rebellious behavior threatened the social and financial status of her family. Though the 1830 census listed the Delilles as white, Henriette's refusal to deny her African ancestry and her public association with Fortière's "colored" school betrayed her family's racial identity. In a time of declining economic and social opportunities for free persons of color, some members of her family passed for white. Henriette's bold activities endangered their mobility.

Instead of securing a favorable alliance with a wealthy and influential white man, Delille insisted on pursuing a religious calling that she proposed to fund with her inheritance. In her family's view, the young woman would forfeit her financial security and diminish the household's fortunes by such a course of action. They refused to cooperate, but she persisted. Jean, Henriette's brother, bitterly resented his sister's actions. By 1850, after the death of his mother and sister Cecilia, Jean had disowned Henriette and moved his family away from New Orleans.

At Fortière's school, Delille, Gaudin, and their schoolmates immersed themselves in charitable work among the poor and the city's slaves. During the early 1830s, the Aliquot sisters joined the school's staff. The three sisters, Adele, Marie Jeanne, and Félicité Aliquot, an Ursuline nun who had taken the name of Sister St. Francis de Sales, were French emigrés. When Marie Jeanne Aliquot arrived in New Orleans in 1832, a black laborer saved her life when she fell into the river from a ship's gangplank. The terrifying fall and her rescuer's courage prompted Aliquot to dedicate her life and possessions to alleviating the misery of the city's poor blacks and slaves.[84]

Not long after her arrival in the city, Marie Jeanne Aliquot took charge of Fortière's school, and in 1834, she purchased a larger facility, the Collège d'Orléans in the Faubourg Tremé. The women continued the school and their philanthropic activities. In November, 1836, Delille, Gaudin, and six other women of color led by directress Marie Jeanne Aliquot organized another religious order, the Sisters of the Presentation, and requested the church's recognition. Church leaders would not, however, authorize the establishment of an interracial convent.

84. Detiege, *Henriette Delille,* 14–25, 31; Baudier, *The Catholic Church,* 397.

In 1830, the state legislature affirmed that any white person found guilty of attempting to "destroy that line of distinction which the law has established between the several classes of this community" would be charged with engaging in a high misdemeanor. Violators of the statute would be subject to a $300 to $1,000 fine and a six-month to three-year term of imprisonment. A free person of color convicted of the same offense would be charged with a $1,000 fine and a three- to five-year term of imprisonment at hard labor. At the end of confinement, the violator would be banished from the state for life.[85]

At the time of the founding of the Sisters of the Presentation, two highly provocative religious publications came to the attention of civil authorities in New Orleans: "A Report of the Committee on Religious Instruction of the Colored Population" and "The Annual Report of the Missionary to the Negroes." Concluding that the pamphlets violated the 1830 ban on the dissemination of inflammatory reading materials, city officials offered a reward for apprehending the pamphleteers and urged the attorney general to use his "best exertions to bring such offenders to punishment." [86]

In such a climate, Catholic leaders refused to sanction the Sisters of the Presentation. The interracial religious order and the nature of their work among free blacks and slaves clearly violated "the line of distinction . . . between the several classes" of society. Church officials dispatched Marie Jeanne Aliquot to Jefferson and St. John Parishes, where some Catholic slaveholders desired religious instruction for their slaves. From her rural exile, Aliquot maintained contact with her colleagues.

In New Orleans, Delille and Gaudin made Bishop Antoine Blanc aware of their intention to establish a religious order, and they continued their missionary work in the city. The women urged slaveholders to permit their bondsmen to enter into the Catholic sacrament of matrimony, although civil law forbade slave marriages. The two women served as witnesses in a number of such marriages. They also encouraged young women of color to

85. M. Boniface Adams, "The Gift of Religious Leadership: Henriette Delille and the Foundation of the Holy Family Sisters," *Cross, Crozier, and Crucible: A Volume Celebrating the Bicentennial of a Catholic Diocese in Louisiana,* ed. Glen R. Conrad (New Orleans, 1993), 365; Detiege, *Henriette Delille,* 26–27; *Acts of the State of Louisiana,* 1830, 92.

86. Detiege, *Henriette Delille,* 28–29.

marry men of their caste, and even though civil statutes prohibited racially mixed marriages, the women persuaded members of the clergy to wed such couples.

Finally, in tandem with the founding of a new Catholic church in the Faubourg Tremé, St. Augustine's, Bishop Blanc authorized the establishment of a racially segregated congregation of women of color. In November, 1842, Henriette Delille, the foundress of the order, and Juliette Gaudin received formal authorization in a religious ceremony in the new edifice, shortly after it was completed. Intent, no doubt, upon erasing the new community's interracial origins, church officials insisted on changing the name of the order to the Sisters of the Holy Family. In 1852, Delille, Gaudin, and Josephine Charles took their formal vows in St. Augustine's.[87]

Their first priority was "the teaching of the poor slave children, and a great deal was accomplished." Under slavery, catechism constituted the only means of permissible instruction for Catholic missionaries. An 1830 state law prohibited anyone from teaching slaves to read or write under penalty of imprisonment. Even though Louisiana law did not ban religious instruction, many slaveholders condemned such activities. In 1843, A. D. Megret, a priest in Lafayette, reported that "hell seems to be let loose" when he attempted to teach catechism to his black communicants. Though other issues were involved, the incident brought matters to a head. One of Megret's white parishioners confronted him in a public thoroughfare, upbraided him in abusive language, and beat him up.[88]

In New Orleans, missionary work among the city's slaves also involved hazards. The nuns and their allies risked public retribution as a consequence of their activities. Indeed, in a number of instances, Delille and her associates encountered ridicule and racial harassment. Yet conditions in the city enabled the women to continue their work. Keenly aware of prevailing laws and attitudes, they proceeded cautiously. Before undertaking

87. *Ibid.*, 28–34; Baudier, *The Catholic Church,* 365, 397; Toledano and Christovich, "The Role of Free People of Color," in *Faubourg Tremé,* ed. Christovich and Toledano, 100.

88. Detiege, *Henriette Delille,* 46; Florence E. Borders, "Black Louisiana's Legacy from Three Women of African Descent," *Chicory Review,* I (Spring, 1989), 11; Randall M. Miller, "A Church in Cultural Captivity: Some Speculations on Catholic Identity in the Old South" in *Catholics in the Old South,* ed. Miller and Wakelyn, 22; quotation from Baudier, *The Catholic Church,* 347.

instruction, the nuns obtained the required permission from the slaveholder.[89]

Aliquot lent her moral support in letters from the rural parishes, also providing the struggling nuns with financial assistance and gifts of sugar, syrup, and other commodities. Her continued association with the women of color convinced church authorities to send Aliquot to Mobile to enter a white convent, the Visitation Sisters. The effort failed, and in 1847, Aliquot returned to New Orleans, where she divided her time between life with the Sisters of the Holy Family and missionary work on plantations east of the city. In addition to assisting her colleagues in their business affairs, Aliquot engaged in other humanitarian deeds. In 1852, for instance, she purchased the freedom of three slaves, Annette Bouron and her two daughters, Henriette and Angéla Bouron. Though Delille and her fellow nuns referred to the French emigré as "Sister Aliquot," the church would not allow her to join the order. Finally, not long before her death in 1863, Aliquot took up permanent residence in the convent.[90]

During the 1860s, the nuns encountered a new set of difficulties in their efforts to educate former slaves for, as Juliette Gaudin explained, "after emancipation . . . the masters who had previously sent their slaves to us to be instructed, wished us to refuse to give them any more lessons." This request, Gaudin maintained, was "asking too much of our Sisters." She continued: "We as Sisters are more obliged than others to teach all. . . . We would work in vain if we were to seek to please the rich and neglect the poor."[91]

As Delille, Gaudin, and Charles struggled to maintain their religious order during the 1840s, they received crucial support from many of the same Afro-Creole leaders who had established the Couvent school. As with the incorporation of the Ecole des Orphelins, François Lacroix, Etienne Cordeviolle, Joseph Vigneaux-Lavigne, Jean Pierre Lanna, Chazal Thomas, and a number of other men and women—including Joseph Dumas, François Boutin, and the white French emigrés Agathe Mager

89. Toledano and Christovich, "The Role of Free People of Color," in *Faubourg Tremé,* ed. Christovich and Toledano, 99; Detiege, *Henriette Delille,* 19, 39.

90. Detiege, *Henriette Delille,* 36–39; Toledano and Christovich, "The Role of Free People of Color," in *Faubourg Tremé,* ed. Christovich and Toledano, 100; Act of Sale, June 4, 1852, Notary Philippe Lacoste, New Orleans Notarial Archives.

91. Detiege, *Henriette Delille,* 47.

Collard and her brother Jean Mager—organized a religious society in July, 1847, called the Association of the Holy Family. Under the provisions of the 1847 incorporation law, the association acted in the same capacity as the Société Catholique pour l'Instruction des Orphelins dans l'Indigence. The organization obtained corporate status for the Sisters of the Holy Family. As with the Couvent school, the patronage of the Catholic Church shielded the congregation from the 1850 state law, which revoked the status of religious societies incorporated by free persons of color.

Leading Romantic writers Michel Saint-Pierre, Michel Séligny, and Louis Nelson Fouché, as well as black Creole leaders Paul Trévigne, François Boisdoré, Bazile Crokère, Louis F. Liotau, and Joseph Bazanac contributed to the construction of the congregation's first hospice. Over the years François Lacroix, Thomy Lafon, and Dr. Louis Charles Roudanez made considerable contributions to the religious order as the nuns expanded their facilities. During the 1840s and 1850s, many of these same intellectuals, artisans, and philanthropists were also actively involved in the Couvent school. The two institutions and their supporters shared numerous goals and concerns.[92]

Afro-Creole intellectuals advocated education as a means to counteract the damaging effects of an increasingly oppressive social and political order. The Couvent school extended educational opportunities to poor children of color. Although the Sisters of the Holy Family placed greater emphasis on religious instruction, they shared a commitment to education. Restricted in their work among the slaves, the women maintained a free school as well as an orphanage for indigent children of color. Their efforts, like those of their secular counterparts at the Couvent school, represented another aspect of the movement for racial uplift underway within the French-speaking free black community.[93]

As Afro-Creole intellectuals struggled to insure their community's stability, they, like Delille's sisterhood, viewed plaçage as a demoralizing

92. *Association de la Sainte Famille* (New Orleans, 1847), in Archives of the Sisters of the Holy Family, New Orleans; Toledano and Christovich, "The Role of Free People of Color," in *Faubourg Tremé,* ed. Christovich and Toledano, 99–100; "Loterie pour aider à l'érection d'un hospice," 1–7, in Archives of the Sisters of the Holy Family; *Lafon Nursing Home of the Holy Family* (New Orleans, 1973), 18.

93. Detiege, *Henriette Delille,* 47.

influence and condemned the practice in poems and short stories. For their part, the Catholic nuns attacked the tradition of interracial concubinage and urged women of color to marry within their caste. Together with literary artists of color, Delille's Sisters of the Holy Family repudiated plaçage as a threat to the social fabric of the free black community.

The newly founded religious order and Lanusse's Couvent school received crucial support from slaveholding as well as nonslaveholding members of the free black community. Indeed, it is highly unlikely that black Creole leaders like Delille and Lanusse could have succeeded without the assistance of prosperous slaveholders like François Lacroix, Joseph Dumas, and J. Manuel Camps. The involvement of these men in the humanitarian activities of free black reformers stemmed in part from their Catholic heritage.

In nineteenth-century New Orleans, Afro-Creole leaders remained committed to policies introduced into Louisiana during the colonial era. Though Catholicism sanctioned slavery, colonial church officials had encouraged slave manumissions and placed considerable emphasis on the slaveholder's moral obligation to treat his bondsmen with benevolence and justice. Church doctrine also required religious instruction and the observance of Sundays and other Catholic holy days.

In New Orleans, Delille and her colleagues continued the church's doctrinal commitment to the humane treatment of slaves. The women insisted that slaves receive religious instruction and the Catholic sacraments, including the sacrament of marriage. Throughout the Catholic South, conscientious clerics like Delille generally met with intense opposition in their efforts to implement such measures. Within the city's Afro-Creole community, however, Latin European religious practices remained well entrenched, and a different pattern of behavior prevailed. Even wealthy black slaveholders like Lacroix and Camps supported mission work among slaves as well as other philanthropic activities. Such activities ran counter to the mounting conservatism of the American Catholic Church.[94]

In Louisiana, as elsewhere in the South, the Americanization of the Catholic Church reinforced an increasingly harsh slave regimen. When

94. John Tracy Ellis, *American Catholicism* (Chicago, 1956), 87–90; Detiege, *Henriette Delille,* 30–31; Randall M. Miller, "The Failed Mission," in *Catholics in the Old South,* ed. Miller and Wakelyn, 152–57.

Pope Gregory XVI reiterated the church's condemnation of the slave trade in December, 1839, southern extremists accused Catholics of abolitionist sympathies. In South Carolina, one of the South's most influential Catholic leaders, Bishop John England, hastened to reassure church critics; defining slavery as a political issue, England acknowledged the state's primacy concerning the fate of the institution. In matters of state, the church was obligated to support civil authorities.

With few exceptions, southern church leaders defended planter hegemony and endorsed the racial values of their conservative white congregations. Recognizing the planter as the sole arbiter of slave discipline, the church all but abandoned its advocacy of lenient manumission policies and the humane treatment of slaves. In such an environment, most Catholic masters neglected the spiritual life of their slaves.[95]

The Americanization of Louisiana's slave regime prompted some observers to complain of an erosion of political and social values. *L'Album*'s commentators had condemned the dehumanizing effects of the Anglo-American order and deplored the decline of American revolutionary principles and the spread of materialism, poverty, and institutionalized injustice. On a visit to the city in 1848, the British abolitionist and Presbyterian minister Ebenezer Davies agreed with such views when he wrote that "Southerners seem to have no heart—no feeling, except that of love to the almighty dollar." Like French-speaking intellectuals, Davies attributed the city's social evils to the increasing prevalence of Anglo-American influences. The British clergyman regretted the decline of Latin European culture and institutions he regarded as more constructive and humane.[96]

Given the declining status of Louisiana's free black population, feelings of discontent were widespread among persons of African descent. Leading black Creoles associated their deteriorating condition with the ascendancy of the American institution of slavery. Historian Rodolphe L. Desdunes, a product of the antebellum Afro-Creole community, later explained that the profitability of slavery attracted a new breed of immigrants to the city and fostered conditions that promoted "exploitation and profit."

95. Ellis, *American Catholicism,* 87; Miller, "A Church in Cultural Captivity," and "The Failed Mission," in *Catholics in the Old South,* ed. Miller and Wakelyn, 15, 157–70.

96. Timothy F. Reilly, "Heterodox New Orleans and the Protestant South, 1800–1861," *Louisiana Studies,* XII (Spring, 1973), 537.

Under such circumstances, slavery was to "be saved at any price!" Desdunes observed that "every transaction revolved around slavery: business, politics, and even religion."

As the new migrants and their resident allies acceded to positions of power, they labeled slavery a "divine institution." Under their influence, Desdunes observed, the system became increasingly oppressive and race prejudice intensified. The new power elite became "most domineering, overbearing, and cruel" toward free persons of color as well as slaves.[97]

Although resident free black intellectuals did not openly attack the institution of slavery during the prewar years, disaffected Romantic writers repudiated the Anglo-American social order and promoted the interests of their caste. Ignoring class differences and even racial barriers, they joined with other Catholic activists to alleviate some of the consequences of the American slave regime. While the Romantic literary movement served as a means of expression for discontented Afro-Creole intellectuals, the lingering influence of the city's Latin European religious culture enabled French-speaking black activists to create institutional alternatives to an increasingly harsh racial order.

97. Desdunes, *Our People,* 111–12.

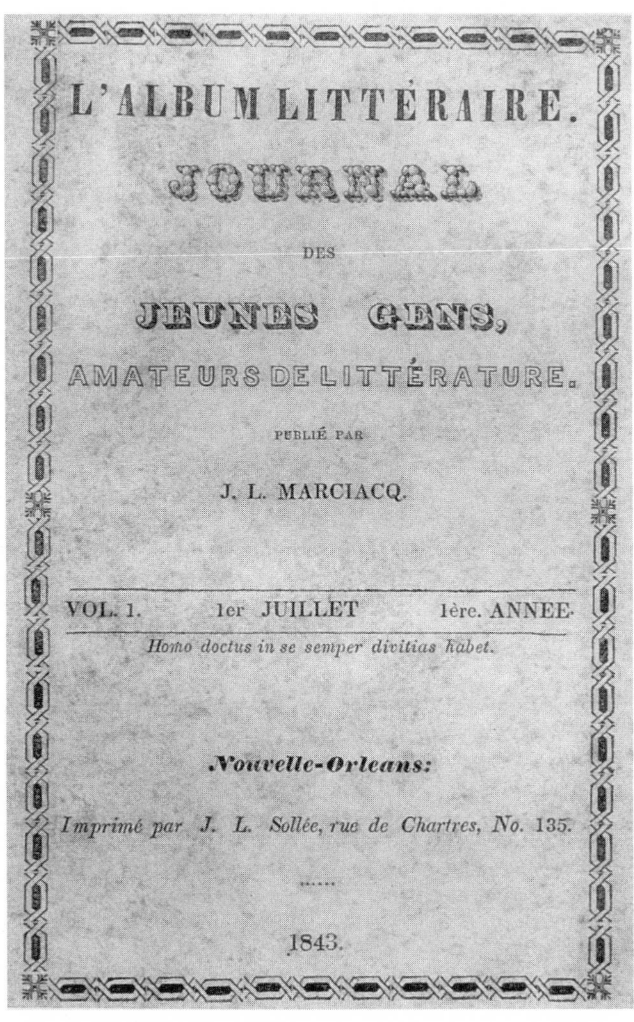

L'ALBUM LITTÉRAIRE.

JOURNAL

DES

JEUNES GENS,

AMATEURS DE LITTÉRATURE.

PUBLIÉ PAR

J. L. MARCIACQ.

VOL. 1. 1er JUILLET 1ère. ANNEE.

Homo doctus in se semper divitias habet.

Nouvelle-Orleans:

Imprimé par J. L. Sollée, rue de Chartres, No. 135.

......

1843.

Cover of *L'Album littéraire: Journal des jeunes gens, amateurs de littérature,* published in New Orleans, July 1843

Courtesy W. S. Hoole Library, Tuscaloosa, University of Alabama Libraries

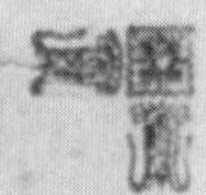

LES

CENELLES.

Choix de Poésies indigènes.

Et de ces fruits qu'un Dieu prodigue dans nos bois
Heureux, si j'en ai su faire un aimable choix!

A. MERCIER.

NOUVELLE ORLEANS.

Imprimé par H. Lauve et Compagnie.

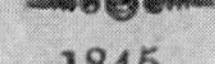

1845.

Cover of *Les Cenelles,* edited by Armand Lanusse, New Orleans, 1845

Courtesy Howard-Tilton Memorial Library, Tulane University

Henriette Delille, founder of the Sisters of the Holy Family

Courtesy Sisters of the Holy Family Motherhouse and Novitiate, New Orleans

44

Ecrit chez moi 1er Decembre 1858.

La vie dans le monde invisible.

Lorsque nous nous sommes détachés de la matière, nous entrons dans le monde invisible, chacun selon la conduite qu'il a mené sur terre. Nous avons différentes Sociétés selon les sympathies qui font tels et tels Esprits se réunir ensemble. La fraternité existe chez nous, sauf chez ceux dominés encore par la matière. Celui qui eut de belles et charitables pensées, qui sut chercher les moyens de soulager ses frères, à peine entré dans le monde invisible, reçoit nos instructions, et sa progression dans les sphères se fait rapide. Voyez cet enfant, à peine au début de sa carrière, il lui faut laisser votre vie; sa mission est incomplète; il lui faut terminer, Eh bien, il s'attache à une âme sympathique qu'il guide durant la vie; à qui il se manifeste; Cette voix qui vous conseille, qui vous suggère de belles pensées, est la sienne; n'entendez-vous pas parfois deux opinions bien différentes l'une à l'autre, vous venant à l'idée; ce sont ses conseils et ceux d'Esprits désireux de vous voir comme eux.

Spirit communication, December 1, 1858

Courtesy Earl K. Long Library, University of New Orleans

Louis Charles Roudanez, publisher of *L'Union* and the New Orleans *Tribune*

Reproduced from Rodolphe Lucien Desdunes, Nos Hommes et Notre Histoire *(Montreal, 1911), courtesy Howard-Tilton Memorial Library, Tulane University*

Henry C. Warmoth, governor of Louisiana, 1868–1872

Courtesy Library of Congress

Rodolphe Lucien Desdunes, literary artist and political activist

Reproduced from Rodolphe Lucien Desdunes, Nos Hommes et Notre Histoire *(Montreal, 1911), courtesy Howard-Tilton Memorial Library, Tulane University*

P. B. S. Pinchback, delegate to the constitutional convention of 1867–1868, lieutenant governor (1871–1872), and governor (December 9, 1872–January 13, 1873) of Louisiana

Courtesy Library of Congress

5

French Freemasonry and the Republican Heritage

Freemasonry is not a religious sect, nor mere ceremonial rites, as I used to suppose; freemasonry is the best, the only expression of the highest, eternal aspects of humanity . . . freemasonry is the teaching of Christianity, freed from its political and religious fetters; the teaching of equality, fraternity, and love.

—Pierre to Prince Andrey, in Tolstoy's *War and Peace*

In *Les Cenelles* the Afro-Creole poet Mirtil-Ferdinand Liotau depicted turmoil within St. Louis Cathedral in the poem entitled "An Impression":

Church of Saint-Louis, old temple, shrine,
You are today empty and deserted!
Those who were entrusted in this world to your care,
Scorning the needs of the sacred tabernacle,
Have led the Christian army elsewhere. . . .

Your splendid altars, your ancient images,
Your crosses, your ornaments, your sacred relics.
Will, alas! remain in profound oblivion
Which is already enveloping them in its immense folds! . . .

O shrine which saw me as a child within these walls
Receive on my forehead the signs of baptism;
Alas! did I grow up to see you today
Deserted, abandoned perhaps forever? . . .

Since we never pray to the Almighty in vain,
Christians, let us unite; when this tutelary God

Had shed all His blood for us on Calvary,
Let us hope that today, all mighty and strong,
Granting our prayers, He will change our destiny;
Let us pray if, through His mercy we wish Him
To destroy among us hatred and discord. . . .

Christians, another effort will tip the scale
Undoubtedly toward peace, we can be sure of that;
And we will see again, as in the past,
The people every day fill up the forsaken temple![1]

Liotau's poem dramatized the outcome of a prolonged struggle between the American church hierarchy and St. Louis Cathedral's church wardens for control of the city's dominant religious institution. The crisis had profound consequences for the free black population. During the clash, Creoles of color and other French-speaking Catholics withdrew from the church. The free black community, as Liotau's poem indicated, had identified with the Latin European religious culture centered in the cathedral. With the further erosion of that culture and the triumph of the conservative American faction, Creoles of color supported the founding of a new church in the Faubourg Tremé on the outskirts of the French Quarter. Some black Catholics, completely disillusioned by events in the church, turned to an alternative form of religious expression.

The church crisis also signified a deep-seated sense of alienation within the white Gallic community. The Americanization of the city, a process accelerated, ironically, by the surge of foreign immigrants into New Orleans after 1830, eroded the status of French-speaking whites. As their ethnic, economic, and political influence declined, they struggled against the emergent status quo. Like their Afro-Creole counterparts, they resented the increasing dominance of Louisiana's planter autocracy. They remained, like Creoles of color, susceptible to radical influences from Europe.

The city's Catholic leaders, like church leaders elsewhere in the South, consolidated their authority over church affairs by identifying their inter-

1. Latortue and Adams, eds., *Les Cenelles,* 89–91.

ests with those of the region's slaveholding elite. In this respect, the struggle over control of St. Louis Cathedral pitted the conservators of the church's liberal religious tradition against the bearers of a distinctly southern brand of religious conservatism. The church dispute and its aftermath served to illustrate the nature of French radicalism.

In France, militant republicans remained committed to the ideals of the First Republic. Despite government repression, they continued to pursue their political agenda under the cover of national and international secret societies. Remembering that during the French Revolution the Catholic Church had opposed the republic, they remained, therefore, unreconciled to the Roman Church and bitterly anticlerical. During the early decades of the nineteenth century, radical republicanism combined with an emergent socialism to produce a broader sociopolitical agenda. To the republican insistence on political equality, socialists added a demand for economic justice, arguing that the private enterprise system vested too much power in the hands of entrepreneurs. Laissez-faire competition led to economic exploitation of workers and maldistribution of wealth.

Saint-Simon, one of the earliest French socialists, argued for socializing the means of production, abolishing the right of inheritance, and expropriating landed property. The industrial state, organized according to socialist principles, Saint-Simon argued, would produce a new social order in which profit was distributed according to productive capacity. Such measures would insure economic and social equity. Though the socialist systems formulated by Charles Fourier, Louis Blanc, and Pierre Proudhon varied in application, their theories shared an underlying faith in the ideal of fraternity. The ills of society would be remedied by an association of men working together in harmony toward socialist goals. In New Orleans, as in France, republican zealots preserved the ideals of the French revolutionary heritage; they constituted an influential faction within the city's extensive network of masonic lodges. In their renewed struggle with the Catholic Church hierarchy during the 1840s, they reaffirmed their French political heritage.[2]

In New Orleans in the church schism of 1805, Catholic freemasons had dominated the board of church trustees (marguilliers), the body of lay

2. Joseph G. Tregle, Jr., "Creoles and Americans," in *Creole New Orleans,* ed. Hirsch and Logsdon, 145–66; Evans, *Social Romanticism,* 9–29.

officials that had seized control of St. Louis Cathedral. The marguilliers handled cathedral finances and insisted on the right to accept or reject church-appointed pastors. Although canon law vested complete authority over pastoral appointments in the bishops, the marguilliers defied the jurisdictional claims of the American church. They remained in power during the early decades of the nineteenth century, and the masonic influence contributed to the strong current of religious ecumenism in St. Louis Cathedral. In the early 1840s, the marguilliers and the Catholic hierarchy resumed their dispute. The struggle served to illustrate masonry's emphasis on religious tolerance and democratic principles.

Unable to dislodge French-speaking church wardens in New Orleans after the Louisiana Purchase and faced with similar schisms in other areas of the nation, ecclesiastical officials in Baltimore reinforced the American church authority by cultivating friendly relations with the federal government. The first Catholic bishop in the United States, John Carroll, elicited praise from Thomas Jefferson after Carroll appointed priests to Louisiana who were sympathetic to American interests.[3]

In 1829, Catholic leaders undertook a major campaign to consolidate their control over church affairs when they met in Baltimore at their first Provincial Council. During the proceedings, church officials severely curtailed the powers of lay trustees and asserted their authority over church affairs. Intent upon warding off persistent charges of un-Americanism, the Catholic hierarchy also reaffirmed the church's need to adapt to the predominant Anglo-American culture.

Theologian Antoine Blanc accelerated the implementation of the Provincial Council's decrees beginning in 1835, when he assumed the office of bishop of the diocese of New Orleans. In 1833, Blanc's predecessor, Bishop Leo de Neckere, founded the first English-speaking parish, St. Patrick's, for the city's large Irish population. Five years later, Blanc laid the cornerstone for a new parish church and established a close relationship with St. Patrick's Irish congregation. Convinced that the future of Catholicism depended upon the support of the church's English-

3. Baudier, *The Catholic Church,* 256–60; Greene, *Masonry in Louisiana,* 76; James J. Pillar, "Catholicism in the Lower South," in *The Americanization of the Gulf Coast, 1803–1850,* ed. Lucius F. Ellsworth (Pensacola, Fla., 1972), 38–39; *New Catholic Encyclopedia* (New York, 1967), III, 152.

speaking members, Blanc considered it "highly important to the interests of religion in New Orleans to uphold especially the influence of the Catholic portion which speaks English. That portion will always sustain the Bishop." [4]

As Blanc directed the laying of St. Patrick's cornerstone in 1838, he also drew up plans to establish another church in the Faubourg Tremé to attract the area's French-speaking residents. At the outset, Blanc agreed to recognize Henriette Delille's religious community in association with the founding of the new church, St. Augustine's. As a consequence, Delille and other members of Tremé's large free black population joined enthusiastically in the fund-raising campaign. Creoles of color rented half the pews in the new church.

The construction of new churches under Blanc's sole authority strengthened the bishop's hand considerably. The departure of Catholics from St. Louis diminished the size of the cathedral congregation and weakened the influence of the marguilliers. In August, 1842, the death of Father Aloysius Leopold Moni, the pastor of St. Louis, signaled the onset of hostilities. Cathedral church wardens had confirmed Moni in 1829 as Père Antoine's successor. With Moni's demise, Blanc prepared to do battle with the French-speaking marguilliers for control of St. Louis.[5]

The showdown began when the marguilliers refused to accept Blanc's appointee to the cathedral post. A heated public debate ensued, and the feud became increasingly acrimonious. After a squabble broke out during religious services in the cathedral, Blanc ordered the clergy to withdraw from the church. Angry supporters of the marguilliers accused the departing clergy of stealing religious ornaments and other church properties. Between November, 1842, and January, 1843, Blanc refused to assign

4. Baudier, *The Catholic Church,* 263, 317, 327–35; Michael Doorley, "The Irish and the Catholic Church in New Orleans, 1835–1918" (M.A. thesis, University of New Orleans, 1987), 11–12, 13. In 1835, the diocese of New Orleans included all of Louisiana (Pillar, "Catholicism in the Lower South," in *The Americanization of the Gulf Coast,* ed. Ellsworth, 36).

5. Baudier, *The Catholic Church,* 336, 365; Detiege, *Henriette Delille,* 32; Dolores Egger Labbé, *Jim Crow Comes to Church: The Establishment of Segregated Catholic Parishes in South Louisiana* (2nd ed.; Lafayette, La., 1971), 14; John Gilmary Shea, *A History of the Catholic Church Within the Limits of the United States* (1886–92; rpr. New York, 1978), III, 676–77.

a priest to the cathedral. The bishop finally relented when the church wardens acceded to some of his demands.

During the religious dispute, many of the city's newspapers sided with the Catholic trustees. In November, 1842, Abbé Napoleon Joseph Perché, one of Blanc's subordinates, started a church newspaper, *Le Propagateur Catholique,* to win public support for the bishop; the following August, hostilities between Blanc and the church wardens resumed when Abbé Perché attacked the marguilliers in its pages. As in the earlier schism, the new skirmish revealed the prominence of French-speaking freemasons in church affairs.[6]

In early August, the French-language newspaper *L'Abeille* (*The Bee*) described a masonic ceremony in a Catholic cemetery. The event commemorated the laying of a cornerstone for a large masonic tomb for lodge members. E. A. Canon, a state legislator, city alderman, and prominent freemason, addressed the gathering. Within days of the ceremony, Abbé Perché condemned the event in the *Propagateur* in an exchange of views under the heading "Scandalous Profanation."

Siding with the abbé, an anonymous contributor to the newspaper noted the masonic function and observed that "according to the principles of freemasonry all men, whatever may be his religious or anti-religious principles, can be admitted into these secret societies," in which case, the writer concluded, "a Protestant, a Jew, a Moslem could be buried in this tomb." But, the irate writer declared, "I have always heard it said that the laws of the church prohibited the burial in Catholic cemeteries of those who were not members of the Catholic Church."

The ceremony, the *Propagateur*'s editor answered, was a "slovenly and scurrilous mockery of Catholicism and deserves to be stigmatized by all men of honour of whatever religious faith." Canon law prohibited Catholics from joining masonic lodges. Furthermore, Abbé Perché informed his readers, "if infidels, if Jews are buried in a Catholic cemetery, it is, according to the laws of the church, a profanation and the cemetery can no longer be considered a holy place." To make matters worse, he continued, the grand master of the state's freemasons, Canon, was none other than the president of St. Louis Cathedral's marguilliers, and other mem-

6. Baudier, *The Catholic Church,* 336–38; Tinker, *Bibliography,* 69.

bers of the church trusteeship were also freemasons. The revelations produced an uproar among English-speaking Catholics.[7]

In September, the death of the recently appointed pastor of St. Louis, Father Ferdinand Bach, brought matters to a head. Once again, Blanc asserted his primacy in church affairs, and once again, the marguilliers disputed his authority. In this highly inflamed atmosphere, Blanc refused to assign a new pastor to St. Louis. In mass meetings and public statements, the marguilliers and their supporters denounced Blanc's actions and disputed papal authority. Their leader, Canon, insisted on the sovereignty of church members, maintaining that the "voice of the people" was the true "voice of God." Church members should choose their own spiritual leader.[8]

The mounting dispute led to lawsuits. After Abbé Perché took legal action against the clergy's detractors, the wardens filed a twenty-thousand-dollar damage suit against the bishop for his refusal to assign a priest to the cathedral. Tensions in the city reached a dangerous level as the highly emotional quarrel spilled over into the newspapers, the courts, and the legislature. According to some accounts, over a thousand members of St. Patrick's Church volunteered to march on the French Quarter and "clean out" the cathedral. Irish Catholics remained loyal supporters of the bishop throughout the crisis. Blanc later confided in a letter to a fellow bishop that the "Irish and Americans have always sustained us and will always be on the side of authority."[9]

In 1844, the Louisiana judiciary resolved the crisis. When a parish judge rejected the suit against the bishop in February, the trustee's attorneys addressed an appeal to the state supreme court. In their petition, representatives for the marguilliers including Canon and Pierre Soulé, a prominent political leader and freemason, based their argument on Spanish precedents. Under colonial rule, the Spanish king had reserved the right to appoint qualified clergymen to church offices. With the transfer of the territory, this "right of patronage" had passed to the people of Louisiana and their designated representatives, and in 1805, the Catholics of New Orleans took possession of the cathedral.

7. *L'Abeille,* August 7, 1843; *Propagateur Catholique,* August 12, 1843; Baudier, *The Catholic Church,* 339.

8. Baudier, *The Catholic Church,* 341, 343.

9. Doorley, "The Irish and the Catholic Church," 13.

Lawyers for the marguilliers contended that the "ultramontane law, or . . . the purely papal law . . . has never been in force either in Spain or in France, nor in the American colonies . . . but has on the contrary always been resisted and repudiated by prelates and dignitaries of the church in those countries where an attempt has been made to introduce it." The pretensions of Bishop Blanc, in his capacity as a representative of the papal authority, constituted a threat to American institutions. The bishop's avowed intention of advancing the interests of religion was a ploy. Instead, the petitioners argued, Blanc sought "to secure to himself a despotic and absolute authority." In this way the bishop could "extend the secular influence of the court of Rome over this republic, in violation of all our laws and usages, and in violation of our religious liberty, and to make the dicta of the court of Rome, even in temporal matters, paramount to the constitution and laws of this State."

In June, the Louisiana Supreme Court ruled in favor of the bishop. In their decision, the justices distinguished between the civil and religious jurisdictions and upheld ecclesiastical authority in church affairs. In October, the clergy returned to the cathedral, but even though defeated, the marguilliers maintained control of some church properties until 1883.[10]

The marguilliers' continued possession of church property notwithstanding, the court's decision dealt a staggering blow to the authority and prestige of the French lodges. Ousted from St. Louis Cathedral and denounced in the Catholic press, they struggled to recover from the defeat. In November, 1845, in an attempt to salvage their public image and win converts to their cause, French-speaking lodge leaders founded a masonic journal, *Le Franc-Maçon* (*The Freemason*).

In the prospectus, the editors called upon lodges and individual members to contribute to the publication. No longer, the editors explained, would "the enemies of human equality" benefit from the order's penchant for secrecy. The founders of the new journal proposed to publicize the true nature of their movement. They expressed confidence that an enlightened public would support masonry's humanitarian principles and lofty goals. The extended series of essays published during the journal's

10. *Petition of the Wardens of the Church of St. Louis of New Orleans* (New Orleans, 1843), 5–6, 13, 14; Baudier, *The Catholic Church,* 342–44.

tenure describing masonry's objectives, philosophy, and history revealed the origins of the city's radical French lodges in Enlightenment France and the French revolutionary experience.[11]

For many Catholics in both Louisiana and nineteenth-century France, freemasonry reconciled deeply held religious beliefs with Enlightenment thought and the gains of the revolutionary era. The advancement of mankind toward a more equitable and civilized earthly existence, a dominant theme of eighteenth-century thought, transformed Christian values. Religious tolerance and new theories of mankind's destiny challenged traditional Christian views of the nature of human relations. In the newly secularized view of society and the past, the individual contributed to humanity's advancement through acts of humanitarian benevolence.

The state, the prime instrument of change, would undertake political and educational reform and promote an enlightened social environment. Since all men shared the same natural rights and powers of reason, all peoples would participate in the progress toward a uniform and humane civilization. Ultimately, mankind would achieve unity. As a consequence of this worldview, concepts of political and religious universalism proliferated, and freemasonry became one of the key purveyors of the new concept of progress.

In eighteenth-century Europe, freemasons discouraged rebellion against civil authority and advocated change through self-improvement and benevolence. They considered their movement a center of union through which men of different religions, political views, and nationalities could combine to promote the welfare of humanity. Upon the basis of freedom, political equality, and comradeship, masonry's adherents were to meet, as the masonic maxim declared, "upon the level."[12]

As a foundation for virtue and morality, early masons formulated a minimal set of religious principles upon which men of different faiths could agree. In 1815, the masonic leader Pierre Chevalier articulated this view: "In masonry, Mecca and Geneva, Rome and Jerusalem are indistinguishable. There are neither Jews, nor Moslems, nor Papists, nor Protestants . . .

11. *Le Franc-Maçon,* November, 1845, p. 1.

12. Margaret C. Jacob, *The Radical Enlightenment: Pantheists, Freemasons and Republicans* (London, 1981), 26.

there are only brothers who have sworn before God, the Father of us all, to remain brothers always."[13]

In Enlightenment France, Andrew Ramsey, one of the founders of eighteenth-century French masonry or Scottish rite freemasonry, conceived of the order as an ancient depository for humanity's collective wisdom. Masonry, Ramsey maintained, possessed essential moral, scientific, and religious truths. By sharing this knowledge with all peoples, the movement would unite mankind. Ramsey perceived in masonry a basis for the establishment of a universal republic made up of a family of nations.[14]

In France, the number of masonic lodges tripled between 1776 and 1789. Though masonry's idealized notion of social equality represented a theoretical repudiation of aristocratic privilege, the movement appealed to the aristocracy as well as to the bourgeoisie. Even members of the Catholic clergy ignored the pope's condemnation of the movement and joined masonic lodges. During the revolution, freemasonry's egalitarian tenets contributed to the emergence of a radical new democratic sociability in Jacobin France.[15]

In New Orleans during the 1790s, French-speaking freemasons secretly organized the earliest known lodges in Louisiana. In 1793, one of the first, Parfaite Union (Perfect Union), looked for recognition to a branch of Anglo-American freemasonry headquartered in Charleston, South Carolina. In 1794, a second lodge, Etoile Polaire (Polar Star), applied to Parisian leaders for official approval. The Terror, however, gripped France, and the accompanying turmoil delayed a response from the French capital. Not until 1796 did leaders in Marseille forward a provisional charter to Etoile Polaire.[16]

Spain's Catholic monarchs had strictly upheld papal bulls condemning freemasonry, and Spanish authorities in New Orleans attempted to quash the movement. In 1799, Charles IV reacted angrily to a report from Bishop Luis Penalver on conditions in the colony. In it, the bishop accused

13. Daniel Ligou *et al.*, *Histoire des francs-maçons en France* (Toulouse, France, 1981), 206.

14. Mildred J. Headings, *French Freemasonry Under the Third Republic,* Johns Hopkins University Studies in Historical and Political Science, LXVI (Baltimore, 1948), 28–30.

15. Jean Touchard, *Histoire des idées politiques* (8th ed.; Paris, 1981), II, 386; Lefebvre, *The French Revolution,* I, 64; Ran Halévi, *Les Loges maçonniques dans la France d'Ancien Régime: Aux origines de la sociabilité démocratique* (Paris, 1984), 9–10.

16. Greene, *Masonry in Louisiana,* 31–39.

freemasons of undermining the moral authority of the church and pointed to the profligacy of military officers engaged in masonic practices. Commanding officials of the garrison lived openly with their mulatto concubines, boldly presenting the offspring of these illicit unions at parish churches to be registered as their natural children. The bishop noted that such scandalous behavior had spread to the civilian population. The king ordered the destruction of the lodges and issued strict instructions to military officers to attend to their religious obligations. The king's orders and the papacy's condemnation notwithstanding, freemasonry remained popular in New Orleans.[17]

After the Louisiana Purchase, the process of Americanization intensified rivalries among the different lodges. Whereas American-based lodges identified with Jeffersonian republicanism, the French lodges remained faithful to the republican ideals of revolutionary France. American freemasons, associating French masonry with the revolution and Bonapartism, regarded their French-speaking counterparts as a subversive and potentially destabilizing element. In fact, radical tendencies persisted within French freemasonry. Throughout the nineteenth century, Etoile Polaire and a number of associated lodges maintained their allegiance to French masonry.[18]

In January, 1846, the leaders of the French lodges published an article in their new journal, *Le Franc-Maçon,* which was written in 1797 by Abbé Grégoire; he had been Bishop John Carroll's French correspondent in 1815. Whereas contributors to *Le Franc-Maçon* wrote contemptuously of the established church and papal authority, they applauded the support of Catholic clerics like the Abbé Grégoire and Antonio de Sedella. In the preface to the journal's second edition, a masonic historian expressed admiration for the deceased Sedella. The anonymous author of "Précis Historique de la Franc-Maçonnerie à la Louisiane" ("Historical Summary of Freemasonry in Louisiana") described Sedella as an enlightened man who had risen above "fanaticism's prejudices." According to masonic tradition, the essayist continued, Sedella was a freemason and had often visited Parfaite Union.[19]

17. *Ibid.*; Bernard Fay, *Revolution and Freemasonry, 1680–1800* (Boston, 1935), 191–92; Robertson, ed., *Louisiana Under the Rule,* I, 353–57; Baudier, *The Catholic Church,* 244–45.

18. Greene, *Masonry in Louisiana,* 82–87.

19. *Le Franc-Maçon,* January, 1846, pp. 18–19, December, 1945, pp. 1–2. Although this statement is undocumented, it is possible that Sedella was a freemason; more likely, however, he sympathized with masonic principles and held views similar to those of Grégoire.

In Grégoire's article, titled "Sur la Franc-Maçonnerie et ses propriétés encore inconnues" ("On Freemasonry and Its As Yet Unrecognized Virtues"), the radical republican cleric sympathized with masonry's tenets. At the time the essay was published in France, Grégoire, the leader of the revolutionary clergy, was struggling to restore the Constitutional Church. In the early stages of the revolution, Grégoire opposed the aristocrats among the bishops in the Estates General, defended religious liberty, and campaigned against slavery and racial prejudice. For Grégoire, all peoples belonged to the family of mankind and shared the same rights. Ultimately, Grégoire believed, humanity would join together in a regenerated, universal Christianity. He viewed republicanism as the most appropriate political form; in an enlightened state, artificial distinctions would disappear, and a society of free and equal men would evolve.

Like Maximilien Robespierre, Grégoire envisioned the creation of a model republic founded on virtue. Both men believed that a political revolution could take place only from the basis of a moral revolution, and they used religious institutions to promote civic virtue. Unlike Robespierre, however, who advocated a state-supported religious cult, the bishop hoped to preserve the organized church. Under the mantle of an all-embracing church, individual nations would ensure the realization of an egalitarian society grounded in a transcendent Christian morality.[20]

In the essay published in New Orleans, Grégoire criticized French revolutionary leaders for repudiating Catholicism without proposing an alternative to the traditional church. Based on the notion of charity, masonry had already overcome the most serious obstacles to the establishment of a religious sect. With its far-flung network of lodges, a capable leadership class, a favorable public image, and a religious tone, masonry offered an institutional framework for establishing a new religion.

Grégoire also recommended masonry as a force for peaceful and gradual political change. Through the agency of freemasonry, he contended, one could have "brought about a less brilliant, and less rapid revolution

20. *Ibid.*, January, 1846, pp. 18-19; Necheles, *The Abbé Grégoire,* xii–xiii, 140. In revolutionary France, the Civil Constitution of the Clergy of July, 1790, established a French national church; this legal or Constitutional Church was opposed by orthodox Catholics who sided with the papacy and created a rival Refractory Church.

than ours has been; but, to be sure, it would have been much happier . . . and then, blood would not have reddened the soil of our beautiful France."[21]

Radical members of the city's French lodges shared Grégoire's view of masonry as a successor to the established church. They agreed with French revolutionary leaders who had condemned traditional Catholicism. In the February, 1846, issue of *Le Franc-Maçon,* in an article signed "Veritas" and titled "Qu'est-ce que Dieu?" ("What Is God?"), one contributor lashed out.

Down through the ages, ambition and pride led evil men to create the "double scourge of a vain aristocracy and a dangerous theocracy." In their craving for power, wealth, and material comfort, such men had obtained their goal of perverting God's essence and his message. The Protestant minister assured his family of the "luxury and the prosperity of the material world" by making "use of the Gospel like the lawyer makes use of the law and the merchant of his balance sheet." In Catholic Rome and in the dioceses under its authority, the "priesthood sells the forgiveness of sins, the blood of God that it worships, and the rights that virtue alone gives us to the inexpressible joys of the future life."[22]

The ancient founders of masonry escaped the tyranny of theocratic despotism. They organized their fraternity to preserve and perpetuate God's truth on earth. Basing their beliefs on the notion of brotherly love and biblical study, the writer continued, the members of the society practiced their faith without ostentation and knew "neither a Christian nor a Jew, neither a Protestant nor a idolater." They extended to all "a benevolent and charitable hand."[23]

In another article, one of *Le Franc-Maçon*'s contributors depicted freemasonry as a conservator of ancient political as well as religious truths. Throughout the ages, the writer explained in an essay titled "De l'institution maçonnique" ("Concerning the Masonic Institution"), masonry served as a depository for the liberal traditions of the early republics. Freemasonry repudiated caste privileges and introduced the concept of equality. Members of the society addressed one another as

21. *Le Franc-Maçon,* January, 1846, pp. 18–19.

22. *Ibid.*, February, 1846, pp. 11–12.

23. *Ibid.*, 13.

brothers, and they enjoyed the right to choose their own leaders in masonic elections.[24]

The concept of equality possessed a sacred significance for freemasons. Since God had created all men in his image, all men were equal. For mankind to accord a superior status to one of their equals would be an affront to God's divine eminence. Masonry's sanctification of the principle of equality prepared the way for human progress.

A study of political revolutions since the late eighteenth century, the writer went on, would show that the great ideas and institutions forming the basis for the American republic and the French nation had originated in masonic lodges. Still, the promise of true equality remained unfulfilled. In an enlightened century, the humble worker acquired the right to say "to princes, to dukes, to gentlemen, and to the highest public officials . . . 'you are no better than I, for the law has made me your equal.' " Economic disparities persisted, however, and the maldistribution of wealth produced intolerable conditions. Life remained an endless cycle of toil and misery for the working classes. Theories designed to regulate labor and relieve the plight of the common worker proliferated. As with the achievement of legal and civil equality, freemasonry would be at the forefront of change.[25]

While *Le Franc-Maçon*'s theorists reformulated republican ideology, the masonic rank and file drew inspiration from religious dissidents like the Abbé Grégoire and Antonio de Sedella. Estranged from the Catholic Church after their ouster from the cathedral in 1844, members of the French-speaking fraternity viewed masonry as a secular religion compatible with their republican ideals. They withdrew into their lodges to practice their religious-political rites. For the remainder of the antebellum period, their struggle against the conservative dispensation of the city's church leaders translated into opposition to the region's planter elite. Events in Europe, while reinvigorating their movement, served to dramatize the differences with their political antagonists.

As the contributors to *Le Franc-Maçon* revealed, members of the city's French lodges were keenly aware of political currents in post-Napoleonic

24. *Le Franc-Maçon,* November, 1845, p. 3.
25. *Ibid.*

France. Their views echoed the sentiments of utopian socialists, republicans, and radical freemasons in Europe who deplored economic injustice and advocated a fairer distribution of wealth. In fact, European radicals reinforced the ranks of the city's Scottish rite lodges. Orazio de Attelis, for instance, a freemason of international standing and the head of masonry's first Supreme Council in New Orleans in 1839, had served as a high-ranking officer in the revolutionary republican forces that swept southern Italy and established the Neapolitan Republic in 1799.[26]

In 1848, events in France inspired a new spirit of republican idealism among the exiled emigrés and their native-born colleagues. In Paris on February 22, republican firebrands and working-class elements took to the city streets to protest government opposition to the staging of a huge "reform banquet"; such banquets, at which political agitators demanded change and drafted antigovernment resolutions, had become popular public events. Enraged Parisians threw up barricades and confronted government forces; the ensuing revolt brought down the government. On February 24, Louis Philippe abdicated.

Revolutionary leaders gathered in the offices of two radical newspapers and organized an interim government that included the Romantic writer Alphonse de Lamartine and the socialist theorist Louis Blanc. The new regime proclaimed the Second Republic and called for elections in April for a National Constituent Assembly on the basis of universal male suffrage. On February 25, the revolutionary leadership recognized the right of all French citizens to work and set about organizing a system of national workshops to resolve the problem of unemployment.

Republican leaders Lamartine, Alexis de Tocqueville, and Victor Schoelcher were ardent abolitionists, and they now exerted their influence. On March 4, within a week after the new regime was established, the provisional government called for the immediate emancipation of the slaves.

26. For references to France's radical masonic lodges, see Ligou *et al.*, *Histoire des Francs-Maçons,* 220–21; significantly, Ligou also notes that all the members of the Second Republic's provisional government, except for Alphonse de Lamartine and Alexandre-Auguste Ledru-Rollin, were freemasons. *Annual Grand Communication of the Supreme Council* (New Orleans, 1859), vi; Robert B. Folger, *The Ancient and Accepted Scottish Rite, in Thirty-Three Degrees* (New York, 1862), 218. In French Scottish rite freemasonry, a supreme council composed of high-ranking masonic officials served as a superior governing body, with ultimate authority over lodges under its jurisdiction.

A subsequent decree on April 27 prohibited French citizens, including those residing in foreign countries, from possessing, buying, or selling slaves upon penalty of forfeiting their French nationality.[27]

In April elections, all males over the age of twenty-one, including the newly freed slaves, voted for deputies to the new unicameral National Constituent Assembly. Accorded direct representation in the parliament, each West Indian island sent three representatives to France. With the exception Victor Schoelcher, one of France's most zealous white abolitionists, all the elective officials were men of African descent. Martinique voters chose Schoelcher, Cyril Bissette, Pierre Pory-Papy, and an alternate, Mazuline. The newly enfranchised citizens of Guadeloupe elected Schoelcher, François Perrinon, Charles Dain, and alternate Louisy Mathieu.[28]

On March 24, 1848, news of the February revolution in Paris reached Louisiana. Astounded by the unexpected and abrupt collapse of Louis Philippe's government, New Orleanians responded in disbelief to initial reports from France. In certain quarters of the city, however, enthusiasm for the new republic mounted rapidly. Supporters of the revolutionary government organized a number of public events to demonstrate their solidarity with the new regime. French freemasons, among the most ardent backers of France's provisional government, played a leading role in the festivities.[29]

On March 26, Pierre Soulé and Robert Preaux, leaders of the city's Gallic community, addressed an enthusiastic *assemblée républicaine* in the rotunda of the St. Louis Exchange. Soulé's evocation of the events of the French Revolution of 1789 induced a spontaneous chorus of "La Marseillaise" and repeated outbursts of "Bravo!" from the audience. Preaux followed Soulé to the podium and elicited an equally emotional response from the excited crowd. After the speeches, an assembly organizer announced that the city's Franco-American population, "having learned that a glorious revolution has, on February 24 and 25, overthrown the back-

27. McCloy, *The Negro in the French West Indies,* 147; Guillaume de Bertier de Sauvigny, *La Révolution parisienne de 1848 vue par les américains* (Paris, 1984), 140.

28. McCloy, *The Negro in France,* 146–47; J. H. Parry and Philip Sherlock, *A Short History of the West Indies* (3rd ed.; New York, 1971), 218; for a discussion of the abolition of slavery in the French Caribbean, see Blackburn, *The Overthrow of Colonial Slavery,* Chap. 12.

29. Sauvigny, *La Révolution parisienne,* 100.

ward and oligarchical power whose selfish and corrupting despotism burdened France for far too long," proposed to hold a public celebration and a "patriotic banquet." Everyone, the speaker continued, "of whatever political party and of whatever nationality, for whom the worship of liberty is the most sacred of all religions, are invited to this fraternal and patriotic celebration." [30]

The assembly's most popular speakers, Soulé and Preaux, shared a long-standing commitment to the republican cause. Soulé, a Democratic Party leader and a Scottish rite mason, had fled political persecution in France. The son of Joseph Soulé, a battalion commander in the French republican army, Pierre was born in 1802 in Castillon, France. His penchant for politics began at an early age; at fifteen he spent over a year in hiding to escape imprisonment for his activities in a secret society. When the controversy subsided, he resumed his education and studied law in Paris, where in 1822 he was admitted to the bar. The ultraconservatism of the Bourbon regime discouraged the highly politicized Soulé from entering a legal career. Instead, he joined with a number of radical journalists to resurrect a satirical, prorepublican paper, *Le Nain Jaune* (*The Yellow Dwarf*), which the government had suppressed. In 1825, *Le Nain* replaced the earlier publication.[31]

Within a month of the paper's appearance, Soulé published an extreme attack upon the church and state. Like stones from a slingshot, Soulé's brother-in-law Alfred Mercier later wrote, the polemic "shattered the windows of the Tuileries and the Archbishopric with such a crash" that the king's ministers ordered his arrest. Convicted, fined ten thousand francs, and sentenced to three years in Sainte-Pélagie Prison, Soulé appealed the decision and obtained a reduced sentence of four months in prison and a fine of three hundred francs. With the help of his republican colleagues and a jailer, Soulé escaped to Great Britain. A brief and disappointing stay in

30. *Courrier,* March 27, 1848.

31. For Soulé's masonic affiliation, see *Le Franc-Maçon,* July, 1846; Amos A. Ettinger, *The Mission to Spain of Pierre Soulé, 1853–1855* (New Haven, 1932), 101–102; Alfred Mercier, *Biographie de Pierre Soulé, Sénateur à Washington* (Paris, 1848), 11–13; Tinker, *Les Ecrits,* 434–37. See also Arthur Freeman, "The Early Career of Pierre Soulé," *Louisiana Historical Quarterly,* XXV (October, 1942), 971–1127, and J. Preston Moore, "Pierre Soulé: Southern Expansionist and Promoter," *Journal of Southern History,* XXI (May, 1955), 203–23.

London convinced the journalist to return to France. "Farewell to the skies of Great Britain," Soulé was reported to have exclaimed on his departure; "I much prefer the ceiling of Sainte-Pélagie." [32]

Upon his arrival in Havre, Soulé's associates persuaded him to leave France. Supplied with letters of recommendation from Abbé Grégoire, he set sail for Haiti. Though the president of the republic, Jean-Pierre Boyer, extended him a warm welcome upon his arrival in Port-au-Prince in September, 1825, Soulé soon set out for the United States, arriving in Louisiana in November.

By the early 1830s, Soulé had married into the Mercier family, one of the city's most prominent Creole families, and joined Louis Moreau-Lislet's prestigious law firm. Moreau-Lislet, a leader of the Gallic community and a prominent member of French freemasonry, recruited Soulé into masonry. By 1832, Soulé had achieved high office within the ranks of the city's French lodges. Nevertheless, despite his success in New Orleans, Soulé still yearned to enter politics in France. He convinced his wife, Armentine Mercier, to move to Europe, and he purchased property in his native Castillon. As the couple prepared to depart for Havre, however, the panic of 1837 swept the city. Ruined in the debacle, Soulé remained in New Orleans and decided upon a political career in Louisiana.[33]

During the 1840s, Soulé joined Louisiana's Democratic Party and succeeded Moreau-Lislet, his law partner, as political spokesman for the state's Gallic inhabitants. After serving as a delegate to the state constitutional convention of 1845, he won a seat in the state senate. When United States senator Alexander Barrow died in office in 1846, the legislature chose Soulé to complete the Louisiana senator's unexpired term of three months. Soulé's involvement in state politics did not diminish his interest in the revolutionary cause in Europe; in 1848, he welcomed news of the republican triumph in Paris.[34]

Robert Preaux, Soulé's fellow speaker at the 1848 republican assembly in New Orleans, was, like Soulé, a prominent member of the city's

32. Ettinger, *The Mission to Spain,* 104; quotations are in Mercier, *Biographie de Pierre Soulé,* 16, 19.

33. Ettinger, *The Mission to Spain*. 104–105; Tinker, *Les Ecrits,* 437–39; *Le Franc-Maçon,* May and July, 1846.

34. Ettinger, *The Mission to Spain,* 108–109; Hunt, *Haiti's Influence,* 61; Tinker, *Les Ecrits,* 439.

French-speaking community and a high-ranking freemason noted for his oratorical skills. Preaux had delivered the graveyard address when schismatic freemasons laid the cornerstone for a masonic tomb in 1843 in the Catholic cemetery. Born in Guadeloupe to a prominent French family, Preaux migrated to Louisiana and began a legal career. By the 1840s, he enjoyed considerable influence within the French-speaking community. Though a longtime Louisiana resident, he also clung proudly to his French republican heritage.[35]

The *Courrier de la Louisiane,* the city's oldest French-language newspaper and the organ of the first municipality, the Vieux Carré, also celebrated "the glorious events in Paris" and applauded the "unsullied and sincerely democratic" leaders of the provisional government. The *Courrier* noted that in "all the cities of the North, the establishment of the French Republic has been greeted with ecstasy and a multitude of resolutions have been addressed to the Provisional Government." The newspaper urged New Orleanians to attend a series of public meetings, to demonstrate Louisiana's solidarity with the northern cities in supporting France.[36]

The *Courrier* rejoiced at the outpouring of sympathy in the North and reported on the debate in Congress over a declaration of support for the Second Republic. On March 30, John P. Hale, a Free Soil senator from New Hampshire, had introduced a resolution congratulating the new French government for its abolition of slavery. Hale's resolution represented a menacing rebuke to the South's slaveholding interests, and South Carolina senator John C. Calhoun succeeded in having the measure tabled. In his opposition to the measure, Calhoun evaded the question of slavery, maintaining instead that congratulations would be premature until republican forces consolidated their victory.[37]

Joined by Senate Whigs, representatives of slaveholding states also opposed a set of resolutions introduced into the Senate by Senator William Allen of Ohio. When Allen introduced a proclamation commending the French people on the establishment of their new republic, Calhoun, John

35. *Le Franc-Maçon,* December, 1845; *L'Abeille,* August 7, 1843; Testut, *Portraits littéraires,* 169.

36. Sauvigny, *La Révolution Parisienne,* 98; *Courrier,* April 7, 8, 1848.

37. *Courrier,* April 7, 1848.

Bell of Tennessee, Thomas H. Benton of Missouri, and Andrew P. Butler of South Carolina blocked its consideration. In view of the French Republic's abolition of slavery, the basis of such opposition was easily understood. Still, the *Courrier* attacked congressional leaders who opposed a declaration of support. "Your readers will here perceive," the paper's Washington correspondent wrote, "that the ultra wings of the democratic senatorial army [Calhoun Democrats] went over to the enemy [Senate Whigs] on this occasion, and prevented the success of a really important measure of democratic principles." The newspaper bemoaned the Senate's "disgraceful backwardness" and reminded its readers to attend the republican celebrations and "speak a few words to our wise men in the Senate, and to Mr. Calhoun, who joined them, in throwing cold water upon the most glorious triumph that Freedom has achieved since the fourth day of July, 1776." [38]

The public ceremonies began in St. Louis Cathedral on April 10, with funeral services for the revolutionaries who perished in the uprising. Afterwards, the crowd gathered on the Place d'Armes, where soldiers fired a cannon in a twenty-one gun salute. Standard-bearers carrying the French and American flags, French consul Aimé Roger, and other dignitaries led French partisans from the cathedral to the Garden of Saint Helena for a banquet. When the procession reached the St. Louis Exchange, a gathering place for the city's Gallic community built by Soulé, the band played the "Marseillaise."

At Saint Helena's, French freemasons presided over the banquet. Freemason Pierre Chevalier, the master of ceremonies, and Consul Roger opened the festivities with introductory remarks. Chevalier, though over eighty years of age, sang a song he had composed for the occasion. Preaux and a fellow lodge member, Louis Caboche, delivered the opening addresses. Caboche, like Preaux, Soulé, and other emigrés, welcomed the triumph of republicans in Paris.

Caboche, born in France in 1791 during the revolution, was raised in Paris. He attended medical school for a time but became disillusioned and turned to teaching; in 1829 he opened a school. An ardent republican and self-described "revolutionist," Caboche participated in a number of republican secret societies. He lost everything as a consequence of the 1830

38. *Courrier,* April 10, 15, 1848.

July Revolution in Paris and three years later moved to Louisiana. In New Orleans, he resumed his teaching career, wrote, and edited several newspapers.[39]

Caboche's political idealism prompted his literary colleague Charles Testut to eulogize his views: "Monsieur Caboche is a progressive in the full meaning of the word and in all good faith. For him, there are not twenty peoples; there is only one people. There are not twenty governments; there is only one government. There are no interests of time, places, castes, countries; there is only the interest of all, the goal to which he marches with confidence, with courage, with perseverance, with hope."[40]

At Saint Helena's, the four hundred banqueters cheered Caboche's tribute to France's Second Republic. The festivities continued until late into the night, when the revelers marched to Consul Roger's residence to sing the "Marseillaise" amidst cries of "Vive la République!" The city's French partisans resumed their celebration the following evening when a crowd engulfed the large rotunda of the St. Louis Exchange.[41]

With the French and American flags draped side by side overhead, Mayor A. D. Crossman and other city officials addressed the exuberant crowd. Preaux, called upon once more to speak, extolled the virtues of fraternity and yielded the floor to his friend Soulé. A spontaneous chant of "Monsieur Soulé! Monsieur Soulé!" arose, and the gifted orator rewarded his audience with an impassioned and stirring address.[42]

Referring to the Parisian workers who had toppled Louis Philippe's government on February 24, Soulé declared that in one day the "rough and bony hands of a few vigorous artisans" had completed the work begun by the French revolutionaries of 1789. "Unveil thy head, beloved France!" he continued, the "entire world beholds thee with admiration, and on thy radiant brow anxiously seeks to discover the signet of your deliverance and emancipation."

Monarchical Europe, Soulé warned, would not tolerate a republican France. He urged the French people to unite with their republican allies in Ireland, Italy, Poland, and elsewhere in Europe to wage a war of liberation.

39. *Ibid.*, April 10, 11, 1848; Tinker, *Les Ecrits,* 64; *Annual Grand Communication,* xxiii.

40. Testut, *Portraits littéraires,* 94.

41. *Courrier,* April 11, 1848.

42. *Ibid.*, April 12, 1848.

France, he declared, must lead the way toward a new political order: "Let thy shield, O France! cover and protect the oppressed throughout Europe. Be the exemplar and teacher of nations that sigh after their emancipation." The audience greeted the speech with outcries of "Bravo!" and thunderous applause. As Soulé descended from the podium, a crowd of well-wishers rushed to congratulate him.[43]

In a gesture intended to memorialize events in France, a common workingman, Louis-Sébastien de Vevey, followed Soulé in speaking. Parisian workers had played a leading role in the February Revolution, and a worker representative, buttonmaker Alexandre Martin, was named to the provisional government. "Oh how happy I am," Vevey began, "to be able to speak in the midst of a gathering so large and so capable of appreciating the significance of the questions that I touch on and the prejudices that I fight." Although the audience howled in approval, one spectator noted, Vevey delivered his remarks with dignity and restraint.[44]

The presiding officer proposed that the assembly forward a set of resolutions to the people of France, then named a committee to draw up the measures. Near the end of the meeting, Thomas J. Durant, the committee's reporter, read the proclamation to the assembly. In Europe, the opening declaration began, "a ray of liberty has come to shed its regenerative warmth over nations long weighed down under the detested yoke of slavery." The citizens of New Orleans, the document continued, congratulated the people of France in their victory over tyranny. Resistance to oppression was "the most sacred of obligations." The heroism and dignity of the French people would ensure the rejuvenation of their country and the triumph of republicanism.

The resolutions praised the provisional government for its declaration of universal male suffrage. "Man possesses the natural and inalienable right of self government" and the French, having asserted these rights, would serve as a model for other European peoples struggling against political oppression. The proclamation also applauded the new republic's labor policy. One of the primary duties of government, Durant continued, was to "protect the rights of the worker and assure him of the greatest possible prosperity." The actions of the provisional government in attempting

43. *Ibid.*, April 12, 15, 1848.

44. Sauvigny, *La Révolution parisienne,* 120.

"to resolve the great social problems related to the organization of labor and capital" demonstrated its "concern for the needs of the French people and the interests of humanity."

Finally, New Orleanians proclaimed the principles of *liberté, égalité, fraternité*. The assembly approved the resolutions by public acclamation. As the meeting drew to a close, the audience sounded three cheers for France, three cheers for freedom, and three cheers for the United States. Their hurrahs and applause, one spectator noted, seemed to echo through the city.[45]

On April 15, the outpouring of sympathy for the new French Republic culminated in a huge banquet. An immense transparency portraying the Goddess of Liberty ornamented a wall of the Orléans meeting hall, where seven hundred representatives of the city's French, German, Italian, and American ethnic groups gathered in a show of fraternal solidarity. The participants delivered speeches and toasts while girls, costumed to portray Liberty and Charity, collected donations for victims of the February revolt. Once again, the plight of the working class emerged as a major theme. This time, T. Wharton Collens delivered the tribute and toasted the French socialist, Charles Fourier: "To the great genius who as early as 1808 proclaimed the idea of industrial association which the triumph of republican France today assures;—to the one whose sublime reason and philanthropic soul has known how to resolve the problem of harmonizing the interests of the capitalist with the rights of the laborer, to the author of the treatise on usury and universal unity, to the founder of the eternal bases of well-being for the worker, to the apostle of social harmony, to the immortal Charles Fourier!"[46]

In New York, Washington, Boston, and Philadelphia, republican enthusiasts like those in New Orleans celebrated the news from France in banquets and other public assemblies. The *Courrier*'s New York correspondent described the gatherings and spoke glowingly of Albert Brisbane's participation in the festivities. Noting that the French-speaking Brisbane had "paid homage in the most felicitous of terms to the devotion

45. *Courrier,* April 12, 1848.

46. Sauvigny, *La Révolution parisienne,* 122–23; *Courrier,* April 17, 1848. Collens is referring to Fourier's *Théorie de l'unité universelle* published in four volumes between 1841 and 1843; it was originally published in two volumes in 1822, under the title *Traité de l'association domestique-agricole*.

of France to the cause of humanity," the reports described him as a "Franco-American at heart." Brisbane, a leader of the Fourierist movement in the United States, championed the cause of France's working class. His colleague, Charles A. Dana, offered an insight into the popular uprising. Whereas the 1789 revolution overturned the feudal order, the 1848 revolution aimed to "destroy the moneyed feudalism and lay the foundations of social liberty." The sympathetic response of Brisbane and his associates to the French Revolution of 1848 undoubtedly delighted their followers in New Orleans.[47]

An American, Brisbane had studied in Europe under Victor Cousin and G.W.F. Hegel. Concerned over the plight of the American working class, he had readily absorbed the doctrines of the early-nineteenth-century French socialist Charles Fourier. For Fourier, the dehumanizing effects of contemporary capitalism reduced wage earners as well as slaves to a condition of barbaric servitude. Circumstances warranted a complete reconstruction of society. The French socialist proposed the creation of model communities called phalanxes, in which a communal lifestyle and joint-stock ownership would ensure personal freedom and an equitable distribution of wealth. The success of the utopian communities would guarantee their spread. An age of harmonious "Association" would gradually replace a shameful era of competitive greed and human degradation.[48]

Like Fourier in France, Brisbane believed that American society tottered on the brink of destruction as economic exploitation widened the gap between rich and poor. Only a root and branch solution, he reasoned, would remedy the nation's ills. Fourier's holistic and cooperationist approach appealed to Brisbane and other American reformers who desired thoroughgoing changes but deplored extremism and the use of force.[49]

47. Sauvigny, *La Révolution parisienne,* 108; *Courrier,* March 31, April 13, 1848; Dana's remark is cited in Merle Curti, "The Impact of the Revolutions of 1848 on American Thought," *Proceedings of the American Philosophical Society,* XCIII (June, 1949), 210.

48. Mark Holloway, *Heavens on Earth: Utopian Communities, 1680–1880* (2nd ed.; New York, 1966), 140. For a discussion of Fourier's ideas, see Jonathan Beecher, *Charles Fourier: The Visionary and His World* (Berkeley, 1986); for specific references to Fourier's condemnation of slavery, see pp. 52–53, 324.

49. Michael Fellman, *The Unbounded Frame: Freedom and Community in Nineteenth-Century American Utopianism* (Westport, Conn., 1973), 4–7; Holloway, *Heavens on Earth,* 141–42.

In New York, Brisbane, Horace Greeley, and other northern reformers popularized Fourier's ideas and organized the American Union of Associationists. During the early 1840s, they encouraged the establishment of over thirty Fourierist communities. They also solicited the views and assistance of Louisiana Fourierists in formulating a solution to the problem of slavery. In New Orleans, T. Wharton Collens, Thomas J. Durant, and other members of an important circle of Louisiana Fourierists forwarded money and advice to the national leadership in New York.[50]

Collens was a native New Orleanian of English and Creole descent. Born in 1812, he had imbibed the religious Gallicanism and free-thought militancy of the city's French-speaking community. During the 1830s, he practiced law in New Orleans and immersed himself in the doctrines of Robert Owen, Charles Fourier, and other socialist writers. In 1841, he condemned "Religion and her companions Superstition, Bigotry, Intolerance and Persecution" and organized a discussion group, the Atheneum, for those "who desire the welfare of the human race." By 1848, Collens was a founding member of a Louisiana chapter of Fourierists and one of the most prominent members of the French masonic lodges.[51]

Collens' fellow Associationist Thomas J. Durant was a native of Pennsylvania. He had arrived in New Orleans in 1831 at the age of fourteen as a consequence of an economic disaster that dispersed his family. During the 1830s, the enterprising Durant published a partisan Democratic journal, the New Orleans *Southerner and People's Friend,* and aspired to political office. In 1846, President James K. Polk named him federal attorney for the Eastern District of Louisiana.[52]

Like Brisbane and other Fourierists, Durant perceived a profound crisis in American society. He denounced the "morality of competitive commerce" and envisioned a society that would "apply the laws of love and charity to the social relations of men." During the 1840s, he organized the

50. Carl J. Guarneri, "Two Utopian Socialist Plans for Emancipation in Antebellum Louisiana," *Louisiana History,* XXIV (Winter, 1983), 7–10.

51. Robert C. Reinders, "T. Wharton Collens: Catholic and Christian Socialist," *Catholic Historical Review,* LII (July, 1966), 215; *Le Delta Maçonnique,* February–March, 1861.

52. Joseph G. Tregle, Jr., "Thomas J. Durant, Utopian Socialism, and the Failure of Presidential Reconstruction in Louisiana," *Journal of Southern History,* XLV (November, 1979), 485–87.

Louisiana chapter of Fourierists, became politically active, and voiced his views. In the presidential campaign of 1840, he attacked the Whigs at a workers' rally as that "portion of the people who derive their substance from financial scheming and traffic[k]ing in the fruits of our fields and the labor of our hands." The earth, he told his audience, "is the beneficent gift of heaven to man." When coal merchants charged excessive prices during the harsh winter of 1845, he expressed outrage. Can anything, he asked, "cause more to lament 'man's inhumanity to man' than the woeful spectacle of the few making fortunes from the freezing limbs of the suffering many?" In the epidemic of 1849, he railed against a city newspaper that, "in the cold bloodless selfishness so characteristic of civilization, did not hesitate to make the brutal remark that *no respectable person* died of cholera." [53]

Durant, like Brisbane and other utopian socialists, viewed slavery as an absolute evil plaguing humanity; however, he advised Brisbane that a frontal assault would stiffen slaveholder resistance and that such a strategy was destined to lead to disaster. Gradually, through education and the example of model communities, slavery's debilitating effects would become apparent, and ultimately, white southerners would recognize Fourierism's superior advantages.

In 1847, Durant shared his views with Brisbane: "You ask me 'Should we or should we not attack slavery openly and strongly, as one of the great evils of civilization . . . or had we rather, try and conciliate the South?' Try to conciliate nothing that you believe to be wrong. Have some confidence in the reformers of the South; believe that the Southern people are men and brethren, not altogether unmindful of the evils of their social institution." [54]

What good, Durant asked, "would accrue to the cause of Association or of humanity, by the overthrow of the Constitution, and the probable consequence, Civil War?" Rather, Durant argued, "Convince them [slaveholders] that there is another and better mode, and you may be sure that they will adopt it." Upon the advice of Durant and other Louisiana Fouri-

53. Jean-Charles Houzeau, *My Passage at the New Orleans "Tribune": A Memoir of the Civil War Era,* ed. David C. Rankin and trans. Gerard F. Denault (Baton Rouge, 1984), 38; Tregle, "Thomas J. Durant," 486, 490.

54. Tregle, "Thomas J. Durant," 491.

erists, Brisbane approved a plan in 1847 for the gradual abolition of slavery. The four-point program included slaveholder compensation, slave education, and a post-emancipation support system.[55]

Fourierism's popularity among a number of planters in south Louisiana's sugar-growing region encouraged Associationists to anticipate the gradual extinction of slavery and the triumph of utopian principles. Sugar planters John D. Wilkins and Thomas P. May contributed thousands of dollars to the Fourierist movement in New York; the enthusiastic Wilkins even proposed to mortgage his plantation in the interest of the utopian cause. Another planter sent his son to Massachusetts to be educated in the utopian community of Brook Farm. In 1844, the editor of the Franklin *Planter's Banner,* Robert Wilson, endorsed Fourierism in his weekly paper and corresponded with Associationist leaders in New York.[56]

In the mid-1850s, Durant and his colleagues held out hope for the success of a model community at Reunion, Texas. Victor Considérant, the colony's renowned founder, had launched the Fourierist movement in France during the early 1830s. In 1854, the French socialist led his followers to Texas to establish a utopian community, but despite the energetic assistance of Durant and other reformers, the short-lived Reunion experiment ended in failure.[57]

During the 1850s, the Fourierists and French freemasons who had played a leading role in the republican celebrations of 1848 gravitated to the wing of the Democratic Party led by Senator Stephen A. Douglas of Illinois. Like them, Douglas had applauded the popular uprising in France and, within a month of it, had urged his Senate colleagues to signal a prompt show of support for the French republican cause. Douglas' enthusiasm for the Second Republic and his sympathy for the liberal European revolutions of 1848 enhanced his reputation with the Soulé wing of Louisiana's Democratic Party. When Douglas visited New Orleans in June, 1848, to campaign in behalf of Democratic presidential nominee Lewis Cass, he enjoyed a warm reception. Soulé escorted Douglas to the podium in the St. Louis Hotel ballroom, where an enthusiastic audience

55. *Ibid.*, 492; Guarneri, "Two Utopian Socialist Plans," 12–13.

56. Guarneri, "Two Utopian Socialist Plans," 9–10.

57. Tregle, "Thomas J. Durant," 492–93; Holloway, *Heavens on Earth,* 139; William A. Hinds, *American Communities and Co-operative Colonies* (3rd ed.; Philadelphia, 1975), 249.

cheered his speech. The visit marked the beginning of an important political alliance.[58]

Some southern conservatives noted events in Louisiana with alarm. In January, 1849, after a fact-finding mission through the South, H. W. Conner expressed his concern. While assessing the strength of the southern-rights movement, he described his impressions to his fellow South Carolinian, Senator John C. Calhoun. Although assured by Louisiana politicians and planters that their state was dedicated to the southern cause, Conner concluded otherwise: "I fear for Louisiana. New Orleans is almost Free Soil in their opinions. The population is one half Northern Agents, another 1/4 or 1/3 are Foreigners. The remnant are Creoles who cannot be made to comprehend their danger until the negroes are being taken out of the fields. . . . Louisiana will be the last if at all to strike for the defense of the South."[59]

Subsequent events did not bolster conservative confidence. In June, 1850, Louisiana failed to send a delegation to the southern-rights convention in Nashville, Tennessee, and Pierre Soulé, elected to the Senate in 1848, continued to promote the revolutionary cause in Europe. His efforts coincided with a movement in Congress to adopt a more forceful stand in the interest of Europe's democratic insurgencies. And of all the popular uprisings launched in 1848, none captured the American public's sympathy as completely as the struggle of Hungarian nationalists.[60]

In March, 1848, Hungarian insurgents led by Louis Kossuth rebelled against Austrian domination. After the nationalists declared their independence from the Austrian Empire, Emperor Francis Joseph invited Tsar Nicholas I of Russia to intervene. In August, 1849, Russian troops crushed the Hungarian army and Kossuth fled to the Ottoman Empire, where he was jailed. In the Senate in 1850, Soulé appealed to American officials to intervene in Kossuth's behalf; when Turkish authorities released him the following year, a congressional resolution authorized the

58. Robert W. Johannsen, *Stephen A. Douglas* (New York, 1973), 329; Freeman, "Early Career of Pierre Soulé," 1106–1107.

59. J. Franklin Jameson, ed., "Correspondence of John C. Calhoun," *Annual Report of the American Historical Association* (Washington, 1900), II, 1189.

60. M. J. White, "Louisiana and the Secessionist Movement of the Early Fifties," *Proceedings of the Mississippi Valley Historical Association,* VIII (1914–15), 282–83.

government to transport him to the United States. Kossuth arrived in New York in December. Only the wild excitement that accompanied Lafayette's visit twenty-five years earlier matched the public outpouring for Kossuth. Amidst torchlight parades and huge demonstrations, his admirers compared him to George Washington and likened Hungary's independence movement to the American Revolution.[61]

On January 20, Senator Cass introduced a resolution into the Senate favoring Hungarian independence and criticizing Russian intervention. Supporters of the measure argued for a more aggressive foreign policy in the interest of European republicanism. By tapping public enthusiasm for democratic revolution in Europe, American nationalists hoped to submerge regional differences and revive a spirit of cross-sectional unity. During debates on the resolution, Soulé voiced a passionate plea for its passage. It was in the nation's interest, he exclaimed, "to keep alive . . . that reverence for the institutions of our country, that devout faith in their efficacy, which looks to their promulgation throughout the world." Soulé, alone among southern Democrats, supported the Cass resolution, and of all the cities of the South, only New Orleans welcomed the Hungarian leader with an official greeting.[62]

Throughout the South, most slaveholding southerners remained unsympathetic to Kossuth and the revolutionary cause. Noting the rising tide of antislavery sentiment in Europe, they feared that intervention in European affairs might invite outside interference with the institution of slavery. In revolutionary France, such attitudes had resulted in emancipation in the French Caribbean. Indeed, the French decrees abolishing slavery had already given new impetus to the antislavery movement in the North.[63]

The excitement over Kossuth's arrival and the attendant congressional debates prompted a number of dissatisfied Democrats to launch a new political movement. Young America, as the maverick Democrats described themselves, identified with the nationalistic and democratic aspirations of

61. Johannsen, *Stephen A. Douglas,* 329–30; Merle Curti, "Impact of the Revolutions of 1848," 212.

62. Merle E. Curti, "Young America," *American Historical Review,* XXXII (October, 1926), 36–37, 39; Curti, "Impact of the Revolutions of 1848," 211; quotation from Ettinger, *The Mission to Spain,* 314–15.

63. Curti, "Impact of the Revolutions of 1848," 213.

the Young Germany, Young Italy, and Young Ireland movements in Europe. Frustrated by the stultifying effects of sectional conflict, Young America leaders sought national unity on the basis of territorial expansion, economic growth, and the promotion of republican ideals abroad. They criticized their party's "old fogy" politicians and demanded bold new leadership. In 1852, they chose Stephen A. Douglas as their candidate for the Democratic Party's presidential nomination.[64]

Pierre Soulé, a Young America zealot, readily endorsed Douglas' candidacy and espoused his cause in Louisiana. Like Douglas, Soulé advocated an aggressive foreign policy that emphasized territorial expansion and support for republican movements abroad. In August, 1852, he shared his enthusiasm for the candidate with fellow Louisianian Charles Gayarré: "In siding with Douglas, I was prompted to give my help in a struggle whose object was the overthrow of the old party-dynasties that had assumed power, and lost all elasticity of mind, all energy of will, all courage in action, so necessary to those who wish to govern a great people." [65]

On the question of slavery, Soulé's position coincided with Douglas' stance. Apparently sharing Douglas' belief that American expansionism would render the institution of slavery obsolete, Soulé attempted to steer a middle course in the mounting sectional dispute. In his public statements, he acceded to southern opinion by advocating local autonomy and state sovereignty and by turning a blind eye to the moral issue of slavery. In the Compromise of 1850, he sanctioned the doctrine of popular sovereignty and defended slaveholding on the basis of states' rights.

Attacked by his local political rivals for his role in the compromise struggle, Soulé defended his actions in a speech in 1851 in Opelousas, Louisiana. Echoing Douglas' harsh view of radicals in both sections, Soulé argued that an unjust compromise had been "forced upon us by the anti-slavery power of the North and North-West, aided and abetted by those of the South who had been the loudest in their condemnation of it [the compromise], when it first made its appearance." Though he recognized the

64. Curti, "Young America," 34–42; Johannsen, *Stephen A. Douglas,* 344–46.

65. For a discussion of Douglas' views on American expansionism and European republicanism, see Johannsen, *Stephen A. Douglas,* 321–57; for further insight into his manifest destiny views, see Harry V. Jaffa, *Crisis of the House Divided* (Seattle, 1959), Chap. 4. Soulé quoted in Ettinger, *The Mission to Spain,* 130.

rights of the states, as the original parties to the constitutional compact, to "make and unmake the Government," he opposed secession: "I am not for breaking this Confederacy; I am not for advising this State to join in any secession movement which may be made by other States." Louisianians could prevent further depredations upon their rights by maintaining a forbearing yet dignified and resolute attitude—an attitude that would command the North's respect.[66]

While Soulé's Opelousas speech may have calmed the fears of some conservative Louisianians, at least one observer noted an air of ambivalence in his proslavery stance. In January, 1852, A. N. Poole of Baton Rouge forwarded a copy of the speech to Charles Sumner. Poole considered the address "a specimen of what an ultra Pro-Slavery man can say of the domestic institutions." He noted the irony in Soulé's position: "Is it not strange that a man like Mr. S[oulé], escaped from France to enjoy the pure air of liberty in this Republic, can be so blind to the freedom of the black Republican." Still, Poole reminded Sumner, Soulé "is a public Southern man—and speaks a good deal for Buncam [bunkum]. I doubt if he really speaks the sentiments of his heart." [67]

In December, Harriet Beecher Stowe regretted that Soulé did not champion the abolitionist cause in the South: "*Can* it be that no man of honor—no man thirsting for immortal fame will yet rise *from the South*—and win himself eternal glory by being the leader of a movement for *universal* freedom—Can such a man as Soulé—I know not if I have rightly

66. For Douglas' views on popular sovereignty and slavery and for references to Soulé's role in the Compromise of 1850, see Johannsen, *Stephen A. Douglas,* 278–81, 289–92, 347; [Edward C. Wharton], *Thoughts on the Slavery Question and the Clay Compromise* (Washington, D.C., 1850), 2–8. Quotations from *Mr. Soulé's Speech at Opelousas, Louisiana Delivered on September 6, 1851* (New Orleans, 1851), 8, 14–15, 18. Ettinger maintains that at the time of the Compromise of 1850, Soulé was a states' rights secessionist and the political heir of John C. Calhoun, but he goes on to present evidence that throws doubt on his assertions (Ettinger, *The Mission to Spain,* 115–17).

67. Ettinger, *The Mission to Spain,* 121. Tinker's conclusions strengthen the view that Soulé was ideologically opposed to slavery: "In theory, Soulé was opposed to slavery; in practice, he felt compelled to defend the interests of the South and to struggle for the rights of the States"; he also cites statements in which Soulé condemned the slave trade as a "cursed traffic," referred to slaves as "victims," and described the presence of slavery in the South as a "plague" (Tinker, *Les Ecrits,* 442).

conceived of him, but I think of him as an impersonation of nobility and chivalry, can he be the tool of tyranny and the leader of despotism—when Freedom is holding up an unfading crown to be worn by some *deliverer*?"[68]

When Douglas failed to win his party's presidential nomination in 1852, he and his followers threw their support to Franklin Pierce, who triumphed in the fall election. In his inaugural address, Pierce alluded to the acquisition of Cuba and proclaimed that his presidency would not "be controlled by any timid forebodings of evil from expansion." Owing to his gratitude for their support and his sympathy with their expansionist policies, Pierce rewarded his Young America allies with a number of important diplomatic posts. Soulé, Douglas' lieutenant in Louisiana, received the ambassadorship to Spain.[69]

In July, 1853, Soulé left Washington for his post in Madrid. As he prepared to set sail for Europe, exiled Cuban revolutionaries staged a demonstration outside his New York hotel. In the torchlight procession, the inscriptions on their banners called attention to their cause: "Cuba must and shall be free" and "Young America and Young Cuba." Soulé received the leader of the rally and greeted the crowd. In an impromptu speech from the hotel balcony, the new ambassador sounded a provocative note. The American minister, as a representative of the United States, "has a right to carry wherever he goes the throbbings of that people that speak out such tremendous truths to the tyrants of the old continent." As the speech created a sensation at home and abroad, Soulé sailed for Europe.[70]

During a two-day stopover in London, Soulé met with Kossuth and Giuseppe Mazzini, the republican leader of the Young Italy movement. When he passed through Paris, he opened his apartment to the republican survivors of Louis Philippe's coup d'état and corresponded with Alexandre Dumas and Joseph Méry, a former collaborator on *Le Nain Jaune*. Finally in mid-October, he arrived in Madrid. Even though Soulé's expansionist policies and subversive activities had raised a storm of controversy in Spain and his appointment had created an immediate diplomatic impasse, the Spanish government accorded the American ambassador a courteous

68. Ettinger, *The Mission to Spain,* 121–22.

69. Johannsen, *Stephen A. Douglas,* 368, 374, 378.

70. Ettinger, *The Mission to Spain,* 175–76.

public reception. Behind the scenes, however, Spanish authorities carefully monitored his activities. The French and British, no less alarmed by Soulé's statements and movements, also placed him under police surveillance.[71]

In October, shortly after his arrival in Spain, the new ambassador visited French republican exiles on the island of Jersey in the English Channel. Such open displays of sympathy for Napoleon III's republican enemies angered the French delegation; consequent tensions produced a violent crisis. In November, when Louis Napoleon's son-in-law, the Duke of Alba, insulted Soulé's wife, Soulé and his son Nelvil fought duels with the duke and France's ambassador to Spain, the Marquis de Turgot. Soulé shot Turgot in the leg. He insisted that the entire affair stemmed from the French government's desire to discredit him in his new post, and even though the incident created an international uproar, Soulé remained unfazed.[72]

In Madrid, he opened the doors of the American legation to Spanish insurgents and maintained contact with other European revolutionaries. During the spring of 1854, some observers accused him of complicity in two major uprisings in Spain, and when Spanish revolutionaries seized power in July, he applauded their victory. Though he favored more radical elements, he extended best wishes from Young America to the new liberal leaders, congratulating them on their "triumph over the shameful despotism under which a policy as fastidious as abject crushed the freedom of thought and stifled its most legitimate aspirations." The statement, issued by an ambassador accredited to the royal court, produced a new storm of public indignation. Undeterred, Soulé went even further.[73]

During an attempted insurrection in Madrid on August 28, he hid the leader of the republican uprising in his home. When the revolt failed, both Soulé and his fugitive houseguest, the republican leader José Maria Orense, marquis of Albaida, beat a hasty retreat. Outraged Spanish authorities ignored diplomatic protocol and arrested the American embassy's chaplain, the Abbé Ramonet, who was a republican refugee. Soulé

71. *Ibid.*, 178–79, 190, 196, 315; Tinker, *Les Ecrits,* 444.

72. Ettinger, *The Mission to Spain,* 212, 227–35; Tinker, *Les Ecrits,* 444–45.

73. Robert C. Binkley, *Realism and Nationalism, 1852–1871* (1935; rpr. New York, 1963), 138; Ettinger, *The Mission to Spain,* 302.

had installed the French priest at the embassy, where Ramonet also acted as his personal assistant. Officials suspected the priest was implicated in the plot; intent upon preventing Soulé's return to Madrid, the government proposed to build an airtight case against the ambassador.[74]

In France, meanwhile, Soulé prepared to attend an October conference in Ostend, Belgium, with the U.S. ministers to England and France, James Buchanan and John Y. Mason respectively. The Pierce administration, wanting to discourage a filibustering expedition against Cuba, proposed to adopt a more forceful policy regarding the island's acquisition. The three ambassadors were instructed to draw up a plan for pressuring Spain to relinquish Cuba.[75]

In the Senate, Soulé had been a proponent of Cuban independence. In Spain, he had entered into negotiations with the republican faction for a Cuban settlement. His ally Orense, the leader of the Spanish republicans, had proposed that in return for United States aid to the revolutionary cause, a republican regime in Spain would allow Cubans to determine their own political fate. The Ostend Manifesto repudiated this agreement and recommended the immediate purchase of Cuba. Moreover, if Spain refused to sell the island and if events in Cuba posed a threat to national security, the United States would "be justified in wresting it [Cuba] from Spain."[76]

The document arrived in Washington on election day in November, 1854, as the Pierce administration was experiencing the disastrous political repercussions of the Kansas-Nebraska Act. The Ostend proclamation was interpreted in the North as another ploy to extend the institution of slavery and provoked a new storm of protest. The manifesto fared even worse in Europe.[77]

In France and Spain, Soulé had already worn out his welcome. When he attempted to return to Madrid after the conference, he was stopped at the French border. Citing his subversive activities and the duel with Turgot, the French government refused to allow him to pass through France.

74. For Soulé's subversive activities in Spain, see Ettinger, *The Mission to Spain,* Chap. 9.

75. Johannsen, *Stephen A. Douglas,* 529–30.

76. Basil Rauch, *American Interest in Cuba, 1848–1855* (New York, 1948), 251–52, 291; Ettinger, *The Mission to Spain,* 326, 363–64.

77. Johannsen, *Stephen A. Douglas,* 530.

The Spanish government insisted on his recall. When the details of the Ostend Manifesto became known, the proclamation was universally condemned as an insult to Spain's national honor. Finally in December, the administration repudiated the manifesto and forced Soulé's resignation. In January, 1855, he formally relinquished his post and left Europe.

After his return to New Orleans in the spring, Soulé resumed his law practice, reentered politics, and renewed his masonic ties. For the remainder of the decade, he and his fellow freemasons remained committed to the ideals of the Second Republic, and their lodges continued to attract exiled French republicans. Eventually, their espousal of radical republicanism brought them into conflict with other masonic jurisdictions in the South.[78]

By 1853, French emigré Louis Dufau, one of their recruits, had attained high office within the city's French lodges. A history teacher in Paris, Dufau had also been an influential member of the Society for the Abolition of Slavery, an organization that included such outstanding French abolitionists as Lamartine, Alexis de Tocqueville, and Victor Schoelcher. He arrived in New Orleans at the time of the 1848 revolution and resumed his teaching career while launching into a number of journalistic ventures.

In 1852, he accepted the directorship of the Collège de la Louisiane on Dauphine Street in New Orleans. A bitter opponent of the Catholic Church, Dufau undoubtedly welcomed the opportunity to teach at a secular institution with a reputation for religious skepticism. In 1853, he hired a newly arrived refugee, Jean-Sylvain Gentil, to teach history and Romance languages at the college.[79]

Gentil, a native of Blois in France and an ardent republican, studied law in Paris during the 1840s and embarked upon a journalistic career.

78. Ettinger, *The Mission to Spain,* 414–15, 449–72; Rauch, *American Interest in Cuba,* 295.

79. *Masonic Delta,* February–March, 1861; Tinker, *Les Ecrits,* 148, 246; Viatte, *Histoire littéraire,* 374. For references to Dufau's abolitionist activities, see *Société française pour l'abolition de l'esclavage: Extrait du procès-verbal de la séance du 1er juillet 1840* (Paris, 1841). The terrible yellow fever epidemic of 1853 convinced Dufau to move the Collège de la Louisiane away from the city, and he transferred the institution to the empty buildings of the failed Jefferson College in rural St. James Parish. In 1857, however, financial difficulties forced him to close the college (Earl F. Niehaus, "Jefferson College in St. James Parish, Louisiana, 1830–1875" [M.A. thesis, Tulane University, 1954], 73–77).

Under the Second Empire, he was arrested when Napoleon III muzzled the press. The revolutionary socialist Auguste Blanqui visited him in prison, and he continued his subversive activities after his release. When police attempted to arrest him again for a seditious speech at an underground rally, he fled. Censured for his misconduct, he was banished from France, and in 1853, he emigrated to Louisiana where he joined Dufau at the Collège de la Louisiane, which had been moved to St. James Parish. By 1857, he, like Dufau, was a high-ranking member of the city's Scottish rite lodges.[80]

In New Orleans, Gentil, Dufau, and other radical freemasons nurtured their republican beliefs within the city's French lodges. Though the ideals of the French Revolution remained unfulfilled, Gentil wrote in *Le Delta Maçonnique* in 1858, he expressed confidence in their ultimate triumph. History taught that "humanity,—religiously, politically and socially,—will in the end shake off, in the name of absolute liberty, every soiled mantle, every slave chain, every crushing dogma, every morbid and monastic discipline, every authority incompatible with the spirit and liberty of man." [81]

In an instructional pamphlet published in 1859, *Les Principes de la Franc-Maçonnerie* (*Principles of Freemasonry*), Gentil's colleague Dufau elaborated upon their beliefs and practices. Masonry's objectives, "the physical, intellectual, and moral progress of the individual as well as the political, religious, and social emancipation of all peoples," required an enlightened membership. Accordingly, the lodges studied the most advanced political theories, including the doctrines of French socialists Pierre Proudhon, Etienne Cabet, Victor Considérant, and Louis Blanc. In freemasonry and in the profane world, Scottish rite masons sought the "immediate and universal application of three words—Liberty, Fraternity, Equality." [82]

Noting the growing radicalism of the city's French lodges, conservative Scottish rite freemasons in Charleston, South Carolina, mounted a campaign to discredit the renegade faction in New Orleans. In the struggle, masonic leaders in Charleston charged the New Orleanians with subversion and proclaimed jurisdictional primacy over all of the South's Scottish rite lodges. During the 1850s, French emigré James Foulhouze headed the

80. Tinker, *Les Ecrits,* 246; *Masonic Delta,* February–March, 1861.

81. *Le Delta Maçonnique,* May, 1858.

82. Louis Dufau, *Principes de la Franc-Maçonnerie* (n.p., 1859), 1, 6, 12–13.

movement against the Charlestonians and their official sponsor, the Grand Orient of France.

As a youth, Foulhouze had attended St. Sulpice Seminary in Paris, where he was ordained a Catholic priest. Disillusioned with the priesthood, however, he renounced the church and studied law. On a visit to France in 1845, he received high honors from France's Scottish rite masons. After his return to the United States, he moved to New Orleans and opened a law office; in 1848, he was elected head of the city's Scottish rite lodges. While Foulhouze and his fellow emigrés Dufau and Gentil fortified Scottish rite's republican heritage, a new government in France laid plans to destroy the city's reinvigorated French-speaking lodges.[83]

In France, after the coup d'état of 1851, Louis Napoleon's cousin, Prince Lucien Murat, was designated to head France's masonic lodges. As tensions mounted in New Orleans and the French lodges struggled to maintain their autonomy, Murat issued a decree on June 1, 1858, affirming the Charleston faction's jurisdictional primacy over the southern states and repudiating the city's Scottish rite lodges.[84]

The decree enraged New Orleans' French freemasons. They spurned the Second Empire as well as the Grand Orient: "The principles of true Scotch Free Masonry, which our Supreme Council strictly follows, cannot agree with the form of government which now prevails in France, and that the Grand Orient, which never was but the humblest servant of all the various forms of government (without excepting the most despotic) . . . cannot at this time work but on a bastard and courtier like Masonry." [85]

In October, the city's French lodges revolted and declared their complete independence. Foulhouze defended their actions and refuted the charge that their beliefs fomented "dangerous revolutions both in the Church and State." To the contrary, he declared, he and his fellow lodge members deplored violence. They refused, however, to compromise their principles. They affirmed their commitment to universal education and suffrage and the right of the working classes "to a nobler position in society." [86]

83. James B. Scot, *Outline of the Rise and Progress of Freemasonry in Louisiana* (New Orleans, 1873), 3–4.

84. Ligou *et al.*, *Histoire des Francs-Maçons,* 236; Folger, *The Ancient and Accepted Scottish Rite,* 328–30.

85. Folger, *The Ancient and Accepted Scottish Rite,* 331.

86. *Ibid.*, 330–33; *Annual Grand Communication,* xxi–xxii.

In rejecting the leadership of "Prince Lucien Murat and his Romish Confreres," Foulhouze proclaimed his faith in masonry: "What I look for in Free Masonry is political and social truth—in a word: the science of MAN, DUTY and RIGHT as understood and practiced in the sense of LIBERTY, EQUALITY and FRATERNITY. For that, I hope nothing from Princes and their courtiers in Free Masonry. In a country like ours, where the right of discussion is warranted by law, one must rely on time, reason, progress, and the friends of the people." [87]

Apparently in a further attempt to suppress the dissident faction, the opposition accused the city's French lodges of admitting black members. In view of the background and attitudes of some members, it is quite likely that interracial lodges existed in antebellum New Orleans. In a lodge meeting in May, 1867, the white freemason B. J. Jauquet recalled the presence within his lodge of two black freemasons. The findings of Afro-Creole historian Charles Roussève sustained Jauquet's assertion. In *The Negro in Louisiana,* published in 1937, he wrote that "when, before the Civil War, the Scottish Rite Masons in New Orleans, many of whom were Frenchmen, avowed abolitionists, and enemies of the Roman Catholic Church, adopted a resolution to admit free Negroes as members on terms of absolute equality and brotherhood, a number of free men of color forsook Catholicism for Freemasonry." [88]

Other evidence indicates that as early as 1820, Pierre Roup, a free man of color and a well-connected member of the Saint Domingue emigré community, played a leading role in the establishment of Perseverance masonic lodge. Together with white Saint Dominguan immigrants, Roup served as a high-ranking officer of the lodge. Roup's marriage to Catherine Lafitte, the daughter of Jean Lafitte's brother Pierre and Pierre's

87. *Annual Grand Communication,* 133.

88. For mention of the racial controversy, see Walkes, *The History of the Prince Hall Grand Lodge,* 47–49, 325 *n*22. Though Walkes does not present documentary evidence, he maintains that in 1858 the city's French lodges opened their doors to all persons regardless of nationality, race, or color. For Jauquet's comments, see Polar Star 1 Minutes Book, 1858–68, May 10, 1867, in the George Longe Collection, Amistad Research Center, Tulane University, hereinafter cited as Polar Star Minutes Book. Roussève, *The Negro in Louisiana,* 41. James Scot's account, which describes the antebellum schismatic faction of French freemasons as the predecessor for an 1867 interracial organization, tends to support the assertions of Walkes and Roussève (Scot, *Outline of the Rise and Progress of Freemasonry,* 96).

quadroon mistress Marie Louise Velard, typified the kinds of ties that often existed between free blacks and whites.[89]

In any event, the race-baiting and charges of subversion produced the desired effect. Opponents of the city's freemasons denounced the defiant lodges and questioned their legitimacy. While the refractory lodges remained steadfast in their defiance, the perception that links existed between prominent freemasons and members of the city's free black community was well founded. Soulé and two of his associates, fellow freemason Anthony Fernandez and political ally Thomas Durant, maintained important links to the Afro-Creole community. Soulé himself had encouraged the artistic career of the black sculptor Eugène Warbourg, whom he knew through the artist's father, Daniel Warbourg, a member of a prominent German Jewish family. Eugène's mother, Marie Rose Blondeau, was Daniel Warbourg's mulatto slave mistress. After his son's birth, the father freed his mistress and child and maintained the couple's common-law relationship.

When mounting racial hostility convinced the highly successful Eugène Warbourg to leave the city in 1852, Soulé encouraged the artist to move to Paris and provided him with a recommendation. After six years of study in the French capital, Warbourg moved to London, where he came into contact with the circle of philanthropists and abolitionists centered at Stafford House, the residence of the Duchess of Sutherland, Harriet Leveson-Gower. The duchess, an admirer and friend of Harriet Beecher Stowe, commissioned him to sculpt a series of bas-reliefs depicting scenes from *Uncle Tom's Cabin*. When he completed the project in 1857, Warbourg moved to Florence, Italy, to further his career. Again, Soulé assisted the sculptor; like the duchess and Harriet Beecher Stowe, he furnished Warbourg with a letter of recommendation.[90]

89. Toledano and Christovich, "The Role of Free People of Color," in *Faubourg Tremé*, ed. Christovich and Toledano, 102; Lyle Saxon, *Lafitte the Pirate* (New York, 1930), Chap. 15.

90. In 1863, both Fernandez and Durant referred to their long-standing ties to the free black community (Tunnell, *Crucible of Reconstruction*, 37–38). In supporting suffrage rights for free blacks in 1863, Durant declared that "I have had long and intimate business relations with the leading freemen of African descent in this city, and I believe that I enjoy their confidence to as great an extent as any other in the city" (Peyton McCrary, *Abraham Lincoln and Reconstruction: The Louisiana Experiment* [Princeton, N.J., 1978], 182). Christian, "A Black History," Chap. XXI, 1; Desdunes, *Our People*, 70; Patricia Brady, "Black Artists in Antebellum New Orleans," *Louisiana History*, XXXII (Winter, 1991), 20–23.

During the 1850s, the struggle within Scottish rite masonry mirrored mounting political tensions. At the time of Soulé's return from Europe in 1855, a coalition of slaveholders and wealthy businessmen dominated the state's political economy. Aided by a number of his masonic and Fourierist allies, Soulé channeled his republican zeal into a campaign to counteract planter dominance and stem the secessionist tide.

In the 1845 state constitutional convention, in one of his earliest challenges to planter power, Soulé had campaigned for universal male suffrage and the apportionment of legislative seats on the basis of the number of voters. Ultimately, however, slaveholding planters and their commercial allies introduced a system of representation that assigned senate seats on the basis of the total population, including all of the slaves. This new scheme assured slaveholders the greatest representation in the state legislature. In the constitutional convention of 1852, they consolidated their political dominance by having the same method of representation introduced into the house.[91]

In the decade before the Civil War, John Slidell, Soulé's political nemesis, headed this conservative slaveholding elite and controlled Louisiana's Democratic Party. Soulé, still committed to Stephen Douglas and backed by an antiplanter alliance of urban middle-class professionals, small farmers, and immigrant laborers, battled Slidell for party leadership. When Slidell advocated secession and orchestrated an attempt to remove Douglas from the Democratic leadership in the late 1850s, friction between the two factions escalated. In the gubernatorial campaign of 1859, the Soulé coalition openly revolted. In April in New Orleans, they convened at the Odd Fellows' Hall in an attempt to break the Slidell faction's dominance of the party. At the meeting, Soulé denounced his powerful rivals as a "contemptible and grovelling oligarchy." They believed, he continued, that they had "grown too big and powerful to be resisted, and are so insolent in their official bearing and despotism, that they will not allow the least manifestations of a will . . . that be not modelled on their own." Soulé invited all political factions to unite upon the basis of states' rights and popular sovereignty.[92]

91. Freeman, "The Early Career of Pierre Soulé," 1007–1022; Shugg, *Origins of Class Struggle,* 130–39.

92. Shugg, *Origins of Class Struggle,* Chap. 5; McCrary, *Abraham Lincoln,* 22, 48; A. L. Diket, "Slidell's Right Hand: Emile La Sere," *Louisiana History,* IV (Summer, 1963), 197; quotation in *Address from the Democratic Executive Committee of the Parish of Orleans* (New Orleans, 1859), 9.

Slidell's outraged supporters retaliated. In May, they met in Baton Rouge and repudiated the Soulé-led movement: "If those who vindicated the squatter sovereignty at the Odd Fellows' Hall knew what they did, they are not fit political associates for Southern men." Undaunted by the victory of Slidell's candidate, Thomas O. Moore, in the gubernatorial race, the Soulé coalition continued its crusade. Relations between the two factions approached a flash point after the 1860 Democratic national convention, when Soulé fought for Douglas' nomination and the Slidell forces supported John C. Breckinridge.[93]

During the presidential campaign, the *Daily Delta,* a Breckinridge backer, attacked Soulé for "preaching Douglasism" to rural Louisianians and declaring that "nobody but the slave-holder has an interest in the preservation of slavery." By this line of reasoning, the editorial continued, Soulé endeavored to "stimulate the jealousy of one portion of our population against another portion" and prepare "it for the reception of Abolition doctrines, and disloyalty to Southern institutions." Douglas Democrats, the paper intimated, "would be the basis of a Black Republican organization" if Lincoln triumphed in the election. This observation proved prophetic. After the fall of the city to federal forces in April, 1862, Douglas' supporters formed the core of the state's wartime Republican Party.[94]

Soulé remained in New Orleans and assisted city officials in their negotiations with General Benjamin F. Butler, the commanding officer of the occupying army. Butler, who distrusted Soulé and apparently viewed him as one of Louisiana's foremost secessionists, had the former senator arrested and imprisoned in the North. Not long after his internment, however, President Lincoln paroled him on condition that he not return to Louisiana. Upon his release, Soulé slipped through the blockade and made his way to Charleston, where he joined the staff of General P.G.T. Beauregard, his fellow Louisianian. At the end of the war, he returned to New Orleans.[95]

93. Van D. Odom, "The Political Career of Thomas Overton Moore, Secession Governor of Louisiana," *Louisiana Historical Quarterly,* XXVI (October, 1943), 987.

94. *Daily Delta,* November 1, 1860; McCrary, *Abraham Lincoln,* 52.

95. Historians differ over the details of Soulé's wartime activities. Tinker maintains that during negotiations between Butler and city officials, Soulé referred to Butler as a "disgrace to humanity," and as a consequence, the general had him arrested and imprisoned in Fort Lafayette in New York Harbor (Tinker, *Les Ecrits,* 447–48). According to James Parton, however, Soulé addressed the general courteously during the talks, and

In the city's antebellum lodges, French-speaking freemasons nurtured a republican philosophy consistent with political currents in France. They fought the Catholic Church's mounting conservatism, the region's political economy, and masonry in the South and in France. After their resounding defeat at the hands of the Catholic Church hierarchy, they derived new vigor from the revolution of 1848. Their criticism of economic injustice, their advocacy of working-class solidarity, and their penchant for the free labor theories of French socialists flew in the face of southern realities.

Soulé and his republican colleagues equated their struggle against the state's slaveholding elite with the popular challenge to monarchical authority in Europe. For all of their ideological fervor, however, a number of these republican zealots, including Soulé himself, refused to recognize the aspirations of slave laborers and free black republicans. Still, their idealization of the principles of *liberté, égalité, fraternité* disputed the intellectual and moral legitimacy of a slave-based society. The French republican political culture they had helped sustain would produce some of the most radical leaders of the Civil War era. In Reconstruction Louisiana, French freemasons and their Creole allies would push masonry's ideal of fraternity to its fullest expression.

Butler, who viewed Soulé as a secessionist, arrested the former senator after the negotiations, sending him to Fort Warren in Boston Harbor, not Fort Lafayette (Parton, *General Butler in New Orleans* [New York, 1864], 290–338).

For Soulé's movements after his release, see Moore, "Pierre Soulé," 204, and Edwin J. Putzell, Jr., "Cui Bono: A Study of Secession in Louisiana" (Typescript, Howard-Tilton Memorial Library, Tulane University), 23.

6

Spiritualism's Dissident Visionaries

The human soul has need of the supernatural. Reason alone cannot explain its sad condition here below.

—Alphonse de Lamartine

In the fall of 1858, a bitter rivalry between the city's Catholic leaders and the advocates of spiritualism, a radical new religious sect, culminated in a confrontation between J. B. Valmour, a black Creole medium, and police authorities. The free man of color, highly acclaimed for his success in "the laying on of hands and in the transmission of spiritual messages," enjoyed a reputation as one of the city's most renowned healing mediums. Late-night disturbances outside of Valmour's blacksmith shop near the outskirts of the city and complaints from the Catholic clergy prompted city police to take action. Accusing the Creole leader and his followers of practicing voodoo, they threatened to suppress spiritualist assemblies. The incident forced the celebrated medium to curtail his activities.[1]

For Valmour and other members of the French-speaking free black community, American spiritualism offered an enlightened alternative to the increasing conservatism of the city's Catholic Church. An anarchical religious movement based on uniquely egalitarian principles, spiritualism repudiated orthodox religion as well as other forms of institutionalized authority. Spiritualist leaders advocated a new "catholic" faith based on the Christian ideal of universal brotherhood. As the movement increased in popularity in New Orleans during the 1850s, Valmour and many other

1. *Le Spiritualiste,* October, 1858; Geoffrey K. Nelson, *Spiritualism and Society* (New York, 1969), 16–17; quotation from Desdunes, *Our People,* 53.

Afro-Creoles assumed leadership roles as spiritualist mediums. The social and political implications of their unorthodox new belief system represented a radical challenge to the South's entire social edifice.

Nineteenth-century American spiritualism originated in New York in the mid-1840s and swept North America and Europe during the subsequent decade. The doctrine behind the new movement represented a synthesis of the thought of three European thinkers: Franz Anton Mesmer, Emanuel Swedenborg, and Charles Fourier. The three philosophers had derived much of their inspiration from the scientific advances of the seventeenth century.[2]

In his theory of universal gravitation, the British scientist Sir Isaac Newton described a physical universe operating under the influence of invisible, mechanical laws. The new physics shattered previously held notions of the material world; its social and political impact was equally profound. Newton's synthesis gave new direction to human relations. The scientist's startling description of the "most subtle spirit which pervades and lies hid in all gross bodies" in the 1713 edition of his *Principia* captivated the public mind. Though the scientist himself was at a loss to explain the essence of this natural phenomenon, the existence of a transcendent and mysterious power suffusing the physical world fired the popular imagination.[3]

Less analytical but no less influential minds devised belief systems to accommodate the new scientific realities. The enthusiasm with which the discovery of a universal force in nature was received reflected an ancient and enduring quest to discover fundamental truths in nature—truths that revealed the universality of human experience and consciousness. This tendency persisted as an integral aspect of Western society.

Key social and intellectual movements within European society readily absorbed the impact of the scientific and philosophical revolution. In the

2. Ernest Isaacs, "A History of Nineteenth-Century American Spiritualism as a Religious and Social Movement" (Ph.D. dissertation, University of Wisconsin, 1975), 5–58; Ernest Isaacs, "The Fox Sisters and American Spiritualism," in *The Occult in America: New Historical Perspectives,* ed. Howard Kerr and Charles L. Crow (Urbana, Ill., 1983), 79–81.

3. The impact of Newtonian physics and the scientific revolution is discussed in Jacob, *The Radical Enlightenment,* Chap. 1; Robert Darnton, *Mesmerism and the End of the Enlightenment in France* (Cambridge, Mass., 1968), 11.

eighteenth and nineteenth centuries, philosophers, artists, and other thinkers elaborated upon spirit-in-matter beliefs and universalist notions abstracted from Newtonian physics. Their efforts demonstrated a widespread craving in Western society to break free of a restrictive and archaic social order.[4]

In France in the decades leading up to the French Revolution, devotees of a new healing science called mesmerism combined the idea of a universal force in nature with discoveries involving magnetism, the flow of electricity, and the human psyche. The originator of the new medical therapy, Franz Anton Mesmer, a Viennese doctor, arrived in Paris in 1778 and announced his discovery of an etherlike substance that permeated the universe and served as a medium for gravity. Carrying light, electricity, and magnetism, the cosmic substance suffused all physical objects. In the human being, sickness resulted from an internal obstacle to the natural flow of this fluid through the body. Health, the state of man's harmony with nature, returned when the fluid's natural flow resumed.

Mesmer's treatment involved the transmission of this invisible fluid or energy by means of a technique he termed animal magnetism. In mesmerist séances, the doctor's patients sat around a large oak tub filled with a solution of water and iron filings. The fluid in the tub, Mesmer maintained, harnessed the energy of the cosmic ether. Movable iron rods extending from the tub transmitted the magnetic force to the participants when they applied the end of the rod to the body's diseased area. During the magnetic healing treatment, the mesmerizer directed the flow of concentrated fluid through the body and dispersed the internal obstacle (the disease), thereby restoring the patient's health. By manipulating magnets and engaging in an early form of hypnosis, Mesmer induced a psychological crisis in his subjects. Some patients suffered convulsions, others entered into hypnotic states of semiconsciousness, and some described sleeplike trances in which the ethereal fluid enabled them to commune with spirits of the dead. In his 1799 *Memoir,* Mesmer portrayed animal magnetism as a proven scientific technique that unleashed latent powers and enabled the subject to experience clairvoyance, to comprehend universal truths, and to heal.

4. For insight into the influence of the new physics on Enlightenment culture, see Jacob, *The Radical Enlightenment,* Introduction.

In eighteenth-century France, Mesmer "cured" hundreds of patients and achieved considerable popular acclaim. But his influence extended beyond the realm of medical therapy. By the eve of the French Revolution, his notion of harnessing nature's forces to alleviate human suffering had inspired a number of political philosophers and social reformers as well.[5]

Mesmerist Jean-Louis Carra based his political theory upon Mesmer's notion of a pervasive substance that acted on the political body in much the same way it affected the human body. In the invisible and superior realm of nature, the mechanism of the universe operated according to republican principles. Conveyed by the mesmeric fluid, nature's forces would, therefore, produce a revolution. Ultimately, Carra predicted, natural laws would bring the political body into harmony with the physical-moral forces of the universe. In the early 1780s, Carra, soon to be a leader in the French Revolution, prophesied that France would become a republic "because the great physical system of the universe, which governs the moral and political affairs of the human race, is itself a veritable republic." In the coming republican millennium, Carra described how the king and the shepherd would be "two men in the true state of equality, two friends in the true state of society."[6]

Mesmerism remained influential during the postrevolutionary era, when utopian socialists incorporated mesmerist concepts into their political theories. Although Charles Fourier criticized mesmerists for misunderstanding their science, he nonetheless assimilated their ideas into his own works; his view that human society could be cured of its ills by being brought into harmony with the physical universe coincided with mes-

5. Darnton, *Mesmerism,* 3–14; Robert S. Ellwood, Jr., *Alternative Altars: Unconventional and Eastern Spirituality in America* (Chicago, 1979), 92. The term *animal* in animal magnetism derives from the Latin word *anima,* which refers to soul or some other life force; it is in this context that the term *animal magnetism* was used to describe mesmerism (Ellwood, *Alternative Altars,* 85). Mesmerists believed that magnetized subjects could see their internal organs, diagnose their illnesses, and predict the time of their cures (Nicholas P. Spanos and Jack Gottlieb, "Demonic Possession, Mesmerism, and Hysteria: A Social Psychological Perspective on Their Historical Interrelations," *Journal of Abnormal Psychology,* LXXXVIII [1979], 529–30). Since mesmerists often associated ill health with moral evil, they sometimes conceived of themselves as opponents of injustice and agents of moral as well as physical healing.

6. Darnton, *Mesmerism,* 108, 110.

merist beliefs. And like Carra's theory, Fourier's philosophy of the physical-moral laws of nature included an apocalyptic transformation in which it would be necessary to "throw all political, moral and economic theories into the fire and to prepare for the most astonishing event . . . FOR THE SUDDEN TRANSITION FROM SOCIAL CHAOS TO UNIVERSAL HARMONY."[7]

In the first half of the nineteenth century, mesmerists exhibited their healing science at well-advertised demonstrations throughout Europe and the United States. By the time the practice crossed the Atlantic, however, French innovators had largely dispensed with the use of magnets, magnetized water, and baths. Instead, they employed more advanced techniques in hypnosis to induce sleeplike states of consciousness in their subjects. The notion of an ethereal fluid remained, however, and mesmerizers believed that this mysterious substance brought their patients into direct communication with a superior otherworldly intelligence. They described extraordinary feats of clairvoyance and telepathy in which their patients diagnosed illnesses, prescribed remedies, and communicated with distant persons and the spirits of the dead.[8]

In the United States during the mid-1840s, mesmerism underwent a unique transformation as a consequence of the experiences of a Poughkeepsie shoemaker's apprentice, Andrew Jackson Davis. Born in 1826, the uneducated Davis began to experience spontaneous trances and visions at the age of twelve. In 1843, he embarked upon a career as a medical clairvoyant after witnessing a mesmerist demonstration. In hypnotic states induced by a mesmerizer, the teenaged Davis diagnosed illnesses and prescribed cures. Although he enjoyed relative success as a seer and healer, his clairvoyant experiences took on a new character after a couple of years.

Between 1845 and 1847, under the guidance of radical Universalist ministers, he dictated a series of trance-lectures. In 1847, Davis and his associates published the spirit communications in a two-volume work entitled *The Principles of Nature, Her Divine Revelations, and A Voice to Mankind, by and Through Andrew Jackson Davis*. In the *Divine Revelations*

7. *Ibid.*, 143.

8. R. Laurence Moore, *In Search of White Crows: Spiritualism, Parapsychology, and American Culture* (New York, 1977), 9; Robert C. Fuller, *Mesmerism and the American Cure of Souls* (Philadelphia, 1982), 10; Darnton, *Mesmerism,* 58.

and more than thirty other books, Davis drew upon Mesmer's healing science, Swedenborg's theology, and Fourier's socialism to lay the theoretical foundation of the spiritualist movement.

Divine Revelations met with a mixed response when it first appeared in July, 1847, but Davis and his fellow reformers forged ahead regardless. They launched a paper, dispatched field missionaries, and announced their intention to bring about the "establishment of a universal system of Truth, and the Reform and Reorganization of Society." Their movement received little notice until the spring of 1848, when events in western New York attracted international attention.[9]

On a farm in Hydesville, two teenaged sisters, Margaret and Kate Fox, heard mysterious rappings on the walls of their room. The sisters and many witnesses attributed the strange noises to the spirits of the dead. The knockings and the teenagers' telepathic abilities created an immediate sensation and transformed spiritualism. Within two years, the movement had spread to most major American cities. While public attention remained fastened on the Hydesville rappings and other spirit-induced phenomena, Davis and his associates elaborated upon their vision of an earthly utopia. In the spiritualist synthesis, Emanuel Swedenborg's theology served as the basis of their new religion.[10]

During the 1740s, Swedenborg, an eminent eighteenth-century Swedish scientist, had experienced a series of visions that convinced him of the failure of orthodox religion. Guided by his mystical revelations, he described three orders of being: the natural, the spiritual, and the divine. On the basis of his doctrine of "correspondences," Swedenborg proposed to establish the transcendent unity of the three realms. Everything in the natural world, he asserted, corresponded to a higher spiritual reality. The material realm was merely an image of the superior spiritual world. The highest realm, the divine, produced and sustained the two lower orders, with God and man sharing a common spiritual essence in the life of the soul. Natural law, like the natural world, was a reflection of its superior correspondent in the upper realms. By living in harmony with divine law, the individual achieved salvation.

9. Isaacs, "A History of Nineteenth-Century American Spiritualism," 26–55, 52.

10. *Ibid.*, 57; Ellwood, *Alternative Altars,* 84.

A highly respected physicist and astronomer, Swedenborg considered theology a science, but a literal interpretation of the Bible produced discrepancies between scientific knowledge and the sacred text. Swedenborg sought to clear away these inconsistencies by revealing the true meaning of biblical scripture. The Bible, he maintained, possessed a spiritual or inner meaning that his powers as a seer had enabled him to decipher. In his reinterpretation of the holy book, Swedenborg found the Bible to agree with science. In nineteenth-century America, the Swedish seer's unitive philosophy resonated in the thought of spiritualists, Transcendentalists, utopian socialists, and other reform-minded idealists.[11]

Inspired by Swedenborg's doctrine of correspondences, spiritualist philosopher Andrew Jackson Davis incorporated the notion of a superior spiritual realm into his "Harmonial Philosophy," a master plan for the radical transformation of existing social, economic, and religious institutions. Embodied in Davis' *Divine Revelations,* the Harmonial Philosophy represented the collective wisdom of the advanced societies of the upper realms.

Davis accepted Swedenborg's concept of a hierarchy of seven spheres. These concentric bands surrounded the earth and represented progressive stages of spiritual enlightenment. When a person died, the inner being of the deceased entered these invisible realms, and to the extent that the believer's spiritual life harmonized with divine law, the soul advanced through the spheres toward ultimate redemption. In the physical world, the soul of a medium during a clairvoyant trance could migrate to the spirit realm and achieve higher states of inner illumination.

Sharing Swedenborg's view of theology as a science, Davis and his followers formulated the mechanistic basis of their belief system with analogues to the physical sciences. In the spiritualist synthesis, electrical energy linked the spiritual and material worlds. Vital electricity, nature's life-giving force, permeated the universe and served as a medium of correspondence between the two realms. In mediumistic trances, the believer communed with the spirits of the dead by means of this electrical force. With the gradual loss of vital electricity, the physical body deteriorated. In

11. J. Stillson Judah, *The History and Philosophy of the Metaphysical Movements in America* (Philadelphia, 1967), 34–41; Sydney E. Ahlstrom, *A Religious History of the American People* (New Haven, 1972), 483–86; Ellwood, *Alternative Altars,* 84–89.

death the soul migrated from the body to become the new abode of the spirit. Freed from its earthly domain, the spirit entered a new state of existence.[12]

Even though Davis, like Swedenborg, postulated a scientific basis of theology, he rejected the Swedish scientist's biblical exegesis. Whereas Swedenborg had attempted to reconcile the inconsistencies between science and biblical scripture, Davis considered such differences insurmountable. He found the doctrines of original sin, predestination, and eternal damnation completely incompatible with the true essence of human spirituality. He therefore rejected any plan of salvation based upon scriptural teachings. He described the Old Testament as "primitive history" and denied the sanctity of the Bible and the divinity of Jesus Christ. In the tradition of Confucius, Zoroaster, Muhammad, Swedenborg, and Fourier, Christ was a "great and good Reformer" who had sought the betterment of the human condition. He had died a martyr "to the cause of love, wisdom, and virtue." [13]

Davis reserved his harshest attacks for the Christian clergy. "It is a deplorable fact that all the miseries, the conflicts, the wars, the devastations and the hostile prejudices existing in the world are owing to the corrupting situation and influence of Clergymen." While science and natural religion contributed to mankind's advancement, the Bible and organized religion served as an obstacle to humanity's progressive development. Religious reform was fundamental to societal regeneration.[14]

Swedenborg's view of God's immanence in the universe also underlay Davis' concept of human spirituality. Human souls were "detached individual personifications of the Deific Nature and Essence" that would attain realization by progression through the spheres. Since all human beings possessed a share of God's divinity, all persons were equal members of a great human brotherhood. Davis admonished spiritualists to "do good and har-

12. Robert W. Delp, "Andrew Jackson Davis and Spiritualism," in *Pseudo-Science and Society in Nineteenth-Century America,* ed. Arthur Wrobel (Lexington, Ky., 1987), 100–102; Judah, *The History and Philosophy of the Metaphysical Movements,* 55–56; Isaacs, "A History of Nineteenth-Century American Spiritualism," 166–210.

13. Isaacs, "A History of Nineteenth-Century American Spiritualism," 44–45; Frank Podmore, *Mediums of the Nineteenth Century* (published in 1902 as *Modern Spiritualism: A History and a Criticism;* rpr. New York, 1963), I, 164; Robert W. Delp, "Andrew Jackson Davis's *Revelations,* Harbinger of American Spiritualism," *New York Historical Society Quarterly,* LX (July, 1971), 220.

14. Slater Brown, *The Heyday of Spiritualism* (New York, 1970), 90.

monious works, for the redemption and ennoblement of your fellow-men." Such works were to be undertaken "because the Human Race is but One Family—all members of one body—in which there is neither Jew nor Gentile, Nazarene nor Greek, Ethiopian nor Anglo-Saxon." In both life and death, the soul possessed the capacity for limitless growth. Davis' rejection of Hell opened the possibility of salvation to everyone. The believer's continuous advancement toward God formed the basis for all true progress, since the regeneration of the spirit would lead to the regeneration of society.[15]

While Swedenborgianism formed the basis for spiritualist theology, Fourierism served as a model for Davis' social theory. During the early nineteenth century, Fourier, who considered himself Newton's successor, proclaimed his discovery of "God's plan" for the universe. He insisted that a social analogue to Newton's principle of gravitational attraction held the key to the correct organization of society. Fourier proposed such an analogue in his theory of "passionate attraction." The principle of passionate attraction acted upon society in the same way that Newton's principle of gravitation acted upon the physical universe. Since human passions were the agents of personal happiness and social harmony, the free expression of these passions would result in a state of "unlimited philanthropy and universal fellow feeling." The repression of these benevolent instincts by civilized society had resulted in every manner of evil. Yet, salvation was at hand. Fourier boldly proclaimed his mission: "I come as the possessor of the book of Destiny to banish political and moral darkness and to erect the theory of universal harmony upon the ruins of the uncertain sciences."[16]

Like Fourier's system of Universal Harmony, the principles of Davis' Harmonial Philosophy were intended "to unfold the Kingdom of Heaven on earth, to apply the laws of planets to individuals; to establish, in a word, in human society the same harmonious relations that are found to obtain in the planetary world."[17]

15. Judah, *The History and Philosophy of the Metaphysical Movements,* 39, 56; Isaacs, "A History of Nineteenth-Century American Spiritualism," 236, 238.

16. Beecher, *Charles Fourier,* 65–67, 74, 226, 237–38; Isaacs, "A History of Nineteenth-Century American Spiritualism," 11.

17. Robert W. Delp, "A Spiritualist in Connecticut: Andrew Jackson Davis, The Hartford Years, 1850–1854," *New England Quarterly,* LIII (September, 1980), 350–51.

Davis argued that contemporary society, instead of conforming to natural law, was divided into competing and antagonistic classes. The exploitation of the laboring poor had resulted in great inequalities. Wealth was concentrated in the hands of "*Capitalists,* for the wealth which the poor create is accumulated by them, and held within their grasp. Wealth that rightly belongs to those who create it, is thus given to those who earn it not, and hence have no natural title to it." The working class was uneducated and "chained in the degrading shackles of superstition, and enslaved by laws imposed by government."[18]

Davis' blueprint for the evils afflicting American society reflected the influence of Albert Brisbane, a regular attendant at Davis' lectures and the country's leading proponent of Fourierist ideas. The interests of capital and labor would be reconciled upon the basis of Associationism. Initially, agricultural laborers and artisans would implement "the law of association—which is the rudimental principle of Nature." When Fourierism's benefits were evident, all professions would join the movement toward "SOCIAL HAPPINESS AND SPIRITUAL ELEVATION."[19]

The failure to recognize nature's harmonious laws—a failure fostered by orthodox religion—led to intemperance, war, slavery, racial oppression, and other forms of human misery. When the organization of society conformed to the harmonious structure of the universe "the human race will display Light and Life, which are *Love,* and order and form, which are *Wisdom*. Thus will be established *universal happiness*—because the whole race will represent the harmony of all created things, and typify the express majesty of the Divine Creator."[20]

In the spiritualist journal *Univercoelum,* published between 1847 and 1849, contributors announced plans for economic reorganization along socialist lines as a first step toward establishing an ideal society. The editors of the journal published articles on socialism, trade unionism, and other

18. Delp, "Andrew Jackson Davis's *Revelations,*" 214–15; Isaacs, "A History of Nineteenth-Century American Spiritualism," 47.

19. Isaacs, "A History of Nineteenth-Century American Spiritualism," 46, 48. For Brisbane's role in the American Fourierist movement, see Carl J. Guarneri, *The Utopian Alternative: Fourierism in Nineteenth-Century America* (Ithaca, N.Y., 1991), 25–32.

20. Isaacs, "The Fox Sisters," in *The Occult in America,* ed. Kerr and Crow, 81; Delp, "Andrew Jackson Davis's *Revelations,*" 215–16.

cooperative organizations. They also indicated the seriousness of their reform efforts: "We are in earnest in the advocacy of general reforms and the reorganization of society, because such is the natural counterpart and outer expression of the interior and spiritual principles which we are endeavoring to set forth." [21]

Davis associated spiritualism with other reform efforts and viewed abolitionism, feminism, and the temperance and peace movements as aspects of a generalized progression toward the ideal society. At the Free Convention of 1858 in Rutland, Vermont, he explained this view: "My belief in Spiritualism is simply the door to my acceptance of the various reforms for which this convention has assembled and I trust that to you all Spiritualism is a broad and glorious triumphant archway leading in all directions into freedom, and a universal enjoyment of a heaven in the world." Similarly, Davis maintained that advances in science, the creations of artists, writers, and musicians, and the guidance received through mediums would contribute to the advancement of human society.[22]

While Davis pressed forward in the North, his followers encountered hostility and threats of violence in the South. Spiritualism's opposition to slavery, its egalitarian ideals, and its popularity among free blacks and slaves aroused southern fears. In 1859 and 1860, spiritualist lecturer Emma Hardinge Britten and her cohorts received threats of lynching during visits to Tennessee and South Carolina. The Charleston *Courier* unleashed a violent attack on the "incendiary practices of the abhorrent Spiritualists." At the same time, the Alabama state legislature passed a statute forbidding spiritualist demonstrations under the penalty of a five-hundred-dollar fine. During the 1850s, opposition to the movement in New Orleans forced spiritualists to confine most of their séances to private residences. Nonetheless, by the eve of the Civil War, the city had acquired a reputation as a spiritualist stronghold.[23]

As in the North, the mesmerist movement paved the way for the emergence of spiritualism in New Orleans. During the late 1820s, French mesmerists introduced animal magnetism into the United States. Mesmer's

21. Podmore, *Mediums,* I, 173.

22. Delp, "Andrew Jackson Davis," 47, 48, 52.

23. Moore, *In Search of White Crows,* 61–62; Boston *Banner of Light,* March 13, April 3, 1858; quotation from Nelson, *Spiritualism and Society,* 17.

followers probably acquainted New Orleanians with the practice during the late 1830s, and in July, 1843, the *Daily Picayune* reported that the "city at the present time is in a perfect state of Mesmerism." The editorialist continued: "Hard times, temperance societies, and of course we must add, the growing intelligence of the age, have made strange revolutions lately." [24]

Two years later in April, 1845, Joseph Barthet, a French emigré and mesmerist propagator, organized a mesmerist society in New Orleans, the Société du Magnétisme de la Nouvelle-Orléans. Following the establishment of their formal organization, Barthet and the society's French-speaking membership corresponded with societies in Paris and elsewhere, publicized their case studies, opened a library dedicated to mesmerist works, staged public demonstrations, and preached the therapeutic value of animal magnetism in the treatment of human ailments. By 1848, the Société du Magnétisme counted seventy-one members of French extraction.[25]

While the city's conservative Catholic Church leadership opposed mesmerism, some members of the city's clergy viewed the movement favorably. One Catholic cleric, the Abbé Malavergne, belonged to the Société du Magnétisme, and a number of other priests referred sick church members to the group for treatment. Barthet, who considered mesmerism "a powerful auxiliary to religion," encouraged this relationship by describing magnetic therapy as a valuable treatment for the "sickness of the soul." During the height of mesmerism's popularity in New Orleans, Barthet and his colleagues attempted to demonstrate mesmerism's compatibility with Catholicism. He and other mesmerists furnished the city's newspapers with accounts of magnetism's acceptance among church leaders in France. Such testimonials notwithstanding, the city's Catholic leaders remained steadfast in their opposition.[26]

24. Brown, *Heyday of Spiritualism,* 12–15; Fuller, *Mesmerism,* 17–20; Wallace K. Tomlinson and J. John Perret, "Mesmerism in New Orleans, 1845–1861," *American Journal of Psychiatry,* XII (December, 1974), 1403; New Orleans *Daily Picayune,* July 16, 1843.

25. Tomlinson and Perret, "Mesmerism," 1403. For information on Barthet, see Manuscript Census Returns, Census of 1850, in Record Group 29, Records of the Bureau of the Census, National Archives.

26. Tomlinson and Perret, "Mesmerism," 1403–1404; *L'Abeille,* March 15, October 22, 1847; *Propagateur Catholique,* August 9, 1851, June 26, 1852. The involvement of Catholic clerics in mesmerism may be attributed to Jansenism's continued influence in nineteenth-century New Orleans. Jansenism, often seen as a precursor to mesmerism, stressed a direct

The editor of the church's official organ, Abbé Perché, conceded in the *Propagateur Catholique* that the Holy See had refrained from an outright denunciation of mesmerism and that prominent members of France's clergy tolerated the movement within their dioceses. He also noted, however, that the Congregation of the Index had condemned the works of a prominent French mesmerist, Alphonse Cahagnet, and he expressed his belief "in the imminent dangers and in the frequent abuse of magnetism." In a subsequent editorial, he cautioned his Catholic readership to beware of the "very great moral dangers" that might accompany the practice of magnetism.[27]

In May, 1852, under the cover of foreign commentary, the *Propagateur* published a particularly violent attack on mesmerists in a book review titled "Freemasonry." French author Francis Lacombe lambasted the "utopians, the *convulsionnaires,* the magnetizers, and the ecstatic somnambulists . . . the Rosicrucians, the freemasons, and the Illuminati, the avant-garde of an army of evil," which had attempted to conquer the world under the inspiration of Enlightenment thought. In the nineteenth century, these bearers of the revolutionary tradition sought the overthrow of the established order. Their esoteric confederacy carried forward the "completely subversive intentions of the French Revolution." Emboldened by their partial success in 1848, Lacombe warned, these secret societies openly pursued their aims. In relation to the avowed purposes of Barthet and other mesmerists in New Orleans and France, these accusations contained a strong element of truth.[28]

Barthet, as president of the mesmerist society, maintained direct correspondence with the Baron du Potet in Paris, who was one of mesmerism's leading proponents in France and editor of the *Journal du magnétisme*. In

---

relationship between God and the believer, and the trancelike states of magnetized subjects closely resembled the visionary experiences of Jansenist mystics. Such similarities surely predisposed many of the city's Catholics to mesmerism's influence (Darnton, *Mesmerism,* 36, 61).

27. *Propagateur Catholique,* August 9, 1851, June 26, 1852.

28. *Ibid*., May 15, 1852. During the religious excitement of the eighteenth century, the phenomena of convulsive shaking and gasping accompanied spiritual revelation for a group of religious ecstatics, or *convulsionnaires,* within the French Jansenist movement (Clarke Garrett, *Spirit Possession and Popular Religion* [Baltimore, Md., 1987], 10–11, 26).

1850, du Potet offered a highly encouraging account of Barthet's progress in New Orleans. He noted that "of all the institutions founded in the last few years outside of Paris for the propagation of mesmerism, the one which has succeeded best is, without doubt, the Society of Magnetism in New Orleans." Du Potet attributed its success to Barthet, whom he considered "a zealous and capable man." [29]

For magnetists like Barthet and the Baron du Potet, mesmerism's benefits extended far beyond the boundaries of medical and spiritual healing. Mesmerism, they believed, would contribute to the transformation of society. To this end, du Potet and his colleagues in Paris drew parallels between mesmerism and utopian socialism. They published extracts from the works of Fourierists and Saint-Simonians, and they welcomed the conversion of utopian socialists to their cause. In 1853, du Potet published Robert Owen's mesmerist experiences in the *Journal du magnétisme* and offered an account of his changeover. Though Owen "had been until now a materialist in the strongest sense of the word," he had been "completely converted to the belief in the immortality of the soul by the conversations he has had with members of his family, who have been dead for years." Owen himself described séances in which the spirits of Benjamin Franklin and Thomas Jefferson explained "that the object of the current general manifestations is to reform the population of our planet, to convince all of us of the truth of another life and to make us all sincerely charitable." [30]

Even mesmerism's founder, du Potet revealed, had viewed magnetism as a means for bringing about a social revolution. Between 1846 and 1848, du Potet published installments in his journal of a manuscript Mesmer had written during the French Revolution: *Notions élémentaires sur la morale, l'éducation et la législation pour servir à l'instruction publique en France* (*Elementary Rudiments of Morality, Education, and Legislation for Use in Public Instruction in France*). In it, Mesmer had outlined a radical blueprint for creating an ideal republic; he had even submitted the document to the French National Convention.

With the revolution of 1848, du Potet's *Journal du magnétisme* railed against academic and political tyranny: "Our learned men wanted nothing to do with mesmerism, just as other men wanted nothing to do with

29. Tomlinson and Perret, "Mesmerism," 1403.

30. Darnton, *Mesmerism,* 145–46.

liberty . . . [but] the links of the despotic chain that science did not want to break have burst into splinters." The journal continued: "Rejoice mesmerists! Here is the dawning of a great and beautiful new day . . . O Mesmer! You who loved the republic . . . you foresaw this time, but . . . you were not understood." [31]

With the rapid spread of spiritualism in the United States after 1848, Barthet became an ardent proponent of the new phenomenon. He forwarded glowing accounts of the movement to his colleagues in Paris, and in 1852, he published an instructional manual on spirit communication, the *ABC des communications spirituelles*. Before the end of the year, Barthet could report the conversion of an important new member, Charles Testut, a white French emigré and literary colleague of the Afro-Creole writer Camille Thierry.[32]

Testut, like other Romantic writers including Victor Hugo, proved especially susceptible to spiritualism's influence. The Romantic movement had fostered the belief that the artist possessed exceptional powers of moral and spiritual insight. In this view, the creative act enabled the poet or artist to commune directly with the animating spirit in nature—a spirit that permeated and unified all things. His poetic images were symbolic representations of a reality grounded in thought and moral experience that functioned as the unseen counterpart of the external, material world.

Unlike eighteenth-century classicism, which had presupposed an objective and rational reality, the Romantic movement emphasized the artist's inner impulses and passions. The urge to discover the authentic self in an act of spontaneous creativity overtook the desire to imitate accepted models of perfection. The superior value placed on the essence of things as opposed to their physical manifestation blurred the dualism of flesh and spirit. The stress on instinct, emotion, and feelings led to a fascination with the human subconscious and the ethereal.[33]

31. *Ibid.*, 146, 148.

32. Auguste Viatte, *Victor Hugo et les illuminés de son temps* (Montréal, 1942), 29; Tinker, *Les Ecrits,* 30.

33. In political exile on the English Channel island of Jersey from 1852 to 1855, Victor Hugo and his fellow French *proscrits* (proscribed republicans) engaged in spiritualist seances similar to those of their contemporaries in New Orleans, recording communications with the spirits of Molière, Dante, Racine, Marat, Charlotte Corday, Muhammad, Jesus Christ, Plato, and others. And much like Testut, Hugo in his capacity as a spiritualist

For leading European and American intellectuals, the Romantic view of human spirituality also engendered religious-political consequences. Romantic writers believed, like French socialists, that the Christian spirit was an essential element of societal progress. "La charité," Lamartine wrote in 1834, "c'est le socialisme." At a banquet in Paris in 1842, he toasted religion as one of the forces that "facilitate the divine unity, that is to say, the confraternity of all races and all men!" While French Romantics such as Lamennais and Lamartine considered themselves devoted Christians, the Catholic Church viewed their writings as heretical. In 1835, the Vatican condemned the work of Lamennais and placed the writings of Lamennais, Lamartine, and Victor Hugo on the papal Index.[34]

In New Orleans, Testut's literary works and his social vision, like that of his Afro-Creole contemporaries, embodied many of these Romantic tendencies. In his book of poetry published in 1851, *Fleurs d'été,* Testut used the examples of Béranger, Lamartine, and other famous French writers to portray the poet as the embodiment of Christian charity—a seeker of truth and justice endowed with superhuman powers of insight and courage. In its preface, Testut introduced this image: "The true poet is the child of God; happy or suffering, he loves his neighbor; he does not envy the rich, he does not scorn the poor; his conscience is not steeped in injustice, nor his hands in blood." The poet-hero "praises the Homeland, Glory, Liberty. In the martial clamor of their poetic fanfare, they inflame hearts, bolster courage, conceal danger and pave the way to victory. In the sphere that they have chosen, they always march ahead, as if some powerful and invisible influence thrust them to the forefront of the conflict." [35]

In "The Poet," a poem dedicated to free man of color Camille Thierry, Testut indicated his belief in the poet's sacred mission:

But still, man for his soul
Has need of nourishment:

---

medium conceived of himself as a prophet who had been chosen to lead humanity. For Hugo's exile in Jersey and mention of Pierre Soulé's visit to the island see Philip Stevens, *Victor Hugo in Jersey* (Chichester, Eng., 1985), 72. For Hugo's spiritualist activities, see André Maurois, *Olympio: The Life of Victor Hugo,* trans. Gerard Hopkins (New York, 1956), Chap. 36; Stromberg, *An Intellectual History,* 213–14; Talmon, *Romanticism and Revolt,* 136–45.

34. Evans, *Social Romanticism,* 39–40, 81.

35. Testut, *Fleurs d'été,* xiii–xiv.

God created the celestial flame
Which must survive in the nothingness!
In days full of frights,
Full of torments and of tears:
Who will come to console him? . . .

It is Jesus Christ! It is the poet
Because his voice is always ready
To console the outcast;
Apostle of mercy
He dies and says: "Hope
Because our soul survives us!"[36]

In December, 1852, Testut attended his first spiritualist gathering, which he later described. He and a large number of other guests crowded into a room, where over a dozen men and women sat around a large oblong table with their open hands resting on the table's surface. After a period of complete silence, each person posed a question. With each question, the side of the table opposite the questioner rose an inch or two from the floor and struck the ground once for "no" and twice for "yes." Though Testut suspected trickery, he remained fascinated and continued to experiment.

His conversion occurred in the privacy of his home. He described his experience:

> I sat down at my table, alone, at my home. I collected my thoughts, I slowly banished all images of material things—and I waited. Soon I felt myself transfused by some kind of warm and flowing liquid; a new sense of well-being overcame me, and, at the same time, I experienced an urge to move the fingers of my right hand. . . . And new ideas gradually arose in my mind, all of justice, of love, and of mercy, and I finished by imagining that I poured a shower of gold over all of the wretched of the earth.[37]

Next, Testut experienced an overwhelming desire to write. He resolved to persevere, and the following night, equipped with a pencil and paper, he resumed his seat at the table. After several moments of meditation, his

36. *Ibid.*, 102–103.
37. *L'Equité,* May 21, 1871, p. 6.

right hand began to shake. He seized the pencil and closed his eyes while the pencil glided over the paper, then fell from his hand. He scanned the seemingly indecipherable scribblings, and when he reached the bottom of the page, he discerned the words, "Not alone."

The phrase triggered a revelatory experience. Testut explained: "These two words inundated me with light. I understood the necessity of being surrounded by brothers . . . so that our combined ardor might lead to a more complete result. Union was necessary. . . . What a lesson in these two words: *Not Alone!* Sacred Fraternity! you are indispensable to the pursuit of good here below." [38]

Within days of his revelation, Testut organized a spiritualist circle. From the beginning, the group met on a regular basis to receive and transcribe their spirit communications. By the time they gathered for a Christmas celebration the following year, the circle numbered over three dozen members. At their holiday banquet they sang, recited poetry, and drank to the "fraternity of all people." Near the end of the evening, they proposed to hold a spiritual séance with Testut acting as the medium. After a prayer and a reading, Testut lapsed into a mesmeric trance. His automatic writing produced a startling communication.

The message began with a blessing and then assumed a prayerful character: "Let the oppressed soon feel the links of their chains fall away! Let war lead to peace, and tyranny to liberty! Look to heaven and you will see. Ask God and he will answer you: You have voices now in another sphere. You are unaware of what you have done and what you do! God, who sees and hears you, knows—and the Good Spirits surround you like a shield. . . . Eight [*sic*] centuries ago I began the mission that you continue. . . . [Signed] Jesus Christ." [39]

The communication rendered the participants speechless. Bolstered by this inspirational experience, they opened their séances to the public and transcribed their spirit messages from Christ, St. Vincent de Paul, and other spirit guides. In a further effort to propagate their beliefs, Testut published their communications in 1854 in a book titled *Manifestations spirituelles*. These "teachings" touched "on all social questions which bear on the present happiness and future felicity of humanity" and represented

38. *Ibid.*, May 28, 1871, p. 6.

39. *Ibid.*

the "quintessence of wisdom, democracy, and love." The group remained together for five years.[40]

Testut, a productive Romantic writer whose literary works often served as propaganda vehicles, later incorporated his spiritualist ideals into an antislavery historical novel that he wrote in 1858, shortly after his arrival in February in New York City. In the work entitled *Le Vieux Salomon; ou, Une Famille d'esclaves au XIXe siècle* (*Old Solomon; or, A Slave Family in the Nineteenth Century*), Testut described an underground religious society in Louisiana called the Brothers of the Universal Faith. The members of the international, interracial organization engaged in abolitionist activities and adhered to an all-embracing belief system with a religious-political mission. Testut summarized the main tenets of his fictitious religion: "The Universal Faith deals with everything: fraternity, charity, liberty, happiness, the present, the future, the greatness of man on earth and his bliss in heaven; possible equality in the social order. . . . It teaches us to love God, to honor men of good will, to scorn ill-gotten riches." [41]

Its members repudiated organized religion, and like spiritualists in New Orleans, they held the Catholic Church in particular contempt. One member offered the view that without "the adverse influence of the priests, perhaps the French colonies would soon be purged of the leprosy of slavery." His colleague responded, "What! them again! . . . They will always be, of course, on the side of injustice and tyranny, these agents of Satan who conceal themselves in the mantle of Christ!" [42]

Near the time of the publication of *Manifestations spirituelles,* Testut also embarked upon a career as a healing medium. At his *consultations spirituelle,* his patients dictated their symptoms. After compiling and numbering their individual ailments, Testut entered into a mesmeric trance and scribbled out prescriptions. He claimed that thirty-four of the thirty-five patients who came the day he opened his practice were healed. His only failure occurred, he alleged, when a patient expired before receiving his prescription from a messenger. Yet Testut's fame as a

40. *Ibid.*, May 21, 1871, 6.

41. Lagarde, "Charles Testut," 26–27, 78–79; Charles Testut, *Le Vieux Salomon ou une famille d'esclaves au XIX siecle* (New Orleans, 1872), 95. For a good summary of Le *Vieux Salomon,* see Jones, *Slavery and Race in Nineteenth-Century Louisiana,* 81–94.

42. Testut, *Le Vieux Salomon,* 97.

healing medium paled beside that of J. B. Valmour, a black Creole blacksmith.[43]

As early as 1852, Valmour enjoyed a reputation as a highly successful healing medium. The sick and the curious flocked to his blacksmith shop on Toulouse Street. At times, the eager visitors overran his small apartment and forced him to perform his spiritual healings in an outdoor courtyard. Usually, however, he and his ailing visitors sat around a large round table. After being seated, the medium lapsed into a deep state of prayerful meditation. Valmour described the nature of these trancelike states when Joseph Barthet and other mesmerists sought his advice in treating one of their patients. He advised them: "Forget that you have magnetized, because that would only mislead you; it is necessary to direct one's thinking toward God, wish for the well-being of one's neighbor, and God will do the rest." [44]

Some of Valmour's "patients" described instant cures and others returned for subsequent sessions. Upon the rare occasions when he prescribed a treatment for a sufferer's ailment, the remedy was always simple. At times the large crowds that gathered at his blacksmith shop brought his business to a complete halt. Despite these costly interruptions and his modest income, he refused to accept any form of compensation.

Valmour's admirers marveled at his powers. Barthet pleaded with the blacksmith's followers to build larger, more comfortable accommodations for the medium and his audiences. He viewed the Creole as a Christlike figure whose meager residence reminded him of the birthplace of "the great Nazarene." The white French emigré compared Valmour's lifestyle and healing feats to the life and work of a renowned magnetist in Pau, France, named Laforgue. Like the Frenchman, Barthet noted, Valmour practiced blacksmithing, possessed neither medical nor scientific training, engaged in mediumistic healing, and obtained "*miracles* of the same kind." Unlike Valmour, however, Laforgue suffered censorship under Napoleon III's government, when it cracked down on French magnetists. Shortly before his death in 1853, police authorities forced the French medium to suspend his activities. According to Barthet, Laforgue died "with the sorrow of having been unable, up to his last day, to do good for

43. *L'Equité,* June 3, 1871.

44. *Le Spiritualiste,* May, July, 1858, pp. 136, 195–96.

his fellowmen; because he was a 'true Christian,' having, like Jesus, more religion than his persecutors, though he didn't go to mass." Barthet attributed Valmour's freedom of action to the "very good Catholics" of wealth and influence among the Creole spiritualist's followers. As sectional tensions mounted during the prewar years, however, even such well-placed friends could not protect the New Orleans medium from suffering a similar fate.[45]

During the early 1850s, spiritualism's rapid spread through the city and the emergence of Valmour and other powerful mediums alarmed church officials. While Catholic leaders had demonstrated a relative degree of restraint in their dealings with mesmerists, they showed no tolerance for spiritualists. In the fall of 1852, reports of a sudden flurry of spiritual manifestations involving a number of leading citizens convinced church officials to voice their opposition.

In setting forth the church's position on spiritualism, a Catholic spokesman acknowledged the intervention of spirits at séances. Indeed, Catholicism professed the existence of spirits and possessed an age-old tradition of spiritual mysticism. Such tendencies contributed to spiritualism's popularity with the city's large Catholic population, as a New Orleans observer noted: "Spiritualism has made much more rapid progress among the Creole and Catholic portions of our population than the Protestant; first, because most of them have more time for investigation than the rushing, hurrying, money-making American, and secondly, the creed of the Catholic Church does not deny the possibility of spirit communion." [46]

Although the Catholic spokesman conceded a spiritual presence at séances in the phenomenon of automatic writing, he attributed such occurrences to the work of the devil. As proof of this charge, he cited a communication in which the Islamic prophet Muhammad was compared with Jesus Christ. Certainly, the outraged writer continued, this blasphemy and

45. *Ibid.*, July, 1858, pp. 195–96; Viatte also mentions the French government's crackdown (Viatte, *Victor Hugo,* 32). Laforgue gave an account of his run-in with the law in a letter to Cahagnet dated September 5, 1852; in the same letter, he also described an emotion-filled visit to his Pau residence on September 1 by four New Orleanians (Alphonse Cahagnet, *Encyclopédie magnetique spiritualiste* [Paris, 1856], 107–108).

46. Ann Braude, *Radical Spirits: Spiritualism and Women's Rights in Nineteenth-Century America* (Boston, 1989), 29–30. For a similar contemporary view of spiritualism's popularity with the city's Catholics, see *Le Spiritualiste,* April, 1857, p. 112.

other unmentionable profanations demonstrated the satanic influence of evil spirits. Biblical prophecy, he reminded his readers, warned of the coming of false prophets and an Antichrist who would perform "*great marvels and astonishing things, to lead into error . . . even the chosen*." He cautioned his fellow Catholics that spiritualist beliefs ran counter to the teachings of the Bible, church instruction, and the example of Catholic saints. Spirit communication resembled practices that fell into the category of divination and sorcery in the Bible—practices that "the law of Moses punished by death, that the Church has always severely condemned, and that the Saints have always held in horror." [47]

In the *Propagateur,* a subsequent editorial ridiculed the movement's "spiritual investigations" into religious matters and equated spiritualists with socialists. Their efforts, the article continued, paralleled the "social investigations" of the socialists who labored "to lay the basis for society after human society has existed for six thousand years, and after Catholic society has operated for eighteen centuries." Spiritual investigations, the piece concluded, "will only lead to foolishness and absurdities; and please to God that they do not lead to calamities and crimes!"[48]

In 1840 in Rome, Catholicism's Congregation of the Inquisition had issued a decree aimed at discouraging mesmerist practices. The church reiterated its position in a subsequent decree in 1847, and in July, 1856, the Congregation prohibited spiritualist practices. Church leaders admonished Catholic bishops to suppress the "evocation of departed spirits and other superstitious practices of spiritism" in order that "the flock of the Lord may be protected against the enemy, the deposit of faith safeguarded, and the faithful preserved from moral corruption." [49]

In New Orleans, spiritualism flourished despite the condemnation of papal authorities, the dire threats of the city's Catholic leaders, and the region's hostile environment. The movement produced two national leaders, New Orleanians Thomas Gales Forster and J. Rollin M. Squire, and two local periodicals: *Le Spiritualiste de la Nouvelle-Orléans* and *Le Salut* (*Salvation*). Both Forster and Squire joined the editorial staff of Boston's

47. *Propagateur Catholique,* October 23, 30, 1852.

48. *Ibid.*, November 13, 1852.

49. M.D. Griffin, "Spiritism," *New Catholic Encyclopedia* (1967), 577.

nationally renowned spiritualist journal, *Banner of Light,* in 1857, then traveled widely as spiritualist lecturers.

Le Spiritualiste made its debut in January, 1857; *Le Salut,* edited by G. F. Simon, a French-speaking white and close friend of the Romantic writer and black Creole medium Joanni Questy, did not appear until after the Civil War. Emboldened by the movement's success, *Le Spiritualiste* editor Joseph Barthet propagated the new religion in the pages of his monthly journal, explaining the main tenets of spiritualism, reporting on experiences of communicants, and publishing spirit communications, news, and articles from spiritualists in the North and in France. The harmonial concepts of Charles Fourier and Andrew Jackson Davis underlay the movement's religious philosophy and worldview.[50]

The spirit communications of Barthet's spiritualist circles dominated the pages of the new publication. In the articles and editorial essays accompanying these messages, Barthet and his colleagues described the nature and purpose of spiritualist beliefs. Societal regeneration, they explained, hinged on mankind's ability to live in harmony with natural laws that govern the universe. The discovery of these principles through spiritual investigation and scientific progress "is our interest, our right, and our duty." While they stressed the importance of scientific inquiry, they emphasized the greater advantages of spiritualist séances: "'Science is the apperception of the harmonies of the universe,' and we understand that human science is far from complete. There is a science superior to official science; the good *mediums* are its ministers and it can be found everywhere. Seek it; study this occult science in order to teach it; enlighten yourselves and enlighten others on the *inflexible* laws which govern the world."[51]

Spirit guides from the upper realms, acting through the agency of spiritualist mediums, would lead mankind toward a future millennium of brotherly love and harmonious human relations. These superior spirits possessed great foresight and recognized "that if we want to bring about Fraternity on Earth, we must look outside of our Capitols, where they endlessly make and unmake injurious laws; outside of our Churches,

50. Braude, *Radical Spirits,* 29–30, 211*n*49; newspaper clipping of Joanni Questy obituary, n.d., Charles B. Roussève Collection, Amistad Research Center, Tulane University.

51. *Le Spiritualiste,* October, 1857, p. 261, August, 1858, p. 197.

where they remain too faithful to old errors and absurd practices!" These spirit teachers were virtuous men "who preached on earth in earlier times, and who are no more *dead* than the truths that they taught." They wanted "to pursue from on high the noble task that they considered imperative.... Their goal is to regenerate humanity by correcting and advancing our knowledge; their language is what we call *Spiritual Manifestations*." In the tradition of the Old and New Testaments, these communications, delivered at séances through spiritualist mediums, would make up a third book of the Christian Bible.[52]

Spiritualists acknowledged that the Hebrew prophet Moses, the Islamic prophet Muhammad, and the religious philosopher Gautama Buddha had possessed knowledge of the creator's transcendent laws; still, they esteemed the doctrines of Jesus Christ as the foremost expression of these precepts. Spiritualism, a synonym for Christianity, sought to restore Christ's ideals to their original purity. Down through the ages established religion had distorted his doctrines: "Spiritualism ... is the same doctrine as Christ's, whereas the precept of Rome is nothing more than the selfish design of the Pharisees who crucified the reformer and grotesquely cloaked themselves later in the garb of Christians in order to suppress the truth and to restore the world to another kind of idolatry [the idolatry of man]."

This deception had promoted ignorance, prejudice, and most of the other evils that afflict humanity: "From infancy they deceive us; they pervert our judgement; they inculcate prejudices that most of us maintain all of our lives and, owing to our ignorance, that lead to most of the evils which afflict us. It will be otherwise when we take more care to enlighten our reason in order that we may be guided by it."[53]

The severity of *Le Spiritualiste*'s attacks upon the church shocked many Catholic readers. In Canada, an outraged Catholic priest seized two issues of the journal from one of his parishioners and burned them. A transatlantic correspondent attributed the publication's poor circulation in France to the anti-Catholic extremism of the spirit communications. "We can do nothing about that," Barthet replied, "the spirits have often told us

52. *Ibid.*, January, February, 1857, pp. 3–4, 30.

53. *Ibid.*, June, October, 1857, pp. 149–50, 261–64, January, 1857, p. 3.

that they see much further than we do and that they know better than us that which mortals require." [54]

In New Orleans, spiritualism's public repudiation of church authority angered Catholic leaders, and tensions mounted as the two religious factions attacked each other in the pages of their respective journals. In May, 1857, when the Abbé Perché made a disparaging reference to women spiritualists, a medium who identified herself as "Marie Bar . . ." penned a stinging rebuttal in which she mimicked Perché: "A woman who thinks . . . what a monstrosity! And who writes what she thinks—what shamelessness! A woman who dares occupy herself with God, with his grandeur, with his goodness, with his essence, with his mercy, with his works, for shame! This is degrading I tell you! Go, Madame, go mend your stockings, make your preserves, beat your Negresses, tattle on your neighbors, and say your rosary. That is what is appropriate to a woman, that is what makes 'the glory of our population,' that is what will earn for you our favour in this world and paradise in the other." [55]

Spirit communications from bygone figures of French history—Catholic reformers of the French Reformation and leaders of the Enlightenment and the age of democratic revolution—dominated the pages of *Le Spiritualiste*. In an attempt to counteract spiritualism's idealization of France's dissident past, the Abbé Perché related his own version of French history in a series of articles entitled "On Liberty"; these began in the fall of 1857 and appeared in *Le Propagateur* for nearly a year. In the wake of the Protestant Reformation, the abbé explained, subversive elements in France nurtured the spirit of revolt during the era of the Catholic Reformation. Conditions worsened at the time of the Enlightenment "when Voltaire appeared, surrounded by an arrogant and foul mob of philosophes." Under the influence of these free thinkers, notions of independence and revolt proliferated. Their advocacy of freedom of thought paved the way for "decadence and ruin."

In the "terrible explosion" of the French Revolution, "the churches were closed, devastated, stripped of everything they possessed, and mutilated when they were not demolished" in the name of liberty. The

54. *Ibid.*, May, 1858, p. 114, September, 1857, p. 234.

55. *Ibid.*, May, 1857, p. 145. "Marie Bar" was undoubtedly Marie Barthet, wife of spiritualist leader Joseph Barthet.

revolutionaries' rallying cry of fraternity was as lethal as their ideal of liberty. They "had taken for a motto: fraternity or death. They should have said: fraternity is death. For, their fraternity was that of Cain." As for equality, "it was equality in servitude and misery," an equality obtained by the "equalizing level of the revolutionary guillotine."

The large numbers of "demagogues, anarchists, radicals, communists, socialists," and other present-day revolutionaries conspired to resume the agenda of the Terror: "Thus, they work ceaselessly to maintain and to increase in the masses these feelings of independence and insubordination, this hatred of all restraint, this contempt for all authority, which form the basis of the revolutionary spirit; and they succeed only too well in this work of iniquity."[56]

In a subsequent essay in April, 1858, in a thinly veiled attack on *Le Spiritualiste,* Abbé Perché accused the journal of destroying the moral authority of the church and called upon government officials to suppress the publication. Surely, he maintained, local authorities "would not tolerate a journal here which would set itself up with the avowed purpose of preaching abolitionism." In a sharp rebuke, Barthet noted the irony in Perché's comparison, writing that it is certain "a Christian would have chosen another example while discoursing 'On Liberty' [the title of the article]." Barthet scoffed at Perché's allusion to abolitionism, although *Le Spiritualiste*'s enthusiastic endorsement of antislavery writers and their works appeared to confirm the abbé's accusations.[57]

In *Le Spiritualiste,* Barthet openly eulogized the life and works of Andrew Jackson Davis, an avowed opponent of slavery, and Louis Cortambert, an ardent white abolitionist, fellow French emigré, and the radical republican editor of the *Revue de l'ouest* (*Review of the West*) in St. Louis, Missouri. Barthet considered Cortambert a "great writer" and published extracts of his articles on spiritualism and education reform in *Le Spiritualiste*. The French-born author shared Barthet's view of the Catholic Church hierarchy, and he joined in the attack on Perché in the March issue of the *Revue:* "One [Perché] could not be more downrightly, more logically, and, we believe, more sincerely absurd."[58]

56. *Propagateur Catholique,* January 30, 1858.

57. *Ibid*., April 3, 1858; *Le Spiritualiste,* May, 1858, p. 115.

58. *Le Spiritualiste,* September, 1857, p. 233, January, March, May, June, August, 1858, pp. 5–6, 59–61, 115, 167, 199–205, 207.

In its bibliography, *Le Spiritualiste* also recommended works by spiritualist radicals in France, including the Baron du Potet, Alphonse Cahagnet, and Allan Kardec. In July, 1857, Barthet glowingly endorsed Kardec's *Le Livre des esprits* (*Book of Spirits*) published in Paris earlier that year, in which the author condemned slavery, an institution he found inconsistent with natural law: "The human law which consecrates slavery is a law contrary to nature since it likens man to an unreasoning beast and degrades him morally and physically." Except for the question of reincarnation, Barthet found Kardec's philosophy in "perfect accord" with the beliefs of New Orleans spiritualists. Barthet considered *Le Livre des esprits* one of the best books on spiritualism and "more than worth its weight in gold," encouraging his readers to purchase a copy.[59]

If *Le Spiritualiste*'s endorsement of antislavery publications tested the limits of the 1830 state law prohibiting dissemination of seditious reading materials, the presence of an unorthodox interracial religion posed an equally provocative challenge to prevailing racial strictures. Segregationist sanctions notwithstanding, the black Creole medium Valmour assumed a leadership role within the movement as a spiritualist healer and presided over interracial séances at which he "performed many wonderful cures simply by the laying on of hands." Other members of the black Creole community, including Paul Trévigne and Constant Reynès, patronized white mediums and furnished public statements of their experiences. *Le Spiritualiste* published testimonials by Constant Reynès, Louis Courcelle, and François Carlon, black Creoles all, alongside those of their white co-religionists. While spiritualists in New Orleans did not openly attack slavery and other forms of racial oppression, their antiauthoritarian attacks on church and state, their advocacy of self-autonomy as a precondition for individual perfectionism, and their movement's interracial makeup posed a radical challenge to the attitudes, customs, and institutions of the slaveholding South.[60]

During the spring and summer, *Le Spiritualiste* responded angrily to Perché's attacks. Labeling the *Propagateur Catholique* an ultramontane

59. *Ibid.*, January, 1857, p. 27, January, June, August, 1858, pp. 6–7, 166, 223; quotations from Allan Kardec, *Le Livre des esprits* (1857; rpr. Montreal, 1979), 369, and *Le Spiritualiste,* July, 1857, p. 202.

60. *Banner of Light,* April 3, 1858; *Courrier de la Louisiane,* July 1, 1857; *Le Spiritualiste,* May, October, 1858, pp. 137–38, 278.

journal, the spiritualist monthly referred to the series "On Liberty" as the abbé's crusade against those "that he calls 'free thinkers,' 'liberators,' 'Voltairians,' and 'revolutionaries.'" Perché, the paper charged, "in proceeding from absurd assumptions, necessarily arrives at absurd conclusions." The abbé, it continued, "does not like the 'Free Thinkers' that he also calls 'liberators'; he requires Slave Thinkers." *Le Spiritualiste* appealed to its readers to think for themselves and to "take part in the revolution, wholly of peace and of love, that spiritualism is carrying out; make this beacon of salvation glow in the eyes of peoples still deceived, and no longer go to church, unless it be, in the example of Christ, to spread the *good news* and drive from the temple the merchants who prostitute it."[61]

In August, church leaders retaliated. In a public campaign launched from the pulpit, Catholic leaders labeled spiritualists "imbeciles" and complained to the police. They described Valmour's healing feats as "monkeyshines" and accused the medium of practicing "gris-gris." In response, the authorities confronted Valmour and threatened to quash the movement.[62]

Barthet fulminated against the police and "a certain curé whose church is nearly deserted." He dared spiritualism's enemies to suppress the movement—"as if these little despots had the right!" He lamented that Valmour would be forced to confine his activities to private séances, even lashing out at the medium's followers; in their refusal to proclaim Valmour's healing powers, they had failed the spiritualist cause.[63]

The rancorousness of the religious feud and the threat of police action forced the movement underground. In December, *Le Spiritualiste* folded. The paper's most oft cited spirit guide, Pére Ambroise, delivered the final spirit communication, concluding thus: "Finally, we end in wishing the best for all men, without distinction of race or of religion and we make the most fervent plea for the triumph of our principles because we are deeply

61. *Le Spiritualiste,* May, June, 1858, pp. 114, 117, 141.

62. *Ibid.*, September, October, 1858, pp. 225, 279. The term *gris-gris* is a voodoo expression meaning an evil spell; voodoo, an African-American folk religion, appeared in New Orleans in the eighteenth century (Gwendolyn Midlo Hall, "The Formation of Afro-Creole Culture," in *Creole New Orleans,* ed. Hirsch and Logsdon, 85–87).

63. *Le Spiritualiste,* October, 1858, p. 279.

convinced that they alone can achieve and consolidate the work of regeneration that we have undertaken. So be it!"[64]

Even though the demise of *Le Spiritualiste* ended an acrimonious public debate, spiritualism continued to thrive within the Creole community. Because personal revelation produced social regeneration, Barthet and his colleagues viewed spiritualist circles as a powerful means of social reform, and the journal encouraged its readers to make "temples" of their homes. During the 1850s, such circles flourished in private residences. Black Creole mediums Joanni Questy, Nelson Desbrosses, Adolphe Duhart, Octave Rey, Paulin Durel, and Charles Veque participated in such a circle at the home of Henry Louis Rey, their fellow medium.[65]

In 1858, Henry Rey at twenty-seven was a well-educated member of one of the Faubourg Tremé's most prominent families. His father, Barthélemy Rey, had played a leading role in the establishment of the Couvent school, the Sisters of the Holy Family Convent, and St. Augustine's Church. At St. Augustine's, the Rey family held a pew and had financed one of the stained-glass windows. During the 1850s, however, as spiritualism spread through the Creole community, Henry Rey and other members of his family converted to the new religion. Rey described the events that led to his changeover.

He recalled that during his youth his mother, Rose Agnes Rey, a devout Catholic, frequently experienced visions in which her deceased children appeared to her. At the time, Rey dismissed these episodes as flights of imagination. He took a more sympathetic view of his mother's mystical-religious experiences, however, after his father died in 1852. The tragedy plunged the family into a state of emotional and economic distress. Rey's mother compounded the family's difficulties when, encouraged by a

64. The identity of Père Ambroise is unknown; in a historical note, Barthet wrote that Ambroise was born in Tours, France, in 1570 and died there in 1638. Given the chronology, it is possible that Barthet is referring to Dom Ambroise Tarbourier, a Benedictine monk and Catholic reformer of the seventeenth century. See *Le Spiritualiste,* August, 1858, p. 209, December, 1858, p. 327.

65. *Ibid.*, May, 1857, p. 115, March, 1858, pp. 73, 206; *Christian Spiritualist* (New York), May 13, 1854, p. 3; *Banner of Light,* April 3, 1858. For the spirit communications of these mediums, see the Spiritualist Registers, September, 1857–May, 1860, René Grandjean Collection, Earl K. Long Library, University of New Orleans.

priest, J. M. Morisot, she lavished the family's remaining finances on an elaborate Catholic funeral.

The grief over his father's death, anger at the church's role in his mother's extravagance, and his new responsibilities as head of the household triggered a response in Rey similar to his mother's clairvoyance, and he began to experience visions of his deceased father. These mystical occurrences coincided with the emergence of spiritualism in the city, prompting Rey to attend séances. He participated in a number of sessions with the black Creole spiritualist Charles Veque and other friends and relatives, including Jean François Chatry, his sister Josephine's white common-law husband. With the assistance of Chatry, a spiritualist medium and a French emigré, Rey achieved promising results. Yet his success with automatic writing and other physical manifestations frightened him. Though he found such phenomena fascinating, he remained skeptical. Finally, with spiritualism's spread through the Afro-Creole community, a dramatic experience in the spring of 1857 transformed Rey.

In April, Soeur (Sister) Louise, a popular medium and a neighbor, enticed Rey to attend a séance at her home. Under her direction, Rey took a place at the table, picked up a pencil, and laid his hand on a sheet of paper. Suddenly, he later recounted, he felt a large invisible hand seize his own. Under the power of this unseen force, his hand scribbled furiously across the paper. In the background he heard a soft, sweet voice speaking words of great wisdom. When an overwhelming sense of fatigue interrupted his concentration, his father's voice admonished him: "Write under our dictates, you are not tired." The experience confirmed Rey's belief in spiritualism and led him to become a dedicated spiritualist medium.[66]

With his conversion to the new religion, Rey opened his home in the Faubourg Tremé to a spiritualist circle that included his wife and two sisters, Alphonsine and Sylphide, and other prominent members of the Creole community. Rey's wife, a cousin of Henriette Delille and the daughter of Pierre Crocker, belonged to one of the city's most distinguished black Creole families. Nelson Desbrosses was a contributor to *Les Cenelles* and a medium whose healing feats rivaled those of Valmour, his mentor. Rey's

66. Toledano and Christovich, "The Role of Free People of Color," in *Faubourg Tremé,* ed. Christovich and Toledano, 94; see Rey's autobiographical sketch in his spirit communications of October 26, 1859, Spiritualist Registers, Grandjean Collection; see also *ibid.*, November 28, 1858.

brother Octave and his friends Charles Veque and François Estève were community activists.

In accordance with their belief in individual perfectibility, spiritualists advocated education and educational reform as an accompaniment to religious regeneration. Not coincidentally, therefore, Rey's circle of black Creole spiritualists also included prominent members of the Couvent school's teaching staff. Joanni Questy, the noted Romantic writer, was Armand Lanusse's assistant principal at the facility, and spiritualists Adolphe Duhart, Constant Reynès, and Joseph Lavigne were Questy's fellow instructors. While expressing reservations, their colleague Samuel Snaer also visited the circle.[67]

Believing that their communications constituted sacred texts, Rey carefully preserved the group's messages in hardcover books. The transcribed entries generally began with the date of the communication and included the location of the séance, name of the medium, and subject of the message. The spirit guide's name appeared at the end of the essay. Consistent with the spirit messages published in *Le Spiritualiste,* the Creole communications combined an unrelenting attack on orthodox religion with the egalitarian, liberal ideas of representative figures of France's Catholic Reformation, Enlightenment, and age of democratic revolution. Unlike the published correspondences of Barthet's journal, however, the communications of the séance registers contained messages from deceased members of the black Creole community. These spirit manifestations reflected the belief that the spirits of the dead could share their otherworldly intelligence with relatives and friends. Likewise, the registers contained a large number of correspondences from Antonio de Sedella, revealing the depth of the former church leader's influence among Creoles, even though Père Antoine's communications did not appear in *Le Spiritualiste,* Barthet, who generally considered all clergy as the "most persistent enemy of progress," described him as an "excellent man" and "a courageous and praiseworthy Capuchin." [68]

67. Spiritualist Registers, October, 1859; Toledano and Christovich, "The Role of Free People of Color," in *Faubourg Tremé,* ed. Christovich and Toledano, 87, 99; Desdunes, *Our People,* 52–53. For *Le Spiritualiste*'s advocacy of educational reform, see the August, 1858, issue, pp. 197–206; Christian, "A Black History," Chap. XIV, 13–15.

68. *Le Spiritualiste,* August, 1858, p. 209; in the registers, Sedella is affectionately referred to as "Père Antoine."

Like Davis, Barthet, and other spiritualists, Rey and his fellow mediums viewed the instructions received in the séances as guidelines to advance human society. In this regard, their communications produced a utopian formula for change based on Christian humanitarianism, universal brotherhood, and political republicanism. In November, 1857, a spirit communication attributed to Bernardin de Saint-Pierre, an Enlightenment intellectual whose works influenced Charles Fourier, admonished the prosperous to share their wealth with the less fortunate and described spiritualism as the "only way to create a new world order and begin a '*New Era* for humanity' in which all will be brothers and sisters and form a single family. . . . Selfishness will make way for Love of the Public Welfare; all will be Peace Harmony, Progress." [69]

The spiritualist engaged in neither the "vain and insipidly superficial practices of a Catholic nor in the bigotry of a Puritan," another spirit intoned. Rather, he exercised "a *reproachless conduct* full of charity towards his brothers and sisters and love for God and his fellow beings. He is truly a Christian and not a feigned one; which is to say, he follows the moral precepts of Jesus."

In other communications, the spirits of the Creole séances assured their listeners of mankind's advancement toward spiritualist ideals: "Everything in life progresses; the spirit rises, see the enormity of what we have done since Jesus." In keeping with spiritualism's view of technological advances as a key factor in humanity's social regeneration, the spirit messages glorified the discovery of the printing press, the steam engine, and the telegraph. These inventions had facilitated a freer flow of information and goods and had contributed to humanity's intellectual and material progress.

The communications pointed to events in Europe as evidence of advances in the political realm. The messages recalled the most radical phase of the French Revolution, when republican leaders proclaimed universal male suffrage and the abolition of slavery: "The Revolution of 93 contributed a great deal to human progress despite the grave mistakes of its leaders." In contemporary Europe, the correspondence continued, Italian

69. For Bernardin de Saint-Pierre's influence on Fourier, see Beecher, *Charles Fourier,* 70, 342–43, 346; Spiritualist Registers, November, 1857.

patriots nurtured the revolutionary cause while Russia "substantiates the social pace by the emancipation of its serfs." France, "more intelligent, more advanced in its progress, has long ago abolished these unjust laws."

The spirit messages gloried in the republican ideal. One transcription showered praise on Guiseppe Garibaldi, the leader of republican forces in Italy, for his unsparing devotion to the revolutionary cause: "Garibaldi! great hero, the new Washington, you only fight for your country and not for self-aggrandizement." And though the message ascribed divisions within the republican ranks to the egotism of the "great men of the Republican party, Lamartine, Hugo, Mazzini, and all the others," it nonetheless praised them as "ardent patriots of the Universal Republic. . . . Children, always be Republicans." [70]

Roman Catholicism, an ally of Europe's monarchical regimes and the religion "in least harmony with the laws of nature," posed the greatest impediment to social regeneration. The institutional church was the "gnawing ulcer which obstructs the progression of society." The entry warned: "Your turn is coming, like Charles X and Louis Philippe, your collapse will be heavy, the edifice will collapse and crush you under its debris." [71]

A subsequent communication inspired by Père Antoine and delivered by Rey sustained the condemnation of the church. Titled "The Ignorance of Men," the essay repudiated orthodox religion and affirmed the righteousness of spiritualist beliefs. The deity of orthodox religion, a manifestation of human egotism and ambition, was an "unjust and cruel being." Only spiritualism, the communication concluded, could reveal God's true nature. Apparently even from the grave, Père Antoine fomented schism and rebellion among French-speaking Catholics.[72]

Another communication, by the medium Paulin Durel, addressed more immediate concerns. In an allusion to plaçage, a spirit message ascribed to Denis Affre, the radical republican archbishop of Paris who was killed during the 1848 revolution, encouraged correct behavior in sexual relations

70. Spiritualist Registers, February, 1858; December 6, 1858; December 30, 1859, February 5, 1860.

71. *Ibid.*, November 28, December 6, 1858. The monarchy of Charles X of France (1824–30) collapsed in the July Revolution. French King Louis-Philippe (1830–48) was overthrown in the February Revolution of 1848.

72. *Ibid.*, November 25, 1858.

as a prerequisite to spiritual progress. The essay advised women to shun the material luxuries and fleeting pleasures of illicit relationships. A marriage based on natural law and spiritual love produced conjugal bliss, family stability, and harmonious human relations—the crucial preconditions for realizing the spiritualist ideals of "love, peace, and universal brotherhood."[73]

The spirit messages produced by Creole séances also contained a stinging critique of contemporary society. A number of Rey's communications noted the contradictions between existing realities and the Christian ideal of brotherhood. In a séance in November, 1858, at the home of spiritualist J. Martino, Rey produced a communication explaining that the phrase "Our Father," which was synonymous with the concept of God, proved "that we all flow from the same source, that we are the children of the same father." Why, then, the communication continued, "these distinctions which exist among us? Why this thirst for domination over your brothers? Why the selfishness with which you repulse them [your brothers] in their pain, in their afflictions, in their needs? Why still these contradictions among you?"

In a séance at Adolphe Duhart's home the following month, Rey's spirit guides resumed their attack on social injustice: "By what rights, Oh men, do you dominate your brother? By what rights do you chain him? . . . Each man in his sphere wants to dominate and yet he admits that God has created us all equal. . . . Oh! mankind when will you cease to be blind to the point of misapprehending that God created the sun for everyone and that his vast creation was made to satisfy the needs of all."

Finally, on May 1, 1860, Rey recorded his last and most prophetic communication before the outbreak of the Civil War. The spirit consoled Rey and his fellow spiritualists: "God sees with pain the calamities which you must endure, He thinks also of the injustices committed by those who dominate the unfortunate classes and who will soon know the sufferings that they [the unfortunate] are forced to endure."[74]

Denied access to traditional avenues of communication and political empowerment, Creole leaders employed nontraditional modes of expression to voice their discontent and affirm their aspirations. They seized

73. *Ibid.*, October, 1858.

74. *Ibid.*, November 19, December 19, 1858; May 1, 1860.

upon spiritualism's universal and immutable principles to repudiate the established order. Having derived ideological inspiration from sustained upheaval in France and the French Caribbean and imbued with a messianic religious zeal, they stood poised to pursue their social and political objectives. In the cataclysm of the Civil War, they anticipated the realization of their ideals.

7

War, Reconstruction, and the Politics of Radicalism

On February 6, 1860, in Port-au-Prince, Haiti, Eugène Heurtelou, a leading Haitian journalist and the republican editor of *Le Progrès,* addressed a letter to France's renowned Romantic writer Victor Hugo. Heurtelou thanked Hugo for his appeal to the United States government on behalf of John Brown. Brown's insurrectionary attack on Harpers Ferry and his arrest had evoked an outpouring of public sympathy in Haiti. After Brown's execution in December, 1859, Haiti's new president, Fabre-Nicolas Geffrard, ordered flags flown at half-mast. Haitians draped their homes in black, and over three thousand mourners, including the presidential family, crowded into the National Chapel for commemorative services.[1]

Though a stranger to Hugo, Heurtelou greeted the exiled French writer as his "Fellow-citizen and Brother." He thanked him for his efforts on behalf of Brown and predicted the demise of slavery and all forms of political repression: "We are on the eve of a great social revival; everything announces it and discerning minds have a presentiment of it. Everywhere, an unseen work is underway, eroding, demolishing, one by one, the ideas, the beliefs which still sustain aristocracies of every kind. On the horizon of each people, three stars gleam . . . *Liberté, Egalité, Fraternité.*" The idea of unity, the writer continued, distinguished nineteenth-century thought: "The fusion of peoples and of races through fraternity, their union in a great and universal republic . . . is this not the pass-word, the rallying cry that thinkers who embody the spirit of their country communicate to one another from one end of the world to the other!"

1. Evans, *Social Romanticism,* 36; Maurois, *Olympio,* 343; Benjamin Quarles, *Allies for Freedom: Blacks and John Brown* (New York, 1974), 146.

Deeply moved by Heurtelou's stirring words, Hugo responded with equal emotion: "We are brothers! It is for this truth that John Brown is dead. It is for this truth that I struggle." He continued: "I love your country, your race, your liberty, your revolution, your republic. . . . [Haiti] serves as a great example: it has crushed despotism. It will help us to destroy slavery! Henceforth, servitude in every form will disappear." In the United States, the execution of Brown sealed the fate of the nation: "From today the American Union may be considered dissolved. . . . Between the North and the South there is the gibbet of Brown. Solidarity is no longer possible." Within a year of their prophetic exchange, Heurtelou and Hugo witnessed the onset of the American Civil War.[2]

In New Orleans, Afro-Creole leaders savored the letters. With the Federal takeover of the city in the spring of 1862, they rallied to the Union cause. In September, they launched a French-language newspaper, *L'Union,* and in a show of solidarity with Heurtelou and Hugo, they featured the correspondence on the front page of the paper's premier issue. Indeed, the radical views of the two writers resonated in the pages of the new journal as contributors defined their antislavery/republican stance.

Along with the letters, *L'Union* published a front-page condemnation of slavery. The editorial essay, entitled "Slavery," blasted the slaveholding South. In Louisiana, the article explained, retrograde laws had favored the growth of slavery. These laws, "which prohibited the slave from cultivating his intelligence and which finally robbed him of all hope of freedom," had virtually banished the bondsman "from the human family and, making property of him, reduced him to the level of a farm animal."

The nation's founders, the writer continued, recognized the contradictions between human bondage and democratic institutions. At the time of the Constitutional Convention, they attempted to discourage slavery's spread by providing for suppression of the slave trade. After 1808, however, slavery's rapid expansion engulfed all efforts to bring about its gradual demise. Creoles of color, imbued like the founding fathers "with the republican ideal," had favored the peaceable extinction of slavery. But "the wisdom of our men of State, of our fathers, and of ourselves, had come to grief against the enormous and uninterrupted growth of this cursed demon."

2. *L'Union,* September 27, 1862.

As planter dominance mounted in the South, "hatred for kings, princes or potentates, the horror of tyranny, equal rights before the law, freedom of conscience, freedom of the press, all of these things were necessarily trampled underfoot and spat upon by the slaveholding power of this country." To safeguard its control, the South's slaveholding authority "showed an excessive severity wherever it exercised its control, inflicting on all those who opposed it punishments of all kinds—banishment, degradation, forced labor, the death penalty—it even extended its arm into the free States."

With the ultimate aims of seizing control of the nation, reestablishing the African slave trade, and extending slavery into foreign territories, the South rose up against the Federal government. But the Rebels had miscalculated: "The truth can be concealed for a time and trampled underfoot but it must be redeemed." The paper confidently predicted the South's defeat and the destruction of slavery, as well as the dawning of a new age when the United States "will represent a noble and eminent civilization which perhaps will announce the approaching reign of the social harmony towards which generous souls naturally tend and whose sweetness the human species must one day taste." [3]

Far from content with the abolition of slavery, Creole editors demanded equal rights for free blacks. Paul Trévigne, *L'Union*'s editor in chief and a language teacher at the Institution Catholique des Orphelins Indigents, summed up their arguments in a subsequent issue. In his editorial, "On Slavery and Caste Prejudice," Trévigne traced the origins of race prejudice to slavery. After stigmatizing an entire race with the taint of bondage, the apologists of slavery insisted upon the racial inferiority of all persons of African descent; following this line of reasoning, they had deprived men of color of their civil rights. Trévigne noted the irony in these developments: "What! you deprive men of color of any participation in the benefits of a democratic and *free* government under the futile pretext that they are descended from a race that your laws have degraded?" Pointing to the accomplishments of Alexandre Dumas, Victor Séjour, and other men of renown, he repudiated the charge of racial inferiority. Then taking his argument to the doorstep of the White House, Trévigne challenged presidential policy.[4]

3. *Ibid.*

4. Roussève, *The Negro in Louisiana,* 118–19; *L'Union,* October 25, 1862.

In December, 1861, Abraham Lincoln had urged Congress to appropriate funds for the voluntary deportation of free blacks and liberated slaves. The following August, in a highly publicized discourse before a five-member, free black delegation from the District of Columbia, the president put forward a plan to resettle African Americans in Chiriqui, a province in present-day Panama. In attempting to persuade free blacks to emigrate to Central America, Lincoln insisted upon the intractability of race prejudice and the necessity for the complete separation of the races: "There is an unwillingness on the part of our people [whites], harsh as it may be, for you free colored people to remain with us. . . . It is better for us both, therefore, to be separated."[5]

Trévigne refuted the president's contention that race prejudice posed an insurmountable obstacle to black aspirations. True, Trévigne conceded, blacks had never enjoyed equal rights in the United States. In the South, the "politics of extinction" had proceeded to the extent, he sardonically exclaimed, that southern legislatures had adopted laws "which permit a free born man to choose a master!" Yet events in France and the French Caribbean demonstrated the possibility of racial reconciliation.

In the wake of the Second Republic's emancipation and enfranchisement decrees, whites and people of color in the French Antilles had resolved their differences. Trévigne challenged the notion that the new racial order infringed upon the status of whites or that the presence of men of color in France's National Assembly had lessened the prestige of the French nation. Nor had racial egalitarianism diminished the stature of Victor Hugo, France's "inspired apostle of universal liberty." He called attention to Hugo's letter to Heurtelou and disputed the idea that Hugo's reputation had been compromised by calling a black man his brother.[6]

François Boisdoré, another prominent Afro-Creole leader, also pointed to events in France and the French Antilles and repeated demands for emancipation and racial equality, while denouncing Lincoln's colonization

5. For Lincoln's colonization project, see Benjamin Quarles, *Lincoln and the Negro* (New York, 1962), 108–23, and James M. McPherson, *The Negro's Civil War: How American Negroes Felt and Acted During the War for the Union* (1965; rpr. Urbana, 1982), 89–97. Roy P. Basler, ed., *The Collected Works of Abraham Lincoln* (New Brunswick, N.J., 1953), V, 372.

6. *L'Union,* October 25, 1862.

project. Opening his essay with a quotation from Lamartine's poem "Liberty," Boisdoré, a renowned Creole orator, issued a stirring appeal: "Brothers! the hour strikes for us; a new sun, like the one of 89, must soon appear on our horizon: Let the cry which electrified France in the taking of the Bastille, resound today in our ears." He urged his compatriots to follow the example of the Antillean abolitionist Cyril Bissette: "Rise up brothers, rise up. . . . Preach to our compatriots that they must follow the path that Bissette has laid out for us, this apostle of liberty in the French colonies." [7]

Noting the presence of black representatives in the French Constituent Assembly of 1848, Boisdoré attacked Lincoln's colonization project:

> Cast a backward glance on the French Chamber in 48, while this noble France was a Republic: we see there these monumental geniuses, Dupont de l'Eure, Victor Hugo, Lamartine, Lamennais, and others . . . seated on the same bench, alongside Pory-Papy, Mazaline, Charles Dain, Louisy Mathieu, Périnen, and other celebrated negroes and mulattoes, also representing their native country! . . . Ah! France in proclaiming the liberty of blacks, has not sought to expatriate them, to colonize them in Chiriqui: they have wanted to make them men and fellow citizens that it has the honor of possessing. . . . Nations of America! whatever may be your systems of government in the name of Christianity copy your fundamental principles from those of France and, like it, you will arrive at the apogee of civilization!

Like Trévigne, Boisdoré assailed the notion of black inferiority, then launched into a more pointed attack on caste prejudice: "Compatriots! the era in which we live boldly exhorts us to combine all our efforts for the cause of liberty, union, and justice" and to "unhesitatingly expel from our hearts all caste hatred as the gardener skillfully uproots . . . from his garden the tree whose fruit is a deepgoing poison." In the name of God, he continued, demand "that wise legislators replace iniquitous laws . . . with laws established for the good of all . . . that they fight the insane prejudices of caste; and that each, according to his talents, his learning, his virtues, his morals, may be able to seek respect; that one may be protected from these persecutions, from these unprecedented, savage outrages unworthy of a civilized people." [8]

7. *L'Union,* October 18, 1862.
8. *Ibid.*

As their radical agenda for restructuring American society demonstrated, Trévigne, Boisdoré, and other Afro-Creole intellectuals had carefully kept abreast of events in France and the French Antilles. Their awareness of the repercussions of the February Revolution was sharpened by colleagues with firsthand knowledge of developments in Europe and the Caribbean. The perspective of these colleagues reinforced *L'Union*'s radical bent.

Not long after the paper's debut, Trévigne and his associates confirmed its bold outlook by inviting Jean-Charles Houzeau, a white Belgian journalist, scientist, and utopian socialist, to join *L'Union*'s staff. Houzeau, "an ardent apostle of 1848," had been dismissed from his post at the Belgium Royal Observatory in 1849 for his role in a Fourierist secret society. During scientific field studies in Texas in the late 1850s, Houzeau became involved in the antislavery underground. In January, 1863, he fled to New Orleans after Confederate authorities discovered his involvement in rescuing a Unionist prisoner.[9]

The radical group centered at the newspaper's offices immediately impressed Houzeau with the depth of their convictions. He "liked to spend time with these pariahs of the proslavery society." Conceiving of their cause as another chapter in "the great universal fight of the oppressed of all colors and nations," he joined their struggle.

In describing his early experiences at *L'Union,* the Belgian journalist hesitated to single out any one of his associates for praise: "Hearts were so well disposed, intentions so solidly fixed, and nearly everywhere such generous devotion to the cause, that it would be unjust to separate a few of them from the group that surrounded and fortified them." Nonetheless, he named some of the paper's staunchest supporters, including Blanc F. Joubert, John Racquet Clay, Joseph Tinchant, Francis E. Dumas, and Dr. Louis Charles Roudanez. These "educated men," he later wrote, "whose intelligence had been developed not only by study but by travel and knowledge of foreign countries, shuddered at the thought of themselves being rejected and scorned." They refused to accept an inferior status in their native land.[10]

9. Houzeau, *My Passage,* 5–11, 18; Alfred Lemonnier, *Notice biographique sur Jean-Charles Houzeau* (Mons, Belgium, 1889), 12.

10. Houzeau, *My Passage,* 75, 73.

Tinchant, who "spoke with the fire of a tribune," had been educated in France. He and Dumas became active agents of liberation in the Union army. In midsummer, 1863, when Rebel forces threatened to attack the city, Tinchant, a successful merchant, closed his business and raised an entire regiment of black Creole soldiers within two days. Convinced, however, by the race prejudice he encountered in the Union army that "the man of color has no rights that a white is bound to respect," he emigrated to Mexico before the end of the war.[11]

Dumas had "imbibed his Republicanism and principles of the equality of men" in France, where he was born, raised, and educated. Before the war, he returned to New Orleans to help manage a family clothing store. When General Benjamin F. Butler invited free blacks to enlist in August, 1862, Dumas, one of the wealthiest free black Creoles in the state, joined the Union army.[12]

Like Tinchant and Dumas, another of *L'Union*'s supporters, Dr. Louis Charles Roudanez, had spent considerable time in France. The son of a wealthy French planter and a free woman of color, Roudanez attended the Faculté de Médecine de Paris, where he came under the influence of the faculty's most renowned proponents of French republicanism. Roudanez and his classmates took to the barricades in the 1848 revolution; after his return to New Orleans in the 1850s, the doctor established a flourishing medical practice.[13]

In New York, the antislavery *Messager Franco-Américain* welcomed *L'Union* into the ranks of the nation's handful of radical French-language newspapers. Pointing to the dangers of taking an antislavery stand in one of the slaveholding South's major cities, the northern journal commended *L'Union* for its courage. The *Messager* endorsed the black Creole contention that human bondage contradicted the nation's founding principles and that slavery's survival was incompatible with the preservation of the Union. Following this line of reasoning, the *Messager* agreed with the free black demand for equal citizenship: "Democracy, taken in the

11. *Ibid.*, 73; New Orleans *Tribune,* August 25, 1864.

12. Logsdon and Bell, "The Americanization of Black New Orleans," in *Creole New Orleans,* ed. Hirsch and Logsdon, 221; Houzeau, *My Passage,* 48; Christian, "A Black History," Chap. XVI, 29.

13. Houzeau, *My Passage,* 27–29; New Orleans *Crusader,* March 22, 1890.

true meaning of the word, implies the civil equality of the races and national unity."[14]

Horace Greeley's New York *Tribune* joined the *Messager* in hailing *L'Union*'s appearance. The *Tribune* praised the paper for its abolitionist stance and noted the publication of the Heurtelou/Hugo exchange in its first issue. That the free black journal had succeeded in publishing the views of an internationally acclaimed opponent of slavery in a major southern city astonished the northern newspaper. Both the *Tribune* and the *Messager* expressed solidarity with *L'Union* and praised the paper's call to arms. In New Orleans, the paper's readers rallied to the Union war effort.[15]

In 1860, the city's 10,939 free blacks had represented approximately 6 percent of an urban population of 144,601 whites and 14,484 slaves. Free people of color were in a distinct minority, and confronted with threats of violence, expulsion, and confiscation in the secession crisis, they mobilized to safeguard their community. In the spring of 1861, Afro-Creole leaders volunteered their services to Confederate officials in a defensive action. By November, the state's Confederate governor, Thomas O. Moore, had enrolled fifteen hundred free black soldiers in the 1st Native Guards, Louisiana Militia, Confederate States of America. Rebel authorities refrained, however, from assigning the men arms and uniforms and confined their activities to company drills.

Early in 1862, the Native Guards confirmed Rebel fears of their allegiance. In January, Confederate authorities noted a high rate of absenteeism within the free black militia, and when David G. Farragut's naval bombardment forced the Confederates to withdraw from New Orleans in April, the Native Guards refused to leave. Shortly after the occupation of the city, black Creole leaders sent a four-man delegation composed of Henry and Octave Rey, Edgar Davis, and Eugène Rapp to meet with the commanding officer of the Union army, General Benjamin F. Butler. The four Native Guard officers, the chosen representatives of the free black militia, proffered their arms and their services to the Union general. Through an interpreter, St. Albain Sauvinet, they assured Butler that "their people could not have any other feelings except those of perfect loyalty to the Federal cause." In the absence of a Federal policy, Butler

14. *Messager Franco-Américain,* cited in *L'Union,* December 6, 1862.

15. New York *Tribune,* cited *ibid.*

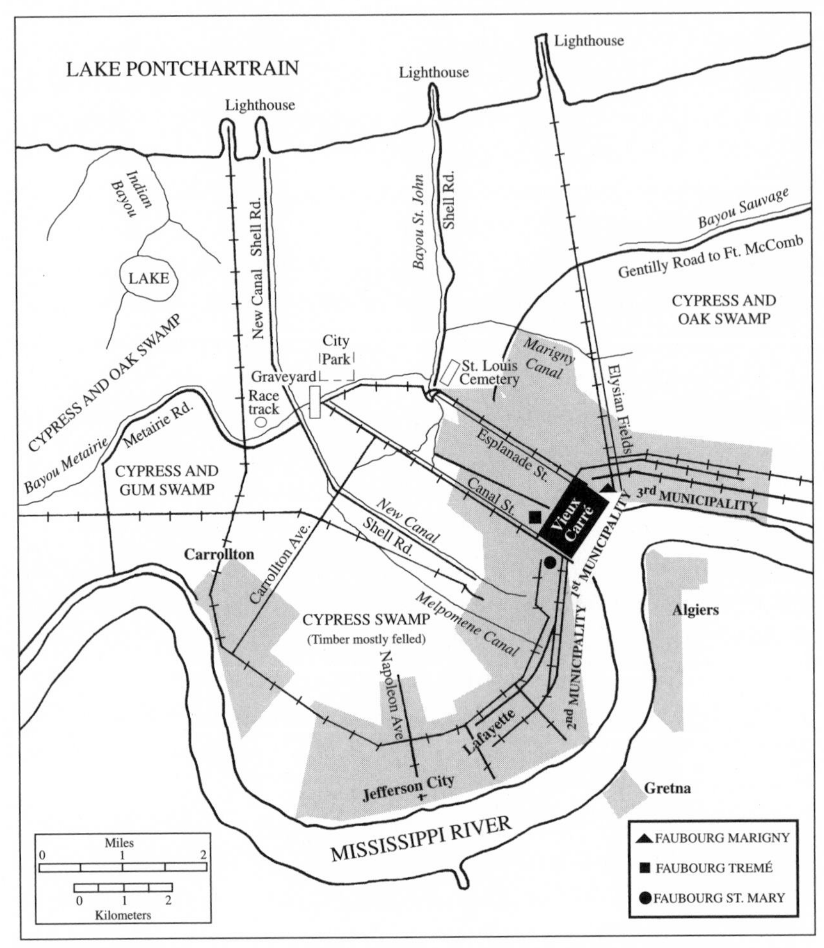

LAKE PONTCHARTRAIN
Lighthouse
Lighthouse
Lighthouse
Indian Bayou
LAKE
New Canal
Shell Rd.
Bayou St. John
Shell Rd.
Bayou Sauvage
Gentilly Road to Ft. McComb
CYPRESS AND OAK SWAMP
CYPRESS AND OAK SWAMP
City Park
Graveyard
Race track
St. Louis Cemetery
Marigny Canal
Elysian Fields
Bayou Metairie
Metairie Rd.
CYPRESS AND GUM SWAMP
Esplanade St.
Canal St.
Vieux Carré
3rd MUNICIPALITY
1st MUNICIPALITY
Carrollton
Carrollton Ave.
New Canal
Shell Rd.
Melpomene Canal
CYPRESS SWAMP
(Timber mostly felled)
Napoleon Ave
Lafayette
2nd MUNICIPALITY
Algiers
Jefferson City
Gretna
MISSISSIPPI RIVER
Miles
0
1
2
0
1
2
Kilometers
FAUBOURG MARIGNY
FAUBOURG TREMÉ
FAUBOURG ST. MARY

New Orleans in 1863

declined their offer. Still, the interview allayed the general's fears. Though pro-Confederate newspapers had convinced him of the regiment's secessionist loyalties, his meeting with the officers of the Native Guards led the general to reassess his first impression. In a letter of May 25, Butler mentioned his change of mind to Secretary of War Edwin M. Stanton: "We have heard much in the newspapers of the free-negro corps of this city organized for the defense of the South. From this a very erroneous idea may have been derived." [16]

By the end of the summer of 1862, military necessities as well as the urgency of Creole requests to enlist in the Union army prompted Butler to authorize the induction of free black recruits. In August, as the general prepared for the official induction of free black soldiers, he asked officers of the Native Guards why they had volunteered for the Confederate army. They replied that they "were ordered out and dared not refuse, for those who did so were killed and their property confiscated." Not long afterward, Captain Henry Rey, a newly enlisted Union officer, backed up their assertions when he responded to white ridicule of the 1st Native Guards. In a letter to *L'Union*'s editor, Rey recounted how Rebel leaders threatened the men and their families. "Quickly, organize into companies," Rey recalled them saying, "otherwise you and your children are done for." Another Unionist who had formerly served in Louisiana's Confederate militia, the radical white Fourierist Thomas Jefferson Durant, supported the claims of the free black soldiers. All those who resisted Rebel authority, he explained to General Butler, did so at the "peril of their lives." [17]

On the basis of pro-Confederate newspaper reports and the seemingly voluntary organization of the free black regiment, later historians have tended to portray the Native Guards as self-serving opportunists who

16. For population figures, see table in Chap. 3; Howard C. Westwood, "Benjamin Butler's Enlistment of Black Troops in New Orleans in 1862," *Louisiana History,* XXVI (Winter, 1985), 13; Mary F. Berry, "Negro Troops in Blue and Gray: The Louisiana Native Guards, 1861–1863," *Louisiana History,* VIII (Spring, 1967), 167–69; quotations from Desdunes, *Our People,* 119, and Benjamin F. Butler to Edwin M. Stanton, May 25, 1862, in *The War of the Rebellion: A Compilation of the Official Records of the Union and Confederate Armies* (Washington, D.C., 1880–1901), Ser. I, Vol. 15, p. 442.

17. Berry, "Negro Troops," 172; *L'Union,* October 18, 1862; Tregle, "Thomas J. Durant," 494*n*34.

sided with the Confederacy until the Union occupation of the city, when they shifted their allegiance to the Federals. Apart from overlooking the historical origins of Creole dissent, this view ignores a considerable body of firsthand testimony. Still, fear of retribution was not the only factor in the decision of black Creoles to enlist in the Rebel military. In some instances, Native Guards attributed their enlistment to fear of an invading army and ethnic pride. One former Native Guard touched on these reasons: "Driven by the noble feeling which impels every man to defend his native country when threatened with invasion, urged on by the desire to protect their families that they believed were in danger, fearing the coming of men from the North that southern newspapers compared every day to the furious hurricane which destroys in its rage the abode of the innocent as well as the guilty, men of color of this city organized . . . a regiment with the name of 'Native Guards.'"[18]

Armand Lanusse, head of the Ecole des Orphelins, expressed similar sentiments. In a letter to *L'Union*'s editor in October, 1862, Lanusse regretted taking up arms against his fellow Louisianians "because of an attachment to the native earth and because of past memories." Yet, he continued, the Afro-Creole community would be "foolish . . . to offer our cooperation . . . to the preservation of a prejudice which, praise be to God, disappears each day from every civilized country of the earth." As the tes-

18. For the view of black Creole soldiers as a self-seeking elite, see Donald E. Everett, "Ben Butler and the Louisiana Native Guards, 1861–1862," *Journal of Southern History,* XXIV (May, 1958), 202–204; Berry, "Negro Troops," 166–67; Tunnell, *Crucible of Reconstruction,* 69–70. For other evidence that Afro-Creole soldiers sided with the Confederacy under duress, see the statement quoted by Benjamin F. Butler in his appearance before the American Freedmen's Inquiry Commission, May 1, 1863, in Manoj K. Joshi and Joseph P. Reidy, "'To Come Forward and Aid in Putting Down This Unholy Rebellion': The Officers of Louisiana's Free Black Native Guard During the Civil War Era," *Southern Studies,* XXI (Fall, 1982), 328 *n*4. In another instance, an anonymous contributor to the New Orleans *Tribune* conceded that free blacks had contributed to the Confederate cause and joined the Rebel army; but, the writer continued, "it is known to all under what pressure of public opinion, under what threats uttered by the promoters of secession, this was done" (*Tribune,* December 7, 1864). For similar accounts, see the wartime remarks of Arnold Bertonneau in James G. Hollandsworth, Jr., *The Louisiana Native Guards: The Black Military Experience During the Civil War* (Baton Rouge, 1995), 3–4, and the congressional testimony of Charles W. Gibbons cited in Robert M. Fogelson and Richard E. Rubenstein, eds., *Mass Violence in America* (New York, 1969), 126.

timony of Lanusse clearly demonstrates, the Afro-Creole community's loyalty to Louisiana should not be interpreted as support for the Confederate cause.[19]

Within two weeks of the general's call to arms on August 22, 1862, Creole soldiers filled a thousand-man regiment. In the Latin European tradition of military recruitment, Francis Dumas, a newly appointed major, enlisted his slaves. He was reported to have assembled the bondsmen and asked if they would fight to "break the bonds of their fellow men." When they said yes, he organized them into an entire company. Near the end of the month, Butler informed General in chief Henry W. Halleck that the "only drawback to two regiments of these Native Guards (colored) is the fear in their minds that the President will not sustain my action—a story, by the by, which is industriously circulated by the rebels here to prevent the enlistment of these loyal citizens."[20]

Under the inspiration of Romanticism and spiritualism, Henry Rey, now an officer of the 1st Native Guards, celebrated his enlistment with a poem entitled "Ignorance." *L'Union* published it the day of his regiment's official mustering into the Union army. The poet portrayed the war as an expiatory necessity:

> It [ignorance] is the evil of Humanity,
> It is the ever-gnawing canker which consumes it,
> That which always controls it,
> And suppresses Liberty. . . .
>
> It was by a decree of Ignorance
> That Jesus, the divine apostle,
> In wanting human progress,
> Suffered an ignoble sentence;
>
> That Joan d'Arc, Socrates and others,
> Christopher Columbus, Swedenborg,
> The apostles of truth
> Were either mocked or put to death!

19. *L'Union,* October 1, 8, 1862.

20. Parton, *General Butler,* 517; *Tribune,* July 2, 1867; Westwood, "Benjamin Butler's Enlistment of Black Troops," 15. For a description of the 1st regiment, see Berry, "Negro Troops," 174–76.

Yes, in the political,
Social or religious world,
As in the artistic world,
Ignorance is enthroned everywhere. . . .

But this enlightened century
Wishes to judge everything at its bar;
And our reason, free and proud,
Now penetrates everywhere.

From its solemn deliberations
Emerges the judgement of truth:
Liberty, universal peace,
Human happiness, fraternity!

What does it matter if the cannon roars,
If on all sides a sepulcher opens:
It is the departure of an evil world,
The dawning of another more beautiful one![21]

The pages of *L'Union* overflowed with words of encouragement and commendation for the newly enlisted soldiers. In one display of patriotic fervor, *L'Union* published a series entitled "The Catechism of the Soldier," in which a catechist instructed a recruit by means of questions and answers. Designed for memorization, like a religious lesson, the exercise taught that the Declaration of Independence had outlawed slavery by declaring that all men were created equal and endowed with inalienable rights. When the instructor posed the question, "What proof have we that the terms of the Declaration of Independence should be applied to Negro slaves as well as to all other individuals?" the soldier replied: "That necessarily results from the term itself; it says: 'all men,' and to permit exceptions would be to deny the precise thought that this language embodies." Pointing to the Declaration again, the catechist asked the soldier to explain how his fight for emancipation could be seen as a fight for his country. "The Declaration affirms," the recruit responded, "that liberty is one of the unalienable rights of all men and that 'it is to assure these rights that governments are established among men'; this is why, in

21. Berry, "Negro Troops," 168; *L'Union,* September 27, 1862.

fighting to assure the liberty of every human being, I defend the cause of my government." Assuring his pupil that the overthrow of slavery and the preservation of the Union were divinely ordained, the catechist concluded the lesson.[22]

Louis Nelson Fouché, a black recruiting agent for the Union army, a business manager for the paper, and, like Rey, an aspiring Romantic writer, summoned the thinker as well as the soldier to the Union cause. In his literary essay "To Work, Laborers of the Future!" Fouché glorified mankind's powers of reason: "Thought! . . . the powerful weapon of the weak against the strong . . . the precious gift of the Divinity! . . . it is under your beneficent auspices that Garibaldi and Victor Hugo, the one with the sword and the other with the pen, have made the benumbed sensibilities of peoples and kings tremble." The writer beckoned to progressive-minded men to hone "your thoughts on the cornerstone of the universal republic" and to "empty into the common urn the products of your humanitarian works."

Mankind stood on the threshold of a new era, for the president of the world's largest republic had "broken the chains of four million slaves, four million men restored to the great human family." With a revolutionary rallying cry, Fouché urged his compatriots forward: "Men of my blood! shake off the contempt with which your oppressors, in their ignorant pride, have ceaselessly covered you. . . . Under the noble folds of the flag of the federation array yourselves. . . . March, live, it is your right . . . it is your duty. . . . Thinkers! to work then! And, tireless laborers, plow in the vast field of the future, the furrow of *Fraternity;* boldly plant there the tree of *Liberty,* whose fruits, gathered by future generations, will be shared in the most perfect *Equality* with the children of the same God." [23]

Black New Orleanians flocked to the training camps daily to watch the soldiers drill, delighting in the afternoon dress parades. Captain Rey encouraged such visits when he invited the editor of *L'Union* to view his regiment at Camp Strong and observe the enthusiasm of the black soldiers. The editor would see "in parade, a thousand white bayonets gleaming in the sun held by black, yellow, or white hands. . . . Be informed that we have no prejudice; that we receive everyone into the camp; but that the

22. *L'Union,* November 1, 1862.

23. *Ibid.*, December 6, 1862.

sight of salesmen of human flesh makes us sick; but, since we know how to behave, though Negroes, we receive them, completely concealing from them the violent internal struggle that their prejudice forces us to wage within ourselves."[24]

While the Creole community rejoiced at the sight of the black soldiers, most whites viewed them with fear and outrage. At the time of Butler's decision to induct the men, the city's largest and most influential daily newspaper, the *Picayune,* editorialized that the proposed plan to enlist black soldiers would "not only bring infamy upon those who so employ a servile and inferior race, against men of their own blood, but it is destined, like all illegitimate and unnatural resorts in war . . . to enure to the injury of the party that invokes such aid in a political struggle between two great sections." In the streets of the city, white crowds jeered and hooted at the men. Even the Catholic clergy joined in the attack.[25]

In 1861, Bishop Jean Marie Odin, head of the city's Catholic Church, and the Abbé Perché, Odin's immediate subordinate and next in line for the bishopric, had sided with the Confederates. Bishop Odin had appealed to the region's priests to serve as chaplains in the Rebel army. In the *Propagateur Catholique,* Perché, an ardent southern nationalist, had fueled secessionist sentiment by depicting abolitionists as fanatical revolutionaries and by portraying Lincoln as an enemy of the South. He described the president's first inaugural address as a "masterpiece of astuteness and hypocrisy filled with contradictions, threats and promises." With the outbreak of hostilities, the Catholic clergy showered praise and blessings on the Rebel soldiers. Contrarily, when the Confederate Native Guards defected to the Union army, conservative priests harassed black Union soldiers and stigmatized the Afro-Creole community.[26]

L'Union reacted furiously to the ostracism. Under the Confederates, the paper charged, when the Native Guards bore arms for the Rebels, the

24. Blassingame, *Black New Orleans,* 40; *L'Union,* October 18, 1862.

25. Everett, "Ben Butler," 209, 214. For further mention of white anger over the enlistment of black soldiers, see letter to the editor from an "Ex-Native Guard," *L'Union,* October 1, 1862.

26. Baudier, *The Catholic Church,* 412–30. Of the eleven Catholic bishops of the Confederate states, only one opposed secession (Aloysius F. Plaisance, "The Catholic Church and the Confederacy," *American Benedictine Review,* XV [June, 1964], 160); quotation from Benjamin J. Blied, *Catholics and the Civil War* (Milwaukee, Wisc., 1945), 71.

churches opened their doors to the soldiers, blessed their flags, and praised them in their sermons calling them the "worthy grandsons of the noble [Joseph] Savary." Now that the soldiers had joined the Union army, the clergy treated them with scandalous contempt: "They spit on them [the soldiers], they close the doors of the temple to them, they freely excommunicate them." In view of such treatment, the paper feared that the church and its Confederate allies "would very gladly carry out now, in an effort to stop them [the soldiers] from taking up arms, the threats which they earlier used to force them to enlist *as volunteers*." [27]

Some of the soldiers' attackers charged that the men would use their military service to demand social equality. While downplaying the highly charged issue of racial integration, *L'Union* insisted that military service entitled the new Union soldiers to political equality. In fact, the paper asserted, recognition of their rights was long overdue. The newly inducted Native Guards, who were almost entirely Creole soldiers, already possessed a legitimate claim to equal citizenship.[28]

Their Haitian ancestors—republican leaders André Rigaud, Louis-Jacques Beauvais, Jean-Baptiste Villate, Jean-Baptiste Mars Belley, and others—the paper proclaimed, had volunteered their services to the American revolutionaries in support of the democratic principles proclaimed in the Declaration of Independence. At Baton Rouge, Mobile, and Pensacola, their Louisiana ancestors had fought on the side of American colonists under Bernardo de Gálvez in the Florida campaigns. In recognition of their distinguished service against the British, First Consul Napoleon Bonaparte provided in Article III of the treaty of cession that all inhabitants of the ceded territory would be received into the United States on terms of complete equality. Again, in the War of 1812 under Andrew Jackson, their forefathers fought valiantly under British fire. Although historians had repeatedly overlooked their ancestral military legacy, this historic birthright entitled the men to equal citizenship. Once again, in fighting with the Union army, Afro-Creole soldiers proposed to assert their claims and obtain their rights. Furthermore, the paper warned, the

27. *L'Union,* December 6, 1862.

28. *L'Union,* October 1, 1862; Roland C. McConnell, "Louisiana's Black Military History, 1729–1865," in *Louisiana's Black Heritage,* ed. MacDonald, Kemp, and Haas, 48.

men had resolved to "protest against all politics which would tend to expatriate them." [29]

In mid-December, 1862, in a change of command that boded ill for the 3,122 officers and men of the three black regiments, General Nathaniel P. Banks replaced Butler as head of the Department of the Gulf. The new commanding officer proposed to win the allegiance of white Louisianians by taking a conciliatory approach to military and civil affairs. Aiming to appease white conservatives, Banks slowed recruitment of black soldiers and reversed Butler's policy of assigning black officers to black regiments.

On the question of recruitment, Banks simply allowed Butler's policy to languish. With the black officers, however, the general moved aggressively. Aware of discontent within their ranks, he acted first against the officers of the 3rd Native Guards. In early February, 1863, he summoned the men to his office and invited them to air their grievances. When they protested their treatment in the military, he advised them to resign.[30]

Stung by Banks's summary dismissal of their charges, the officers resigned en masse. On February 19, in a joint letter of resignation, the men condemned the unrelenting "Scorn and contempt" leveled at them by white soldiers of every rank. Such treatment had "sunk deep Into our hearts. We did not expect It and therefore It is intolerable. We cannot serve a country In which we have no more rights and Privileges given us." General Butler had assured them of equal treatment, and although they had not expected social equality, they "did most certainly expect the Privileges, and respect due to a Soldier who had offered his services and his life to his government." [31]

Ultimately, military necessities forced Banks to reinaugurate Butler's recruitment policy. By the end of the war, with over twenty-four thousand black soldiers enlisting in the Union army, Louisiana furnished more black recruits than any other state in the nation. The contributions of black Louisianians to the Federal war effort notwithstanding, Banks

29. *L'Union,* October 1, 1862.

30. Westwood, "Benjamin Butler's Enlistment of Black Troops," 17–18; McCrary, *Abraham Lincoln,* 110–11, 123; Berry, "Negro Troops," 182, 184; Joshi and Reidy, "To Come Forward," 330.

31. Joshi and Reidy, "To Come Forward," 330.

remained opposed to commissioning black officers. In August, 1863, he complained to Lincoln that the morale of the black regiments had been undermined by "discreditable" officers whose "arrogance and self-assertion" angered white soldiers. Despite sustained pressure from the discharged officers, Banks continued his purge until mid-1864, when he was removed from departmental command. By then he had replaced most of the seventy-five black officers commissioned by Butler.[32]

While Banks orchestrated the officers' removal during the spring of 1863, the men distinguished themselves on the battlefield. In April, several companies of the 2nd Native Guards stationed at Ship Island in the Gulf of Mexico participated in a Union raid on the coastal town of Pascagoula, Mississippi. Union troops advanced into the town until a large company of Confederate cavalrymen attacked the soldiers and forced their withdrawal. The Creole regiment retreated to the waterfront toward the cover of a Union gunboat; at this point, the white crewmen aboard the vessel opened fire on the retreating soldiers instead of shelling the Confederates pursuing them. The vengeful attack stemmed from an incident in which a black sentry had killed some white soldiers at their Ship Island outpost. Major Dumas, perceiving the men's desperate situation, plunged into the fray, wheeled them around, and repulsed the Confederate attack, thereby rescuing the entrapped soldiers.[33]

Omitting mention of the white crewmen's treachery, the regimental commander, N. U. Daniels, praised the soldiers for their valor under fire and singled out Major Dumas and three of his junior officers for special commendation. These men "were constantly in the thickest of the fight, and by their unflinching bravery, and admirable handling of their commands, contributed to the success of the attack, and reflected great honor upon the flag under and for which they so nobly struggled."[34]

32. McCrary, *Abraham Lincoln,* 143; Berry, "Negro Troops," 182; Charles Vincent, "Black Louisianians During the Civil War and Reconstruction: Aspects of Their Struggles and Achievements," in *Louisiana's Black Heritage,* ed. MacDonald, Kemp, and Haas, 88; Joshi and Reidy, "To Come Forward," 333–35; McPherson, *The Negro's Civil War,* 238; quotations from Blassingame, *Black New Orleans,* 44.

33. Christian, "A Black History," Chap. XVI, 14–15; Joseph T. Wilson, *The Black Phalanx* (New York, 1968), 207–11; George W. Williams, *A History of the Negro Troops in the War of Rebellion, 1861–1865* (New York, 1888), 221–23.

34. Wilson, *The Black Phalanx*, 176, 211.

In the Union assault on Port Hudson, a Confederate stronghold twenty miles north of Baton Rouge on the Mississippi River, Captain André Cailloux achieved legendary renown. A highly skilled equestrian and marksman who boasted of the blackness of his skin, Cailloux cut a dashing figure in Creole society. When Butler ordered the recruitment of black soldiers, the well-liked Cailloux quickly raised a company. The general rewarded him and his friend, Henry Rey, with captain's commissions in the 1st Native Guards.

At Port Hudson on May 27, Cailloux' Company E charged Confederate lines repeatedly. During the assault, the Creole officer steadied his men as he moved along the line speaking to them in both French and English. After enemy fire shattered his left arm, he refused to leave the battlefield and led the men forward until, finally, a fatal shot struck him down. Though comrades attempted to recover his body, Confederate sharpshooters prevented the men from removing it until the surrender of the fort six weeks later.[35]

In New Orleans, while the slain captain's body lay exposed on the battlefield, *L'Union* published a literary work entitled "Captain André Cailloux and His Companions in Arms." Signed with the initials "E. H.," the poem lionized the black community's fallen hero:

What! You weep for the brave captain,
Whose valor astonished Port Hudson!
Why, in falling on the open field,
He struck down a vile conjecture.
We console ourselves, we, men of his race,
That before God alone he bent his knee.
Let both Whites and Blacks follow the noble path
Of the brave André Cailloux.

Yes, it was among the cannon-balls, the grapeshot
That this hero of the black brow so proud
Directed his steps, leading in battle,

35. McConnell, "Louisiana's Black Military History," in *Louisiana's Black Heritage,* ed. MacDonald, Kemp, and Haas, 46–53; Steven J. Ochs, "A Patriot, a Priest, and a Prelate: Black Catholic Activism in Civil-War New Orleans," *U.S. Catholic Historian,* XII (Winter, 1994), 53–55; Williams, *A History of the Negro Troops,* 218–19; Desdunes, *Our People,* 124–25; Wilson, *The Black Phalanx,* 176, 214–19.

His black brothers, brave as steel!
It was in the midst of enemy bullets,
Hissing of death, and bearing it everywhere,
That these soldiers, possessed of a thousand lives,
Followed André Cailloux!

God, what ardor! What sublime courage!
Without any help in this bloody battle,
They made the enemy tremble in his rage;
Banks recognized the saviors of the State!!
Six times that day they attempted victory:
A thousand cannons crushed them everywhere.
Those noble dead in the abode of glory!
Always follow Cailloux!

Oh Liberty! Our mother, contemplate
What your children will henceforth be able to do?
Doubt has fled; open your temple to them,
And let the Union bide its time.
Conquered soon the unworthy rebels,
Bloodthirsty men, of your grandeur jealous,
Will disappear, and there will be faithful to you
Over a hundred thousand Cailloux!!![36]

Henry Rey reinforced the image of Cailloux as a martyr-hero through the agency of spiritualism. In a séance following the fall of Port Hudson, the medium transformed his friend's death into an inspiring call to arms. Before the war, Cailloux had made light of spiritualism, but now, Rey related the fallen soldier's conversion in a spirit message. In the medium's communication, the slain Cailloux described his passage into the spiritual realm and assured Rey and the other soldiers: "I have left your world a lover of liberty, fighting for my brothers; I have won the same [liberty] in the spirit world, for God has rewarded me.... I will be with you, dear friends, in the battles, my spirit will be among you to inspire you with a manly courage and an indomitable spirit.... I will be your torch bearer, I will be among those who receive you into our world if you should succumb in the struggle; fight, God demands liberty, our brothers will have it, equality will follow."[37]

36. *L'Union,* July 4, 1863.

37. Spiritualist Registers, July 17, 1863, in Grandjean Collection, UNO.

In a report to Major General H. W. Halleck, Banks praised the black soldiers' performance in the battle: "No troops could be more determined or more daring. They made during the day three charges upon the batteries of the enemy, suffering very heavy losses and holding their position at nightfall with the other troops on the right of our line." Still, Banks remained committed to ousting black officers in the Native Guards. In another apparent concession to white conservatives, he even denied the men permission to emblazon their regimental banners with the Port Hudson battle. In the fall of 1863, Major Dumas and another popular officer, Captain P.B.S. Pinchback, resigned in disgust.[38]

When Cailloux' body was returned to New Orleans after the fall of Port Hudson on July 8, the black community honored its hero with a lavish public funeral. Cailloux' fraternal society, the Friends of the Order, received the body and laid the flower-strewn, flag-draped coffin in state in their large public meeting hall. After religious services, eight soldiers shouldered the casket and carried Cailloux' body through the huge crowd of mourners that had gathered outside. The funeral procession consisted of the 42nd Massachusetts regimental band, two companies of black soldiers of the 6th Louisiana regiment, a large contingent of officers of the Native Guards, about a hundred wounded black soldiers, carriages containing the Cailloux family and a number of army officers, and representatives of thirty-seven black societies. As they escorted the hearse on the way to the Bienville Street cemetery, where the body was interred with military honors, the cortège passed through a throng of mourners that stretched for over a mile on Esplanade Avenue.[39]

A Catholic priest, Claude Paschal Maistre, officiated at Cailloux' funeral. After performing the traditional Catholic rites, Maistre delivered a glowing eulogy of the deceased soldier. The French priest, a committed Unionist who supported Lincoln's Emancipation Proclamation, called upon his listeners to model their actions after those of the courageous Cailloux. Under ordinary circumstances, Father Maistre would have conducted the

38. McConnell, "Louisiana's Black Military History," in *Louisiana's Black Heritage,* ed. MacDonald, Kemp, and Haas, 55; Berry, "Negro Troops," 189; Joshi and Reidy, "To Come Forward," 332.

39. Wilson, *The Black Phalanx,* 214–17; Desdunes, *Our People,* 124–25; Tunnell, *Crucible of Reconstruction,* 71–73.

services and delivered his oration in his parish church, St. Rose of Lima; however, events surrounding the services were anything but ordinary.

At the time of the Federal occupation of the city, General Butler had ordered the closure of churches whose ministers espoused the Confederate cause. Aware of the views of Catholic Church leaders, the general placed Abbé Perché under house arrest and suppressed the *Propagateur Catholique*. It was rumored that Butler was afraid of offending his Irish Catholic troops and thus refrained from arresting Archbishop Odin, but he did place the Catholic leader under surveillance.[40]

Pro-Confederate priests wreaked their vengeance on the Afro-Creole community and its Unionist allies. In St. Mary's Church adjoining the archbishopric, Father Gabriel Chalon, Odin's secretary, introduced a segregated seating arrangement. Infuriated by the priest's insistence on having whites in the front, mulattoes in the middle, and the slaves in the rear, black Creole spiritualist Paul Huard, one of *L'Union*'s contributing writers, reported Chalon's actions in the newspaper. After criticizing the priest for another incident in which he made racist remarks to a mulatto child, Huard extended his criticism to the Church in Rome. He insisted that "the true Church of our dearly beloved Lord Jesus Christ, built by the apostle St. Peter, the Church which flourished in its poverty and its unselfishness and which taught people forgiveness and love of humanity, that is to say the renunciation of oppression, of tyranny, of slavery, of wickedness . . . exists only in name and in memory." Thus, Huard sarcastically concluded, "permit me the liberty . . . of telling you that I do not like the priests of the Roman church, that I do not trust them, and that for a long time this Church ('outside of which there is no salvation') is not my Church."[41]

Other Afro-Creole spokesmen accused members of the clergy of withholding church sacraments from black soldiers. When a delegation of Creole women visited their parish rectory to request a high mass for their men in arms, the priest refused; instead, he cynically volunteered to

40. Ochs, "A Patriot, a Priest, and a Prelate," 49; McCrary, *Abraham Lincoln,* 112; Baudier, *The Catholic Church,* 426, 443; Roger Baudier, "Archbishops Leray and Perche Came Here as Missionaries," New Orleans *Item,* May 5, 1935; Roger Baudier, *Centennial: St. Rose of Lima Parish* (New Orleans, 1957), 20.

41. Baudier, *The Catholic Church,* 402, 412; *L'Union,* May 5, 1863. For Huard's spiritualist views, see *L'Union,* October 18, 1862.

perform funeral services for the soldiers. After this incident, many black Creole Catholics deserted their neighborhood churches and flocked to St. Rose's on the outskirts of the city, where Maistre welcomed them to his congregation.[42]

Pro-Confederate laymen and clerics reacted angrily to Maistre's actions. They accused him of being an abolitionist who preached incendiary sermons to his black congregation. Maistre's enemies threatened to lynch him, and in one instance a priest confided to some of his parishioners that "a rope would be too good for him" and that "his stole [ecclesiastical neckband] would suffice." In an attempt to protect the priest, *L'Union* published these threats and purported to know who had issued them.[43]

While Maistre's fellow clergymen accused him of having "incited the Negroes against the whites," Bishop Odin orchestrated the French priest's removal through official channels. First, the bishop ordered Maistre to cease his abolitionist sermons and his defiance of diocesan rules. Besides advocating emancipation from the pulpit, the refractory priest ignored church regulations requiring separate baptismal and marriage registers for the races. When Maistre ignored Odin's orders and his subsequent reprimands, the bishop suspended the priest and banished him from St. Rose's. Nonetheless, Maistre and his congregation refused to vacate the church. In May, 1863, Odin, backed up by church officials in Rome, ordered St. Rose's closure; the interdiction prohibited Catholics from attending services under the threat of excommunication. In a pastoral letter read to all parishioners of the diocese, Odin condemned the "profanations" committed by the schismatics. Still, Maistre and his black parishioners defied the bishop.[44]

Finally, despite the rough treatment of church leaders at the time of Federal occupation, Odin turned to Union authorities to have Maistre forcibly ousted. Banks, who had replaced Butler in December, 1863, agreed. Hoping to conciliate southern conservatives, the general had ear-

42. *L'Union,* December 6, 1862; Baudier, *The Catholic Church,* 402, 412. For other mention of the ill-treatment of black Catholics, see Paul Huard's letter to the editor, *L'Union,* May 5, 1863.

43. *L'Union,* December 6, 1862.

44. Baudier, *Centennial,* 22; Baudier, *The Catholic Church,* 413. For the gist of Maistre's sermons, see *L'Union,* April 14, May 2, 1863.

lier reopened churches closed by Butler for voicing pro-Confederate sympathies. He now obliged Odin by sending a detachment of soldiers to St. Rose's to end the standoff. With the priest's departure, the bishop padlocked the deserted church.[45]

By the time Maistre officiated at Cailloux' funeral in early July, both he and his congregation had been ostracized from the Catholic Church. Although many Creoles may have anticipated the bishop's actions in the dispute, they were no doubt taken aback by the general's role. His repeated concessions to white conservatives posed a stinging rebuke to black aspirations.

During the religious controversy, *L'Union* deplored the church's treatment of black Catholics, but even before the events at St. Rose, an ideological chasm separated black Creole Catholics from their church leaders. Not long after *L'Union*'s debut, an editorialist had accused Abbé Perché of taking "the side of the oppressors against the oppressed" and of "making himself the champion of treason and rebellion." When one of the church's English-language weeklies, the *Southern Pilot,* repudiated the Emancipation Proclamation, *L'Union* reacted with rage. Referring to a *Pilot* editorial in which the proslavery writer characterized the slave as a "Sambo," the paper unleashed its full fury: "What! you unblushingly portray yourselves as the disciples of Jesus Christ . . . but what is there in common between his sublime teachings and your perverse and barbarous doctrines? . . . Satan has hung some relics and some rosaries at his side, he has donned a three-cornered hat, and he has concealed his hideous face behind a holy mask in order to breathe at his ease his corrupted breath upon those who can no longer recognize him in his disguise." In the tenor of its dispute with the church, *L'Union* closely resembled *Le Spiritualiste*. The similarities to Barthet's defunct journal ran even deeper.[46]

Besides attacking the city's Catholic leadership, *L'Union* published spiritualist writings as well as news and editorials from Cortambert's radical abolitionist tract, the *Revue de l'ouest*. Significantly, the paper also published a full-length biography of St. Vincent de Paul, a highly esteemed spirit guide whom the city's Catholic spiritualists viewed as a prototype of Christian love. The serialized study began in one of the paper's earliest issues; written by the popular French novelist Clémence Robert and

45. McCrary, *Abraham Lincoln,* 112; Baudier, *Centennial,* 24.

46. *L'Union,* November 15, 1862, January 29, 1863.

entitled "The Pastor of the People," it appeared continuously for over six months. Unlike Barthet's journal, however, *L'Union* did not openly proclaim the spiritualist creed. Still, the movement's millennial vision of a republican utopia cropped up repeatedly in the paper's editorials.[47]

In one such essay, a brief article titled "A Step into the Future," an anonymous contributor likened Confederate forces to "barbarian hordes" who warred against "progress, liberty, and mankind's welfare." In attacking "democracy, such as it was preached by Christ," the slaveholding oligarchy attempted to defy the laws of nature and obstruct the spread of republicanism. But God had created men to govern themselves, and the war would usher in an era of social reform. In concluding, the writer prophesied the dawning of a new "millennium" by the turn of the century.[48]

Coincident with their dispute with the church hierarchy and their entry into the military, Creole activists had embarked upon an equally determined campaign for political rights. In September, 1862, in defiance of white conservatives, free black leaders began to assert their political will at "Union meetings." In the wake of the Federal occupation, both black and white radicals saw an opportunity to transform state government and moved swiftly to advance their political agendas.[49]

When the Civil War began, roughly 9 percent of Louisiana's white male population was Unionist. In New Orleans, the Union movement, a white middle-class coalition of urban professionals, businessmen, and workers, was dominated by outsiders: men who had migrated to the city from the North, the border states, or a foreign country. These Unionists quickly organized after the surrender of New Orleans. Led by a cadre of French-speaking radicals, including native New Orleanian Anthony Fernandez and French emigré Louis Dufau, two former members of the Soulé coalition and adherents of French freemasonry, they held a public

47. For spirit communications and articles in *L'Union,* see September 27, October 1, 18, 1862; for reprints from *Revue* articles, see November 1, 1862, April 9, May 30, December 3, 1863, May 28, 1864. *L'Union* published "The Pastor of the People" between October, 1862, and April, 1863. Robert's works often appeared as serialized novels in journals in France (Georges Grente *et al.*, comps., "Clémence Robert," in *Dictionnaire des lettres françaises* (Paris, 1972).

48. *L'Union,* December 6, 1862; for other such essays, see October 8, 1862, August 20, December 1, 1863.

49. Everett, "Demands of the New Orleans Free Colored Population," 44.

rally at the end of May, 1862, one month after the fall of the city. On June 4, they founded the Union Association of New Orleans with the businessman Fernandez as president. A few days later, they released a copy of their new constitution for publication in the city's newspapers.[50]

When Federal authorities called for an election on December 3, 1862, to elect representatives for two New Orleans area congressional districts, the Union Association mobilized. In November, it hosted a rally with the skilled political orator Thomas J. Durant as the keynote speaker. In his address Durant, a Fourierist and another former member of the Soulé faction, explained that even though the drafters of the Constitution had provided for slavery's gradual abolition, the proslavery South had blocked every step in that direction. Ambition and greed, he charged, had given rise to the doctrine of secession. In Louisiana, despite popular opposition to disunion, the slaveholding power had forced the state into the Rebel camp. With a concluding, stirring appeal for the Unionist cause, Durant elicited an outburst of applause from the enthusiastic audience. After the speechmaking, the crowd paraded through the streets carrying torches, flags, and multicolored cloth transparencies.[51]

When Fernandez, a Union Association candidate in the December election, lost his bid for the First District's congressional seat, the radical Durant emerged as the unrivaled leader of the organization. In the spring of 1863, Durant began to press for reestablishing civil government upon the basis of a new state constitution that would abolish slavery throughout Louisiana. With encouragement from the Lincoln administration, he and his fellow Unionists asked General George F. Shepley, the state's military governor, to begin registering voters for the election of delegates to a constitutional convention. On June 12, the general boosted the movement by appointing Durant attorney general and commissioner of registration.[52]

Through their long-standing association with Fernandez and Durant, black Creole leaders at *L'Union* had close ties to the Unionist movement.

50. Tunnell, *Crucible of Reconstruction,* Chap. 1; for a profile of Fernandez, see p. 225. McCrary, *Abraham Lincoln,* 95–96; *La Renaissance* (New Orleans), June 9, 1862; New Orleans *Daily Delta,* June 7, 1862.

51. New York *Times,* November 30, 1862; McCrary, *Abraham Lincoln,* 99–100.

52. New York *Tribune,* December 1, 1862; McCrary, *Abraham Lincoln,* 125–26, 131, 163.

Fernandez, a veteran of the War of 1812 and a prosperous auctioneer who knew many of the Afro-Creole leaders personally, advertised regularly in *L'Union*. For its part, the newspaper printed the association's public notices as well as accounts of its activities. On June 5, 1863, Unionist leaders acknowledged the paper's support by naming *L'Union* the French-language publisher of the association's official announcements. A month later, *L'Union* appeared in both French and English.[53]

Brandishing calls for *liberté, égalité, fraternité, L'Union* pressed its demands for free black voting rights. The paper and its allies seized upon the Unionist movement's proposed election of convention delegates to demand immediate enfranchisement. On November 5, 1963, they sponsored an interracial rally to air their views. The first speaker, a white antislavery Unionist from Texas, touched a raw nerve when he advised the audience to set aside the suffrage issue because there was "a vast amount of prejudice to remove before the question of franchise could be considered." [54]

In an impromptu speech noted for its eloquence, black Creole François Boisdoré rejected all halfway measures. The right of suffrage, he insisted, was long overdue: "When our fathers fought in 1815 they were told that they should be compensated. . . . We have waited long enough. . . . If the United States has the right to arm us, it certainly has the right to allow us the rights of suffrage." Boisdoré threatened that if local authorities denied them their hard-fought rights, they would take their appeal "to a higher power. We will go to President Lincoln, and then we shall know who we are dealing with." The audience approved the Creole leader's address with thunderous applause. P.B.S. Pinchback, a former captain of the Native Guard whom Banks had drummed out of the officer corps, backed up Boisdoré's demand. Black Union soldiers "did not ask for social equality, and did not expect it, but they demanded political rights—they wanted to be men." [55]

Another white Unionist, Anthony P. Dostie, a native New Yorker and New Orleans dentist who had openly opposed Louisiana's Confederate regime, described the suffrage issue as an obstacle to the association's reorganization efforts. Like the first speaker, he asked his listeners to

53. For the association's notices, see *L'Union,* December 25, 1862, February 28, April 11, 14, May 7, 1863; McCrary, *Abraham Lincoln,* 181; Houzeau, *My Passage,* 22.

54. *L'Union,* June 16, July 4, 1863; New Orleans *Times,* November 6, 1863.

55. New Orleans *Times,* November 6, 1863.

postpone their demands. His remarks, though well received, failed to sway the audience. At the end of the meeting, the assembly approved a resolution requesting that General Shepley order the registration of free black voters.[56]

In his closing remarks, Boisdoré offered conditional black support for the free state movement on recognition of their rights: "Gentlemen say that we should wait till we have a free State Government. We offer them our assistance to establish a free State Government, and will they refuse it?" Led by Durant, the Union Association accepted the challenge.[57]

On November 26, before a large black audience in Economy Hall, Durant wheeled his organization behind free black demands for voting rights. Durant was first of a number of white Unionists who addressed the assembly. Greeting his listeners as "fellow citizens," he traced the origins of the war to the sectional dispute over slavery. The immorality of slavery had plunged the nation into a fratricidal conflict. Who, he asked, "cannot see in current events the hand of divine justice?" Before long, the "God of Justice and Liberty will destroy slavery and establish universal liberty."[58]

Toward the end of his speech, the radical Unionist turned to the question of civil rights. Owing to the debilitating effects of slavery, he explained, he did not believe that newly emancipated freedmen should "immediately possess all of the rights and privileges of American citizens." On the other hand, he added, the antebellum free black community—a class of persons who had exercised many of the rights of free men before the war—possessed "the same claims as any other class to the enjoyment of all the civil, political, and religious rights of American citizens." Upon hearing these words, the audience burst into applause.[59]

In a speech before the white Workingmen's National Union League a few nights later, Durant again pressed the issue of free black voting rights. The number of loyal citizens must be enlarged, he insisted, to insure a safe transition to a free state government. Without an expanded loyalist electorate, the free state movement could be sabotaged by returning Rebel

56. Emily Hazen Reed, *Life of A. P. Dostie; or, The Conflict in New Orleans* (New York, 1868), 13; Taylor, *Louisiana Reconstructed,* 13; New Orleans *Times,* November 6, 1863.

57. New Orleans *Times,* November 6, 1863.

58. *L'Union,* November 28, 1863.

59. *Ibid.*

voters. To the surprise of some participants, Durant's large audience of white workers and professionals with working-class backgrounds responded enthusiastically to his radical scheme to expand the electorate. Earlier in the day, in a letter to Salmon P. Chase, Durant had broached the same question with the secretary of the treasury. Although General Shepley had ignored the free black petition, Durant assured his antislavery ally in Washington that free black claims to voting rights were "well founded in justice."[60]

While the Union Association and the free black community moved toward closer cooperation in the second half of 1863, relations between the free state movement and the military establishment deteriorated. Despite instructions from President Lincoln to assist the Durant faction, Banks and Shepley stymied the convention movement by withholding military support. Finally, the slow pace of the association's reorganization efforts as well as Banks's misrepresentations of Unionist activities persuaded President Lincoln to abandon the free state movement. On December 8, 1863, the president issued his Proclamation of Amnesty and Reconstruction, the famous "Ten Percent Plan." The plan offered a full pardon to antebellum voters, with the exception of high-ranking Confederate officials, who took an oath of loyalty and accepted the abolition of slavery. When 10 percent of the number of those who cast votes in 1860 had taken the oath of allegiance, a new state government could be organized. The president's reconstruction plan and his appointment of Banks as the "master" of the state's political reorganization delivered the coup de grâce to the Unionist movement. Durant angrily resigned as attorney general.[61]

With the sabotage of the Union Association's convention movement, Creole leaders made good on Boisdoré's threat to take the suffrage issue to Washington. They launched a petition campaign in December and collected signatures of a thousand free black property holders, twenty-seven veterans of the War of 1812, and twenty-two white radicals, including Durant and Fernandez. In their resolution, the petitioners urged the president and Congress to extend suffrage to Louisiana's freeborn men of African descent.

60. New Orleans *Times,* December 4, 1863; McCrary, *Abraham Lincoln,* 182–85.

61. McCrary, *Abraham Lincoln,* Chap. 5; Tregle, "Thomas J. Durant," 504–508, 509. For a good explanation of the Ten Percent Plan, see Foner, *Reconstruction,* 35–36.

In their original appeal, Afro-Creole leaders had called for the enfranchisement of freedmen as well as the freeborn; however, Durant and other white radicals persuaded them to moderate their demands in this initial campaign. A petition that focused on the rights of antebellum free blacks, their white allies reasoned, was more likely to succeed, since the 1803 treaty had guaranteed citizenship to all of Louisiana's free inhabitants. Finally in mid-February, black Creole leaders dispatched two emissaries, *L'Union* cofounder Jean-Baptiste Roudanez and E. Arnold Bertonneau, a former officer in the Union army, to the nation's capital. Durant supplied the men with a letter of introduction to President Lincoln, in which he supported their appeal for voting rights. Because the men had been unable to "obtain a favorable hearing from those in authority in this quarter," Durant explained, "they deem themselves justified . . . in appealing for relief to the representatives of the nation."[62]

Critics of the city's free black leadership have interpreted the petition drive as part of an overall campaign to obtain the franchise for a self-serving, caste-conscious elite. Proponents of this view have overlooked a summary of an interview with Roudanez and Bertonneau in April, 1864, in the New York *Anglo-African,* a black weekly, in which the two New Orleanians described how the free black petition was formulated. They explained to the *Anglo-African*'s editors that "when the initial step was made in New Orleans to secure the franchise, the ground was boldly taken that the right to vote must be asked for *all,* and not for those only who have all their lives been free." The publicly stated policy of the Union Association sustains this explanation. As noted above, Durant had already set forth the organization's support of limited enfranchisement for the free black class in the November, 1863, Economy Hall meeting.[63]

In Washington on March 10, Roudanez and Bertonneau met with U.S. senator Charles Sumner of Massachusetts and Congressman William D.

62. McCrary, *Abraham Lincoln,* 229–30. For the petition, see the New York *Anglo-African,* April 2, 1864.

63. For the view of Afro-Creole leaders as a power-hungry elite, see Everett, "Demands of the New Orleans Free Colored Population," 50–64, and Rankin, "The Origins of Negro Leadership," in *Southern Black Leaders of the Reconstruction Era,* ed. Rabinowitz, 170–73; for a more thorough discussion of this topic, see Logsdon and Bell, "The Americanization of Black New Orleans," in *Creole New Orleans,* ed. Hirsch and Logsdon, 224–27. Quotation from *Anglo-African,* April 16, 1864.

Kelley of Pennsylvania. Strong proponents of equal suffrage as a precondition for reconstruction, the congressional radicals agreed with the original demands of the Afro-Creole petitioners. After conferring, the men drafted an addendum to the memorial that extended suffrage to freedmen as well as those born free, in all regions of the South. Both justice and political expediency, the new provision declared, required that "full effect should be given to all the Union feeling in the rebel States, in order to secure the permanence of the free institutions and loyal governments now organized therein." Two days later, Roudanez and Bertonneau presented the document to the president.[64]

Though impressed by the black New Orleanians, President Lincoln remained noncommittal. Privately, he encouraged Michael Hahn, Louisiana's newly inaugurated governor, to consider a limited extension of the suffrage: "I barely suggest for your private consideration," the president wrote, "whether some of the colored people may not be let in [granted suffrage]—as, for instance, the very intelligent, and especially those who have fought gallantly in our ranks." The president's recommendation notwithstanding, the constitutional convention, which met during the spring and summer of 1864, refused to sanction black voting rights. Instead, the delegates authorized the state legislature, albeit begrudgingly, to grant limited black suffrage at some unspecified time in the future.[65]

In 1864, the mounting conservatism of presidential reconstruction strategy convinced the city's radicals to gear their own toward congressional intervention. In Washington, Durant lobbied against Louisiana's provisional government in newspaper editorials and meetings with key congressmen, while in Louisiana, Dr. Louis Charles Roudanez and his associates inaugurated a new suffrage campaign by gearing their bilingual, triweekly newspaper to a larger audience. In July, 1864, they reorganized *L'Union* and renamed the paper the New Orleans *Tribune*. Paul Trévigne remained editor in chief, and the paper's managers announced their intention to publish the journal every day except Monday. After a new press arrived in the fall, the *Tribune* became the first black daily in the United States. From their newly expanded forum, the paper's Afro-Creole spokesmen kept Sumner, Kelley,

64. *Anglo-African,* April 2, 1864.

65. McPherson, *The Negro's Civil War,* 279–80; Taylor, *Louisiana Reconstructed,* 52; McCrary, *Abraham Lincoln,* 261–65, 349–50.

and other northerners informed of the government's treatment of black Louisianians and agitated for voting rights.[66]

The *Tribune*'s editors stepped up their attack on presidential reconstruction when New England abolitionist William Lloyd Garrison defended Lincoln's refusal to require black suffrage. In July, 1864, in a public letter to British abolitionist Francis W. Newman, Garrison asserted that the power to extend the suffrage belonged to the states rather than the national government. Even if Lincoln possessed the authority to enfranchise the freedmen, such an action would be ill advised, he warned, since "the white population, with their superior intelligence, wealth and power, would unquestionably alter the franchise in accordance with their prejudices." Furthermore, Garrison continued, "when was it ever known that liberation from bondage was accompanied by a recognition of political equality?"[67]

The *Tribune* countered that Garrison, swayed by political considerations, refused to acknowledge the complexity of Louisiana's black population. Seeking to promote Lincoln's reconstruction policy, he chose to portray all black Louisianians as a vulnerable mass of propertyless, uneducated former slaves. Like most northern whites, the paper continued, Garrison ignored the presence of the antebellum free black class; refusal to distinguish between freedmen and prewar free blacks had led to the arbitrary arrest and imprisonment of free men of color.[68]

In January, 1864, General Nathaniel P. Banks, commanding officer of the Department of the Gulf, issued labor regulations in General Order Number 23, mandating that workers enter into a yearlong labor contract. The agreement required freedmen, under penalty of arrest, to obtain the written consent of their employer, overseer, or provost marshal if they left the plantation to which they were contractually bound. Initially, the *Tribune* had accepted the tight controls on plantation workers as a military necessity and had even applauded the Banks decree. After the first growing

66. McCrary, *Abraham Lincoln,* Chap. 9. The *Tribune* appeared on July 21, two days after *L'Union* halted publication on July 19. In listing reasons for its failure, *L'Union* took a parting swipe at the pro-Confederate clergy and the provisional government (*L'Union,* May 31, 1864). Also see Houzeau, *My Passage,* 19, 22–23, 25*n*34.

67. James M. McPherson, *The Struggle for Equality* (2nd ed.; Princeton, 1995), 294.

68. *Tribune,* August 4, 1864.

season, however, the exploitive nature of the regulations and the realization that the strict worker controls were not temporary convinced the *Tribune* to reject Banks's labor policy. The newspaper expressed outrage as military authorities even began to arrest members of the Baton Rouge and New Orleans prewar free black population for not carrying worker passes.[69]

The *Tribune* likewise rejected Garrison's contention that the extension of voting rights to newly freed slaves would be an unprecedented action. True, the *Tribune* conceded, in English-speaking areas of the world, suffrage had not accompanied freedom. Although the British had emancipated their slaves in 1834, they had not enfranchised the freedmen; however, events in the French-speaking world revealed a different reality. The paper pointed out the French government's action on February 4, 1794, when the revolutionary regime abolished slavery in the French West Indies and declared that "all men, without distinction of colour, domiciled in the colonies, are French citizens and enjoy all the rights assured under the Constitution." The *Tribune*'s editors urged Garrison and his allies to broaden their vision. Insisting that freedom and political equality were inseparably linked, the paper urged the United States to follow the example of France and wondered why the "proud Anglo-Saxon" hesitated "to fulfill an act of justice."[70]

The controversy over black suffrage flared again when one of Garrison's allies in Louisiana, B. Rush Plumly, attacked the black newspaper while defending the reconstruction policies of Lincoln and Banks. The newspaper struck back: "The Garrisonians do not often forget that they belong to the Caucasian race, and seem to say to the Negro: 'now that you are free, you will go no further.' . . . It is in rising up against an arrogant and vindictive race that we sometimes run afoul of the feelings of those who play the part of defenders of the principles of the Declaration of Independence, and who dare not throw off their irrational and absurd prejudices."[71]

When the Garrisonian faction pressed the *Tribune* to compromise and accept a limited extension of the suffrage, the paper refused: "We defend a principle. . . . We can compromise with interests, but we cannot com-

69. Ripley, *Slaves and Freedmen,* 56, 73, 90–93.

70. *Tribune,* January 28, 1865. For a discussion of emancipation in the French Caribbean in 1794, see Blackburn, *The Overthrow of Colonial Slavery,* 224–25.

71. *Tribune,* October 11, 1864.

promise with principles. Assured of the sound basis of our rights, we proclaim them, we uphold them fully and completely, and we will hear nothing of sacrificing them. . . . The revolution moves forward; we await our hour; it will come, and we will enter into the temple not dressed in the garb of the catechumen, led to the altar by a *parrain* [godfather] and a *marraine* [godmother], but in the dress of Uncle Sam's men in arms." [72]

In early 1865, the situation in Louisiana deteriorated further when the lieutenant governor, James Madison Wells, replaced Governor Michael Hahn after the latter's election to the United States Senate. The provisional government's small electoral base convinced Wells, a former planter from upstate Louisiana, to side with the conservatives. After taking office in March, he summarily dismissed municipal and state officials and replaced them with conservative Unionists and unrepentant returning Rebels. With the Confederate surrender on April 9, Wells extended his reactionary regime to the entire state. In mid-May, President Andrew Johnson, the slain Lincoln's successor, sanctioned the conservative coup.[73]

Undeterred by the conservative onslaught, the *Tribune* denounced the Wells regime and praised Congress for withholding recognition of Louisiana's provisional government. The policy of denying voting rights to black Louisianians, the paper insisted, had opened the way for the reactionary takeover. Only universal suffrage could ensure the creation of a loyal state government.

With the end of the war, the paper headed a campaign to organize returning Union soldiers and other loyalists into a political coalition dedicated to universal suffrage. Inviting "Democrats and Republicans, Abolitionists as well as the friends of free labor, white and black, State Rights men and Federalists" to unite under the banner of equal rights for all men, the paper envisioned a party "where the old lines of demarkation, of all kinds, will be obliterated." [74]

At the same time, the *Tribune*'s editorialists urged the Louisiana chapter of the National Equal Rights League to send a black delegate to Washington. In October, 1864, in Syracuse, New York, 144 black representatives from eighteen states including Louisiana had founded the

72. *Ibid.*, November 16, 1864.

73. Tunnell, *Crucible of Reconstruction,* 95–96.

74. *Tribune,* May 25, 1865.

National Equal Rights League, a civil rights federation organized to petition Congress for unqualified black voting rights throughout the nation. In January, 1865, black Louisianians created their own chapter of the national league, with the *Tribune* as the new organization's official organ.[75]

Now, with the failure of presidential reconstruction, the radical black newspaper proposed that the state Equal Rights League send an emissary to the nation's capital. The Louisiana delegate, the *Tribune* insisted, should "be a fair representative not only of intelligence and education, not only of our patriotism and our devotion to our country, but . . . also a representative of the physical type of the great mass of the people of African descent. We want him to be a black man. We want him to be thoroughly identified with the working of slavery." Deprived of self-government, black Louisianians required a permanent, full-time representative to convey their interests and grievances to the president, Congress, and the nation. In fact, the paper maintained, all African Americans required such a spokesman. The other state leagues would undoubtedly follow Louisiana's example once black Louisianians dispatched their representative to Washington.[76]

Soon, however, Afro-Creole leaders at the *Tribune* joined with the Durant faction to organize returning Union soldiers and other loyalists into an interracial political coalition. On June 10, 1865, they founded the Friends of Universal Suffrage. With Durant as their president, they vowed to "deprecate any discrimination founded upon origin or birth." Liberty, they continued, "is but a word as long as taxation, elections, and the whole political machinery are confined into the hands of an enemical [*sic*] race." Everyone must be "given a fair chance in the world, with the same rights before the law; that each one be free and unobstructed to find his own level, according to his education and means."[77]

75. Logsdon and Bell, "The Americanization of Black New Orleans," in *Creole New Orleans,* ed. Hirsch and Logsdon, 231–32; McPherson, *The Negro's Civil War,* 286–87.

76. *Tribune,* May 26, June 1, 1865.

77. F. Wayne Binning, "Carpetbaggers' Triumph: The Louisiana State Election of 1868," *Louisiana History,* XIV (Winter, 1973), 22–23; Philip D. Uzee, "The Beginnings of the Louisiana Republican Party," *Louisiana History,* XII (Summer, 1971), 205; *Proceedings of the Convention of the Republican Party of Louisiana* (New Orleans, 1865), iii–iv; *Tribune,* June 10, 16, 17, July 8, 1865.

With a view to their ultimate objective, the founders of the Friends of Universal Suffrage introduced a policy of proportional representation in the makeup of the new organization's leadership council. They created a Central Executive Committee composed of six representatives from each of the city's four municipal districts. At least one of the six members was to be chosen from the district's black residents; the one-to-six ratio approximated the proportion of black New Orleanians in the city's population.[78]

At their weekly meetings, the Friends planned to hold a "voluntary election" simultaneous with the state's official fall balloting. By boycotting the regular elections and conducting a successful parallel electoral campaign with a significant voter turnout, movement leaders hoped to win congressional support for a new model of reconstruction based on universal suffrage. In the mock registration campaign, radicals enrolled voters of both races for an election on September 16 to choose delegates to a statewide nominating convention.[79]

At the same time, the Friends of Universal Suffrage devised other strategies to assure equality before the law for all black Louisianians. In addition to voting rights, the Central Executive Committee advocated the right to serve on juries and to run for all political offices. "Suffrage," the *Tribune* asserted, "would be but an incomplete franchise if an entire class of voters was excluded from office, and if the nominees had to be taken from among a different—and as the case may be—a hostile class." [80]

Significantly, the coalition's leadership council also urged the proportional representation of black Louisianians in the coming state nominating convention, to be held September 25 in New Orleans. Since black Louisianians constituted nearly half the state's population, the committee recommended selecting an equal number of white and black delegates.[81]

The Friends welcomed members of the Hahn faction, their former opponents, into their camp. The overwhelming momentum of the conservative backlash had converted the besieged Banks coalition to the cause of

78. *Tribune,* June 17, 1865; *Proceedings of the Convention of the Republican Party of Louisiana,* 1–2; McCrary, *Abraham Lincoln,* 316–17.

79. Houzeau, *My Passage,* 112–13; Vincent, "Black Louisianians," in *Louisiana's Black Heritage,* ed. MacDonald, Kemp, and Haas, 92.

80. *Tribune,* July 8, 1865.

81. *Ibid.*, August 22, 1865; *Proceedings of the Convention of the Republican Party of Louisiana,* 9.

black suffrage; following the radicals' example, moderate Republicans founded an interracial political organization, the National Union Republican Club. On June 30, they elected Henry Clay Warmoth, a former Union officer from Missouri, as their president. Warmoth had not favored emancipation and had supported the conservative 1864 state constitution, but he had nonetheless been one of the first moderates to express public support for black enfranchisement. Impressed by his endorsement of voting rights, the Friends organization elected him to the office of corresponding secretary. Though he declined the post, he accepted membership in the group, and he and other moderates ran as candidates in the voluntary election campaign.

At the racially mixed convention of the Friends of Universal Suffrage that met in New Orleans September 25, delegates chose Durant as their president. Taking the podium in the midst of a roaring ovation, Durant assured his listeners that universal liberty and universal suffrage were the only remedies for the nation's ills. He attacked the constitutional legitimacy of the Wells government and asserted that the conservative regime would never compromise on the question of black suffrage. "The only thing left," he insisted, "is to appeal to the decision of the United States Congress." [82]

The delegates approved Durant's strategy, and convention harmony prevailed until a member of the Warmoth group introduced a proposal to merge the Friends of Universal Suffrage with the national Republican Party under a new name, the Republican Party of Louisiana. Wary of the national party's commitment to black suffrage, convention radicals objected to the measure. A heated debate ensued. If the Friends of Universal Suffrage declared themselves Republicans, the *Tribune* maintained, they would be compelled to adopt the party's entire program. The paper opposed this strategy: "Shall we become obedient tools in the hands of a party whose policy is not completely settled on the very question that brought us together in this Convention? . . . And if that party stop half way, and be satisfied with an extension of suffrage to some tax payers, what will become of our main object? Let us be the allies of the republicans, not their tools; let us retain our individuality, our banner, and our name." [83]

82. McCrary, *Abraham Lincoln,* 316–32; Binning, "Carpetbaggers' Triumph," 23; Francis W. Binning, "Henry Clay Warmoth and Louisiana Reconstruction" (Ph.D. dissertation, University of North Carolina, 1969), 17–18; Taylor, *Louisiana Reconstructed,* 53.

83. *Tribune,* September 26, 1865.

Durant argued forcefully for a merger. He dismissed the threat of political betrayal and stressed the advantages of solidarity with the national party. "We are isolated," he declared, "we began our labors all alone, in the heart of a southern state. It is necessary above all to establish connections, to ally ourselves with the great liberal party of the country—the party which in the United States is called the Republican party. . . . We shall inscribe on our flag all the great principles which the northern liberals have determined to defend, and we shall ask the national Republican party to help us to obtain equal rights." [84]

Convention radicals reluctantly yielded after the Warmoth group agreed to a resolution calling on the Republican Party to adopt universal suffrage as the basis of the party's national platform. Before long, however, the moderates precipitated another dispute when Warmoth proposed that the convention adopt a state constitution as a step toward Louisiana's readmission to the Union. Under this plan, the 1864 constitution, revised to enfranchise blacks, would be submitted to the voters for approval in the upcoming parallel election.

Warmoth's audacious challenge alarmed the radicals. Aside from derailing their strategy of seeking a congressional remedy, an amended state constitution would be vulnerable to attack by a conservative state legislature. Moreover, to convene a constitutional convention under existing conditions would invite a violent reaction. They repudiated the proposal. The convention's ultimate goal, delegate Rufus Waples argued, required federal support. Our hope, he concluded, "is in Congress." The convention tabled the proposal.[85]

Next, the assembly called upon Congress to govern Louisiana as a territory and nominated Durant to run for the designated office of "territorial delegate" from Louisiana. But both he and a subsequent nominee, the radical white lawyer William R. Crane, declined the nomination on the grounds they could better serve the movement by remaining in the state. Finally, the convention chose Warmoth to be its standard-bearer.

In the November 4 parallel election, Warmoth garnered a little over 19,000 unofficial votes, as well as approximately 2,500 official votes. By comparison, the official gubernatorial candidate of the Democrats and

84. Houzeau, *My Passage,* 114.

85. McCrary, *Abraham Lincoln,* 334.

Conservative Union Party, the former Whig planter James Madison Wells, polled only about 22,000 votes in the official election, in which a total of almost 28,000 votes were cast throughout the state. In December, congressional Republicans snubbed Louisiana's officially elected delegation, while according Warmoth all the privileges enjoyed by delegates from the western territories.

In the official statewide elections of November, 1865, white voters returned reactionary southern Democrats to power. In the state legislature, the revived white conservatives capped their electoral victory with a revised version of Louisiana's black codes. Designed to restore white dominance, the new decrees relegated freedmen to a condition of semiservitude.

In a municipal election in early 1866, city residents expelled the remaining Unionists from the mayoralty and other city offices. Ousted from power and desperate, conservative Unionists joined forces with moderate Republicans and proposed to fight the former Confederates with a new state constitution. At the end of March, Warmoth, a spokesman for the moderates, revived his call for a constitutional convention and submitted a plan of action to the state Republican Party's executive committee. The territorial delegate encountered opposition, however, when committee member William R. Crane accused him of carrying water for Banks and Hahn. Aware, perhaps, that Warmoth had just returned from meetings in Washington with the two men, Crane attributed the scheme to the general and the ex-governor. Reminding his colleagues of their record on the suffrage issue, Crane cautioned the committee to "beware of such friends!"[86]

The objections of party radicals notwithstanding, Republican moderates forged ahead. They devised a plan to reconvene the constitutional

86. Binning, "Carpetbaggers' Triumph," 24–25; McCrary, *Abraham Lincoln,* 334–41; Tunnell, *Crucible of Reconstruction,* 103, 224; Gilles Vandal, *The New Orleans Riot of 1866: Anatomy of a Tragedy* (Lafayette, La., 1983), 70, 93; Binning, "Henry Clay Warmoth," 96–97; *Tribune,* March 23, 1862. Crane, a close friend of Durant and a native of Washington, D.C., practiced law in antebellum New Orleans and owned four slaves. Later, the Warmoth faction seized upon this fact to undermine his influence with black Louisianians, but the *Tribune,* having earlier described Crane as "a friend of our race, who has his whole soul in the cause of universal freedom," defended the white radical. According to the former slaves, Crane had purchased three of the bondsmen at their own request to save them from the ill-treatment of abusive masters (*Tribune,* February 9, 1865, June 2, 1867).

convention of 1864 with the aim of enfranchising black Louisianians while disfranchising former Rebels. As the radicals had predicted, however, the attempt to extend the suffrage without federal support brought whites and blacks into open conflict.

When the convention movement leaders attempted to convene on July 30 at the Mechanics Institute, violence erupted. At noon the day of the scheduled meeting, a white mob opened fire on a procession of over two hundred black marchers converging on the convention hall. After overcoming them, the white rioters invaded the institute.

Fatefully, members of the Durant faction had assembled inside to observe the proceedings. Although neither the *Tribune* nor Durant favored reconvening the convention, many members of the black community had gathered at the institute in support of black suffrage. Black Creole radical Ludger Boguille, one of the Couvent school's first teachers and a former officer in the Union army, described events inside the auditorium. At first, Boguille and others fought off the invading gunmen with tables and chairs, but after nearly an hour in the besieged hall, Boguille bolted from the building. The mob swarmed over him, beating him with guns and clubs. He escaped, however, when a white northerner caught the mob's attention; as Captain C. Loup, who had commanded a company of black soldiers during the war, appeared at the door of the institute, the mob rushed him; stabbing and beating him, they then shot him to death.[87]

When the rioters first burst into the building, black Creole Victor Lacroix, Boguille's friend, attempted to surrender. The mob killed him outright. The wealthy Lacroix, a former Union soldier and the son of François Lacroix, carried a gold watchchain and a large sum of money. His assassins stripped him of his valuables and mutilated his body. Rufus Waples, who viewed the victims' bodies afterwards, described how Lacroix had been "cut from head to foot," and "butchered and mutilated in the most shocking and barbarous manner."[88]

87. Houzeau, *My Passage,* 124; Taylor, *Louisiana Reconstructed,* 109–10. For other accounts of the riot, see Donald E. Reynolds, "The New Orleans Riot of 1866, Reconsidered," *Louisiana History,* V (Winter, 1964), 5–27, and Vandal, *The New Orleans Riot,* Chap. 6; Fogelson and Rubenstein, eds., *Mass Violence in America,* 154, 199, 364–65, 383–85.

88. Fogelson and Rubenstein, eds., *Mass Violence in America,* 24, 332, 384; Reed, *Life of A. P. Dostie,* 338.

Lucien Jean Pierre Capla, another black Creole Unionist who had raised a black company during the war and whose father had fought in the battle of New Orleans, attended the convention with his son Alfred. When the rioters entered the hall, Capla grabbed the teenager and started to flee the building, but as they struggled down the stairs, the mob seized them. Capla suffered a fractured skull and a gunshot wound in his side; his son lost his right eye from a pistol shot.

Eugène Staès, a black former officer in the Union army, was inside the hall at the time of the attack but managed to escape by jumping from a window to a nearby rooftop. Staès's fellow black Creole, J. Manuel Camps, a community activist identified with the Couvent school, did not—he was beaten and stabbed in the back.

The Belgian editor Houzeau, the *Tribune*'s news reporter at the convention, escaped through a service entrance. As he watched the melee from his hiding place in a nearby shop, he heard the shout, "To the *Tribune*!" At the newspaper's offices, however, a company of black soldiers guarded the journal's printing presses.[89]

The ferocity of the attack persuaded Durant and other well-known radicals to take the death threats they received that day seriously. Upon the advice of a confidant, Durant fled into exile the evening of the disaster; William R. Crane and Rufus Waples, his fellow radicals, also left the city. The deadly riot resulted in over 150 black casualties, with approximately forty-four deaths. Three white Unionists lost their lives. Of the white rioters, only one was killed. General Philip H. Sheridan, commanding officer of U.S. troops in Louisiana, returned to New Orleans within twenty-four hours of the riot. Though he considered the convention leaders troublemakers, the general was appalled by the carnage. He wired his superior in Washington, General Ulysses S. Grant, that the mayor had "suppressed the convention by the use of the police force, and . . . attacked the members of the convention and a party of two hundred negroes with fire-arms, clubs and knives, in a manner so unnecessary and atrocious as to compel me to say that it was murder." It was, he reported the following day, "no riot; it was an absolute massacre by the po-

89. Fogelson and Rubenstein, eds., *Mass Violence in America,* 15, 118–20, 591; Houzeau, *My Passage,* 159.

lice, which was not excelled in murderous cruelty by that of Fort Pillow."[90]

In the aftermath of the bloody assault, policemen or white rioters were reprimanded or arrested. The *Tribune* and its readers demanded justice. The black community lashed out at President Johnson, the city's ex-Confederate mayor John T. Monroe, the city police force, and other local officials. A former slave who was a victim of the attack complained that police and the white mob had "murdered our friends in their own yards, in the presence of their own family, and yet our civil government is still running, and the murderers are still allowed to roam our streets undisturbed. We submit to it, and [are] ruled by a man that was a rebel when Gen. Butler came here, and is a rebel yet." The writer continued: "I feel for one that redress should be had, any way we can obtain it." Another contributor asserted that black New Orleanians could look to neither city officials nor President Johnson for redress; he believed, however, that "THE [American] PEOPLE will yet revenge these outrages upon humanity, and mete out to rebel murderers their just due, *even over the head of 'the dead dog of the White House*.' "[91]

The murder and mutilation of Lacroix, like the death of Cailloux, dealt a wrenching blow to the close-knit black Creole community. Once again, however, religious radicals transformed their loss. They immediately elevated their slain friend to the status of a martyred hero. Within days of the riot, medium Henry Rey entered into a crisis-induced trance in which the deceased Lacroix appeared to him. Raised to the stature of a spirit guide, Lacroix reviled his assassins and urged his comrades forward. The spirit message demanded action. Inspired by such communications, spiritualists Henry and Octave Rey, François and Auguste Dubuclet, Victor Lavigne,

90. Fogelson and Rubenstein, eds., *Mass Violence in America,* 8–9, 12, 174–75, 388. When Durant's enemies criticized him for leaving New Orleans, the *Tribune* defended his decision (*Tribune,* September 9, 1866). See Sheridan's dispatches to Grant, August 1, 2, 1866, in Harvey Wish, ed., *Reconstruction in the South, 1865–1877: First-Hand Accounts of the American Southland After the Civil War, by Northerners & Southerners* (New York, 1965), 52–53. After Union forces at Fort Pillow on the Mississippi River surrendered to General Nathan Bedford Forrest on April 12, 1864, Confederate soldiers executed scores of defenseless black soldiers along with some of the whites.

91. Reynolds, "The New Orleans Riot," 13; *Tribune,* September 1, August 31, 1866.

Rodolphe Desdunes, and Aristide Mary sustained their campaign of political activism in the aftermath of the riot.[92]

The New Orleans riot and a similar rampage in Memphis contributed to a growing sense of alarm in the North. In the congressional elections of 1866, northern voters repudiated presidential reconstruction by increasing the Republican majority to two-thirds in both houses. In 1867, Congress overrode the president and implemented its own plan of restoration. The Reconstruction Acts divided ten southern states into five military districts; General Sheridan assumed command of the Fifth Military District comprising Louisiana and Texas. Sheridan promptly removed the mayor and other officials implicated in the 1866 riot. Then, to pave the way for reorganizing the state government and readmitting Louisiana into the Union, the general ordered the registration of all adult males, black and white, excluding those ex-Confederates disqualified by the Fourteenth Amendment.

With the return of Federal troops to the city, community activists resumed their assault on the color line in public accommodations. Earlier, not long after the Union occupation of New Orleans in 1862, the free black community had embarked upon an unsuccessful campaign to desegregate public schools and the streetcar system. Now, in April, 1867, the *Tribune* inaugurated the new movement by insisting on equal access to political office, the franchise, the jury box, the schoolroom, and public conveyances. The paper demanded action from their purported allies: "All these discriminations that had slavery at the bottom, have become nonsense. It behooves those who understand the new era, and who feel bold enough to shake off the old prejudice and to confront their prejudiced associates, to show their hands, and gain the friendship of the colored population of this State. . . . Friendship, or political alliance, have to show themselves by action."[93]

Within two weeks of the editorial, the black community had launched a full-scale assault on the city's segregated streetcars. Racial tensions approached a flash point as black passengers forced their way onto cars set aside for whites. With the city on the verge of a race riot, French-speaking freemasons took up the *Tribune*'s challenge.[94]

92. Spiritualist Registers, February 21, 1869, Grandjean Collection, UNO.

93. Tunnell, *Crucible of Reconstruction,* 107; Taylor, *Louisiana Reconstructed,* 138–39; Roger A. Fischer, *The Segregation Struggle in Louisiana, 1862–77* (Urbana, Ill., 1974), 22–31; *Tribune,* April 21, 1867.

94. Fischer, *The Segregation Struggle,* 32–35.

On May 2, Eugène Chassaignac, a French emigré and the head of Scottish rite masonry, opened the doors of the city's French lodges to black members. After declaring that masonry should always "march in the forefront of the struggle against prejudice and declare to the world its grand principles of Liberty, Equality and Fraternity," Chassaignac ordered the white lodges under his jurisdiction to welcome all freemasons "without distinction as to race or color."

Pierre Soulé, Louisiana's most outspoken proponent of revolutionary republicanism during the 1840s and 1850s, refused to meet "upon the level" with black Louisianians. He and other members of Polar Star, the city's oldest Scottish rite lodge, resigned rather than honor the new directive. Not long afterward, Soulé, overcome by financial and personal disasters, lost his sanity. He died on March 16, 1870.

The opposition of Soulé and his supporters notwithstanding, French-speaking radicals upheld Chassaignac's command. Together with black Creole leaders Paul Trévigne, Henry and Octave Rey, Louis Nelson Fouché, Lucien Jean Pierre Capla, and Arnold Bertonneau, they founded new, racially integrated lodges.[95]

On June 16, when Chassaignac installed the officers of one of French freemasonry's new affiliates, Fraternité, the *Tribune* described the formal ceremony in glowing terms. Earlier, the paper had published a poetic tribute to French masonry in anticipation of Chassaignac's decree:

The Sacred Triangle

Your pure luster, masonic emblem,
Like a beacon, lights up the heavens;
The better to ascend the steps of the portico.
The unjust gaze towards you.
Traversing the world in your intrepid journey;
Purifying the regenerate man.

95. Grace H. Yerbury, "Concert Music in New Orleans," *Louisiana Historical Quarterly,* XL (April, 1957), 101. The edict is in the Polar Star Minutes Book, May 24, 1867. For an English translation, see the *Perfect Ashlar,* April, 1951, p. 6; also see Scot, *Outline of the Rise and Progress of Freemasonry,* 5. For opposition to Chassaignac's decree, see Polar Star Minutes Book, May 10–December 1, 1867. On Soulé's death, see Tinker, *Les Ecrits,* 448. Membership rosters for Polar Star and Fraternité No. 20 and information on some of the members' background is in the Appendix.

Every Freemason's soul is elevated
When saluting the Sacred Triangle!

Subdued in the bondage which binds him to earth,
Bondman or vassal oblivious of his rights,
Benumbed man endures his misery
While depicted as prescribed by law.
But in an awakening, the solemn hour arrives.
On the horizon, suddenly transformed
Liberty brushes him with its wing
And forms the base of the Sacred Triangle!

Prejudice, its roots are deep-reaching;
How many otherwise good, generous souls
Say: "The black does not belong to the human race,
He is born a slave and truly believes he is happy."
All sons of God; blacks or whites, He loves us,
Over all, according to his revered command,
Equality passes to the supreme level
And takes its place in the Sacred Triangle!

Here comes the holy Fraternity,
Which says: Children, follow my law of love!
From God's bosom, I heard your lamentation;
To be initiated, insist on my return.
Enough blood, death, and war;
Let a little hope return to the embittered heart.
I come to offer happiness to the earth
In completing the Sacred Triangle!

And we, guardians of the luminous symbol;
By its rays, guide the human race;
Teaching mankind the divine word,
By our labors, point the way.
There will come a day, when throughout the heavenly spheres,
Everyone will utter the same cry:
Because It makes us all Equal, Free and Brothers!
Three cheers for the Sacred Triangle![96]

96. *Tribune,* April 28, June 18, 1867.

As word of Chassaignac's action spread through masonry's international network, radical lodges in France, Italy, and Belgium sent their congratulations. In Paris, members of the Rose du Parfait Silence lodge honored Chassaignac. The members, "moved by the grand sentiments of liberty, equality, and fraternity which constitute the strength and glory of our Institution; deeply touched by your efforts to claim, in your *Obédience* [jurisdiction], the human rights unjustly denied, until today, to our Brothers of color," voted unanimously to make the New Orleanian an honorary member of their lodge.[97]

Giuseppe Garibaldi, a high-ranking member of Italian freemasonry, forwarded Chassaignac an equally compelling note of support: "From the bottom of my heart, I join with you in your noble and courageous resolution of admitting all Freemasons without distinction of color into the lodges under your jurisdiction." Garibaldi concluded his message by drawing attention to the struggle for political equality: "It is inconceivable, my brother, that the great republic—the palladium of world liberty—should falter in the path that she has already sanctified through so much blood and heroism."[98]

From Belgium, political exile Victor Hugo added a note of approval to the rising chorus of support. Alluding, however, to the alliance between conservative French freemasons and the regime of Napoleon III, he tempered his praise: "You are right, monsieur, without belonging, in name, to masonry, I am with it in heart. . . . I love your noble goal and your magnificent fraternity, a symbol of the great fraternity of the future. . . . I thank you for having communicated to me the solemn and glorious progress that you have undertaken; the admission of blacks into your ranks commences the equality that the exclusion of princes [from masonry] will consummate."[99]

97. The masonic decree is in *Bulletin de la Maçonnerie Louisianaise,* April–May, 1869, 31; *Tribune,* November 8, 1867.

98. *Bulletin de la Maçonnerie,* 14–15.

99. *Ibid.*, 15–16. For mention of the alliance between masonic conservatives and Napoleon III's government, see Chap. 6; an influx of French republicans into the Scottish rite lodges during the 1860s undermined this conservative partnership. A declaration from the Scottish lodge La Justice on December 1, 1869, offers insight into the political radicalism of some of France's republican lodges: "In the name of Equality, we reject all aristocracies which have ruled and still rule the world: the aristocracy of power, the aristocracy of birth, the aristocracy of money, the aristocracy of science, the aristocracy of color, the aristocracy of sex" (Headings, *French Freemasonry,* 39).

The *Tribune* published the testimonials and depicted Chassaignac's declaration as a dramatic turning point: "One day this document will have a truly historical value. It will be the point of departure for a social transformation, the effects of which we can scarcely foresee." Calculating the influence of masonry's fraternal ideal, the paper continued: "We are in a state of social transition. Society is now being reorganized among us, upon the true principle of freedom, and, to do this great work, we need harmony and friendship, for we want to build up an edifice that will stand, and no one will deny the influence that masonry may have in assisting us in a grand achievement of this much desired object." [100]

In the eyes of Creole radicals, the masonic decree clearly signaled the commencement of a new era. With the convening of the Republican state convention in June, they proposed to translate freemasonry's ideals into a concrete formula for racial equality. If, however, the actions of the French lodges signified a new departure in race relations, the maneuvers of Republican moderates pointed away from meaningful change.

When the Friends of Universal Suffrage merged with the national Republican Party in September, 1865, the radical Durant-*Tribune* faction dominated the organization. In that transitional phase, the names of radical leaders Anthony Fernandez, William R. Crane, Henry Rey, Rufus Waples, Ludger Boguille, Blanc F. Joubert, John Racquet Clay, Aristide Mary, and Armand Lanusse headed the membership roster. In the spring of 1867, radicals remained at the head of the party. With the onset of Reconstruction, however, the drastically improved fortunes of the Republican Party triggered a thoroughgoing takeover by Republican moderates.[101]

In April, 1867, the moderates, backed by the *Tribune*'s new rival, the pro-Warmoth New Orleans *Republican,* began their offensive. Put off by the radicalism and interracial makeup of the official Republican Party, a number of white moderates had founded a parallel organization, the Ben Butler Clubs. When the First Reconstruction Act provided for black suffrage, the clubs began to admit black members and proposed to oust the radicals from control of the Republican Party's leadership council, the powerful Central Executive Committee. The moderates denied the le-

100. *Tribune,* June 23, 1867; some of the testimonials are in English in the *Perfect Ashlar,* April, 1951, 6–7.

101. *Proceedings of the Convention of the Republican Party of Louisiana,* 10–11.

gality of the committee's origins in the 1865 Friends of Universal Suffrage convention, arguing that since black delegates were not citizens at the time of the convention, they were not entitled to vote; their participation, therefore, had undermined the legitimacy of the convention's governing body. They proposed to replace the radical council with an executive committee of their own.[102]

In June, the struggle between the two factions erupted into open conflict at the party's state convention. One of the disputes centered on two platform resolutions introduced by Robert H. Isabelle, a black former army officer; Isabelle's initiatives called for some form of proportional representation for black Republicans. White delegate John Hale Sypher, another former army officer and an ally of Warmoth's, objected. Describing himself as a believer in progress, Sypher declared that the convention should not make any distinctions on the basis of race. Black delegate and former army officer P.B.S. Pinchback joined the debate. As proof that the newly enfranchised citizens required special protection, Pinchback pointed to the army's ill treatment of black soldiers. When Sypher denied that black soldiers had been discriminated against in the army, James H. Ingraham, a black former officer who, like Isabelle and Pinchback, had been drummed out of the military by General Banks, lectured the white delegate.

Despite the mounting challenge from the Right, the radicals prevailed in formulating the party platform. The fifteen-point program committed the party to the "doctrine of perfect equality in the right to hold office." Resolution 14 guaranteed that in view of the party's black majority, "at least one-half of the nominations to elective offices, as well as one-half the appointed offices, shall be taken from that class [of black Republicans], and no distinctions made whether said nominees and appointees were born free or not." On the question of political patronage, Resolution 13 provided that the party "will support no man for office who will not openly and boldly pledge himself to make an equal distribution among white and colored alike of all offices to which he may have power of appointment." Resolutions 4 and 7 ensured black Louisianians equal access to schools and other public accommodations. The party advocated "a complete and thorough revision of the laws now in force in this State, [so] that the legislation of

102. Binning, "Carpetbaggers' Triumph," 26; *Tribune,* April 11, 25, May 14, July 3, 1867.

Louisiana may be consistent with and conducive to the great ends of equal justice to all men, without distinction of race or color." [103]

The party platform's radicalism posed a direct threat to the strategy of Republican moderates. Faced with almost universal opposition from the region's traditional electorate and under pressure from northern Republicans to expand their political base, they undertook conciliatory policies to win white support. During Reconstruction, Republican moderates throughout the South would attempt to build a broader white constituency by awarding political patronage to established local leaders and by obstructing civil rights legislation. In Louisiana, the pro-Warmoth faction moved decisively to purge party leadership of the architects of the platform's one-half guaranty and equal accommodations provisions. In the closing moments of the 1867 convention, they staged a coup engineered by Sypher. As chairman of the reorganization committee, Sypher hurriedly pushed through a scheme to replace the radical executive committee. The new committee's membership roster of forty-six whites and thirty-three blacks listed some of the key opponents of the radical platform, including Governor Benjamin F. Flanders, New Orleans mayor Edward Heath, Reverend John P. Newman, and Warmoth.

Governor Flanders, a friend of Warmoth's, had opposed the "one-half guaranty" embodied in Resolutions 13 and 14 in an address to the convention. Mayor Heath had upheld the color line at the height of the desegregation struggle. On May 15, only weeks before the convention, the mayor had issued a proclamation prohibiting "all persons whatever from intruding into any store, shop or other place of business conducted by private individuals, against the consent and wish of the owners, proprietors, or keepers of the same." [104]

Newman, one of the mayor's most ardent supporters and a key Warmoth ally, had engaged in a fierce feud with the *Tribune* in the weeks leading up to the Republican convention. In an article entitled "Who Shall Rule?" in his weekly newspaper, the New Orleans *Advocate,* the Methodist minister accused the radical faction of promoting a "black republican party." In such

103. Binning, "Carpetbaggers' Triumph," 27; *Tribune,* June 13, 18, 1867.

104. Foner, *Reconstruction,* 346–79; Binning, "Henry Clay Warmoth," 80; *Tribune,* June 29, 1867; Fischer, *The Segregation Struggle,* 40.

a circumstance, Newman warned, "the republican party of this country would abandon its [the Louisiana Republican party's] ranks." [105]

Maneuvering behind the scenes, Warmoth, who later wrote that the radical Republican movement was a plot by Creole extremists "to establish an *African State Government,*" played a major role in ousting the old committee. His political organ, the New Orleans *Republican,* had sided with the Ben Butler Clubs. In October, with the approach of the constitutional convention, the paper would support the city's segregated school system and disavow the party's pledge to "enforce the opening of all schools . . . to all children." [106]

Another member of the new committee, Lionel A. Sheldon, an army comrade of Warmoth's, had testified before the congressional committee that investigated the 1866 riot, in behalf of ex-Confederates Thomas E. Adams and Harry T. Hays, respectively the chief of police and sheriff of Orleans Parish at the time of the massacre. When queried by the committee about political conditions in the state, Sheldon had asserted that the "kindest men in the State of Louisiana towards the blacks are the old slaveholders" and that the real troublemakers and "sneaking rebels" in the region were the advocates of black suffrage.[107]

Sypher's actions infuriated the radicals. Apart from ignoring executive committee policy of assigning half the seats to black Republicans, the makeup of the rival committee presaged the sabotage of the party platform. In a futile attempt to preserve the old executive committee, the *Tribune* retaliated by printing Sheldon's entire testimony before the House committee. In a succession of editorials, the paper protested the new committee's white majority and questioned the credentials of other members of the governing council. "Have bad Republicans been put in because they were white," the paper asked, "and good Republicans been kept out because they were black?" [108]

105. Logsdon and Bell, "The Americanization of Black New Orleans," in *Creole New Orleans,* ed., Hirsch and Logsdon, 246–47; *Tribune,* May 21, 1867.

106. Warmoth, *War, Politics and Reconstruction,* 52; *Tribune,* May 14, 1867; Fischer, *The Segregation Struggle,* 47.

107. Binning, "Carpetbaggers' Triumph," 28. Sheldon's congressional testimony is in Fogelson and Rubenstein, eds., *Mass Violence in America,* 281.

108. *Tribune,* June 20, 1867.

The objections of the radicals notwithstanding, the reconstituted committee chose Governor Flanders as chairman. Within two weeks of the convention's adjournment, the thoroughness of the moderate takeover forced the *Tribune* to concede that even though "the new committee is regarded with distrust, and even with apprehension by a portion of the people," the authority of the old committee "is no longer but a contested and doubtful power."

With the overthrow of the radical committee and the approach of the constitutional convention, the *Tribune* pleaded with its readers to support only those delegates who pledged their support to the party platform. Without the one-half guaranty, the paper warned, it would "soon be done with the colored interest. Office-seekers will rule, and the colored citizens will be but tools." Without school desegregation, the nation would separate into two peoples. "We are, or at least we ought to be one people. . . . Do not make any longer white and black citizens; let us have but Americans." [109]

The radical platform's one-half guaranty assured black Republicans of an equal share of seats at the constitutional convention that convened on November 23, 1867, in New Orleans. In fact, with fifty of the convention's ninety-eight seats, black delegates possessed a slight numerical edge. Together with their white allies, they succeeded in incorporating key elements of the party platform into the state constitution. Laws providing for equal access to places of public accommodation were adopted, and Article 135 prohibited segregation in public schools and required the state to furnish each parish with at least one public school. The measure forbade "separate schools or institutions of learning established exclusively for any race by the State of Louisiana." [110]

Ultimately, however, the radicals lost their struggle to guarantee a quota of state offices to black Louisianians. Still, the faction's advanced demands forced the moderates to pass a resolution requiring state officials to accept the principle of racial equality. Incorporated into Article 100, the

109. *Ibid.*, June 23, 27, 29, July 31, 1867.

110. Tunnell, *Crucible of Reconstruction,* 111–19; Charles Vincent, "Negro Leadership and Programs in the Louisiana Constitutional Convention of 1868," *Louisiana History,* X (Fall, 1969), 342; Fischer, *The Segregation Struggle,* 51.

measure provided that all officeholders take an oath to "accept the civil and political equality of all men, and agree not to attempt to deprive any person or persons, on account of race, color, or previous condition, of any political or civil right, privilege, or immunity enjoyed by any other class of men." [111]

The rejection of the one-half guaranty revealed a growing rift among black Republicans. P.B.S. Pinchback, a native Mississippian and black politician who had acquired considerable influence during the war, had criticized the measure on the grounds that race should not be placed above merit in choosing political officials. Although he ultimately supported the constitution's equal accommodations provision (Article 13), he nonetheless spoke against the measure during the first round of debate. While Pinchback insisted on equal accommodations, he opposed forced integration: "I consider myself just as far above coming into company that does not want me, as they are above my coming into an elevation with them. . . . I do not believe that any sensible colored man upon this floor would wish to be in a private part of a public place without the consent of the owners of it. It is false; it is wholesale falsehood to say that we wish to force ourselves upon white people." Pinchback's position may have represented the thinking of most southern blacks on the question of access to public accommodations, but it put him squarely at odds with party radicals.[112]

While Pinchback advised caution and warned that blacks "could get no rights the whites did not see fit to give them," the *Tribune* forces insisted on a social revolution. They demanded complete equality and issued a warning of their own to Republican moderates: "Halfway measures are done away with. . . . Whoever stops in revolutionary times is soon distanced. All attempts to veneering the old system have thus far been impotent, and have entailed the fall of those who tried to shape new ideas into old forms. We want soldiers of progress and no compromise. . . . We want

111. Fischer, *The Segregation Struggle,* 54.

112. W.E.B. DuBois, *Black Reconstruction in America, 1860–1880* (1935; rpr. New York, 1975), 467–68, 472–73. Tunnell, *Crucible of Reconstruction,* 124; Vincent, "Black Louisianians," in *Louisiana's Black Heritage,* ed. MacDonald, Kemp, and Haas, 100; Howard N. Rabinowitz, *Race Relations in the Urban South, 1865–1890* (New York, 1978), 346–49.

to remodel anew the institutions of the State." Differences between the *Tribune*-led radicals and black leaders like Pinchback helped white moderates to clinch their control of the Republican Party at the state nominating convention.[113]

In New Orleans in January, 1868, Pinchback quashed a move at the party convention to place his name in nomination for governor on the ground that the candidacy of a black man was unwise. He and another influential black leader, native Mississippian James H. Ingraham, threw their support to Warmoth. On the first ballot for governor, Afro-Creole radical Francis E. Dumas, a leader of the *Tribune* faction and a distinguished former officer in the Union army, won with 41 votes. Warmoth followed closely with 37, while three other nominees received a lesser number. On the second round, however, Warmoth narrowly defeated Dumas, winning the gubernatorial nomination 45 to 43.[114]

The radicals charged the Warmoth faction with fraud, accusing the moderates of illegally adding three votes and rejecting one to defeat Dumas, their candidate. They refused to recognize Warmoth's nomination. Convinced of the illegality of the vote and certain that a Warmoth victory would undermine the cause of black civil and political equality, the *Tribune*-led radicals bolted and put forward an independent Republican ticket.[115]

The moderates moved quickly to undercut their rivals. At the end of January, within two weeks of the radical bolt, they purged nine more radicals from the Central Executive Committee and discharged the *Tribune* as the party's official organ. After replacing the radical journal with a pro-Warmoth newspaper, the New Orleans *Republican,* they dispatched an emissary to Washington to complete their takeover of the party press. There, in February, Thomas W. Conway, a nominee on the Warmoth ticket for superintendent of education, succeeded in having the Republican government switch its patronage from the *Tribune* to the *St. Landry Progress,* a pro-Warmoth newspaper.

113. *Tribune,* April 11, 1867.

114. Houzeau, *My Passage,* 72–74; Wilson, *The Black Phalanx,* 176, 211; Foner, *Reconstruction,* 332; Tunnell, *Crucible of Reconstruction,* 76–77, 135, 145; Taylor, *Louisiana Reconstructed,* 156.

115. Taylor, *Louisiana Reconstructed,* 156–57.

With little in the way of party support, the radicals' rival campaign foundered. Warmoth triumphed in the April election, assuring his faction's dominance of the state's Reconstruction government. Stripped of its subsidy, the *Tribune* suspended publication within two weeks of the election.[116]

Through a series of well-calculated maneuvers beginning in April, 1867, the moderates had undercut their radical opponents and seized control of the Louisiana Republican Party. With Warmoth's victory in 1868, their dominance of state government was assured. And with the moderate victory, the prospects for the kind of societal transformation envisioned by Afro-Creole leaders at the war's outset appeared dim indeed on the eve of "radical reconstruction."

116. *Ibid.*, 156–58; Tunnell, *Crucible of Reconstruction,* 135; Binning, "Henry Clay Warmoth," 113–14. Government printing subsidies were essential to the *Tribune* and other pro-Republican newspapers, since a paper could not sustain itself through subscriptions and local advertising. A printing bill enacted in 1868 provided that $1.5 million in state warrants be paid out over a period of three years. These state warrants supported Republican papers like the *Tribune* (Taylor, *Louisiana Reconstructed,* 198–99).

Conclusion

The "reign of knaves and adventurers," Rodolphe Desdunes later wrote of the Warmoth administration, "was of short duration." Besieged by charges of corruption and rent by political factionalism, the regime's downfall began as early as mid-1870. The Louisiana house delivered the fatal blow in December, 1872, when legislators impeached the governor and suspended him from office.[1]

Before his political ouster, Warmoth courted white Democrats and stymied civil rights legislation just as radical Republicans had feared. After taking office on June 27, 1868, the Republican carpetbagger appointed Democrats to political office, curried favor with white conservatives by awarding patronage to local leaders, rejected two civil rights measures, resisted desegregation of the public schools, opposed enforcement of the state constitution's equal accommodations provision, and accumulated a personal fortune by "exacting tribute" from railroad companies.

In September, 1868, within three months of his inauguration, Warmoth vetoed a bill designed to enforce Article 13 of the constitution, which provided for equal access to public accommodations. When the state legislature passed another bill in 1870 providing for criminal prosecution of civil rights violations, Warmoth vetoed that measure as well. The governor's opposition to the legislative enactments of 1868 and 1870, his resistance to the desegregation of public schools, and his concessions to Democratic conservatives prompted Oscar J. Dunn, his black lieutenant governor, to complain that the carpetbagger governor had "shown an itching desire . . .

1. Desdunes, *Our People,* 135; Taylor, *Louisiana Reconstructed,* 209–47. Although charged with bribery and other illegal actions, Warmoth was never convicted (Tunnell, *Crucible of Reconstruction,* 171).

to secure the personal support of the Democracy at the expense of his party, and an equally manifest craving to obtain a cheap and ignoble white respectability by the sacrifice of . . . the masses of that race who elected him." Warmoth was, Dunn continued, the party's "first Ku Klux Governor." In the end, the Warmoth administration's attempts to win the allegiance of white conservatives proved as destructive of black interests as those of the Banks regime.[2]

Warmoth's veto of the 1868 civil rights bill convinced Afro-Creole radicals to revive the *Tribune*. Reappearing near the end of the year, the paper urged state legislators to make the state constitution's public accommodations and school desegregation provisions their top priority. The "*spirit* of slavery" survived, the paper insisted, in attempts to reduce the rights of blacks to the "lowest possible *minimum*." Emancipation would not be complete until segregation and other discriminatory practices were undone.[3]

After the state charter's ratification in 1868, the black newspaper's insistence on its enforcement and the mounting assertiveness of black New Orleanians compelled Warmoth and Superintendent of Education Conway to institute the desegregation of the city's public schools in 1870. By the spring of 1874, hundreds of black and white schoolchildren attended approximately nineteen racially mixed schools. But even before ratification of the Reconstruction constitution in 1868, an Afro-Creole campaign against segregation contributed to real progress in New Orleans; for example, a *Tribune*-led attack on segregated streetcars in 1867 had produced equality on the city's public conveyances.[4]

Although financial difficulties forced Dr. Louis Charles Roudanez and his associates once again to suspend publication of the *Tribune* in 1871, they nonetheless pressed ahead with their radical agenda. In the 1872 governor's race, they put forward Aristide Mary as a candidate for the governorship; Mary was an uncompromising proponent of the "one-half guaranty" and a celebrated Afro-Creole philanthropist. When his bid for the

2. Fischer, *The Segregation Struggle,* 64–72; Taylor, *Louisiana Reconstructed,* 210; Foner, *Reconstruction,* 385; Houzeau, *My Passage,* 56; Vincent, *Black Legislators,* 102; Oscar J. Dunn to Horace Greeley, August 31, 1871, cited in Tunnell, *Crucible of Reconstruction,* 165.

3. Houzeau, *My Passage,* 56; *Tribune,* January 3, 17, 1869.

4. Fischer, *The Segregation Struggle,* 32–41, 119; Tunnell, *Crucible of Reconstruction,* 150, 167–69.

Republican gubernatorial nomination failed, Afro-Creole leaders joined the Louisiana Unification Movement, a bipartisan political coalition organized by the city's white business elite.

With the state on the verge of anarchy and economic collapse after the tumultuous election of 1872, the Unifiers moved to oust the existing Republican-carpetbagger regime and return control of state government to local leaders. Since black votes were essential to the restoration of "home rule," the Unification Movement emphasized racial cooperation and advocated acceptance of black civil and political rights. In the summer of 1873, they invited Afro-Creole leaders Roudanez, Mary, and Lieutenant Governor Caesar C. Antoine to join a platform committee of five blacks and five whites entrusted with formulating the movement's overall objectives.

In return for their support, black committee members exacted remarkable concessions. The approved report, which appeared in New Orleans newspapers on June 17, pledged to guarantee black civil and political rights. It accepted an equal distribution of political offices between the races, and it sanctioned the desegregation of all places of public accommodation including schools, factories, and transit carriers. The agreement even promised to consider the breakup of large landholdings into small farms, so that "our colored citizens and white emigrants may become practical farmers and cultivators of the soil." Such a proposal had been put forward first in 1864, when the *Tribune* had recommended dividing plantations into five-acre plots to be "partitioned among the tillers of the soil." [5]

The Unification platform won significant support from white New Orleanians until Afro-Creoles Roudanez, Mary, Antoine, Paulin C. Bon-

5. Houzeau, *My Passage,* 56; Tinker, *Les Ecrits,* 299; Desdunes, *Our People,* 93–94, 138–41; Rankin, "The Impact of the Civil War," 403–404; T. Harry Williams, "The Louisiana Unification Movement of 1873," *Journal of Southern History,* XI (August, 1945), 350–53; Foner, *Reconstruction,* 545–51; Armstead L. Robinson, "Beyond the Realm of Social Consensus: New Meanings of Reconstruction for American History," *Journal of American History,* LXVIII (September, 1981), 93–94; Fischer, *The Segregation Struggle,* 74–78. An original of the approved Report of the Committee of Fifteen is in the Unification Movement Papers, Louisiana State University, Baton Rouge; *Tribune,* September 24, 1864. When Democrats claimed victory in the fiercely contested gubernatorial election of 1872, the federal government used force to install Republican William P. Kellogg in the governor's office. Violence ensued as many Democrats refused to recognize the Kellogg regime.

seigneur, and E. Rillieux, together with three other representative black leaders, publicly withheld their backing of home rule until "the existing opposition against the enjoyment of our rights . . . shall have ceased." The statement formally ended the Unification Movement. A white supremacist resurgence in the state's rural districts had already ruled out any real chance of a viable interracial coalition.[6]

In 1873, with the retreat from Reconstruction underway in Louisiana, the U.S. Supreme Court inaugurated the federal government's retreat from equal citizenship in the Louisiana *Slaughterhouse* cases, the Court's first interpretation of the Fourteenth Amendment. Though the question of black citizenship was not at issue in *Slaughterhouse,* the ruling largely nullified the intent of the Fourteenth Amendment by curbing federal power and affirming the states' rights tradition. As the Supreme Court surrendered custody of black civil rights to the individual states in the *Slaughterhouse* decision and in an equally disastrous ruling of 1876, *U.S.* v. *Cruikshank* (a case that also originated in Louisiana), violence escalated throughout the South.

White supremacists founded new paramilitary organizations modeled on the earlier Ku Klux Klan and the Knights of the White Camellia to drive black and white Republicans from power. In the face of an unrelenting campaign of terror, northern resolve faltered. Frustrated by its inability to transform an unrepentant and hostile South, the North turned its attention from the plight of southern blacks to national reconciliation and economic expansion.

In the contested presidential election of 1876, Ulysses S. Grant, the country's outgoing Republican president, urged an end to the crisis with a call for "peace at any price." In the compromise of 1877, southern blacks paid the price of peace when Democrats agreed to halt their opposition to the presidency of Republican Rutherford B. Hayes in return for withdrawing federal troops from the South. Thus ended the era of Reconstruction. With its demise, the white-ruled South set about fortifying a political and social system based upon disfranchisement and racial segregation.[7]

6. Williams, "The Louisiana Unification Movement," 354–66. The signed document is in the Unification Papers.

7. Otto H. Olsen, ed., *The Thin Disguise: Turning Point in Negro History* (New York, 1967), 6–7; Foner, *Reconstruction,* 529–31.

In New Orleans, Afro-Creole activists devised a strategy of resistance while nurturing their militant ideology in freemasonry and spiritualism. When Democrats reimposed segregated schools and public accommodations in 1877, they joined with leaders of the English-speaking, Protestant black community to stage large public protests, then sued under the 1868 constitution. After Louisiana lawmakers sanctioned segregated public facilities in the 1879 state constitution, the activists concluded that the federal courts offered the best opportunity to reverse the declining status of black southerners.

In 1891, with Aristide Mary's financial assistance, Afro-Creoles Louis A. Martinet, Caesar C. Antoine, Rodolphe Desdunes, and Arthur Estèves mobilized black resistance to state-imposed segregation with the founding of the Citizens' Committee. The committee proposed to test the constitutionality of a railroad segregation statute, the 1890 Louisiana Separate Car Law. On June 7, 1892, the committee set its plan in motion when Homer A. Plessy, a young black Creole artisan and community activist, boarded the East Louisiana Railway in New Orleans and took a seat in the white coach of the train. When he refused to move to a separate car for black riders, the police hustled him from the train and charged him with violating the segregation law.[8]

With Plessy's arrest, the committee's legal counsel denounced the separate-car law for establishing "an insidious distinction and discrimination between Citizens of the United States based on race which is obnoxious to the fundamental principles of National Citizenship." The segregation statute perpetuated "involuntary servitude as regards Citizens of the Colored Race under the merest pretense of promoting the comfort of passengers on railway trains." In these and other respects, the committee asserted, the separate-car law abridged "the privileges and immunities of Citizens of the United States and the rights secured by the 13th and 14th

8. Logsdon and Bell, "The Americanization of Black New Orleans," in *Creole New Orleans,* ed. Hirsch and Logsdon, 253; Donald E. DeVore and Joseph Logsdon, *Crescent City Schools: Public Education in New Orleans, 1841–1991* (Lafayette, La., 1991), 86–89. Desdunes, *Our People,* 141–44; Citizens' Committee, *Report of the Proceedings for the Annulment of Act 111 of 1890* (New Orleans, [1897?]), 2–3, in Alexander Pierre Tureaud Collection, Amistad Research Center, Tulane University; Olsen, *The Thin Disguise,* 14; Charles A. Lofgren, *The Plessy Case: A Legal-Historical Interpretation* (New York, 1987), 41.

Amendments to the Federal Constitution." When state courts denied their arguments against the 1890 law, the committee proceeded to the nation's highest court.[9]

In view of southern realities and earlier Supreme Court decisions, the prospects for a favorable outcome appeared all but hopeless. Nonetheless, when a despairing supporter of the Citizens' Committee complained that black New Orleanians were engaged in "a battle which is forlorn," black Creole leader Rodolphe Desdunes insisted upon a militant strategy: "Liberty is won by continued resistance to tyranny. . . . [It is] more noble and dignified to fight, no matter what, than to show a passive attitude of resignation. Absolute submission augments the oppressor's power and creates doubts about the feelings of the oppressed." [10]

On May 19, 1896, the Supreme Court upheld the "separate but equal" doctrine and denied that segregation was oppressive. In accordance with the decision, Plessy appeared before the New Orleans Criminal District Court in January, 1897, pleaded guilty, paid a fine of twenty-five dollars, and was discharged. Before disbanding, the Citizens' Committee issued a final public statement: "The majority of the judges of the highest tribunal of this American government have cast their voice against our just appeal in demanding the nullification of a State law which is in direct conflict with the American Declaration of Independence, which declares that 'all men are created free and equal.' Notwithstanding this decision, which was rendered contrary to our expectations, we, as freemen, still believe that we were right, and our cause was sacred. . . . In defending the cause of liberty, we met with defeat, but not with ignominy." [11]

The *Plessy* decision sanctioned a system of enforced segregation that endured for over fifty years. Introduced first into railroads and schools, Jim Crow laws were extended to nearly every facet of southern life, including libraries, restaurants, prisons, playgrounds, hospitals, restrooms, drinking fountains, and even cemeteries. Southern extremists had proceeded, one observer noted, "from an undiscriminating attack upon the Negro's ballot

9. Olsen, *The Thin Disguise,* 14.

10. New Orleans *Crusader,* August 15, 1891, cited in Logsdon and Bell, "The Americanization of Black New Orleans," in *Creole New Orleans,* ed. Hirsch and Logsdon, 260; Desdunes, *Our People,* 147.

11. New Orleans *Crusader,* July 19, 1890; Lofgren, *The Plessy Case,* 207–208.

to a like attack upon his schools, his labor, his life—from the contention that no Negro shall vote to the contention that no Negro shall learn, that no Negro shall labor, and (by implication) that no Negro shall live." [12]

In Louisiana, as elsewhere in the South, state-mandated segregation was extended to virtually all public accommodations during the 1890s. Finally in 1898, a new state constitution stripped black Louisianians of the right to vote. Radical Reconstruction's promise of freedom, opportunity, and equal citizenship had ended in a nightmare of semiservitude, Jim Crow laws, and disfranchisement.[13]

Yet, the *Plessy* case embodied a powerful dissent, one that had been forged in a revolutionary age. In the upheaval of war and Reconstruction, Afro-Creole radicals succeeded in transforming the symbolic ideals of *liberté, égalité, fraternité* into an aggressive campaign for meaningful change. Although their dream of a utopian millennium of racial justice and harmony far exceeded what their state and nation were willing to concede, their actions assured the survival of their protest tradition. Their legacy of dissent had changed the political dynamic during the Civil War and Reconstruction and shifted the expectations of both blacks and whites. This dissent, which would be used to rescue the Reconstruction amendments in later Supreme Court decisions, offered a vision for the future.

12. C. Vann Woodward, *Origins of the New South, 1877–1913* (1951; rpr. Baton Rouge, 1974), 353.

13. Logsdon and Bell, "The Americanization of Black New Orleans," in *Creole New Orleans,* ed. Hirsch and Logsdon, 259–60; Joe Gray Taylor, "Louisiana: An Impossible Task," in *Reconstruction and Redemption in the South,* ed. Otto H. Olsen (Baton Rouge, 1980), 208.

Appendix: Membership in Two Masonic Lodges and Biographical Information

The information in Tables 1, 2, and 3 was taken mainly from the Polar Star #1 Minutes Book, 1858–1868, and the Fraternité #20 Minutes Book, 1868–1873 (both written in French), in the George Longe Collection at the Amistad Research Center, Tulane University. M signifies member; H, honorary member; D, deceased; V, visitor; R, resigned; T, turned away from membership.

TABLE 1. MEMBERSHIP LIST FOR POLAR STAR #1, 1858–1867

The asterisk indicates the lodge member was an officer of the Supreme Council when that body opened Scottish Rite masonry to black members.

NAME	1858	1859	1860	1861	1862	1863	1864	1865	1866	1867
Alexander, Sidney	—	—	—	—	—	—	—	M	—	—
Avila, Manuel Pio*	—	—	—	M	M	M	—	—	—	—
Avril, Ths.	—	M	—	—	—	—	—	—	—	—
Ayneau, E.	M	M	M	—	—	—	—	—	—	—
Bance, H.	M	—	—	—	—	—	—	—	—	—
Baudrias, J.	—	—	M	M	M	—	—	—	—	—
Beer, David	M	—	—	—	—	—	—	—	—	—
Bellezia, Tarq.	—	—	—	—	—	—	—	—	—	M
Berta, François B.*	—	—	—	M	—	M	M	M	M	M
Bienvenu, Charles*	M	M	M	—	—	M	M	—	M	—
Blassonné, Louis H.	—	—	—	—	—	—	—	M	—	—

POLAR STAR #1 (cont.)

NAME	1858	1859	1860	1861	1862	1863	1864	1865	1866	1867
Boudreau, Theo.	—	—	—	—	—	—	M	M	—	—
Boulin, E.	M	M	M	—	—	—	—	—	—	—
Bourges, E.	—	M	M	—	—	—	—	—	—	—
Bretton, F.	—	M	—	—	—	—	—	—	—	—
Brisolara, Manuel	—	—	—	—	—	—	—	M	M	M
Brisolara, Pepe	—	—	—	—	—	—	—	M	M	M
Brosset, J. B.	—	M	M	M	M	M	M	—	M	D
Broue, D.	—	—	—	—	—	—	—	—	M	—
Brown, Sam.	—	—	—	M	M	—	—	—	—	—
Brugier, Romain	M	—	—	—	M	—	—	—	—	—
Brun, Jean	—	—	—	—	—	—	—	M	—	—
Caboche, Louis	M	M	M	M	D	—	—	—	—	—
Caillat, Hilaire	—	—	—	M	M	M	M	D	—	—
Caron, Auguste	—	—	—	—	—	—	—	—	M	M
Carrière, Leopold	—	—	—	—	M	M	M	—	—	—
Castro, Vincent de	M	M	—	—	—	—	—	—	—	—
Cazenavette, Gabr.	—	—	—	—	—	—	—	—	M	R
Chassaignac, Eug.	—	—	—	—	—	—	—	—	—	M
Chemidlin, Joseph	—	—	M	M	M	M	M	M	—	M
Claiborne, Charles	M	—	—	—	—	—	—	—	—	—
Closterman, H. C.	M	—	—	—	—	—	—	—	—	—
Colin, N.	M	M	M	M	M	—	—	—	—	—
Collens, Thomas W.	M	—	—	—	M	—	—	M	M	R
Collon, Feremie	M	M	M	—	—	—	—	—	—	—
Colombet, A.	—	—	—	—	M	—	—	—	—	—
Considerant, Vict.	M	—	—	—	—	—	—	—	—	—
Constance, Henry	—	M	M	—	M	—	—	—	—	—
Crozat, S. E.	—	M	—	—	—	—	—	—	—	—
Dagoret, G. M.	—	—	—	M	M	M	—	M	—	—
Dehezoni, L. E.	—	M	—	—	—	—	—	—	—	—
Delamotte, A.	—	—	—	M	M	—	—	—	—	—
Delpeuch, Alcide	—	—	—	—	—	—	—	—	M	M
Delustre, V. A.	M	—	—	—	—	—	—	—	—	—
Deluzain, L. E.	M	M	—	M	M	—	—	—	M	—
Denis, A.	M	M	M	—	—	—	—	M	—	—
Deverger, P.	M	—	—	—	—	—	—	—	—	—
Deviu, Gustave	—	—	—	—	—	—	—	—	M	—

POLAR STAR #1 (cont.)

NAME	1858	1859	1860	1861	1862	1863	1864	1865	1866	1867
Devron, G.	—	—	—	—	—	—	—	—	—	M
Diamantis, Chris.	—	M	—	—	—	—	—	—	—	—
Dour, Bertrand*	—	—	—	—	—	—	—	M	M	M
Doyen, V. M.	M	—	—	—	—	—	—	—	—	—
Dubuisson, J.	—	M	M	—	—	—	—	—	—	—
Dubuisson, Mistil	M	M	M	—	—	—	M	—	—	—
Dudoussat, A.*	—	—	—	M	M	M	—	M	M	R
Dufau, Louis	M	M	M	M	M	—	—	—	—	—
Dufour, W. C.	—	M	—	—	—	—	—	—	—	—
Dupre, C.	M	M	M	—	M	M	M	M	M	—
Ecrot, F.	M	M	M	—	—	M	—	—	—	—
Fabio, J. G.	—	M	M	M	—	D	—	—	—	—
Fabio, T.	D	—	—	—	—	—	—	—	—	—
Fauquet, F.	M	—	—	—	—	—	—	—	—	—
Ferrier, A.	M	M	M	M	M	M	—	M	—	M
Forget, Philippe	—	—	—	—	—	—	M	M	—	M
Fortier, Charles	—	M	—	—	—	—	—	—	—	—
Foulhouze, James	M	M	M	M	M	—	—	M	—	—
Fouquet, Edouard	—	—	—	—	—	—	M	M	M	M
Fourment, M.	—	—	—	—	—	—	M	M	—	D
Frederic, Anto.	—	M	—	—	—	—	—	—	—	—
Gadet, Celestin	—	—	—	—	—	—	—	M	M	M
Garcia, Benjamin	—	—	—	—	—	—	—	—	—	M
Gardette, James	M	M	M	—	—	—	—	—	—	—
Gentil, Jean	M	M	M	—	—	—	—	—	—	—
Gloeckner, L.	M	M	M	—	—	—	—	—	—	—
Gros, Th.	—	M	—	—	—	—	—	—	—	—
Guerin, Emile	—	—	—	M	M	—	—	—	—	—
Gueydan, François	—	—	—	—	—	—	—	M	—	—
Guinaud, Charles	M	—	—	—	—	—	—	—	—	—
Guns, Th.	—	M	—	—	—	—	—	—	—	—
Habert, H.	—	—	—	M	M	M	—	M	—	R
Helm, Philippe	M	M	M	M	M	M	M	—	—	—
Jacob, Em.*	M	M	M	M	M	M	M	M	M	—
Jamot, A.	—	—	—	—	—	—	—	—	M	M
Jaquet, Alfred E.	—	—	—	—	—	—	—	—	—	—
Jauquet, J.*	M	M	M	M	—	M	M	M	M	M

POLAR STAR #1 (cont.)

NAME	1858	1859	1860	1861	1862	1863	1864	1865	1866	1867
Knabe, C. L.*	—	—	—	—	—	—	—	—	M	—
Lacoste, Belgarde	—	M	—	—	—	—	—	—	—	—
Lacoste, G.	M	—	—	—	—	—	—	—	—	—
Lacroix, Charles	M	—	—	—	—	—	—	—	—	—
Lafon, Pierre	—	—	—	—	M	M	M	M	—	—
Lafond, Ach.	—	—	—	M	M	M	—	M	—	—
Lasalle, G.	M	M	M	—	—	—	—	—	—	—
Latapie, Jean	—	—	—	—	—	M	—	—	—	—
Leblanc, Joseph*	—	—	—	—	—	—	—	—	M	—
Leclair, P. T.	—	—	M	M	—	—	—	—	—	—
Leclerc, E. V.	—	M	—	—	—	—	—	—	—	—
Ledoyen, V. M.	M	M	M	M	M	—	—	M	—	—
Lefoullon, J. J.	—	—	—	—	M	—	—	—	—	—
Lefranc, Emile	—	—	—	—	—	—	—	M	M	M
Leroy, Gustave	—	—	—	—	M	—	—	—	—	—
L'Etang, Hypo. B.	—	—	—	—	—	—	—	—	—	M
Levasseur, F.	M	—	—	—	—	—	—	—	—	—
Levy, Mathias	M	M	M	—	M	—	—	—	—	—
Lisboni, G.	M	—	—	—	—	—	—	—	—	—
Lods, Louis*	—	—	—	—	—	—	—	M	M	M
Lucchesi, Gius.	—	—	—	—	—	—	M	M	M	M
Luneau, A.	M	—	—	—	M	—	—	—	—	—
Lutz, Jacques	—	—	—	—	—	—	M	M	—	—
Lyonnet, Philippe	—	—	—	—	—	M	—	M	—	—
Magnon, G. H.	M	—	—	—	—	—	—	—	—	—
Mandry, Constant	—	—	—	—	—	—	—	—	—	M
Marc, Edouard*	M	M	M	M	M	M	M	M	M	M
Marchant, L. E.*	—	—	—	M	M	M	M	—	M	M
Martinez, F. P.	—	—	—	—	—	M	M	—	M	—
Massicot, J. E.	M	—	—	M	M	—	—	—	—	—
Massore, W. J.	—	M	—	—	—	—	—	—	—	—
Meilleur, M.	M	—	—	—	—	—	—	—	—	—
Menie, Att.	—	M	—	—	—	—	—	—	—	—
Meunier, Auguste	—	—	M	M	M	M	M	—	—	—
Michel, D.	M	M	—	—	—	—	—	—	—	—
Momus, Jean	—	—	—	M	—	—	—	—	—	—
Montasant, G.	—	M	—	—	—	—	—	—	—	—
Morel, Ernest	M	—	—	M	M	—	—	—	—	—

POLAR STAR #1 (cont.)

NAME	1858	1859	1860	1861	1862	1863	1864	1865	1866	1867
Nikol, F. W.	—	—	—	—	—	—	M	—	—	M
Petitjean, P.	—	—	—	M	—	—	—	—	—	—
Queyrouse, L.	—	—	—	M	—	—	—	—	—	—
Raisson, J. A.	—	M	—	—	—	—	—	—	—	—
Rapin, Charles	—	—	M	M	M	—	—	—	—	—
Remy, Henry	M	M	M	M	M	M	M	—	—	—
Remy, Pierre Louis	—	—	—	—	—	M	M	—	—	—
Revol, Emile	—	—	—	—	—	—	—	M	M	M
Robbin, Pierre	—	—	—	—	—	—	—	—	—	M
Rolling, Henry	—	—	—	—	—	—	—	M	—	—
Rooten, Elan	M	—	—	—	—	—	—	—	—	—
St. Marc, F. V.	—	—	—	M	M	—	—	—	—	—
Sallean, Lewis	—	—	—	M	M	—	—	—	—	—
Scessi, Guambas.	—	—	—	—	—	—	—	—	—	M
Seguela, A.	—	M	M	M	M	M	M	—	—	—
Sillan, Edouard	—	—	—	—	—	—	—	—	M	—
Simon, L.	—	—	—	M	—	M	M	M	M	M
Socola, Angelo*	—	—	—	M	—	M	M	M	M	M
Soulé, Nelvil	—	—	—	—	—	—	—	—	M	M
Soulé, Pierre	M	M	M	M	M	M	—	M	M	R
Therin, A. Jean B.	—	—	—	—	—	M	M	M	M	M
Thomas, Armand	M	M	M	—	—	—	—	—	—	—
Ticchi, F.	M	M	M	M	—	—	—	—	—	—
Tournaben, G. F.	M	M	M	M	—	—	—	—	—	—
Trappin, C.	—	—	—	M	—	—	—	—	—	—
Trouard, C.	—	M	—	—	—	—	—	—	—	—
Turpia, J.	M	M	—	M	M	M	M	—	—	—
Vandergriff, J. B.	—	—	—	—	—	—	—	M	—	—
Vanrooten, G.	M	M	—	—	M	—	—	—	—	—
Vaudricosat, A. D.	—	M	—	—	—	—	—	—	—	—
Vedot, J.	M	M	M	—	—	—	—	—	—	—
Vitry, Charles	M	M	M	M	M	M	M	M	—	—
Voisin, A.	—	—	—	M	M	M	M	M	M	M
Waflaer, Auguste	—	—	—	—	—	—	—	—	—	M
Walden, J.	—	M	—	—	—	—	—	—	—	—
White, Charles F.	—	M	—	—	—	—	—	—	—	—
Woolverton, N.	—	—	—	M	M	—	—	—	—	—

TABLE 2. MEMBERSHIP LIST FOR FRATERNITÉ #20, 1867–1873

The asterisk indicates the lodge member was white.

NAME	1867	1868	1869	1870	1871	1872	1873
Adam, Manuel	M	M	—	—	—	M	M
Adzer, Laurence C.	R	—	—	—	—	—	—
Aicard, Justin	M	—	—	—	—	R	—
Armand, Joseph	M	—	—	—	—	—	—
Aubert, Charles	M	—	—	—	—	—	—
Audisson, P. J.	—	M	M	—	M	—	—
Auguste, Myrtile	M	—	—	—	—	—	—
Auld, Joseph J.	M	M	M	M	M	M	M
Avila, Manuel Pio*	H	H	H		H	D	—
Bacas, Paul Albert	M	—	—	—	—	—	—
Barthe, Ant.	—	—	M	M	M	M	M
Barthe, E.	—	—	M	—	—	—	—
Bebee, Luc	M	—	—	—	—	—	—
Bernard, William	M	—	—	—	—	—	—
Berniard, Jules	M	—	—	M	M	M	—
Berry, J. B.	V	—	—	—	—	—	—
Berthelot, Eugene C.	M	—	—	—	—	—	—
Bertonneau, Arnold	M	—	—	—	—	—	—
Bienvenu, P.	—	M	—	—	—	—	—
Blancand, Eug.	M	M	M	M	M	M	D
Blasco, Amedee G.	M	—	—	—	—	—	—
Boissière, Jean	M	—	—	—	M	M	—
Boissière, V.	—	—	—	M	M	—	—
Bonseigneur, Henry	V	V	—	—	—	—	—
Boutin, Gustave	M	—	—	—	—	—	—
Boutin, Jos. A.	M	—	—	M	—	—	—
Camp, Clement	M	—	—	—	—	—	—
Campanel, E.	—	M	M	—	—	—	—
Camps, Henry J.	M	M	M	M	M	M	M
Capla, L.J.P.	M	M	—	—	—	—	—
Carrere, F.	—	—	M	M	M	M	M
Cavelier, Louis	M	—	M	—	—	—	—
Cavelier, Theophile	M	—	—	—	—	—	—
Cavelier, V.	—	—	H	—	—	—	—
Chassaignac, Eugene*	H	H	H	—	—	—	—

FRATERNITÉ #20 (cont.)

NAME	1867	1868	1869	1870	1871	1872	1873
Cheval, Paul	M	M	M	—	M	—	—
Claiborne, Charles S.*	M	M	M	—	M	—	—
Coca, C. B.	M	—	M	M	M	M	—
Cornière, Jacques	M	M	—	—	—	—	—
Courcelle, Charles Jos.	M	—	—	—	—	—	—
Daumoy, A.	M	—	—	—	—	—	—
Daunoy, J. A.	M	—	—	—	—	—	—
Dauphin, Augustin Ovide	M	M	D	—	—	—	—
Deruize, Donatien	M	—	—	—	—	—	—
Dollide, J. E.	M	—	—	—	—	—	—
Dolliole, Jos. Ernest	M	—	—	—	—	—	—
Dominguez, Raphael	M	M	M	—	—	—	—
Dorin, Honore	M	—	—	—	—	—	—
Dorin, Theodore	M	—	—	—	—	—	—
Dorsin, M.	—	M	—	—	—	—	—
Dours, B.*	H	—	D	—	—	—	—
Ducre, G.	—	M	M	M	M	—	—
Dufillo, John B.	M	M	M	—	—	—	—
Dupart, Victor	—	—	—	—	M	M	M
Durnford, Thomas M.	M	R	—	—	—	—	—
Dussuau, E., Jr.	—	—	—	—	M	—	—
Dussuau, Emile	M	M	M	M	M	M	M
Dussuau, J. B.	M	—	—	—	—	—	—
Etranger, F.	—	—	—	—	M	—	—
Farr, Edward D.	M	R	—	—	—	—	—
Fernandez, O.	—	—	—	—	M	—	—
Folk, Armand	M	M	M	—	—	—	—
Follin, Joseph	M	M	—	—	—	—	—
Folque, Armand	M	—	—	—	—	—	—
Fouche, Louis Nelson	M	M	—	—	M	—	—
Fourcade, St. Cyr	V	—	—	—	—	—	—
Frank, S.	—	—	—	—	M	—	—
Freche, G.	V	—	—	—	—	—	—
Gabriel, Julien L.	M	—	M	—	—	—	—
Gabriel, Saintville	M	M	M	M	M	M	M
Gaignard, Charles	M	—	—	—	—	—	—
Gardere, Eug.	M	—	M	M	M	M	M

FRATERNITÉ #20 (cont.)

NAME	1867	1868	1869	1870	1871	1872	1873
Garidelle, Clemine	—	M	—	—	—	—	—
Garidelle, Joseph	M	—	—	—	—	—	—
Glaudin, Meurice	R	—	—	—	—	—	—
Greeves, Felix	M	—	—	—	—	—	—
Grubbs, Joseph G.	M	—	—	—	—	—	—
Herriman, George	M	M	M	M	M	M	M
Herriman, George, Jr.	—	—	—	—	—	M	M
Hewlett, Leopold	M	M	—	—	M	—	—
Icard, Justin	M	M	—	—	—	—	—
Julien, Albert	—	—	—	—	M	—	—
Julien, Faix	—	—	—	—	M	—	—
Labau, Joseph	M	—	—	—	—	—	—
Lafonta, Joseph	M	M	M	—	M	—	—
Lainez, J. O.	M	M	—	—	M	—	—
Laizer, C.	—	—	H	—	—	—	—
Lanabere, Azemar	M	—	—	—	—	M	M
Laprime, Adolphe	M	—	—	—	—	—	—
Lautier, Louis	M	M	M	D	—	—	—
Lavigne, Edouard	M	M	M	M	M	M	M
Leclerc, J. M.	—	—	—	—	—	—	—
Leon, Thomas	M	—	—	—	—	—	—
Lods, Louis*	H	H	H	—	—	—	—
Longmire, John H.	M	M	M	M	M	M	—
Loquet, Ernest	—	—	—	—	M	M	M
McCarthy, Lionel	—	M	—	—	—	—	—
Macarthy, V. E.	—	M	—	—	—	—	—
Mallard, Albert	R	—	—	—	—	—	—
Marc, Edouard*	—	H	H	H	H	H	M
Massicot, J. A.*	—	M	M	M	—	—	—
Mathieu, E.	V	—	—	—	—	—	—
Mathieu, Joseph Ernest	M	—	—	—	—	—	—
Mathieu, S. Henry	M	—	—	—	—	—	—
Meilleur, Eug.	M	M	M	M	M	M	—
Meilleur, V. Albert	M	—	—	—	—	—	—
Merle, Emile	M	—	—	—	—	—	—
Merlet, E.	—	M	—	—	—	—	—
Montieu, Jos. L.	M	—	—	—	—	—	—

FRATERNITÉ #20 (cont.)

NAME	1867	1868	1869	1870	1871	1872	1873
Mouny, F.	—	M	—	—	—	—	—
Noble, J.	—	V	V	—	—	—	—
Noel, Arthur	M	—	M	—	—	—	—
Pavageau, N.	—	—	—	—	M	—	—
Pavageau, Randolph	M	M	—	—	M	—	—
Pavageau, Robert	M	M	—	—	—	—	—
Pavajean, N.	M	—	—	—	—	—	—
Peralt, Anthony	M	M	M	M	M	M	—
Perrault, R. O.	M	—	—	—	—	—	—
Petit, P.	M	—	—	—	—	—	—
Piron, M.	M	—	—	—	M	—	—
Pizero, Elisee	M	—	—	—	—	—	—
Planchard, H.	—	—	—	—	M	—	—
Populus, Ulysse	M	M	M	—	M	M	—
Raphael, A.	M	M	—	—	—	—	—
Raphael, Hermogene	M	M	—	—	—	—	—
Rapp, Eugène	M	—	—	—	—	—	—
Relf, Henry	M	—	—	—	—	M	—
Rene, Louis C.	M	—	—	—	—	—	—
Revoil, C. Arthur	M	—	—	—	—	—	—
Rey, Henry Louis	M	M	M	M	M	M	M
Rey, Hyppolite	M	M	M	—	M	M	—
Rey, Octave	M	M	—	—	—	—	—
Rieriras, J.	—	—	—	—	—	M	—
Rodant, Louis C.	—	—	—	—	V	—	—
Roudes, Sully	M	M	M	M	M	M	M
Rougelot, Alfred	M	M	—	—	—	—	—
Roussel, C.	M	—	—	—	—	—	—
Roussève, Paul	—	—	—	—	M	M	M
Roux, Jos. G.	M	—	—	—	—	—	—
Roux, Vincent	M	—	—	—	—	—	—
Sainez, J. O.	M	—	—	—	—	—	—
Sautier, Louis	M	—	—	—	—	—	—
Sauvinet, C. S.	M	—	—	—	—	—	—
Senegal, H.	—	—	—	V	V	—	—
Siggs, Ed.	M	M	—	—	—	—	—
Snaer, L. A.	M	M	—	—	—	—	—

FRATERNITÉ #20 (cont.)

NAME	1867	1868	1869	1870	1871	1872	1873
St. Amant, Hubert	M	M	—	M	R	—	—
St. Cyr, C. L.	M	M	M	M	M	M	M
St. Leger, Ant.	M	—	—	—	—	—	—
Staès, J. E.	—	—	—	—	—	M	M
Surle, Louis	M	M	M	—	—	—	—
Taylor, Jos. W.	M	M	—	—	—	—	—
Tervalon, Adolphe F.	M	—	—	—	—	—	—
Testut, Charles H. J.*	—	—	—	—	M	M	M
Thezan, Sidney	M	—	—	—	—	—	—
Tissot	V	—	—	—	—	—	—
Tomlinson, E.	—	—	M	M	M	M	M
Trévigne, Paul	M	M	M	—	M	—	—
Veque, Charles	M	M	M	M	M	—	M
Vigers, William	M	M	—	M	—	—	—
Voisin, Terence	M	—	—	—	—	—	—
Xavier, Benjamin	M	M	M	M	M	M	R
Xavier, Joseph F.	—	—	—	M	—	—	—

TABLE 3. BIOGRAPHICAL INFORMATION ON MEMBERS OF FRATERNITÉ #20

Name	Age	Religion	Marital Status	Occupation	Place of Birth	Address
Audisson, P. J.	29	Catholic	Married	Merchant	France	Bayou Lafourche
Barthe, Ant.	44	Catholic	Married	Cooper	La.	401 Grand Hommes
Blancand, Eug.	47	Catholic	Widower	Merchant	La.	Corner Casacalvo & Mandeville Sts.
Blanchard, H.	28	Catholic	Single	—	La.	106 Orleans St.
Camp, Clement	48	Unitarian	Married	Contractor	N.O., La.	2157 Perdido St.
Carrere, F.	20	Catholic	Single	Clerk	La.	88 Mandeville St.
Claiborne, Charles S.	29	—	Married	Merchant	N.O., La.	439 Royal St.
Cornière, Jacques	41	Catholic	Single	Painter	France	9 Ursulines St.
Courcelle, Charles Jos.	47	Catholic	Married	Merchant	N.O., La.	Dumaine & Derbigny Sts.
Daunoy, J. A.	40	Catholic	—	Cigar maker	N.O., La.	371 Orleans St.
Dolliole, Jos. Ernest	22	Catholic	Single	Shoemaker	N.O., La.	174 Villere St.
Dominguez, Raphael	30	Catholic	Married	Cafe owner	Tampico, Mexico	Corner St. Claude & St. Anne Sts.
Dorin, Theodore	22	Catholic	Single	Cigar maker	Santiago de Cuba	223 Dumaine St.
Durnford, Thomas M.	42	—	Married	Farmer	N.O., La.	63 Basin St.
Dussuau, J. B.	48	Catholic	Married	Jeweler	N.O., La.	263 Roman St.
Farr, Edward	32	Catholic	Married	Clerk	N.O., La.	Corner Villery & Laharpe
Folque, Armand	34	Catholic	Married	Mason	N.O., La.	34 Good Children
Gabriel, Saintville	35	Catholic	Single	Cigar maker	N.O., La.	99 Perdido St.
Lafonta, Joseph	30	Catholic	Single	Shopkeeper	La.	20 Bayou St. John St.
Lainez, J. O.	34	Catholic	Married	Teacher	N.O., La.	104 St. Phillip St.
Leclerc, J. M.	53	Catholic	Married	Merchant	N.O., La.	147 Dauphine St.
Leon, Thomas	32	Catholic	Married	Mason	N.O., La.	560 Craps St.
Massicot, J. A.	26	Catholic	Married	Judge	La.	409 Grand Hommes
Montieu, Joseph L.	40	Catholic	Married	Clerk	N.O., La.	158 Gasquet St.
Mouny, F.	23	Catholic	Single	Cigar maker	La.	113 Quarter
Noel, Arthur	21	Catholic	Single	Typographer	N.O., La.	73 Dauphine St.
Peralt, Anthony	46	Catholic	Married	Merchant	N.O., La.	Tremé Quarter, Marais St.

BIOGRAPHICAL INFORMATION (cont.)

Name	Age	Religion	Marital Status	Occupation	Place of Birth	Address
Petit, P.	32	Catholic	Single	Painter	Amiens, France	Corner Bourgoyne & Hospital Sts.
Rapp, Eugène	32	—	—	Tailor	N.O., La.	345 Derbigny St.
Revoil, C. Arthur	37	Catholic	Married	Cigar maker	N.O., La.	402 Good Children
Roudes, Sully	45	Catholic	Married	Cooper	La.	343 Benton St.
Sautier, Louis	36	Catholic	Married	Cooper	N.O., La.	7 & 8 Dryades St.
Sauvinet, C. S.	38	Catholic	Married	Clerk	N.O., La.	4 Kerlerec St.
Siggs, Edward	40	—	Single	Merchant	N.O., La.	118 Toulouse St.
Snaer, J. L.	25	Catholic	Single	Supt. of residential streets	La.	234 St. Claude St.
Xavier, Joseph François	37	Catholic	Single	Cooper	N.O., La.	—

Bibliography

PRIMARY SOURCES

Archival Materials

Amistad Research Center, Tulane University, New Orleans

Longe, George. Collection.

Roussève, Charles B. Collection.

Tureaud, Alexander Pierre. Collection.

Archives of the Sisters of the Holy Family, New Orleans

Association de la Sainte Famille. New Orleans, 1847.

"Loterie pour aider à l'érection d'un hospice," 1848–1851, Financial Records, Association de la Sainte Famille.

Earl K. Long Library, University of New Orleans, New Orleans

Christian, Marcus B. Collection.

Grandjean, René. Collection.

Supreme Court of Louisiana Collection.

Hill Memorial Library, Louisiana State University, Baton Rouge

Wharton, E. C. Papers.

Historic New Orleans Collection

Proceedings of the Convention of the Republican Party of Louisiana. New Orleans, 1865.

Howard-Tilton Memorial Library, Tulane University, New Orleans

Documens relatifs à la colonie d'Eureka, dans l'Etat de Veracruz. New Orleans, 1857.

"Letters of Padre Antonio de Sedella." Typescript translation.

Prospectus de l'institution catholique des orphelins indigents. New Orleans, 1847.

Société française pour l'abolition de l'esclavage. Paris, 1841.

Mr. Soulé's Speech at Opelousas, Louisiana Delivered on September 6, 1851. New Orleans, 1851.

Tableau des ff. composant la r. loge le foyer maçonnique no.4. New Orleans, 1842.

Library of Congress, Washington, D.C.

Jackson, Andrew. Papers.

Jefferson, Thomas. Papers.

National Archives, Washington, D.C.

Messages of Francisco Luis Hector, El Baron de Carondelet. (Translation.)

New Orleans Public Library, New Orleans

Records and Deliberations of the Cabildo. (Translation.)

Public Documents

Acts of the State of Louisiana.

New Orleans Notarial Archives.

U.S. Bureau of the Census. 7th, 8th Censuses.

The War of the Rebellion: A Compilation of the Official Records of the Union and Confederate Armies. 128 vols. Washington, D.C., 1880–1901.

Published Memoirs, Letters, Articles, Documents, Literary Works, and Historical Narratives

Address from the Democratic Executive Committee of the Parish of Orleans. New Orleans, 1859.

Annual Grand Communication of the Supreme Council. New Orleans, 1859.

Basler, Roy P., ed. *The Collected Works of Abraham Lincoln.* 8 vols. New Brunswick, N.J., 1953.

Bassett, John Spencer, ed. *Correspondence of Andrew Jackson.* 6 vols. Washington, D.C., 1926–33.

Beard, Reverend John R. *The Life of Toussaint L'Ouverture, the Negro Patriot of Hayti: Comprising an Account of the Struggle for Liberty in the Island, and a Sketch of Its History to the Present Period.* 1853; rpr. Westport, Conn., 1970.

Butler, Benjamin F. *Butler's Book.* Boston, 1892.

Cahagnet, Alphonse. *Encyclopédie magnetique spiritualiste.* Paris, 1856.

Carter, Clarence Edwin, ed. *The Territory of Orleans, 1803-1812.* Washington, 1940. Vol. IX of Carter, ed., *The Territorial Papers of the United States.*

Citizens' Committee. *Report of the Proceedings for the Annulment of Act 111 of 1890.* New Orleans, [1897?].

Clapp, Theodore. *Autobiographical Sketches and Recollections, During a Thirty-Five Years' Residence in New Orleans*. Boston, 1858.

Desdunes, Rodolphe Lucien. *Hommage rendu à la mémoire de Alexandre Aristide Mary, décédé à la Nouvelle-Orléans, le 15 mai 1893, à l'age de 70 ans*. [New Orleans, 1893].

———. "Mme. Bernard Couvent." Translated by Raoul M. Pérez. *Negro History Bulletin,* VII (October, 1943), 7–9.

———. *Our People and Our History*. Translated and edited by Sister Dorothea Olga McCants. Baton Rouge, 1973.

Dufau, Louis. *Principes de la Franc-Maçonnerie*. N.p., 1859.

Ellis, John Tracy, ed. *Documents of American Catholic History*. 2 vols. Chicago, 1967.

Faye, Stanley, ed. "The Schism of 1805 in New Orleans." *Louisiana Historical Quarterly,* XXII (January, 1939), 98–141.

Folger, Robert B. *The Ancient and Accepted Scottish Rite, in Thirty-Three Degrees*. New York, 1862.

Ford, Worthington C., ed. *Writings of John Quincy Adams*. 6 vols. New York, 1916.

Garreau, Armand. "Louisiana." In Vol. I of *Veillées Louisianaises,* edited by Charles Testut. 2 vols. New Orleans, 1849.

Hamilton, Thomas. *Men and Manners in America*. Philadelphia, 1833.

Hinds, William A. *American Communities and Co-operative Colonies*. 3rd ed. Philadelphia, 1975.

Houzeau, Jean-Charles. *My Passage at the New Orleans "Tribune": A Memoir of the Civil War Era*. Edited by David C. Rankin and translated by Gerard F. Denault. Baton Rouge, 1984.

Jameson, J. Franklin, ed. "Correspondence of John C. Calhoun." *Annual Report of the American Historical Association*. Washington, D.C., 1900.

Johannsen, Robert W., ed. *The Letters of Stephen A. Douglas*. Urbana, Ill., 1961.

Kardec, Allan. *Le Livre des esprits*. 1857; rpr. Montreal, 1979.

King, Grace. *New Orleans, the Place and the People*. 1896; rpr. New York, 1926.

Lanusse, Armand, ed. *Les Cenelles: Choix de poésies indigènes*. New Orleans, 1845.

Lemonnier, Alfred. *Notice biographique sur Jean-Charles Houzeau*. Mons, Belgium, 1889.

Levasseur, A. *Lafayette en Amerique, 1824–1825, ou journal d'un voyage aux Etats-Unis*. 2 vols. Paris, 1829.

M'Caleb, Thomas, ed. *The Louisiana Book: Selections from the Literature of the State*. New Orleans, 1894.

Martineau, Harriet. *Retrospect of Western Travel*. 2 vols. London, 1838.

Mercier, Alfred. *Biographie de Pierre Soulé, Sénateur à Washington.* Paris, 1848.

Nichols, Thomas Low. *Forty Years of American Life.* 1864; rpr. New York, 1937.

Nolte, Vincent. *Fifty Years in Both Hemispheres, or Reminiscences of the Life of a Former Merchant.* New York, 1854.

Olmsted, Frederick Law. *The Cotton Kingdom: A Traveller's Observations on Cotton and Slavery in the American Slave States.* Edited by Arthur M. Schlesinger. New York, 1953.

Parton, James. *General Butler in New Orleans.* New York, 1864.

Petition of the Wardens of the Church of St. Louis of New Orleans. New Orleans, 1843.

Porteous, Laura L., and Walter Prichard. "Index to Spanish Judicial Records of Louisiana, LXXI, September, 1784." *Louisiana Historical Quarterly,* XXIV (October, 1941), 1232–80.

Reed, Emily Hazen. *Life of A. P. Dostie; or, The Conflict in New Orleans.* New York, 1868.

Robertson, James Alexander, ed. *Louisiana Under the Rule of Spain, France, and the United States, 1785–1807.* 2 vols. Cleveland, 1910–11.

Rowland, Dunbar, ed. *Official Letter Books of W.C.C. Claiborne,* 1801–1816. 6 vols. Jackson, Miss., 1917.

Scot, James B. *Outline of the Rise and Progress of Freemasonry in Louisiana.* New Orleans, 1873.

Stuart, James. *Three Years in North America.* 2 vols. New York, 1833.

Testut, Charles. *Fleurs d'été.* New Orleans, 1851.

———. *Portraits littéraires de la Nouvelle-Orléans.* New Orleans, 1850.

———, ed. *Veillées Louisianaises.* 2 vols. New Orleans, 1849.

———. *Le Vieux Salomon ou une famille d'esclaves au XIX siècle.* New Orleans, 1872.

Warmoth, Henry Clay. *War, Politics and Reconstruction: Stormy Days in Louisiana.* New York, 1930.

Warren, Harris Gaylord, ed. and trans. "Documents Relating to the Establishment of Privateers at Galveston, 1816–1817." *Louisiana Historical Quarterly,* XXI (October, 1938), 1086–1109.

[Wharton, Edward C.] *Thoughts on the Slavery Question and the Clay Compromise.* Washington, D.C., 1850.

Willey, Nathan. "Education of the Colored Population of Louisiana." *Harper's New Monthly Magazine,* XXXIII (July, 1866), 244–50.

Williams, George W. *A History of the Negro Troops in the War of Rebellion, 1861–1865.* New York, 1888.

Wish, Harvey, ed. *Reconstruction in the South, 1865–1877: First-Hand Accounts of the American Southland After the Civil War, by Northerners & Southerners.* New York, 1965.

Newspapers and Periodicals

Boston *Banner of Light,* 1858.
Boston *Liberator,* 1853.
Bulletin de la Maçonnerie Louisianaise (New Orleans), 1869.
Genius of Universal Emancipation, 1830.
Harper's New Monthly Magazine, 1866.
L'Album littéraire: Journal des jeunes gens, amateurs de littérature, 1843.
La Renaissance (New Orleans), 1862.
Le Delta maçonnique (Masonic Delta) (New Orleans), 1858–61.
Le Franc-Maçon (New Orleans), 1845–46.
L'Equité (New Orleans), 1871.
Le Spiritualiste (New Orleans), 1857–58.
Louisiana Courier (Le Courrier de la Louisiane) (New Orleans), 1848–57.
L'Union (New Orleans), 1862–64.
New Orleans *Bee (L'Abeille de la Nouvelle Orléans),* 1843–59.
New Orleans *Crusader,* 1890–91.
New Orleans *Daily Crescent,* 1848.
New Orleans *Daily Delta,* 1857–62.
New Orleans *Daily Picayune,* 1843–68.
New Orleans *Louisiana Weekly,* 1938.
New Orleans *Times,* 1863.
New Orleans *Tribune,* 1864–69.
New York *Anglo-African,* 1864.
New York *Christian Spiritualist,* 1854.
New York *Times,* 1862.
New York *Tribune,* 1862.
Niles' Weekly Register (Baltimore), 1825.
Perfect Ashlar, April, 1951.
Propagateur Catholique (New Orleans), 1843–58.
Revue des Colonies (Paris), 1835–37.

SECONDARY SOURCES

Books and Pamphlets

Ahlstrom, Sydney E. *A Religious History of the American People*. New Haven, 1972.
Artz, Frederick B. *Reaction and Revolution*. New York, 1934.
Baker, Derek, ed. *Church, Society and Politics*. Oxford, Eng., 1975.

Baudier, Roger. *The Catholic Church in Louisiana*. New Orleans, 1939.

———. *Centennial: St. Rose of Lima Parish*. New Orleans, 1957.

Beecher, Jonathan. *Charles Fourier: The Visionary and His World*. Berkeley, 1986.

Bellegarde-Smith, Patrick. *In the Shadow of Powers: Dantes Bellegarde in Haitian Social Thought*. Atlantic Highlands, N.J., 1985.

Bennett, Lerone, Jr. *Before the Mayflower: A History of Black America*. Rev. ed. New York, 1986.

Berlin, Ira. *Slaves Without Masters: The Free Negro in the Antebellum South*. New York, 1974.

Billings, Warren M., and Edward F. Haas, eds. *In Search of Fundamental Law: Louisiana's Constitutions, 1812–1974*. Lafayette, La., 1993.

Binkley, Robert C. *Realism and Nationalism, 1852–1871*. 1935; rpr. New York, 1963.

Blackburn, Robin. *The Overthrow of Colonial Slavery, 1776–1848*. London, 1988.

Blassingame, John W. *Black New Orleans, 1860–1880*. Chicago, 1973.

Blied, Benjamin J. *Catholics and the Civil War*. Milwaukee, Wisc., 1945.

Braude, Ann. *Radical Spirits: Spiritualism and Women's Rights in Nineteenth-Century America*. Boston, 1989.

Brown, Slater. *The Heyday of Spiritualism*. New York, 1970.

Burson, Caroline Maude. *The Stewardship of Don Esteban Miró, 1782–1792: A Study of Louisiana Based Largely on the Documents in New Orleans*. New Orleans, 1940.

Callan, Louise. *Philippine Duchesne: Frontier Missionary of the Sacred Heart, 1769–1852*. Westminster, Md., 1957.

Cass, Donn A. *Negro Freemasonry and Segregation: An Historical Study of Prejudice Against American Negroes as Freemasons*. Chicago, 1957.

Christian, Marcus. *The Battle of New Orleans: Negro Soldiers in the Battle of New Orleans*. New Orleans, 1965.

Christovich, Mary Louise, and Roulhac Toledano, eds. *Faubourg Tremé and the Bayou Road*. Gretna, La., 1980. Vol. VI of Christovich, ed., *New Orleans Architecture*. 6 vols.

Coleman, Edward Maceo, ed. *Creole Voices: Poems in French by Free Men of Color First Published in 1845*. Washington, D.C., 1945.

Conrad, Glen R., ed. *Cross, Crozier, and Crucible: A Volume Celebrating the Bicentennial of a Catholic Diocese in Louisiana*. New Orleans, 1993.

Cragg, Gerald R. *The Church and the Age of Reason, 1648–1789*. Grand Rapids, Mich., 1960.

Curry, Leonard P. *The Free Negro in Urban America, 1800–1850: The Shadow of the Dream*. Chicago, 1981.

Dalencour, François. *Alexandre Pétion devant l'humanité: Alexandre Pétion et Simon Bolivar, Haiti et l'Amérique Latine*. Port-au-Prince, 1928.

Darnton, Robert. *Mesmerism and the End of the Enlightenment in France*. Cambridge, Mass., 1968.

Davis, Cyprian. *The History of Black Catholics in the United States*. New York, 1993.

Davis, David Brion. *The Problem of Slavery in the Age of Revolution, 1770–1823*. Ithaca, N.Y., 1975.

Detiege, Audrey Marie. *Henriette Delille, Free Woman of Color: Foundress of the Sisters of the Holy Family*. New Orleans, 1976.

DeVore, Donald E., and Joseph Logsdon. *Crescent City Schools: Public Education in New Orleans, 1841–1991*. Lafayette, La., 1991.

Dominguez, Virginia R. *White by Definition: Social Classification in Creole Louisiana*. New Brunswick, N.J., 1986.

DuBois, W.E.B. *Black Reconstruction in America, 1860–1880*. 1935; rpr. New York, 1975.

Eaton, Clement. *Freedom of Thought in the Old South*. Durham, N.C., 1940.

Ellis, John Tracy. *American Catholicism*. Chicago, 1956.

Ellsworth, Lucius F., ed. *The Americanization of the Gulf Coast, 1803–1850*. Pensacola, Fla., 1972.

Ellwood, Robert S., Jr. *Alternative Altars: Unconventional and Eastern Spirituality in America*. Chicago, 1979.

Ettinger, Amos A. *The Mission to Spain of Pierre Soulé, 1853–1855*. New Haven, 1932.

Evans, David Owen. *Social Romanticism in France, 1830–1848*. London, 1951.

Fay, Bernard. *Revolution and Freemasonry, 1680–1800*. Boston, 1935.

Fellman, Michael. *The Unbounded Frame: Freedom and Community in Nineteenth-Century American Utopianism*. Westport, Conn., 1973.

Fick, Carolyn E. *The Making of Haiti: The Saint Domingue Revolution from Below*. Knoxville, Tenn., 1990.

Fischer, Roger A. *The Segregation Struggle in Louisiana, 1862–77*. Urbana, Ill., 1974.

Fogelson, Robert M., and Richard E. Rubenstein, eds. *Mass Violence in America*. New York, 1969.

Foner, Eric. *Reconstruction: America's Unfinished Revolution, 1863–1877*. New York, 1988.

Fortescue, William. *Alphonse de Lamartine: A Political Biography*. New York, 1983.

Fortier, Alceé. *A History of Louisiana*. 4 vols. New York, 1904.

Fossier, Albert A. *New Orleans: The Glamour Period, 1800–1840*. New Orleans, 1957.

Fredrickson, George M. *White Supremacy: A Comparative Study in American and South African History*. New York, 1981.

Fuller, Robert C. *Mesmerism and the American Cure of Souls*. Philadelphia, 1982.

Garrett, Clarke. *Spirit Possession and Popular Religion*. Baltimore, Md., 1987.

Gayarré, Charles. *History of Louisiana*. 4 vols. New Orleans, 1903.

Geggus, David P. *Slavery, War, and Revolution: The British Occupation of Saint Domingue, 1793–1798*. Oxford, Eng., 1982.

George, Albert J. *Lamartine and Romantic Unanimism*. New York, 1940.

Greene, Glen Lee. *Masonry in Louisiana: A Sesquicentennial History, 1812–1962*. New York, 1962.

Griggs, Earl Leslie, and Clifford H. Prator, eds. *Henry Christophe and Thomas Clarkson: A Correspondence*. New York, 1968.

Grummond, Jane Lucas de. *The Baratarians and the Battle of New Orleans*. 1961; rpr. Baton Rouge, 1968.

———. *Renato Beluche: Smuggler, Privateer and Patriot, 1780–1860*. Baton Rouge, 1983.

Guarneri, Carl J. *The Utopian Alternative: Fourierism in Nineteenth-Century America*. Ithaca, N.Y., 1991.

Haas, Edward F., ed. *Louisiana's Legal Heritage*. Pensacola, Fla., 1983.

Hales, E.E.Y. *Revolution and the Papacy, 1769–1846*. Garden City, N.Y., 1960.

Halévi, Ran. *Les Loges maçonniques dans la France d'Ancien Régime: Aux origines de la sociabilité démocratique*. Paris, 1984.

Hall, Gwendolyn Midlo. *Africans in Colonial Louisiana: The Development of Afro-Creole Culture in the Eighteenth Century*. Baton Rouge, 1992.

Headings, Mildred J. *French Freemasonry Under the Third Republic*. Johns Hopkins University Studies in Historical and Political Science, LXVI. Baltimore, 1948.

Heinl, Robert Debs, and Nancy Gordon Heinl. *Written in Blood: The Story of the Haitian People, 1492–1971*. Boston, 1978.

Hennesey, James. *American Catholics: A History of the Roman Catholic Community in the United States*. New York, 1981.

Hirsch, Arnold R., and Joseph Logsdon, eds. *Creole New Orleans: Race and Americanization*. Baton Rouge, 1992.

Hollandsworth, James G., Jr. *The Louisiana Native Guards: The Black Military Experience During the Civil War*. Baton Rouge, 1995.

Holloway, Mark. *Heavens on Earth: Utopian Communities, 1680–1880*. 2nd ed. New York, 1966.

Hunt, Alfred N. *Haiti's Influence on Antebellum America: Slumbering Volcano in the Caribbean*. Baton Rouge, 1988.

Jacob, Margaret C. *The Radical Enlightenment: Pantheists, Freemasons and Republicans*. London, 1981.

Jaffa, Harry V. *Crisis of the House Divided*. Seattle, 1959.

James, C.L.R. *The Black Jacobins: Toussaint L'Ouverture and the San Domingo Revolution*. Rev. ed. New York, 1963.

Jean-Baptiste, Saint-Victor. *Haiti: Sa Lutte pour l'emancipation*. Paris, 1957.

Johannsen, Robert W. *Stephen A. Douglas*. New York, 1973.

Jones, John Maxwell, Jr. *Slavery and Race in Nineteenth-Century Louisiana French Literature*. Camden, N.J., 1978.

Judah, J. Stillson. *The History and Philosophy of the Metaphysical Movements in America*. Philadelphia, 1967.

Kaplan, Sidney. *The Black Presence in the Era of the American Revolution, 1770–1800*. New York, 1973.

Kerr, Howard, and Charles L. Crow, eds. *The Occult in America: New Historical Perspectives*. Urbana, Ill., 1983.

Krantz, Frederick. *History from Below: Studies in Popular Protest and Popular Ideology*. Oxford, Eng., 1988.

Labbé, Dolores Egger. *Jim Crow Comes to Church: The Establishment of Segregated Catholic Parishes in South Louisiana*. 2nd ed. Lafayette, La., 1971.

Lafon Nursing Home of the Holy Family. New Orleans, 1973.

Latortue, Régine, and Gleason R.W. Adams, eds. and trans. *Les Cenelles: A Collection of Poems by Creole Writers of the Early Nineteenth Century*. Boston, 1979.

Lefebvre, Georges. *The French Revolution*. Translated by Elizabeth M. Evanson. 2 vols. 1951; rpr. New York, 1969.

Ligou, Daniel, *et al., Histoire des francs-maçons en France*. Toulouse, France, 1981.

Lofgren, Charles A. *The Plessy Case: A Legal-Historical Interpretation*. New York, 1987.

Logan, Rayford W. *Haiti and the Dominican Republic*. New York, 1968.

McCloy, Shelby T. *The Negro in France*. Lexington, Ky., 1961.

———. *The Negro in the French West Indies*. Lexington, Ky., 1966.

McConnell, Roland C. *Negro Troops of Antebellum Louisiana: A History of the Battalion of Free Men of Color*. Baton Rouge, 1968.

McCrary, Peyton. *Abraham Lincoln and Reconstruction: The Louisiana Experiment*. Princeton, 1978.

MacDonald, Robert R., John R. Kemp, and Edward F. Haas, eds. *Louisiana's Black Heritage*. New Orleans, 1979.

McPherson, James M. *The Negro's Civil War: How American Negroes Felt and Acted During the War for the Union*. 1965; rpr. Urbana, Ill., 1982.

———. *The Struggle for Equality*. 2nd ed. Princeton, 1995.

Martin, François-Xavier. *The History of Louisiana from the Earliest Period*. New Orleans, 1882.

Masur, Gerhard. *Simon Bolivar*. Albuquerque, N.M., 1948.

Maurois, André. *Olympio: The Life of Victor Hugo*. Translated by Gerard Hopkins. New York, 1956.

Melville, Annabelle M. *Louis William DuBourg: Bishop of Louisiana and the Floridas, Bishop of Montauban, and Archbishop of Besançon, 1766–1833*. 2 vols. Chicago, 1986.

Menn, Joseph Karl. *The Large Slaveholders of Louisiana, 1860*. New Orleans, 1964.

Miller, Randall M., and Jon L. Wakelyn, eds. *Catholics in the Old South: Essays on Church and Culture*. Macon, Ga., 1983.

Mills, Gary B. *The Forgotten People: Cane River's Creoles of Color*. Baton Rouge, 1977.

Moore, R. Laurence. *In Search of White Crows: Spiritualism, Parapsychology, and American Culture*. New York, 1977.

Necheles, Ruth F. *The Abbé Grégoire, 1787–1831: The Odyssey of an Egalitarian*. Westport, Conn., 1971.

Nelson, Geoffrey K. *Spiritualism and Society*. New York, 1969.

Nicholls, David. *From Dessalines to Duvalier: Race, Colour and National Independence in Haiti*. Cambridge, Eng., 1979.

Nolan, Charles E. *Bayou Carmel: The Sisters of Mount Carmel of Louisiana, 1833–1903*. Ann Arbor, 1977.

Olsen, Otto H., ed. *Reconstruction and Redemption in the South*. Baton Rouge, 1980.

———, ed. *The Thin Disguise: Turning Point in Negro History*. New York, 1967.

O'Neill, Charles Edwards. *Church and State in French Colonial Louisiana: Policy and Politics to 1732*. New Haven, 1966.

———. *Séjour: Parisian Playwright from Louisiana*. Lafayette, La., 1996.

Pachonski, Jan, and Reuel K. Wilson. *Poland's Caribbean Tragedy: A Study of Polish Legions in the Haitian War of Independence, 1802–1803*. New York, 1986.

Palmer, R. R. *The Age of Democratic Revolution: A Political History of Europe and America, 1760–1800*. 2 vols. Princeton, 1959, 1964.

Parry, J. H., and Philip Sherlock. *A Short History of the West Indies*. 3rd ed. New York, 1971.

Plummer, Brenda Gayle. *Haiti and the Great Powers, 1902–1915*. Baton Rouge, 1988.

Podmore, Frank. *Mediums of the Nineteenth Century*. 2 vols. 1902; rpr. New York, 1963. Originally published under the title *Modern Spiritualism: A History and a Criticism*.

Pompilus, Pradel. *Manuel illustré d'histoire de la littérature haitienne*. Port-au-Prince, 1961.

Quarles, Benjamin. *Allies for Freedom: Blacks and John Brown*. New York, 1974.

———. *Lincoln and the Negro*. New York, 1962.

———. *The Negro in the Civil War*. 1953; rpr. New York, 1968.

Rabinowitz, Howard. *Race Relations in the Urban South, 1865–1890*. New York, 1978.

———, ed. *Southern Black Leaders of the Reconstruction Era*. Urbana, Ill., 1982.

Rauch, Basil. *American Interest in Cuba, 1848–1855*. New York, 1948.

Ripley, C. Peter. *Slaves and Freedmen in Civil War Louisiana*. Baton Rouge, 1976.

Rose, Willie Lee. *Slavery and Freedom*. Edited by William W. Freehling. New York, 1982.

Roussève, Charles B. *The Negro in Louisiana: Aspects of His History and His Literature*. New Orleans, 1937.

Saintsbury, George. *A Short History of French Literature*. Oxford, Eng., 1901.

Sauvigny, Guillaume de Bertier de. *La Révolution parisienne de 1848 vue par les américains*. Paris, 1984.

Saxon, Lyle. *Lafitte the Pirate*. New York, 1930.

Shea, John G. *A History of the Catholic Church Within the Limits of the United States*. 4 vols. 1886–92; rpr. New York, 1978.

Shugg, Roger W. *Origins of Class Struggle in Louisiana: A Social History of White Farmers and Laborers during Slavery and After, 1840–1875*. 1939; rpr. Baton Rouge, 1968.

Smith, Charles Spencer. *A History of the A.M.E. Church*. 1922; rpr. New York, 1968.

Sterkx, H. E. *The Free Negro in Ante-Bellum Louisiana*. Rutherford, N.J., 1972.

Stevens, Philip. *Victor Hugo in Jersey*. Chichester, Eng., 1985.

Stromberg, Roland N. *An Intellectual History of Modern Europe*. New York, 1966.

Talmon, J. L. *Romanticism and Revolt: Europe, 1815–1848*. New York, 1967.

———. *The Unique and the Universal: Some Historical Reflections*. New York, 1965.

Tannenbaum, Frank. *Slave and Citizen: The Negro in the Americas*. New York, 1946.

Taylor, Joe Gray. *Louisiana Reconstructed, 1863–1877*. Baton Rouge, 1974.

———. *Negro Slavery in Louisiana*. Baton Rouge, 1963.

Tinker, Edward Larocque. *Bibliography of the French Newspapers and Periodicals of Louisiana*. Worcester, Mass., 1933.

———. *Les Ecrits de langue française en Louisiane au XIX siecle.* 1923; rpr. Geneva, 1975.

Touchard, Jean. *Histoire des idées politiques.* 2 vols. 8th ed. Paris, 1981.

Tunnell, Ted. *Crucible of Reconstruction: War, Radicalism, and Race in Louisiana, 1862–1877.* Baton Rouge, 1984.

Usner, Daniel H., Jr. *Indians, Settlers, & Slaves in a Frontier Exchange Economy: The Lower Mississippi Valley Before 1783.* Chapel Hill, N.C., 1992.

Vandal, Gilles. *The New Orleans Riot of 1866: Anatomy of a Tragedy.* Lafayette, La., 1983.

Viatte, Auguste. *Histoire littéraire de l'Amérique Française des origines à 1950.* Paris, 1954.

———. *Victor Hugo et les illuminés de son temps.* Montréal, 1942.

Vincent, Charles. *Black Legislators in Louisiana During Reconstruction.* Baton Rouge, 1976.

Walkes, Joseph A., Jr. *The History of the Prince Hall Grand Lodge of Louisiana, 1842–1979.* N.p., 1986.

Warren, Harris Gaylord. *The Sword Was Their Passport: A History of American Filibustering in the Mexican Revolution.* Baton Rouge, 1943.

Whitten, David O. *Andrew Durnford: A Black Sugar Planter in Antebellum Louisiana.* Natchitoches, La., 1981.

Williams, George W. *A History of the Negro Troops in the War of the Rebellion, 1861–1865.* New York, 1888.

Williams, Loretta J. *Black Freemasonry and Middle-Class Realities.* Columbia, Mo., 1980.

Wilson, Joseph T. *The Black Phalanx.* New York, 1968.

Woodward, C. Vann. *Origins of the New South, 1877–1913.* 1951; rpr. Baton Rouge, 1971.

Wright, C.H.C. *The Background of Modern French Literature*. Boston, 1926.

Wrobel, Arthur, ed. *Pseudo-Science and Society in Nineteenth-Century America*. Lexington, Ky., 1987.

Articles

Berry, Mary F. "Negro Troops in Blue and Gray: The Louisiana Native Guards, 1861–1863." *Louisiana History,* VIII (Spring, 1967), 165–90.

Bettersworth, John K. "Protestant Beginnings in New Orleans." *Louisiana Historical Quarterly,* XXI (July, 1938), 823–45.

Binning, F. Wayne. "Carpetbaggers' Triumph: The Louisiana State Election of 1868." *Louisiana History,* XIV (Winter, 1973), 21–39.

Borders, Florence E. "Black Louisiana's Legacy from Three Women of African Descent." *Chicory Review,* I (Spring, 1989), 10–11.

Brady, Patricia. "Black Artists in Antebellum New Orleans." *Louisiana History,* XXXII (Winter, 1991), 5–28.

Breathett, George. "Religious Protectionism and the Slave in Haiti." *Catholic Historical Review,* LV (April, 1969–January, 1970), 26–39.

Christian, Marcus. "Demand by Men of Color for Rights in Orleans Territory." *Negro History Bulletin,* XXXVI (March, 1973), 54–57.

———. "Dream of an African Ex-slave." New Orleans *Louisiana Weekly,* February 1, 1938.

Cleven, N. Andrew N. "The First Panama Mission and the Congress of the United States." *Journal of Negro History,* XIII (July, 1928), 225–54.

Connor, William P. "Reconstruction Rebels: The *New Orleans Tribune* in Post-War Louisiana." *Louisiana History,* XXI (Spring, 1980), 159–81.

Curti, Merle E. "The Impact of the Revolutions of 1848 on American Thought." *Proceedings of the American Philosophical Society,* XCIII (June, 1949), 209–15.

———. "Young America." *American Historical Review,* XXXII (October, 1926), 34–55.

Dabney, Lancaster E. "Louis Aury: The First Governor of Texas." *Southwestern Historical Quarterly,* XLII (July, 1938–April, 1939), 108–16.

Delp, Robert W. "Andrew Jackson Davis: Prophet of American Spiritualism." *Journal of American History,* LIV (June, 1967), 43–56.

———. "Andrew Jackson Davis's *Revelations,* Harbinger of American Spiritualism." *New York Historical Society Quarterly,* LX (July, 1971), 211–34.

———. "A Spiritualist in Connecticut: Andrew Jackson Davis, The Hartford Years, 1850–1854." *New England Quarterly,* LIII (September, 1980), 345–62.

Diket, A.L. "Slidell's Right Hand: Emile La Sere." *Louisiana History,* IV (Summer, 1963), 177–205.

Din, Gilbert C. "*Cimarrones* and the San Malo Band in Spanish Louisiana." *Louisiana History,* XXI (Summer, 1980), 237–62.

Dorman, James H. "The Persistent Specter: Slave Rebellion in Territorial Louisiana." *Louisiana History,* XVIII (Fall, 1977), 389–404.

Dunbar-Nelson, Alice. "People of Color of Louisiana." Part 1. *Journal of Negro History,* I (October, 1916), 361–76.

———. "People of Color of Louisiana." Part 2. *Journal of Negro History,* II (January, 1917), 51–78.

Everett, Donald E. "Ben Butler and the Louisiana Native Guards, 1861–1862." *Journal of Southern History,* XXIV (May, 1958), 202–17.

———. "Demands of the New Orleans Free Colored Population for Political Equality, 1862–1865." *Louisiana Historical Quarterly,* XXXVIII (April, 1955), 43–64.

———. "Emigres and Militiamen: Free Persons of Color in New Orleans, 1803–1815." *Journal of Negro History,* XXXVIII (October, 1953), 377–402.

Faye, Stanley. "Commodore Aury." *Louisiana Historical Quarterly,* XXIV (July, 1941), 611–97.

———. "The Great Stroke of Pierre Laffite [*sic*]." *Louisiana Historical Quarterly,* XXIII (July, 1940), 732–826.

———. "Privateers of Guadeloupe and Their Establishment in Barataria." *Louisiana Historical Quarterly,* XXIII (April, 1940), 428–44.

———. "Privateersmen of the Gulf and Their Prizes." *Louisiana Historical Quarterly,* XXII (October, 1939), 1012–1094.

Fischer, Roger A. "A Pioneer Protest: The New Orleans Street-Car Controversy of 1867." *Journal of Negro History,* LIII (July, 1968), 219–33.

———. "Racial Segregation in Ante Bellum New Orleans." *American Historical Review,* XXIV (February, 1969), 926–37.

Foner, Laura. "The Free People of Color in Louisiana and St. Domingue." *Journal of Social History,* III (Summer, 1970), 406–30.

Freeman, Arthur. "The Early Career of Pierre Soulé." *Louisiana Historical Quarterly,* XXV (October, 1942), 971–1127.

Geggus, David P. "The French and Haitian Revolutions and Resistance to Slavery in the Americas." *Revue française d'histoire d'Outre-Mer,* LXXVI (1989), 107–24.

Greenleaf, Richard E. "The Inquisition in Spanish Louisiana, 1762–1800." *New Mexico Historical Review,* L (January, 1975), 45–72.

Guarneri, Carl J. "Two Utopian Socialist Plans for Emancipation in Antebellum Louisiana." *Louisiana History,* XXIV (Winter, 1983), 5–24.

Haggard, J. Villansana. "The Neutral Ground Between Louisiana and Texas, 1806–1821." *Louisiana Historical Quarterly,* XXVIII (October, 1945), 1001–1103.

Hanger, Kimberly. "Avenues to Freedom Open to New Orleans' Black Population, 1769–1779." *Louisiana History,* XXXI (Summer, 1990), 237–63.

———. "Conflicting Loyalties: The French Revolution and Free People of Color in Spanish New Orleans." *Louisiana History,* XXXIV (Winter, 1993), 5–33.

Harwood, Thomas F. "The Abolitionist Image of Louisiana and Mississippi." *Louisiana History,* VII (Winter, 1966), 281–308.

Ingersoll, Thomas N. "Free Blacks in a Slave Society: New Orleans, 1718–1812." *William and Mary Quarterly,* XLVIII (April, 1991), 173–200.

Jeanfreau, Vance Lynn S. "Louisiana Know Nothings and the Elections of 1855–1856." *Louisiana Studies,* IV (Fall, 1965), 222–55.

Johnson, Jerah. "*Les Cenelles:* What's in a Name?" *Louisiana History,* XXXI (Winter, 1990), 407–10.

Joshi, Manoj K., and Joseph P. Reidy, "'To Come Forward and Aid in Putting Down This Unholy Rebellion': The Officers of Louisiana's Free Black Native Guard During the Civil War Era." *Southern Studies,* XXI (Fall, 1982), 326–42.

Lachance, Paul F. "The 1809 Immigration of Saint-Domingue Refugees to New Orleans: Reception, Integration and Impact." *Louisiana History,* XXIX (Spring, 1988), 109–41.

———. "The Formation of a Three-Caste Society." *Social Science History,* XVIII (Summer, 1994), 211–42.

———. "The Politics of Fear: French Louisianians and the Slave Trade, 1786–1809." *Plantation Society,* I (June, 1979), 162–97.

Liljegren, Ernest R. "Jacobinism in Spanish Louisiana, 1792–1797." *Louisiana Historical Quarterly,* XXII (January, 1939), 47–97.

Lyttle, Charles H. "Historical Bases of Rome's Conflict with Freemasonry." *Church History,* IX (March, 1940), 3–23.

Marigny, Bernard. "Reflections on the Campaign of General Andrew Jackson in Louisiana in 1814 and '15." *Louisiana Historical Quarterly,* VI (January, 1923), 63–85.

Moore, J. Preston. "Pierre Soulé: Southern Expansionist and Promoter." *Journal of Southern History,* XXI (May, 1955), 201–23.

Ochs, Steven J. "A Patriot, a Priest, and a Prelate: Black Catholic Activism in Civil-War New Orleans." *U.S. Catholic Historian,* XII (Winter, 1994), 49–75.

O'Connell, David. "Victor Séjour: Ecrivain américain de langue française." *Revue de Louisiane,* I (Winter, 1972), 60–75.

Odom, Van D. "The Political Career of Thomas Overton Moore, Secession Governor of Louisiana." *Louisiana Historical Quarterly,* XXVI (October, 1943), 975–1054.

O'Neill, Charles Edwards. "'A Quarter Marked by Sundry Peculiarities': New Orleans, Lay Trustees, and Père Antoine." *Catholic Historical Review,* LXXVI (April, 1990), 235–77.

Pérotin-Dumon, Anne. "Les Corsaires de la liberté." *L'Histoire,* XLIII (March, 1982), 24–29.

Perret, J. John. "Victor Séjour, Black French Playwright from Louisiana." *French Review,* LVII (December, 1983), 187–93.

Plaisance, Aloysius F. "The Catholic Church and the Confederacy." *American Benedictine Review,* XV (June, 1964), 159–67.

Porter, Betty. "The History of Negro Education in Louisiana." *Louisiana Historical Quarterly,* XXV (July, 1942), 728–821.

Rankin, David C. "The Impact of the Civil War on the Free Colored Community of New Orleans." *Perspectives in American History,* XI (1977–78), 379–416.

———. "The Tannenbaum Thesis Reconsidered: Slavery and Race Relations in Antebellum Louisiana." *Southern Studies,* XVIII (Spring, 1979), 5–31.

Reilly, Timothy F. "Heterodox New Orleans and the Protestant South, 1800–1861." *Louisiana Studies,* XII (Spring, 1973), 533–51.

———. "*Le Liberateur:* New Orleans' Free Negro Newspaper." *Gulf Coast Historical Review,* II (Fall, 1986), 5–24.

Reinders, Robert C. "The Churches and the Negro in New Orleans, 1850–1860." *Phylon,* XXII (Fall, 1961), 241–48.

———. "The Decline of the New Orleans Free Negro in the Decade Before the Civil War." *Journal of Mississippi History,* XXIV (January–October, 1962), 88–98.

———. "The Free Negro in the New Orleans Economy, 1850–1860." *Louisiana History,* VI (Summer, 1965), 273–85.

———. "T. Wharton Collens: Catholic and Christian Socialist." *Catholic Historical Review,* LII (July, 1966), 212–33.

Reynolds, Donald E. "The New Orleans Riot of 1866, Reconsidered." *Louisiana History,* V (Winter, 1964), 5–27.

Ricard, Ulysses S., Jr. "Pierre Belly and Rose: More Forgotten People." *Chicory Review,* I (Fall, 1988), 13–15.

Robinson, Armstead L. "Beyond the Realm of Social Consensus: New Meanings of Reconstruction for American History." *Journal of American History,* LXVIII (September, 1981), 276–97.

Schafer, Judith K. " 'Open and Notorious Concubinage': The Emancipation of Slave Mistresses by Will and the Supreme Court in Antebellum Louisiana." *Louisiana History,* XXVIII (Spring, 1987), 165–82.

Schweninger, Loren. "Prosperous Blacks in the South, 1790–1880." *American Historical Review,* XCV (February, 1990), 31–56.

Spanos, Nicholas P., and Jack Gottlieb. "Demonic Possession, Mesmerism, and Hysteria: A Social Psychological Perspective on Their Historical Interrelations." *Journal of Abnormal Psychology,* LXXXVIII (1979), 527–46.

Stahl, Annie Lee West. "The Free Negro in Ante-Bellum Louisiana." *Louisiana Historical Quarterly,* XXV (April, 1942), 301–96.

Tansey, Richard. "Out-of-State Free Blacks in Late Antebellum New Orleans." *Louisiana History,* XXII (Fall, 1981), 369–86.

Thornton, Joseph A. "A History of St. James A.M.E. Church." In *The Jubilee Anniversary Program, St. James A.M.E. Church*. New Orleans, 1945.

Tomlinson, Wallace K., and J. John Perret. "Mesmerism in New Orleans, 1845–1861." *American Journal of Psychiatry,* XII (December, 1974), 1402–1404.

Tregle, Joseph G., Jr. "Thomas J. Durant, Utopian Socialism, and the Failure of Presidential Reconstruction in Louisiana." *Journal of Southern History,* XLV (November, 1979), 485–12.

Tunnell, Ted. "Free Negroes and the Freedmen: Black Politics in New Orleans During the Civil War." *Southern Studies,* XIV (Spring, 1980), 5–28.

Uzee, Philip D. "The Beginnings of the Louisiana Republican Party." *Louisiana History,* XII (Summer, 1971), 197–211.

Viatte, Auguste. "Complement à la bibliographie louisianaise d'Edward Larocque Tinker." *Louisiana Review,* III (Winter, 1974), 12–57.

Vincent, Charles. "Aspects of the Family and Public Life of Antoine Dubuclet: Louisiana's Black State Treasurer, 1868–1878." *Journal of Negro History,* LXVI (Spring, 1981), 26–36.

———. "Black Louisianians: The Uniqueness and Significance of Their History: A Preliminary Analysis." *Griot,* X (Fall, 1991), 44–50.

———. "Negro Leadership and Programs in the Louisiana Constitutional Convention of 1868." *Louisiana History,* X (Fall, 1969), 339–51.

Warren, Harris Gaylord. "José Alvarez de Toledo's Reconciliation with Spain and Projects for Suppressing Rebellion in the Spanish Colonies." *Louisiana Historical Quarterly,* XXIII (July, 1940), 827–63.

———. "Southern Filibusters in the War of 1812." *Louisiana Historical Quarterly,* XXV (April, 1942), 291–300.

Westwood, Howard C. "Benjamin Butler's Enlistment of Black Troops in New Orleans in 1862." *Louisiana History,* XXVI (Winter, 1985), 5–22.

White, M. J. "Louisiana and the Secession Movement of the Early Fifties." *Proceedings of the Mississippi Valley Historical Association,* VIII (1914–15), 278–88.

Williams, T. Harry. "The Louisiana Unification Movement of 1873." *Journal of Southern History,* XI (August, 1945), 349–69.

Yerbury, Grace. "Concert Music in New Orleans." *Louisiana Historical Quarterly,* XL (April, 1957), 95–109.

Manuscripts and Unpublished Papers

Christian, Marcus. "A Black History of Louisiana." Typescript, Marcus B. Christian Collection, Earl K. Long Library, University of New Orleans, n.d.

Lachance, Paul F. "New Orleans in the Era of Revolution: A Demographic Profile." Paper presented at the American Society for Eighteenth-Century Studies Conference, New Orleans, 1989.

Putzell, Edwin J., Jr. "Cui Bono: A Study of Secession in Louisiana." Typescript, Howard-Tilton Memorial Library, Tulane University, New Orleans, 1935.

Vandal, Gilles. "Origins of Black Political Leadership in Louisiana, 1865–1884." Paper presented at the Louisiana Historical Association Conference, Lafayette, La., 1992.

Dissertations and Theses

Binning, Francis W. "Henry Clay Warmoth and Louisiana Reconstruction." Ph.D. dissertation, University of North Carolina, 1969.

Brown, Burton Gates, Jr. "Spiritualism in Nineteenth-Century America." Ph.D. dissertation, Boston University, 1973.

Doorley, Michael. "The Irish and the Catholic Church in New Orleans, 1835–1918." M.A. thesis, University of New Orleans, 1987.

Hopkins, James. "Joanna Southcott: A Study of Popular Religion and Radical Politics, 1789–1814." Ph.D. dissertation, University of Texas, 1972.

Isaacs, Ernest J. "A History of Nineteenth-Century American Spiritualism as a Religious and Social Movement." Ph.D. dissertation, University of Wisconsin, 1975.

Lagarde, Marie L. "Charles Testut: Critic, Journalist and Literary Socialist." M.A. thesis, Tulane University, 1948.

McGowan, James Thomas. "Creation of a Slave Society: Louisiana Plantations in the Eighteenth Century." Ph.D. dissertation, University of Rochester, 1976.

McTigue, Geraldine. "Forms of Racial Interaction in Louisiana, 1860–1880." Ph.D. dissertation, Yale University, 1975.

Miceli, Mary V. "The Influence of the Roman Catholic Church on Slavery in Colonial Louisiana, 1718–1763." Ph.D. dissertation, Tulane University, 1979.

Niehaus, Earl F. "Jefferson College in St. James Parish, Louisiana, 1830–1875." M.A. thesis, Tulane University, 1954.

Rankin, David Connell, "The Forgotten People: Free People of Color in New Orleans, 1850–1870." Ph.D. dissertation, Johns Hopkins University, 1976.

Schafer, Judith K. "The Long Arm of the Law: Slavery and the Supreme Court in Antebellum Louisiana, 1809–1862." Ph.D. dissertation, Tulane University, 1987.

Index

Revolution, Romanticism, *and the* Afro-Creole Protest Tradition *in* Louisiana 1718–1868

CARYN COSSÉ BELL

With the Federal occupation of New Orleans in 1862, Afro-Creole leaders in that city and their white allies seized upon the ideals of the American and French Revolutions and images of revolutionary events in the French Caribbean and demanded *liberté, égalité, fraternité*. Rooted in the egalitarianism of the age of democratic revolution, a Catholic universalist ethic, and Romantic philosophy, their republican idealism produced the postwar South's most progressive vision of the future. Caryn Cossé Bell, in her impressive, sweeping study, traces the eighteenth-century origins of this Afro-Creole political and intellectual heritage, its evolution in antebellum New Orleans, and its impact on the war and Reconstruction, addressing a long-neglected aspect of Louisiana's political history and brilliantly recovering this biracial protest tradition.

Bell explains how colonial New Orleans' Latin European religious culture and tripartite racial order gave rise to one of the most assertive, prosperous, well-educated, and cohesive free black societies in nineteenth-century North America. She explores the broad forces—revolutionary republicanism, literary Romanticism, freemasonry, and spiritualism—that shaped the world view of Afro-Creole activists and their white, French-speaking counterparts. After the Civil War, these leaders played a key role in the struggle to build a model of reconstruction in Louisiana, and their efforts influenced